ACCOUNTING CONTROL SYSTEMS:
A BEHAVIORAL AND TECHNICAL INTEGRATION

ACCOUNTING CONTROL SYSTEMS:
A Behavioral and Technical Integration

edited, with an introduction by

JAN BELL

Columbia University
Graduate School of Business Administration

MARKUS WIENER PUBLISHING, INC.

ISBN 0-910129-02-9
Library of Congress Catalog Card No. 83-061102

Printed in the United States of America

TABLE OF CONTENTS

INTRODUCTION
ACCOUNTING CONTROL SYSTEMS

Planning and control systems are those organizational arrangements and actions designed to facilitate the achievement of high performance with the fewest unintended dysfunctional consequences.

A system should motivate managers to achieve targeted cost, profit or return on investment goals without encouraging them to trade long-run for short-run performance by ignoring key variables (e.g., product quality, delivery or customer service). This is accomplished by designing a control system that coordinates both organizational arrangements (e.g. organizational structures, financial control structures, and information flows) and actions (e.g., the behavioral process of reviewing and approving budgets, analyzing and explaining variances, or giving informal rewards and sanctions).

The interest in designing internal accounting systems originated approximately fifty years ago. Since that time, there have been at least five recognizable and distinctly different frames from which to view planning and control activities. Early systems focused on reporting "the true cost" of cost objectives and strove to develop technical rules for presenting accurate costs which would reflect "economic reality." Next came the realization that different costs should be used for different purposes (the "flexible" approach). Accountants and academic researchers then set out to determine which cost measurement techniques were appropriate in what circumstances. Finally two new approaches (cost-benefit and behavioral) became popular. The cost-benefit or information economics approach concerns itself with how accounting data influence a decision-maker's actions. It treats the accountant as a decision-maker who must identify available information system alternatives, evaluate them against a set of objectives, specify the existence of uncertainty, and select the optimal information system. This approach to control system design treats the information network as the only design variable subject to manipulation. It ignores other structural variables and all behavioral actions. A behavioral approach currently co-exists with the cost-benefit approach. It concerns itself with the behavioral implications of implementing technical information systems by questioning, for example, assumptions about the motivations of workers, their inherent dislike of work, power-authority relationships, and leadership styles. This approach lacks a well-defined useful model of individual behavior within an organization and focuses on achieving control by concentrating only on behavioral variables while treating the information system as constant or neutral.

In the past few years, a few academics have been attempting to integrate these two existing approaches into a new "integrated" approach to control systems design. They are relying heavily on the organization theory literature and treating a control system as an "open system" in constant commerce with its environment. Instead of focusing solely on information network issues or behavioral issues to achieve high performance with fewest dysfunctional consequences, the integrated approach recognizes that the same end result (high performance) can be obtained from many different combinations of organizational arrangements (e.g., organizational structures and information systems) and actions (e.g., behavioral and reward variables).

The articles in this anthology provide an overview of the development of management accounting. They fall into four sections.

The first section contains papers that explain the development of management accounting and competing frameworks to control systems design. The goal of this section is to provide the reader with a look at control system design from three frameworks: 1) technical cost-benefit, 2) behavioral, and 3) integrated.

Section two describes how budgeting and variances analysis are viewed from both cost-benefit and behavioral frameworks. Technical accounting tools are then blended with organizational-behavioral issues to show how an integrated approach facilitates an organization's adaption to its environment.

Information network issues are contained in section three. State-of-the-art technical and behavioral papers are provided, which deal with transfer pricing, cost-volume profit analysis and other quantitative techniques.

The last section is devoted to performance measurement. Most articles contain criticisms of existing methods of performance measurement. Such articles attack—e.g., specific methods of measurement (e.g., ROI), the time dimension of evaluations, and unidimensional evaluation approaches. This is an area where the future integration of technical and behavioral approaches will be most fruitful.

These readings will enrich advanced courses in management accounting at the undergraduate level, introductory managerial accounting at the under-graduate level and introductory managerial accounting courses at the graduate level by providing a historical perspective to control system design and by presenting technical accounting issues from several competing frameworks: cost-benefit, behavioral and integrated. The reader is designed to supplement a basic text, such as Anthony and Dearden, *Management Control Systems,* 4th ed. (Richard D. Irwin, Inc., 1980), Shillinglaw, *Managerial Cost Accounting*, 5th ed. (Richard D. Irwin, Inc., 1982) or Horngren, *Cost Accounting: A Managerial Emphasis,* 5th ed. (Prentice-Hall, 1982).

Jan Bell
Columbia University
June 1983

PART I
AN OVERVIEW OF MANAGEMENT CONTROL SYSTEMS

This section contains articles that trace the historical development of management accounting and provide competing approaches to control systems design. Horngren's paper discusses the changes in management accounting from its infancy up to the co-existence of the cost-benefit and behavioral approaches. The article suggests a control system design framework which treats the technical information structure as the key design variable. Analysis of alternative designs is performed using a non-quantitative cost-benefit approach. Baiman's article on agency theory extends that approach by criticizing the issues studied by both cost-benefit and behavioral researchers. The lack of fundamental economic analysis and the focus on the technical issues resulting from these approaches is attributed to the lack of a well-defined, useful model of individual behavior within an organization. Baiman suggests that the agency theory framework provides such a model. In this model, one or more individuals (principals) hire one or more persons (agents) for the purpose of delegating responsibility. Each member is assumed to act in his own self-interest; agents are presumed to be work-averse (they "shirk"). Agency theory examines the relationship between the firm's information system, its employment contracts, and the welfare of its members. Control is achieved by selecting the proper payment schedule and monitoring mechanism to reward and motivate the agent. The design variable focused upon is again the information structure; other design variables are ignored.

To evaluate the criticisms of the technical cost-benefit approaches levied by behaviorists, the article by Caplan outlines and criticizes the behavior assumptions underlying traditional management accounting (including some assumptions in agency theory) and provides alternative assumptions based on laboratory and empirical studies. Many subsequent behavioral studies tested assumptions and suggestions put forth in this article.

This section is concluded by an article positing an integrated approach to control system design. Ansari discusses the co-existence of structural and behavioral approaches and suggests the need for integration. He identifies the key interacting control-system subcomponents as information structures, leadership style, subordinate personality, and rewards, and discusses the need to focus on their joint fit rather than focusing on control through manipulation of either structural or behavioral subcomponents.

Management Accounting: Where Are We?

CHARLES T. HORNGREN
Stanford University

This paper presents some personal reactions to the evolution of management and cost accounting. My perspective is always changing, so this critique will undoubtedly continue to be modified as the years unfold.

The Development of Management Accounting Courses

The field of management accounting has come a long distance since I first learned accounting during the late 1940s. My early schooling in accounting was like that of thousands of other students--a heavy emphasis on public accounting and the production of accounting data for external purposes. Uses of accounting data internally were given little attention in textbooks and in classes. At that time (1949), there were almost zero courses in management accounting as it is known today.

When I was an undergraduate student, the cost accounting courses and textbooks were largely concerned with how systems could trace costs to products and services for income statements and balance sheets. In an exaggerated sense, the cost accountant's main mission might have been depicted as the pursuit of absolute truth,[1] where truth was defined in terms of getting as accurate or precise costs as possible. Indeed, some "advanced" cost accounting courses were largely concerned with how to track costs in complex production settings (e.g., three or four processes with varying spoilage, shrinkage, and waste in each process).

This absolute truth approach is more accurately labeled as the historical communication approach. The approach aims at producing a unique set of historical information for all purposes. The objective is to use measurement rules that supply unambiguous information in the sense that only one

---

[1] J. Demski, G. Feltham, C. Horngren, R. Jaedicke, **A Conceptual Approach to Cost Determination** (Iowa State University Press, forthcoming in 1976), Chapter 1, pp. 2-3. Also see Report of the Committee on Concepts and Standards--Internal Planning and Control, **The Accounting Review**, (Supplement to Vol. XLIX, 1974), pp. 79-81. Also see Yuji Ijiri, **Theory of Accounting Measurement** (Sarasota, Florida: American Accounting Association, 1975), pp. 30-33.

---

measurement system is acceptable. The user can then supply his or her own adjustments as desired.

This unique historical data phenomenon had a narrowing impact on impressionable students. For example, when I began teaching management accounting in 1953, I encountered several students who (like me) initially resisted the idea that historical costs or book values might be safely ignored in some decision situations. The absolutist phenomenon also hobbled students' ability to see the potential of direct costing or contribution reporting. Inevitably, the students with heavy previous training in accounting offered the strongest opposition. Somehow these ideas were heretical because they challenged a measure that was perceived as a unique and unalterable truth.

During the 1950s, new courses in management accounting were begun in several schools. These courses were required in many MBA programs. During the 1960s and 1970s, management accounting courses have also tended to become required courses in undergraduate programs. Meanwhile, the cost accounting courses were taking on a much heavier management accounting flavor. (This paper will use "management accounting" to encompass all courses and accounting research that stress internal uses of accounting data.)

Consider why management accounting started to flourish. It remedied many defects, including the preoccupation with finding "the" unique cost. The most refreshing contribution of management accounting has been its focus on the potential uses of decisions that might be affected by the accounting data. The theme of "different costs for different purposes" was stressed--a preoccupation with finding **conditional** truth. This conditional truth theme has been labeled as the user decision model approach. Decision models are assumed for output levels, investments, and other purposes. Deductive reasoning is used to isolate and measure relevant data. Thus, accounting became more complex, more fascinating, and more responsive to students' perceived future roles. After all, only a slim percentage of students in accounting courses become lifelong career specialists in auditing or income taxes. Instead, the large percentage become managers or accountants who serve managers.

As I have taught various courses in management accounting through the years, I have been increasingly troubled by its decision model approach. It has too much of an **ad hoc**, or "let's solve this case" flavor that I find unsatisfying. There is no unity, no common element beyond the caveat that each situation "requires" different costs.

I started casting about a more robust conceptual framework that I could apply serenely in this variety of decision settings. My present views are slightly more comforting, but my quest for the grail has failed. My search for a framework will continue, but it will be a look for modest improvements in my slippery grasp of an open-ended subject. My current perceptions are an amalgamation of much influential thinking done by many individuals, too many to name without overlooking somebody. I have tested these perceptions with my classes, so let me test them with you.

Focus on Decisions

As most of us can testify, our individual approaches to professional problems are frequently affected by our readings and by our conversations with colleagues. The authors who recently have influenced me the most have been my colleagues, Joel Demski and Gerald Feltham.[2] They approach these issues with more rigor and abstraction than I can muster. They also may cringe at my simplifications of their ideas. But our general philosophy is similar.

The Demski-Feltham approach has been called information analysis or information evaluation; it might also be dubbed as the "costly truth" approach (as contrasted with the "true cost" approach). They fundamentally regard management accounting as being concerned with how accounting data facilitate rational economic choices by internal decision makers. Their framework focuses on the roles of the decision maker and the accountant. The decision maker selects an

---

[2]See Joel S. Demski, **Information Analysis** (Reading, Mass.: Addison-Wesley Publishing Co. Inc., 1972) and Gerald A. Feltham, **Information Evaluation** (Sarasota, Fla.: American Accounting Association, 1972). The Demski-Feltham approach has influenced the American Accounting Association committee reports on management accounting. For example, see **The Accounting Review Supplements** for 1972, pp. 317-335; 1973, pp. 234-235; and 1974, pp. 79-99. Demski and Feltham have been heavily influenced by the publications of Kenneth Arrow and Jacob Marschak.

action in a specific situation. The accountant provides information to facilitate the decision maker's choice. Of course, the two roles may be performed by the same individual, different individuals, or a group.[3]

The costly truth approach emphasizes a method of analysis that explicitly regards the accountant as a decision maker. He (or she) must identify the information alternatives, evaluate them in terms of some set of objectives, deal with the existence of uncertainty, and choose the most desirable alternative. The information evaluation method can be plainly called a cost-benefit method whereby the accountant predicts the relationships among the accounting system, the decision maker's choice process, the selected action, and the resulting consequences. The central thrust is expressed by the question: In a world of uncertainty, how much are you willing to pay for one information system versus another? What system are you willing to buy?

Accounting Information as an Economic Good

Information is a commodity. Measurement consumes resources. Kenneth Arrow has commented: "...in organizational control, as in automobiles, cuisine, and every other commodity, the benefits of improved quality [of information] must always be compared with their costs."[4]

Accounting data are economic goods (just like cuisine and smog control devices) obtainable at various costs. The manager, therefore, buys accounting data as well as other data. Ideally, we should evaluate various types of information in terms of whether the action choices will be affected by the information in question. For example, if the information will not affect the action choice, it is valueless. On the other

---

3Ijiri, op. cit., p. 45, favors another approach, the information control approach. He states: "In a fourth method which we propose here, the same relationship is observed but is shifted to one level higher. A systems designer will now foresee all optimization behavior of accountants under each alternative rule. He will then select the one method most suitable for achieving the overall goal of the system. We may call this the information control approach, since one of the purposes of issuing rules is to control information processing systems by eliminating much of the discretionary activity of accountants." Ijiri also (pp. 32-33) stresses accountability as what distinguishes accounting from other information systems.

4Kenneth J. Arrow, "Control in Large Organizations," Management Science, Vol. 10, No. 3 (April, 1964), p. 401.

hand, if the information will lead the manager to a better action choice, then its value is measurable in terms of the increase in net benefit (e.g., net profit after deducting the costs of getting the information) obtained with the information as compared to the net benefit obtained without the information. In its most simplified sense, we have described a cost-benefit approach to management accounting issues. The cost of acquiring accounting information includes compilation, processing, and education, which can be enormously expensive.

Consider how the economist approaches the question of buying commodities like butter or internal accounting information. Do we see economics textbooks that tell us how much or what quality of butter the consumer **needs**? No. The economist tells us about the conditions of optimality (e.g., for the consumer to be in equilibrium, the marginal utility of the last dollar spent on each commodity must be equal). In contrast, the accounting literature is more doctrinaire; it is far more willing to tell you how much or what quality butter or accounting to consume. The primary implication of the economist's approach to information is almost philosophical. It is a rejection of both the unique truth and the conditional truth philosophies in favor of the cost-benefit philosophy. The foregoing examples may be trivial, but the cost-benefit approach to information is not trivial.

To see how my views have been reshaped, I reread my thirteen-year old "perspective" article, "Choosing Accounting Practices for Reporting to Management" (**NAA Bulletin**, September, 1962, pp. 3-15). That article summarized a few existing ideas that I continue to emphasize, particularly the idea of gathering relevant data for particular purposes and the idea of motivation in harmony with organizational goals. That article also contained phrasing that I want to disown, such as: "the information needed" and the major sub-title, "relevant information--the basic need." The major weakness of the article was probably its failure to give cost-benefit analysis the prominence it merits.

Even though these cost-benefit decisions are most often made implicitly (sometimes as a rationalization of a decision **ex post**), the underlying philosophy here should not be overlooked. For example, in many places we see opinions about what data are "needed" for making assorted decisions with only passing reference (at most) to the associated "costs" and "benefits".

My distaste for thinking in terms of data "needs" is not a semantic quibble. On the contrary, it is a basic criticism of academic thought and accounting theories that are often incomplete and hence inapplicable. How can we conclude whether accounting data (or perfectly clean air) are "needed" **per se**? Accounting data are economic goods. Many alternatives exist, and choosing one over another is just one more type of decision that must somehow be made.

To illustrate this point, you may encounter arguments from time to time that one way is better than a second way of computing the cost of a product. The first way is "needed" because it provides a "more accurate" or a "truer" approximation of "economic reality." The cost-benefit approach to such an issue does not use "need" or "truth" or "accuracy" as the fundamental method of resolving the dispute. Instead, its method is to ask whether the decisions affected by these costs will differ if the first way is used rather than the second way. The direct costing-absorption costing controversy is an example. More specifically, my preferred way for settling arguments about direct costing versus absorption costing for internal purposes is to predict how each method or system will affect volume, mix, pricing, investment and other decisions in a particular organization. If the decisions will be unaffected, then the less costly alternative is preferable. If the decisions will be affected differently, then the preferable alternative is that which is expected to produce the most net benefit. Management accounting choices are inherently contextual; sweeping generalizations across contexts are alien to the cost-benefit philosophy. For instance, a cost-benefit adherent would refrain from making a generalization such as "direct costing is better than absorption costing."

The cost-benefit approach is especially attractive to me because it provides a starting point for tackling virtually all accounting issues. Furthermore, it can be subsumed under a rich theoretical structure of information economics,[5] which

---

[5]For a description of the theory, and the works in economics from which it sprung, see Demski, op. cit., and Feltham, op. cit., and the ample references therein.

is the application of microeconomic theory to questions of purchasing information. Also, it has practical appeal because accountants, managers, and students find its central ideas easy to accept.

Criticisms of Cost-Benefit Approach

Some critics may claim that there is nothing new here, that cost-benefit analysis has been important in accountants' thinking for years.[6] Perhaps, but too often it has been implicit and too often it has been an "implementation" or "practical" aspect or criterion--not the dominant, central theoretical thrust.

Cost-benefit analysis is anchored to a rationalistic view of organizations, a view that has been assailed by many as being far too simplified and abstract.[7] The information economist will defend the rationalistic view as follows:

"There is no intention of denying that non-rational factors, sociological and psychological, are of utmost importance in the study and development of organizations. But a rational point of view is also needed, and indeed much of the value of studies in group dynamics will only be properly realized in the context of rational design of organizations."[8]

This audience consists of practitioners and academicians. Practitioners may respond to my focus on cost-benefit

---

[6]For example, Robert T. Sprouse, reporter, **The Measurement of Property, Plant, and Equipment in Financial Statements,** Accounting Round Table, April 29-30, 1963 (Boston: Harvard Business School, 1964), p. 22, cited feasibility along with usefulness and objectivity as the three major criteria for the general acceptance of an accounting principle or practice: "In order to merit serious consideration, valuation bases must be capable of practicable and economic implementation. . .Similarly, proposals are unacceptable that are possible of attainment but only at a cost that is clearly disproportionate to any additional benefits relative to less costly alternatives."

[7]Many alternative models have been championed. For example, Michael D. Cohen, James G. March, and Johan P. Olsen, "A Garbage Can Model of Organizational Choice," **Administrative Science Quarterly,** Vol. 17, No. 1 (March, 1972), suggest that some "organizations can be viewed for some purposes as collections of choices looking for problems, issues and feelings looking for decision situations in which they might be aired, solutions looking for issues to which they might be an answer, and decision makers looking for workers."

[8]Arrow, op. cit., p. 399.

analysis by gloating, "That's what I've been using throughout my career. It's about time you professors recognize that we've been operating as sub rosa information economists." Nevertheless, until recently the practitioners' official literature has rarely cited cost-benefit analysis as a major means of resolving issues.[9]

Academicians may have a ho-hum response to my focus on cost-benefit analysis. After all, the information economics model and its cost-benefit simplifications are too hopelessly broad, normative, theoretical, and nondescriptive to be useful template to lay over the discipline of management accounting.

A similar criticism was leveled against the notion or concept of relevance, when it was advanced as a starting point for developing the decision model approach to management accounting during the 1950s. A committee of the American Accounting Association observed:

"There is a temptation to dispense with the whole question concerning concepts underlying internal reports by saying that the only concept of general applicability in this area is the concept of relevance. That is, what is good or bad accounting is decided fundamentally by the usefulness of the result in meeting specific management problems. While this is true of internal reporting, such a general statement hardly justifies stature as an underlying concept. It does not provide guidance to accountants regarding methods to follow nor does it assist users in the interpretation of internal reports. When used with this meaning, the term relevance is more a statement of the problem rather than a solution to it.[10]

Whether you call it a concept, a principle, an insight, or a hackneyed expression, the idea of relevance had immense

_____

[9]During the 1970s the Securities and Exchange Commission and the Financial Accounting Standards Board have explicitly recognized the importance of cost-benefit analysis as one consideration in their decisions. Still, the Trueblood Study Group, **Objectives of Financial Statements** (New York: American Institute of Certified Public Accountants, 1973), gave scant attention to the cost-benefit approach.

[10]Report of the 1961 Managerial Accounting Committee, **The Accounting Review**, Vo. XXXVII, No. 3 (July, 1962), p. 536

impact on our literature and our courses of the 1960s and 1970s. Relevance had been lurking in the wings for years, [11] but until it was stressed by a few individuals, it had little effect on curricula or on setling accounting controversies.

Similarly, cost-benefit analysis has been in the woodwork for years.[12] If it offends you to call it a theory, then call it a state of mind. Along with the idea of relevance, it offers a focus for the 1970s that may help explain and improve management accounting.

Example of Applying Cost-Benefit Analysis

Consider the application of cost-benefit analysis by a control systems designer, who may be an accountant, a manager, or both. A troublesome problem in both internal and external accounting has been asset valuation for performance measurement. Among the alternatives are historical costs, historical costs restated for a general price index, and some version of current value. The accounting literature is replete with exhortations about the infirmities of historical costs and the virtues of one or more of the alternatives.

Ten years ago my criterion for choosing was: which measurement was most directly relevant to decisions? Obviously, I thought, the manager "needs" something beyond historical costs. A web of impeccable logic can be spun that will demonstrate the conceptual superiority (usually under conditions of certainty) of some version of current or future values for decisions.

Although the relevance criterion is appealing, it is not sufficient. Most important, we should recognize that the basic job of accounting systems is to supply information. Furthermore, the system is only one source of information. The issue of comparative advantage must be faced. The acceptance or rejection of historical cost, when compared to some version of current value, would depend on the costs of each alternative set of information in light of the perceived

---

11 J. M. Clark, **Economics of Overhead Costs**, (Chicago: University of Chicago Press, 1923), Chapter 9.

12 An early citation would be appropriate, but my limited search of the literature has produced none.

benefits that might arise from better economic decisions, as well as on what competing sources of information are available.

Given the defects of historical cost, why do organizations continue to use it for evaluating performance of the company as a whole and its subunits? There are several reasons. Some seem unjustifiable, while others make sense. Ignorance has been cited as a likely reason. But I have not encountered a convincing argument as to why this supposed ignorance persists. The routine use of some alternative value entails an extra cost of compiling data. The manager (and some investors) want **routine** data essentially as clues for deciding whether and how to seek (buy) more information. The constraints of generally accepted accounting principles are not as dominant for internal purposes. Still, most managers have regarded historical costs as good enough for such purposes.[13] Major internal decisions to invest or disinvest are not routine decisions. From the viewpoint of the systems designer, it may be more economical to get replacement and net realizable values by conducting special studies as desired rather than by routine recording.

The implications from practice are clear. The use of "defective" data such as historical costs may often make both conceptual and practical sense--even though advocates of the user decision model approach find the idea difficult to swallow. Although current values may indeed be more relevant and even more objective, they still may not be preferable to historical costs if the latter are less costly to compile and will lead to the same decisions.

The advocates of a multiple value or fair value system bear the burden of demonstrating its superiority over historical cost. To my knowledge, the advocates have had few successes in convincing management of its advantages for the internal routine evaluation of performance. This would be the first step in showing that a current value framework can be implemented successfully.

---

[13]John J. Mauriel and Robert N. Anthony, "Misevaluation of Investment Center Performance," **Harvard Business Review**, Vol. 44, No. 2, summarize the practices of 2,658 companies. Only three percent of the companies used some measure that departs from historical cost, such as insurance value or appraisal value.

Two Sets of Accounting Principles

An example from the area of external reporting also may clarify or reinforce my major point. For years, many CPAs have complained that several Accounting Principles Board requirements are often too costly for smaller clients. For instance, the computations of earnings per share statistics and the preparation of a statement of changes in financial position, may be onerous burdens with negative benefit.[14] Also, imagine the possible new burden of adjusting the financial statements for the changes in the general price level.

The replies to these complaints have consistently stated that society should not have a separate set of accounting principles for large organizations and a different set for small organizations. I tended to agree with that position, primarily because I had a knee-jerk reaction as a professor who preferred a universal set for all.

Now I think of this issue in terms of cost-benefit analysis. That is, as organization by organization is examined, there may be convincing reasons in terms of cost-benefit analysis against using the same financial accounting standards for many small organizations.

Does this mean that we would have chaos? No, but it might mean giving a more careful consideration to these complaints of the smaller organizations. Of course, boards like the APB or FASB may still reach the same conclusions in favor of a single set of financial accounting standards. But I would feel more comfortable if those conclusions were framed in terms of the net benefits to society compared with the net cost to individual organizations. That is, the net benefit to society as a whole must be perceived as exceeding the net costs suffered by many organizations from compiling useless data. In a sense then, the smaller organizations are being taxed in the interests of more uniform accounting.

Behavioral Problems and Management Accounting

Cost-benefit analysis is most highly developed in relatively

---

[14]On March 31, 1975, the AICPA's Accounting Standards Division issued a neutral discussion paper on the application of generally accepted accounting principles to smaller and/or closely-held businesses.

abstract, single-person decision situations. Although cost-benefit analysis provides a pervasive general state of mind for judging accounting systems, there still is no tightly-knit framework that gives operational guidance to systems design in the multi-person situations found in complex organizations. Information economics, behavioral science, and welfare economics are applicable to a multi-person setting, but all are better at identifying problems than at supplying operational methods of analysis or solutions. In short, the challenge to cost-benefit analysis is to make it more operational in multi-person settings.

Of course, many unsolved problems exist in management accounting, particularly in complex situations. When I teach my classes, I feel obliged to stress some dimensions of the multi-person problems even though I have no pat answers or even a systematic method for solving the problems. Therefore, my teaching has a strong behavioral focus.

Unfortunately, many management accounting teachers skim or dodge "the behavioral stuff" entirely because it is too messy and too intractable for discussing in a classroom. But I am convinced that students should get a steady exposure to the behavioral implications of the choices of accounting data and systems. A major objective of a management accounting course should be to give students an overview of the important **problems** in the area, even though universal methods of solution are undiscovered or will never be discovered. A comparative advantage of education is to create an awareness of widespread problems that the students are likely to encounter. Unless students are placed on the alert, they will be ill-equipped and will be less likely to see the major behavioral problems that should be identified before choosing a particular acounting system.

In my courses, I have tended to stress the problems of obtaining goal congruence and incentive, which can be wrapped together in one word, **motivation**. Psychologists have defined motivation as the perception of some want or goal together with the resulting drive toward achieving the want. Many authors in the 1950s and 1960s stressed the link between these seemingly foreign ideas of motivation and the design of management accounting systems.[15]

The difference between goal congruence and incentive deserves elaboration. Goal congruence is having two or more persons **aiming** toward the same objective, while incentive is a **striving** toward the given objective, whatever it may be. For example, if you want a subordinate to move through a doorway, you want a measure or a system that will aim him or her accordingly. But you probably do not want the subordinate to take baby steps toward the doorway. You want him or her to **move**--the quicker, the better. So goal congruence and incentive are intertwined, yet they are separable characteristics that warrant attention when appraising or designing a control system.

The distinction between goal congruence and incentive might be clarified by an additional example. Division managers may accept top management goals as their personal goals regarding sales, costs, quality control, research, or other items. So goal congruence may exist. But the incentive problem still remains. A major means of providing incentive is the evaluation of performance. Clearly, the manager is influenced by how his or her performance is appraised. The choices of the content, format, timing, and circulation of performance reports are heavily affected by their probable influence on incentives. For instance, top managers may want to predict the incentive effects of alternative accounting measures of performance (e.g., profit centers, cost centers, cost allocations, human resource accounting, replacement costs).[16]

---

[15]An early effort was R. N. Anthony, "Cost Concepts for Control," **Accounting Review** (April, 1957), p. 234. Anthony has suggested that a control technique can be judged in two ways: by the **direction** and by the **strength** of its motivation. See his **Management Accounting** (rev. ed.; Homewood, Ill.: Richard D. Irwin, Inc., 1960), p. 317. As far as I can determine, Anthony was the first to introduce the now-popular term, goal congruence, to the accounting literature. See p. 362 of the third edition of his **Management Accounting**, 1964.

[16]There is little theory or research available regarding the relationships between management incentives and the evaluation of performance. Arrow, **op. cit.**, p. 400, observes: "There are (at least) two problems in devising incentive systems: (1) an effective incentive system creates new demands for information; the reward is a function of performance, so top management must have a way of measuring performance. (2) Even if the [performance] index is appropriate, the relationship between the reward and the index remains to be determined." Also see E. E. Lawler, **Pay and Organizational Effectiveness** (New York: McGraw-Hill, Inc., 1971). For an overview of accounting and behavior, see Anthony Hopwood, **Accounting and Human Behavior** (London: Haymarket Publishing Limited, distributed by Prentice-Hall International, 1974).

A summary of my general approach to teaching complex cases in management accounting follows. The task of the formal control system is to help provide goal congruence and incentive through the use of technical tools (e.g., budgets, standards, formal measures of performance) that provide information and feedback. The systems designer usually considers various technical proposals (usually at the margin) in a cost-benefit sense. Will the new data or configurations promote a net benefit of more congruence and incentive?

Keep in mind that the approach applies a cost-benefit framework--as a fundamental approach, not as an afterthought. Accounting data and control systems are economic goods. The application occurs in a multi-person setting in a world of uncertainty, so obviously the choices are not easy to justify in comfortable quantitative terms. Generalizations are especially perilous, so we should concentrate on the identification of the key problems and on the **method** for making the hard choices, not on prescriptions that represent widespread solutions. Because definitive answers seem hard to isolate, this approach will never satisfy absolutists or teachers and students who avoid the challenge of pinpointing central problems in untidy situations.

Explaining the Evolution of Systems

The application of cost-benefit analysis and the identification of problems of goal congruence and incentives provide an explanation for the evolution of management accounting systems in many organizations. The sequence frequently is:
1. Physical observation
2. Historical records
3. Static budgets
4. Flexible budgets and standards
5. Profit centers and investment centers
As the sequence occurs, the system tends to become more elaborate and costly because the earlier facets of the system are often retained.

A scenario may occur as follows. A proprietor (or two partners like Hewlett and Packard) may begin a modest enterprise in a garage. The manager's physical observations may provide the sole planning and control system for a day or two. But the simple tracking of cash will require a modicum of historical records. Furthermore, no formal cost-benefit analysis is necessary to convince the manager that sufficient documentation be kept to satisfy the Internal Revenue Service; the benefits are keeping the business as a going concern and staying out of jail.

Historical records may be compared from year to year as a basis for evaluating performance and planning. But many managers find that investing in a formal budgeting system is a cost-effective way to compel planning, promote goal congruence, and improve incentive. Managers often begin budgeting with relatively simple static budgets and, as the net benefits seem apparent, gradually develop flexible budgets and standards.

The incentive criterion is a major justification for taking the next step into some kind of profit center or investment center. Cost centers with flexible budgets and standards have sometimes been found wanting. For instance, some cost center managers have focused on meeting a budget and on keeping costs under control--and nothing more. When the cost centers are transformed into profit centers, managers may continue to care about costs, but they may give new attention to production schedules and important marketing factors. Top managers have sometimes found that pep talks and cajoling do not get subordinates to accept top management goals. But giving profit responsibility works better because it crystallizes goals and provides better incentives. That is, goal congruence may exist in a vague, half-hearted fashion but profit centers provide the formal system that is so often the most persuasive means of communicating top management's goals and boosting incentives.

Professors and managers can spend hours delineating the weaknesses of profit centers and transfer pricing schemes, especially when the managers have little local autonomy. Nevertheless, despite their manifold defects, profit centers may often be the most cost effective way to obtain the desired goal congruence and incentives.[17]

------

[17]Incidentally, profit centers and decentralization are sometimes erroneously used as if they were synonymous terms. Decentralization is the relative freedom to make decisions. Although it seems strange at first glance, profit centers can be coupled with a highly centralized organization, and cost centers can be coupled with a highly decentralized organization. So the labels of profit center and cost center can be deceptive as indicators of the degree of decentralization.

In addition to the questions of using profit centers or cost centers, other accounting issues may be assessed by using the approach advocated here. For example, more detailed or elaborate overhead rates usually are developed in a cost-benefit framework. The key question is not which is the most accurate cost allocation. Rather, it is how much accuracy is justified by potential uses.

Another much-publicized development is human resources accounting. Much of the literature focuses on whether human resources can qualify in an accounting framework as assets and on how they should be valued. To me, the attractions of human resource accounting must focus on whether this more costly system will have the desired impact on decisions.[18] I hope that such evaluations of these human resource experiments are forthcoming soon.

Above all, the cost-benefit theme dominates the evolution of systems. When somebody's money is at stake, accounting systems get renewed attention. For example, the current boom in the installation of cost accounting systems in the health services industry is primarily explained by the growth of government-sponsored health care programs. To get reimbursed by government agencies, the health care institutions often have to use cost accounting to justify their claims. The net benefit of cost accounting has rapidly become obvious throughout an entire industry.

My illustrations here have pointed to cost-benefit analysis as being a major explanation of the evolution of management accounting systems. Practitioners and managers have been operating as information economists. A survival of the fittest mechansim may be at work. The "markets" for management accounting information, models, and specialists may be influenced by an invisible hand. In contrast, the existence and survival of financial accounting is often legislated via a quasi-political system.

Summary and Conclusion

The best accounting measure or system is that which

18An example of this focus is Nabil Elias, "The Effects of Human Asset Statements on the Investment Decision: An Experiment," **Empirical Research in Accounting: Selected Studies,** 1972, pp. 215-240.

produces the most benefit after deducting the costs of obtaining the data. We should incessantly ask the question: How much are you willing to pay for one accounting method or system versus another?

These implicit cost-benefit tradeoffs can be uncovered throughout the evolution of accounting. However, until recently we have given insufficient attention to the central importance of explicitly recognizing the choice among accounting alternatives as an economic decision made under conditions of uncertainty.

Some predictions are usually a part of this kind of paper, so I offer some at absolutely no incremental cost to you. Keep in mind that they are worth their cost.

Management accounting evolved from an absolute truth (numerical) emphasis to a conditional truth (contextual) emphasis. Currently, much attention is being given to the question of whether a cost-benefit (analytical) emphasis will be productive. The next step will probably be a stronger multi-person (behavioral) emphasis.[19]

The cost-benefit approach does not take us very far when we try to apply it in the multi-person setting of large organizations. The application of welfare economics and behavioral science holds some promise. However, the vast complexity of the subject matter defies any convincing synthesis. Still, I think progress is evident. Despite the absence of a tightly-knit operational framework, management accounting, which is still in its infancy, has become an increasingly strong part of accounting curricula and accounting research.

Management accounting courses and textbooks will probably encompass more of the approach of information evaluation and cost-benefit analysis as a general philosophy or point of view. If this occurs, it will be another illustration

---

[19]Accounting researchers are conducting research on human information processing that often can be linked with cost-benefit analysis. Some of this work has been influenced by M. J. Driver and S. Streufert, "Integrative Complexity: An Approach to Individuals and Groups as Information-Processing Systems," **Administrative Science Quarterly**, Vol. 14, No. 2 (June, 1969), pp. 272-285.

of how research--which is frequently highly abstract--eventually affects curricula.

The challenge facing the cost-benefit researchers is how to extend their method of analysis from single-person decision situations to multi-person situations. You can make your own predictions of their likelihood of success.

Of course, as the information economists and their advocates in accounting ease into the multi-person scene, they inevitably must contend, by definition, with complicated behavioral ramifications. Similarly, as management accounting curricula and research push beyond the rudiments of highly simplified situations, they face intricate behavioral problems. So our improvements in management accounting will primarily depend on how we embed behavioral accounting in our thinking.

I have taken no polls, and I have compiled only scattered, cocktail party evidence. Nevertheless, my hypothesis is that the teachers of management accounting are divided into two polar camps regarding the importance of behavioral considerations, a small camp that gives hearty attention to them and a large camp that almost ignores them. Furthermore, my weaker hypothesis is that the practitioners have an even smaller camp that gives attention to behavioral considerations. If these hypotheses are valid, our next step is probably to persuade teachers to give some serious attention to behavioral implications in their management accounting courses.

Although management accounting has thrived during the past twenty years continued progress will depend on whether researchers and teachers can improve our methods for analyzing multi-person situations. As a minimum, I hope that we can identify the major problems more clearly. To do so, the behavioral implications (such as effects on goal congruence and incentives) of our choices of accounting systems deserve front and center attention. Above all, management accountants should communicate the central role of the behavioral problems in management accounting to students, managers, and other interested persons--at least to the extent that individuals become highly sensitive to the idea that accounting may be as closely related to the behavioral sciences as to economics and the decision sciences.

Agency Research In Managerial Accounting: A Survey

STANLEY BAIMAN*

University of Pittsburgh

I. INTRODUCTION

Managerial accounting texts advocate the use of several different types of procedures including overhead allocation, flexible budgeting, standard costing, and cost-volume-profit analysis. Managerial accounting texts also advocate a cost-benefit approach toward the choice, design, and implementation of such procedures. (See, for example, [Horngren, 1977, p. 7]). Until recently, however, managerial accounting research has not attempted to assess formally the value of these procedures by applying this cost-benefit philosophy to them. Rather, managerial accounting research has tended to assume their usefulness and value and has concentrated on (a) studying the attributes of specific ways or techniques of implementing these procedures, (b) generalizing the standard techniques, and (c) generating new variations of the standard techniques. For example, the recent game theoretic overhead allocation literature has suggested new methods of overhead allocation and new criteria for evaluating different procedures (see [Moriarity, 1975] and [Hamlen, et. al., 1977]). Dopuch, et. al. [1967] and Demski [1967] generalized variance computations. However, in none of the cited studies is there a formal demonstration of the value of the standard procedure or of the extensions advocated by the authors.

Cost-benefit analysis has not been rigorously applied to these procedures because the fundamental economic analysis on which such cost-benefit computations must be based has only recently been attempted in a systematic manner. Horngren [1977] implicitly admits this when he states: "Admittedly the measurement of these cost and benefits is an imposing, complex undertaking that may often be infeasible." [Horngren, 1977, p. 7]. "The cost-benefit way of thinking is widely applicable even if the costs and benefits defy precise measurement." [Horngren, 1977, p. 7, fn. 2]. One reason for this absence of fundamental economic analysis of managerial accounting procedures has been the lack of a well-defined, useful model of individual behavior within an organization. Both "well-defined" and "useful" are important characteristics which have been absent from models of human behavior previously suggested as frameworks for evaluating managerial accounting procedures. For example, Ronen and Livingstone [1975] suggested the expectancy model as a basis for the design of budgets. Hayes [1977] suggested contingency theory as a framework for managerial accounting. Both these behavioral models are so loosely defined that few precise and unam-

* This paper would not have been possible without the continuing intellectual stimulation provided by Joel Demski. Harry Evans and James M. Patton made significant improvements to this paper as a result of their comments and criticisms. The comments of Barry Lewis, Katherine Schipper, the Editor and an anonymous referee also significantly improved this paper. Finally, Bob Kaplan made numerous helpful suggestions on an earlier draft of this paper.

biguous implications have been derived from them. At the opposite extreme, models of the firm based on mathematical programming formulations have been suggested (see [Hamlen, 1980]), but these models are so complex and intractable that few managerial implications have been derived from them. Because managerial accounting information is produced and used by individuals within a multiperson organizational setting, the benefit and cost of installing a managerial accounting procedure depends upon how people react to and use its output in that setting. The agency model of the firm is based on a description of individual behavior within a multiperson organization. Analysis of the managerial accounting function based on this model has recently begun. The purpose of this paper is to survey and synthesize the subset of agency literature that has implications for managerial accounting.

Agency theory research focuses on the optimal contractual relationships among members of the firm, where each member is assumed to be motivated solely by self-interest. (The concepts of optimality, rationality, and efficiency used in agency research are discussed later in the paper). In the agency model of the firm, one or more individuals (the principal(s)) hire one or more persons (the agent(s)) for the purpose of delegating responsibilities to the latter. The rights and responsibilities of the members of the firm are specified in the firm's mutually agreed upon employment contracts. Agency research examines the relationship between the firm's information systems, its employment contracts, and the welfare of its members. In the agency model, the firm's employment contracts are optimal functions of the information supplied by the firm's managerial accounting information system. Further, in the agency model each individual chooses his actions optimally (in his own self-interest) based upon his own information (in part supplied by the firm's managerial accounting information system) and the chosen employment contracts. Agency theory therefore provides a model from which uses of managerial accounting information can be derived and studied.

In agency theory the firm is viewed not as an individual, but merely as an overlapping set of contracts among principals and agents, each of whom is assumed to be motivated solely by self-interest. Therefore the behavior of the firm is the outcome of the process that brings into equilibrium, via the agreed upon contracts, the (possibly) conflicting self-interests of the principals and agents. In fact, much of the early agency research was devoted to analyzing the reasons for the existence of the firm as an alternative to strictly market-mediated transactions [Alchian and Demsetz, 1972, Williamson, et. al. 1975]. While this early research was insightful and must be credited with developing the agency perspective (along with Jensen and Meckling [1976]), most of its results were based on casual rather than rigorous analysis.[1] The literature surveyed in this essay builds upon these early studies by specifying the agency model more carefully and analyzing it more rigorously.

---

[1] This is especially true of the Williamson, et. al. [1975] research. However, it is also true of the Jensen and Meckling [1976] research, since much of their analysis was based on graphs that they failed to justify. Further, while much of their analysis was in the form of comparative statics, they restricted the entrepreneur to a fixed nonoptimal employment contract.

This survey concentrates on those papers whose analyses have implications for managerial accounting. Results that are basically methodological are discussed only briefly. The survey does, however, critically analyze possible limitations of the agency model. Because of space limitations, the survey is limited to only the formal analytical agency research within nonprice (nonmarket) mediated settings.

The multiperson information economics literature studies the use and value of information in both small groups and in competitive markets. The latter generally studies the existence and characteristics of market equilibria in the presence of unequally distributed information. For example, see [Hakansson, 1977; Ng. 1975; Gonedes and Dopuch, 1974; Grossman and Stiglitz, 1976; Amershi, 1980b; and Riley 1979]. Atkinson and Feltham [1981] examine the agency problem within a capital market setting. While this literature is certainly important for understanding the efficient functioning of the economy, questions of market equilibrium are of tangential interest to the managerial accountant faced with choosing an information system. As a result, in this paper only the literature dealing with a small number of participants is surveyed. In addition, the literature dealing with behavioral experiments to measure the effects of different information systems is not surveyed in this paper. Schelling [1960] has been the source of many of the hypotheses tested. Harnett and Hamner [1973] survey some of this literature and provide their own results. Further, since members of a firm can always base their employment contracts on the chosen accounting system, this paper does not consider the literature that assumes a fixed contractual relationship and hence is more suitable to an analysis of the role of information in oligopolies (see, for example, [Baiman, 1975; and Ponssard and Zamir, 1973]).

This survey is potentially valuable for four reasons. First, because the area of agency research is new, the literature contains different perspectives, emphases, and sets of assumptions. A paper that classifies the existing work, pointing out similarities and differences, would be most helpful to future research. Second, the paper develops some positive implications of the agency research for commonly used managerial accounting procedures and for the philosophy on which they are based. That is, one purpose of this survey will be to analyze the extent to which the use of some familiar managerial accounting procedures is consistent with the agency model of the firm. Third, surveying the results of recent agency research will provide a basis for evaluating the potential of the agency model as the foundation for a rigorous normative theory of managerial accounting. Finally, the paper identifies some unanswered managerial accounting questions that may be amenable to the type of analysis discussed here.

In the social sciences a theory may be evaluated as either a normative theory or positive theory or both. A normative theory would describe how managerial accounting procedures should be designed. A positive theory would predict how people would react to given procedures as well as predict the form and use of observed procedures. The second purpose for the survey, as stated above, is to evaluate the agency model as a basis for a positive theory. The third purpose is to see whether a fruitful normative theory of managerial accounting can be based on the agency model. These two purposes are complementary since the degree to which we can have confidence that our normative suggestions will lead to the desired outcomes depends upon how well we understand (can predict) how people behave within an organizational setting. Further, a finding that the results of agency research are consistent with observed managerial accounting procedures (a positive statement) does not eliminate the usefulness of the agency model as a basis for a normative theory of managerial accounting. The agency model only describes the current equilibrium solution. New technology will bring down monitoring costs and make new monitoring alternatives available. The agency model in its normative role can help to evaluate these new alternatives and to attain the new equilibrium point more efficiently than might be possible without the formal agency model guiding our analysis.

In order to put the agency model in perspective, the second section discusses some other analytical models that have been suggested as possible frameworks for a theory of managerial accounting and compares them to the agency model. The third section contains a more formal description and discussion of the agency model. The fourth section contains the survey together with the classification scheme used to organize the literature. The fifth section provides the summary and conclusions.

II. NONAGENCY ANALYTICAL MODELS SUGGESTED AS FRAMEWORKS FOR A THEORY OF MANAGERIAL ACCOUNTING

In order to emphasize the distinctive features of the agency model, it will be helpful to first discuss briefly other analytical models that have been suggested as frameworks for the managerial accounting and control process. These include the Decision Theory model, the Syndicate Theory model, the Information Evaluator-Decision Maker model, the Team Theory model, and the Demand Revelation model. In each of these frameworks, a model of the firm (including a model of individual behavior within the firm) is described and then used to derive the demands for (i.e., uses of) managerial accounting information implied by that model. Each model can then be analyzed to determine how the managerial accounting information system should be designed in order to supply the kinds of information demanded.

The uses of managerial accounting information should be a derivable implication of the model rather than an assumption of the model. A model may lack internal consistency if it merely assumes the demand for an accounting procedure. For example, in the game-theoretic cost allocation litera-ture, the demand for cost allocations is assumed to exist. This literature then analyzes different allocation procedures in terms of various criteria. But the analyses invariably take place within the context of a model in which a strict improvement could be achieved (according to the chosen crite-ria) by not allocating costs. The assumed demand for the allocation of costs is inconsistent with the model in which the different allocation procedures are evaluated (see [Baiman, 1981] and [Demski, 1981] for critiques of this literature). This internal inconsistency leaves the model's implications suspect.

One test of the usefulness of any proposed model is whether its derived de-mands for information include those uses of managerial accounting information that are observed. This is a reasonable test because a model of the managerial accounting process whose derived demands for information do not include uses that are observed is probably based on an overly restrictive view of the manage-rial accounting process and therefore is likely to lead to the choice of suboptimal managerial accounting information systems and procedures. In this section these alternative analytical models are evaluated by comparing each of their derived demands for managerial accounting information to three observed uses, which are described next.

Managerial accounting information has at least three observed uses. The first use is to improve a manager's *ex ante* assessment of the production environ-ment in order to improve his production decisions. This is the *belief revision* use of managerial accounting information. For example, a plant manager may base his make versus buy decision on a forecasted incremental cost analysis, which is an output of the managerial accounting system. The manager revises his beliefs about the production environment based on this incremental cost analysis. (This belief revision use of information is comparable to the problem-solving use dis-cussed in [Simon, et. al. 1954].) The second use is to help supervisors *motivate* subordinates. The third use is to facilitate the *allocation*—among members of the firm—*of the risk* inherent in operating in an uncertain production environment. These *motivational* and *risk-sharing* uses of information are interrelated in that a subordinate's motivation can be influenced by the amount of financial risk im-posed on him. For example, a plant manager's compensation may depend upon a comparison between his plant's actual production cost and its cost budget, both of which are outputs from the same managerial accounting system as the previously mentioned incremental cost analysis. The financial *risk* to the manager (the un-certainty with respect to his compensation) will differ according to whether his cost budget is fixed or flexible. As a result, the plant manager's *motivation* to cut discretionary costs such as repair and maintenance will differ according to whether he is evaluated relative to a fixed or a flexible budget. Thus, the plant manager's motivation is affected by the financial risk that is imposed on him, and both motivation and risk are affected by the managerial accounting information that is collected and how it is used. Since the *risk-sharing* and *motivational* uses of information are interrelated, hereafter they will be jointly referred to as the *performance evaluation* use of managerial accounting information. (The performance evaluation use of information includes the scorekeeping use discussed in [Simon, et. al., 1954].)

Assume that one's preference ordering over a set of information systems when the signals of each are to be used only for belief revision purposes is different from one's preference ordering over the same set of information systems when the signals of each are to be used only for performance evaluation purposes. If this assumption is true,[2] then any model whose derived demands for information do not include *both* the belief revision and the performance evaluation uses will, in general, lead to incorrect managerial accounting information system choices because one use of the system's output is ignored. For each of the alternative models, its derived uses of information are compared to the observed uses of belief revision and performance evaluation.

The Decision Theory model [Feltham, 1968] was the first model in management accounting in which the demand for information was formally derived rather than assumed. In the Decision Theory model the firm is viewed as a single individual who is playing a game against nature. Prior to his own action choice, the individual may gather information, which he can use to revise his beliefs about nature's chosen action. While this model derives the belief revision use of managerial accounting information, it ignores the performance evaluation use because performance evaluation is meaningful only in a multiperson firm.

Syndicate Theory [Wilson, 1968; Demski and Swieringa, 1974; and Demski, 1976] models multiperson firms. In the Syndicate Theory model several individuals jointly choose a set of actions and a method for sharing the resulting uncertain outcome (the sharing rule). Each individual is interested in maximizing his own expected utility through the choice of the action and the sharing rule. The belief revision demand for information can again be derived. In addition, the choice of the action and the sharing rule will have an important effect on the total risk borne by the Syndicate and how that risk is allocated among its members. Since the sharing rule can be based only on jointly observed information, the Syndicate Theory model can be used to derive the risk-sharing use of information. The motivational use of information is still ignored because all motivational problems are assumed away. In particular, all information is assumed to be publicly available and the action is assumed to be jointly chosen and implemented.

The multiperson context is preserved in the Information Evaluator-Decision Maker literature [Demski and Feltham, 1977] and the Mathematical Programming literature [Bailey and Boe, 1976; Hamlen, 1980]. These models include an owner who delegates the action choices to one or more agents. The owner or information evaluator is assumed to act in his own best interest. Each agent, however, is assumed to act in a *exogenously specified* manner. No model of individual behavior is provided to explain why the firm's agents act in the assumed

---

[2] As will be discussed later in the paper, the ordering of information systems for belief revision purposes and for performance evaluation purposes are, in general, not the same.

manner.[3] Assuming rather than deriving the agent's decision rule creates difficulties if the agent is assumed to act contrary to his own best interests. Since these models do not explicitly state the agent's utility function, the reader does not know whether the agent is assumed to act in his own best interest. Therefore, any motivational implications derived from these models are suspect.[4]

In the Team Theory model [Marschak and Radner, 1972], as in the Syndicate Theory model, several individuals come together to choose a set of actions and share the resulting payoff. Unlike the Information Evaluator-Decision Maker model, each individual is assumed to act in his own best interests. Further, unlike the Syndicate Theory model, in a Team setting the individual action choices are delegated to *different* individuals who may separately acquire private information on which each can base his decision. Each individual bases his action choice only on the information available to him. But the welfare of the team depends upon the successful coordination of the individual action choices. The problem for the team is to choose the individual decision rules in order to maximize the team's welfare in the presence of decentralized information. Clearly, the belief revision use of information can be derived from the Team model, but there is no motivational role for information in the Team model since all individuals are assumed to have the same preferences. Each team member will therefore implement whichever decision rule is given to him. Further, the assumption of identical preferences implies that technological constraints are the only impediments to the full sharing and utilization of the privately acquired information. That is, when information can be transmitted in a Team setting, it is assumed to be transmitted honestly. In a more realistic setting, self-interest as well as technology may prevent the full and honest communication of information within a firm.

The Demand Revelation model [Loeb, 1975; Groves, 1975; Groves and Loeb, 1979] is the same as the Team Theory model *without* the assumption of identical preferences. The issue of interest is how to induce (motivate) the agents to reveal their private information honestly and to use the information to maximize the profits of the firm. Thus both a belief revision and motivational use for information is derived in the Demand Revelation model. Since the objective is to maximize the firm's profit, *unadjusted* for the compensation paid to the agents rather than the owner's residual claim to the firm's profits after compensating the agents, the Demand Revelation model is more appropriate for analyzing worker cooperatives than capitalist firms. (See [Groves and Ledyard, 1976] for a discussion of other problems with the Demand Revelation model).

---

[3] As Demski and Feltham [1977, p. 30] note: "With the evaluator's outcome generally dependent upon his as well as the decision maker's choice, we have a game situation. Although we do not explore determination of η^* (the optimal information system) and $\chi(\eta)$ (the decision maker's decision rule) in a game setting system (but, for simplicity treat $\chi(\eta)$ as exogenously given), it should be clear that such an approach would provide a more thorough analysis of the class of problems we are addressing."

[4] For example in the Dantzig and Wolfe [1960] decomposition model each agent is *assumed* to reveal truthfully his demand for each resource given the prices announced by the owner. Jennergren [1971] shows that each agent may be acting against his own best interests by responding honestly.

In summary, the nonagency analytical models proposed as frameworks for the managerial accounting process all have drawbacks. The use of information for performance evaluation (specifically motivational) purposes is either (1) ignored (the Decision Theory, Syndicate Theory, and Team Theory models) or (2) constrained by the use of *assumed* rather than derived decision rules for subordinates (the Information Evaluator-Decision Maker and Mathematical Programming models) or alternatively (3) the model of the firm is inappropriate (the Demand Revelation literature). These problems are all avoided by the agency model. The agency model represents the firm as an overlapping set of contracts between self-interested individuals. Further, there is an owner of the firm who is interested in his *residual* claim (after compensating the agents) to the firm's income. Therefore the agency model is based on a reasonable representation of the capitalist firm. In addition, because the firm's employment contracts are optimal functions of the information produced by the firm's managerial accounting information system and because each individual acts in his own best interest based on his own information (some of which he receives from the firm's managerial accounting information system) and his employment contract, the performance evaluation and belief revision uses of information observed in practice can be derived from the agency model.

III. THE AGENCY MODEL

In this section the agency model is discussed in more detail and an example of what will be called the basic agency problem is offered. This basic agency problem is then formulated mathematically and the formulation is discussed and criticized. Finally, generalizations of this basic agency problem are discussed.

III.1 The Sources of Conflict and Cooperation in the Agency Model

Although the agency model assumes that all individuals (whether principals or agents) are motivated by self-interest, this does not preclude there being a common interest among the members of the firm. As Fama [1980, p. 289] notes: "In effect, the firm is viewed as a team of individuals whose members act from self-interest but realize that their destinies depend to some extent on the survival of the team in its competition with other teams."

In Fama's description of the firm, self-interest motivates each individual so that the potential for intrafirm conflict is recognized. However, since each individual's welfare is dependent upon the success of the firm, increased cooperation among the members of the firm might result in an increase in the welfare of some members without a decrease in the welfare of any of the others—i.e., in a Pareto improvement.[5] The contractual relationships agreed upon by the members of the firm determine the extent to which self-interested and cooperative behavior diverge; hence the interest of agency research in optimal contractual relationships.

---

[5] The Prisoner's Dilemma (Luce and Raiffa [1957] is the classic example in which self-interest precludes cooperative behavior even though each prisoner would be strictly better off by cooperating.

If individuals are motivated by self-interest and if engaging in cooperative behavior would increase the welfare of some individuals but not decrease the welfare of any individuals, why would the individuals not engage in cooperative behavior? That is, why may there be a divergence between self-interested and cooperative behavior? To explain this phenomenon it is first necessary to explain more fully what is meant by cooperative behavior.

The behavior of the members of the firm is defined to be cooperative when:

(1) all members honestly share all information.

(2) all members act in the manner agreed upon; that is each member implements the action rule he is assigned (see (3) below).

(3) all members agree on a set of individual action rules and a method of sharing the uncertain outcome resulting from their individual actions such that no one can be made better off without making someone worse off. That is, they agree to a *Pareto optimal* set of action rules and sharing rules.

A cooperative solution is obtained when all members engage in the agreed upon cooperative behavior. For any situation, there may be many possible cooperative solutions since there may be many alternative Pareto optimal sets of action rules and sharing rules. *But the cooperative solution ignores motivational problems.* The Pareto optimal sharing rules agreed to in Rule (3) are not necessarily such that it is in each member's *self-interest* to reveal his information honestly (as *assumed* in Rule (1)) and to implement the action rule he is assigned (as *assumed* in Rule (2)). That is, if all other members of the firm behave cooperatively, it may still be in the self-interest of one member, *given his sharing rule*, to act in a manner different from that agreed to. If this is true for one or more members of the firm and if they are motivated by self-interest, then each will *not* act cooperatively but rather act differently—in a purely self-interested manner—possibly making *all* members worse off than if they had acted cooperatively. The problem is that the cooperative behavior agreed upon may not be *enforceable* (may not be in the self-interest of each member to implement) given the cooperative sharing rules agreed upon. More generally, the environment in which the firm operates may be such that there exists *no* set of sharing rules and action rules based on cooperative behavior such that it is in the self-interest of each member to reveal his information honestly and to implement his assigned action rule. Thus cooperative behavior need not be enforceable (i.e., achievable) for the self-interested individuals who make up the firm. Again, agency research focuses on the design of employment contracts to mitigate the divergence (i.e., conflict) between the cooperative behavior that will maximize the welfare of the individuals and the self-interested behavior that is achievable.

This divergence between self-interested and cooperative behavior may arise for either of two reasons. Both reasons result from the principal hiring the agent to perform some duties but not being able to *motivate* the agent appropriately to perform those duties. The principal hires an agent in order to delegate to him the responsibilities for providing inputs to the firm's production process and possibly for gathering and processing information for decision-making purposes. First, assume that the agent is hired only to provide inputs to the firm's production process. If the inputs supplied by the agent are observed by the principal, then the amount supplied can be used as the basis for contracting between the principal and agent. In this case, the agent can be appropriately motivated to supply the inputs since he is paid only for inputs he actually supplies. However, some variable other than the agent's actual input may have to serve as the basis for contracting between the principal and agent, as when the principal cannot observe the input supplied by the agent. The use of this surrogate as the basis for contracting between the principal and agent may result in a reduction of the agent's incentive to supply the input (it may increase his incentive to shirk) and result in a loss of welfare for *both* the principal and the agent. This resulting reduction in the welfare of *both* individuals indicates a divergence between self-interested and cooperative behavior; that is it indicates imperfectly resolved conflicts between the two individuals. When motivational problems and conflicts arise as a result of basing contracts on imperfect surrogates of behavior, the problem of *moral hazard*[6] is said to arise.

The second possible reason for the divergence between cooperative and self-interested behavior may arise even if the principal can verify the amount of input supplied by the agent and can base the agent's employment contract on his input. For if the agent bases his input supply decision on private information that cannot be verified by the principal, then the principal cannot determine whether the observed input was the appropriate choice given the action rule that the principal wants the agent to use and given the agent's actual private information. This situation arises in decentralized firms in which subordinates are typically *better informed* about the production environment or the marketing environment than are their supervisors. If the agent is motivated to misrepresent his private information in order to successfully implement an input action rule different from that desired by the principal (again, possibly in order to shirk) then the problem of *adverse selection* is said to arise.

Both moral hazard and adverse selection are information-based problems. If the principal's information system accurately reports the agent's input choice and private information, moral hazard and adverse selection can be eliminated. For example, the principal and agent would agree on the desired input decision rule and payment due to the agent for implementing that decision rule. Since the principal can observe both the agent's input and information, he can verify whether the agent has in fact fulfilled his contract. If the agent has fulfilled his contract, the principal pays the agent the agreed upon amount; if the agent has not, the principal pays a smaller amount. This is termed a forcing contract. In this situation the principal and agent's relationship is effectively reduced to a market-mediated transaction. Agency theory's concern with the welfare of the

---

[6] The problem in the Prisoner's Dilemma presents a moral hazard: Both individuals would be better off if neither confessed. But such behavior is not enforceable because the two prisoners cannot write an enforceable contract between themselves based on their confessing behavior. That is, each individual's action choice is whether to confess or not. But in the Prisoner's Delemma, the individuals cannot write a contract between themselves which punishes or rewards each based on their respective action choices.

firm's members leads to its interest in the use of information in contracts to mitigate the welfare-reducing problems of moral hazard and adverse selection.

III.2 An Example of an Agency-Type Problem

In this section an example of an agency-type problem that is representative of the types of problems analyzed in much of the extant agency literature is presented. This example should make clearer to the reader the kinds of problems amenable to an agency-type analysis. Further, the more detailed description of the agency model and the survey of the agency literature that follow in later sections will be made more concrete by discussing them in terms of the simple agency-type problem presented next.

The firm consists of two individuals, a principal and an agent, and operates in a single-period world. One person (the principal) owns a fully automated machine that lasts only one period. The principal hires a second person (the agent) to perform preventive maintenance on the machine. This preventive maintenance is to be performed at the start of the period. The agent is hired solely for his labor. Any information that the agent has about the machine is also known by the principal. If the machine breaks down during the period, it remains down for the duration of the single period. The agent cannot repair the machine once it breaks. The market for the machine's output is competitive with a known price per unit. The sales value of the machine's output (x) is a random variable that is a function of the amount of preventive maintenance supplied by the agent (e) and the machine's realized breakdown parameter (Θ, the state realization), where $x = x(e, \Theta)$. For a given state realization, the more preventive maintenance supplied by the agent, the longer the machine will run before it breaks down and therefore the greater the sales value of the machine's output during the single period. Likewise, for a given amount of preventive maintenance, the greater the state realization, the greater will be the sales value of the machine's output during the single period.

The agent receives no additional information about the machine's breakdown parameter between the time when he is hired and the time when he performs the preventive maintenance. The principal cannot directly verify the amount of preventive maintenance provided by the agent, nor can he directly verify the machine's realized breakdown parameter. The principal is assumed to sell the output of the machine himself and therefore to observe directly the machine's sales output (x). In addition, the firm has an information system, (η), which reports a signal ($y \in Y$) at the *end* of the period to both the principal and the agent. This *public post-decision* information system (η, hereafter also referred to as the *monitoring system*) produces signals that may convey information about the amount of preventive maintenance actually supplied by the agent (e) and/or about the realized breakdown parameter (Θ). Thus, depending on the form of monitoring system, the agent may not learn the machine's sales output.

33

The principal values only his residual claim on the firm's cash flow, the difference between the firm's sales output (x) and the amount paid to the agent $(I(\bullet)^7$). The agent values his income $(I(\bullet))$ but dislikes providing preventive maintenance. Both individuals are expected utility maximizers. The principal's decision problem is to choose the agent's payment schedule $(I(\bullet))$ and the monitoring system (η) so as to maximize his own expected utility subject to inducing the agent to work for him. The agent's problem is to supply that amount of preventive maintenance (e) that will maximize his own expected utility given the chosen payment schedule and monitoring system. In evaluating any payment schedule-monitoring system repair, the principal must consider what level of preventive maintenance the agent (acting in his own best interest) will be induced to supply given that repair.

In this simple example a moral hazard problem may arise because the principal cannot directly verify the amount of preventive maintenance activity supplied by the agent and therefore may have to contract with the agent based on some surrogate measure of his preventive maintenance activity. No adverse selection problem can arise because the principal has access to all the information on which the agent bases his preventive maintenance decision.

Before this problem can be analyzed within an agency context, the environment in which the firm operates and the assumptions underlying agency analysis must be discussed more fully. For example, what restrictions are there on the kinds of contracts into which the principal and agent can enter? What are the characteristics of the agency solution concept? This more thorough discussion of the agency model, within the context of the preventive-maintenance problem outlined here, is presented next.

III.3 Description of the Basic Agency Problem

The agency model of the firm is distinguished from other models by its description of the individual members of the firm and of the world in which they operate. The preventive maintenance example given above and its description are representative of the class of problems, hereafter referred to as the *basic agency problem*, which is the focus of much of agency research. In this section, the description of the basic agency problem will be illustrated within the context of the preventive-maintenance example. Criticisms and generalizations of this basic agency problem will be discussed later.

The description of the basic agency problem can be divided into three major categories. The first category ((a) and (b) below) consists of the description of the principals and agents, their relationship, preferences, and belief. The second category ((c) through (i) below) includes the description of the production, informational, and legal environment in which the firm operates. The final category ((j) through (1) below) consists of the specification of the solution concept used in the agency literature. The basic agency problem, consists of the following:

---

[7] The arguments in the agent's schedule $(I(\bullet))$ are left unspecified until later.

(a) *Description of the two individuals*:

   i) The principal or residual claimant of the firm who supplies the production process (the machine, in the preventive maintenance example).

   ii) The agent who is hired by the principal and to whom is delegated the responsibility for supplying productive inputs (preventive maintenance, in the example) and possibly information (for example, knowledge about the machine's breakdown parameter). In the basic agency problem and preventive maintenance example, the agent is *not* hired to gather or process information.

Both individuals subscribe to the expected utility hypothesis. That is, they both exhibit rationality and can peform all necessary computations costlessly. The principal values only consumption and is risk averse. His utility function for income is assumed to be $G(x - I(\bullet))$. The agent also values consumption and is assumed to be strictly risk-averse. Further, the agent gets disutility from providing preventive maintenace services, i.e. he dislikes the task. His utility function for income and preventive maintenance services is assumed to be $U(I(\bullet), e)$.

The principal hires the agent to perform the preventive maintenance task, and it is assumed that the principal cannot directly observe the service provided by the agent. The principal can influence the agent's actions only to the extent that he can control the agent's payment schedule ($I(\bullet)$) and the monitoring system (η) and hence can influence the agent's *motivation* to provide the preventive maintenance.

(b) *Description of the initial distribution of information and beliefs.*

In the basic agency problem and in the preventive maintenance example, prior to the formation of the firm the principal and agent possess exactly the same information and beliefs about the stochastic process generating the machine's realized breakdown parameter and about the characteristics of each feasible information system.[*] That is, neither individual has *private pre-contract* information. Alternatively stated, there is no *asymmetry* of pre-contract information. The principal is assumed to know the agent's preferences and beliefs.

(c) *Description of the number of periods.*

The basic agency problem assumes a one-period world.

(d) *Description of the firm's production function.*

The firm's production function relates the following to the machine's sales output (x):

   i) the amount of capital supplied by the principal (the machine)

   ii) the agent's level of preventive maintenance, e and

---

[*] If the principal's and agent's assessed probability distributions over some uncertain event differ strictly because of different information, they are said to have different beliefs. If they differ for reasons other than different information, they are said to have different opinions. The distinction is important in that the existence of different opinions raises possibilities of side betting on the state realization between principal and agent. Most of the agency literature assumes identical opinions and therefore suppresses the use of information for side-betting purposes. Homogeneous opinions will be assumed throughout this paper. For analyses that do assume heterogeneous opinions, see [Wilson, 1968] and [Amershi, 1979].

iii) an exogenously determined uncertain state realization (the machine's breakdown parameter, Θ).

(e) *Description of the feasible set of actions from which the agent chooses.*

In the basic agency problem it is assumed that the level of preventive maintenance supplied by the agent can be represented as a nonnegative, bounded scalar.

(f) *Description of the labor and capital markets.*

Each individual has access to a market in which he can sell his labor or capital for a given expected utility. The agent's opportunity cost of joining the firm is foregoing an expected utility of K by selling his services in the labor market. The principal's opportunity cost of devoting his machine to the firm is foregoing an expected utility of C by selling the use of his machine in the market.

(g) *Description of the feasible set of information system.*

Information can be acquired by the principal or agent at any of three times. Each may acquire *pre-contract* information prior to joining the firm. As was stated earlier, in the basic agency problem it is assumed that the principal and agent join the firm with the same information and beliefs; that is, they have symmetric pre-contract information and beliefs. Once the principal and agent join the firm they may jointly or separately acquire information at either or both of two times.

Before the agent makes his preventive maintenance decision, the firm's *pre-decision* information system may provide a signal with information about the machine's realized breakdown parameter, say as a result of conducting a test of the machine. The signal may be observed by both individuals or only by one of them. In the basic agency problem and the preventive maintenance example it is assumed that the firm has *no* pre-decision information system. The information on which the agent bases his maintenance decision is therefore merely his pre-contract information, which was assumed to be identical to the principal's pre-contract information.

Subsequent to the agent supplying his maintenance services, the firm's post-decision information system (i.e., the monitoring system) may supply a signal, y, with information about one or more of the following: the machine's sales output, the realized breakdown parameter, or the amount of maintenance supplied by the agent. This signal is reported *publicly* (i.e. to *both* the principal and the agent). The principal is assumed to sell the machine's output personally and therefore is assumed always to observe the sales output (x) directly. Since the agent is not involved in selling the machine's output, he is not assumed to observe directly the sales output (x). Therefore, the signal produced by the monitoring system is the *only* jointly observed signal produced within the firm. That is, while the principal's post-decision information consists of (x,y), the agent's consists only of (y). The monitoring system (η) is the only information system that is a choice variable (rather than a given) in the basic agency problem. (As will be discussed in later sections, the basic agency model can be expanded to include those situations in which the pre-decision information system is a choice variable as well.) Further, in the basic agency problem it is assumed that for each feasible monitoring system ($\eta \epsilon \; \Xi$), both individuals agree on the probability distribution of x and y given e (as represented by $\phi(x,y|e,\eta)$).

(h) *Description of the legal system*

The central focus of agency theory is the employment contract (which includes the agent's payment schedule and the monitoring system). Contracts are enforced by legal institutions.[*] The decision of legal institutions as to whether an employment contract has been honored or violated depends upon the evidence that can be submitted by the contracting parties to the legal enforcement mechanism. The legal system specifies what is admissible evidence. This specification clearly influences the set of contract types that would be considered by the contracting parties. For example, the agent would never agree to an employment contract in which the agent's payment schedule was a function of inadmissible data. In the basic agency problem it is assumed that only *jointly* observed data can serve as the basis of contracting, i.e. are admissible data. The monitoring signal (y) is the only jointly observed piece of data and therefore that signal is the only piece of data on which the principal and agent can contract. If the monitoring signal (y) does not include the amount of preventive maintenance supplied by the agent, the potential for moral hazard arises.

The legal system also specifies the types of behavior that can be legally enforced. For example, can the agent credibly commit himself *now* to perform some act *in the future* from which *neither* principal nor agent would *then* benefit, if the principal does not now agree to the agent's most desired employment contract? If the agent can, then he can engage in such strategic or threatening behavior in order to improve his bargaining position with respect to his payment schedule and the monitoring system.[10] The agent makes such threats credible if he can use the legal system to put himself into a position in which he *has* to carry out his threat if his demands are not met by the principal. In the basic agency problem, it is assumed that the legal system does not give the agent the option of committing himself to engage at some future time in behavior that would not *then* be in his self-interest. Thus, it is assumed that the agent cannot credibly engage in strategic behavior in order to influence the principal's choice of the employment contract.

---

[*] Contracts, or more generally behavior, may also be enforced by social pressure and reputational effects. See [Schelling, 1978] for discussion of these.

[10] This is an example of "first-mover's" advantage or the advantage one can gain in negotiation situations by reducing one's own options. See [Schelling, 1960] for additional discussion of these and other game-theoretic issues.

For example, can the agent commit himself to destroy the principal's machine if the principal does not agree to the agent's most desired contract? If the agent would go to jail for this act, he might not go through with such a plan even if the principal did not agree to the agent's most desired contract. In this case the threat is not credible. If the agent had already hired an arsonist to destroy the machine if the principal did not agree to the desired contract and if the agent has no way of subsequently communicating with the arsonist but the arsonist can independently observe the contract to which the principal and agent have agreed, then the threat is enforceable and credible and may cause the principal to capitulate, thereby assuring that the threat would never be carried out.

(i) *Description of the feasible set of payment schedules.*

In the basic agency model, the principal chooses the payment schedule and the monitoring system to reward and motivate the agent. The information and legal restrictions on the feasible set of payment schedules were discussed earlier. It is important to emphasize the relationship between the chosen monitoring system and the feasible set of payment schedules. If a certain type of information is not publicly reported by the chosen monitoring system (say the sales value of the output (x)), then any contract based on that information is not enforceable and thus not feasible. Finally, there may also be technical restrictions on the set of feasible payment schedules. In the basic agency problem these restrictions are quite weak. For example, the payment schedule is not even required to be a continuous or differentiable function.

The usual assumption is that the payment schedule must be chosen from the set of bounded and measureable functions. An experiment is a set S of elements or outcomes τ. Events are subsets of S to which probabilities are assigned. Let A and B be events and A^c be the implement of A. Field F is a nonempty class of sets such that:

i) if $A \in F$, then $A^c \in F$
ii) if $a \in F$ and $B \in F$, then $A \cup B \in F$

A real-valued function whose domain is in the space S such that the set $\{x < \tilde{x}\}$ is an event for any real number $\tilde{x}$ is called measurable in the field F. See [Papoulis, 1965].

(j) *Description of the solution to the basic agency model.*

The solution to the basic agency problem consists of:
   i) the employment contract, which incorporates:
   1. the payment schedule for the agent;
   2. the information system choices ($\eta \in \Xi$ for the basic agency problem);
   3. specification of how the agent *promises* to act;
   ii) the agent's actual action

Since the payment schedule and information system choices that are implemented are jointly observable and admissible data, the agreed upon payment schedule and information system choices are legally enforceable. That is, it can be assumed that the principal and agent legally commit themselves to the agreed upon payment schedule and information system choices. However, if the agent's action choice is not jointly observable, the agent cannot credibly commit himself to any action that is not in his best interest to implement.

The remaining descriptions relate to the assumed behavior of the principal and the agent and to the solution concept employed in agency research. These specifications are the essential defining characteristics of the agency framework and are common to all agency work, not just those dealing with the basic agency problem.

(k) *The role of self-interest.*

Each individual acts in his own best interest. That is, each individual's choices are endogenously derived (rather than assumed) and are based only on his own self-interest. Further, each individual expects all other individuals to act solely in their own best interests, and therefore each chooses his own action based on that expectation. Each individual's expectations about the choices made by the others must therefore be in equilibrium. Thus, the principal chooses the payment schedule and monitoring system that best exploits (based on the principal's own interest) the agent's self-interested behavior. In short, agency theory exploits the power of self-interest as a stabilizing and predictive force.

(l) *The solution concept and the nature of optimality.*

While each individual acts in his own best interest (according to expected utility maximization) based on the expectation that all others will act in their own best interest, the nature of this expectational equilibrium must be further specified. To do so, the forces of self-interest and shared interest must be reconciled.

Agency theorists have accomplished this reconciliation by using the intersection of two game-theoretic solution concepts. *First*, agency theory restricts the set of feasible employment contracts to those that are self-enforcing as defined by the *Perfect Nash solution concept*, which has the following assumptions:

> (i) It is assumed that the agent cannot engage in credible strategic or threatening behavior in order to influence the principal's choice of the employment contract. This follows from the assumed legal environment discussed in (h), above. Therefore, it is assumed that the agent will always choose to supply that level of preventive maintenance service that maximizes his expected utility *given* the chosen employment contract and his own information.
>
> (ii) It is assumed that the principal restricts his choice of the employment contract to be from that set of contracts such that the agent actually supplies (i.e. finds it in his own best interest to supply) the level of preventive maintenance that he *promised* to supply when he agreed to the contract.[11]

The self-enforcing aspect of the Perfect Nash solution concept comes from the fact that the chosen payment schedule-monitoring system pair is such that the agent does (i.e. from Part (i) finds it in his own best interest to do so at the time that he must act) what the principal expects him to do (from Part (ii)). We call such a $(\eta, I(\bullet), e)$ triple a self-enforcing triple or a self-enforcing contract.

Second, from this set of Perfect Nash self-enforcing employment contracts, it is assumed that all contracts that are Pareto-inferior to at least one other contract in the set of self-enforcing contracts are eliminated from consideration. The employment contract chosen will be selected from the subset of contracts remaining after these two stages.

---

[11] The agent's *promised* as well as actual behavior is part of the agency solution.

It may be helpful to illustrate the use of this agency theory solution concept within the context of the preventive maintenance example. For a given feasible monitoring system, η_1, the principal enumerates *all* feasible payment schedules and the agent's optimal preventive maintenance response to *each* monitoring system-payment schedule pair. Each triple $(\eta_1, I(\bullet), e)$, will generate a pair of expected utility points, one for the principal, one for the agent. From this set the principal eliminates all those triples that produce Pareto inferior expected utility pairs. The principal is then left with the Pareto frontier for the given monitoring system, η_1. The principal then repeats this exercise for each feasible monitoring system. If the Pareto frontier for any monitoring system is everywhere dominated by the Pareto frontier of any other system (the frontier of the first is everywhere to the left of the frontier of the second), the dominated one is eliminated. If one Pareto frontier remains, then that is the Pareto optimal monitoring system and the principal and agent bargain over the particular feasible payment schedule (or a randomization over payment schedules if the frontier is not concave).[12] If there is more than one Pareto frontier left (for example, two or more frontiers cross) then the principal and agent must bargain over randomizations of payment schedule-monitoring information system pairs in order to produce an overall concave Pareto frontier. In summary then, all Pareto comparisons between information systems are comparisons between Pareto frontiers, not between individual expected utility pairs.

Both the cooperative solution concept and the agency solution concept arrive at a solution by applying the Pareto criterion to a set of contracts, i.e. $(\eta, I(\bullet), e)$ triples. The cooperative solution is arrived at by applying the Pareto criterion to all possible combinations of η, $I(\bullet)$ and e subject only to $I(\bullet)$ being feasible given η (as was indicated in the discussion of the relationship between the set of feasible payment schedules and the monitoring system). The agency solution is arrived at by applying the Pareto criterion to all possible combinations of n, $I(\bullet)$ and e subject to: (1) $I(\bullet)$ being feasible given η *and* (2) e being the agent's optimal response to η and $I(\bullet)$. It is this additional second constraint imposed by the agency solution concept that captures the idea of self-interested behavior and that causes the divergence between the cooperative solution and the self-interested, agency solution discussed above. The cooperative solution ignores motivational considerations while the agency solution concept considers them (via this second constraint).

The use of the Pareto criterion in the agency solution concept defines the notion of firm efficiency; efficiency is defined in terms of the expected utilities of the principal and agent. The utility of the principal is a function of the probability distribution of his residual claim $(x - I(y))$, while the utility of the agent is a function both of his preventive maintenance activity (e) and of the probability distribution of his payment $(I(y))$. Therefore, not only is the firm's probability distribution of sales output an important consideration of the chosen

---

[12] With a pure payment schedule, for any given observed signal y, the agent would receive a specified amount $I(y)$. With a randomized payment schedule, for any given observed signal y, the agent would receive a specified *lottery* or gamble.

employment contract, but also the payment schedule ($I(y)$), which specifies how the risk of this sales output probability distribution will be shared is important. The choice of the firm's employment contract most often is the result of a trade-off between its productive efficiency (the distribution of x induced by the contract via its effect on the agent's incentive to provide preventive maintenance) and its risk-sharing efficiency. For example, if the agent is paid a flat fee, he has no motivation to provide preventive maintenance and bears no financial risk. In order to achieve a more preferred sales output probability distribution, the principal may have to increase the agent's incentive to provide preventive maintenance by increasing the agent's financial risk. The agent's motivation to provide preventive maintenance will be maximized if he pays a flat fee for the use of the machine and keeps the balance of the sales output for himself. Such an arrangement greatly increases the financial risk that the agent must bear. Because the agent is risk averse, this latter arrangement might not be Pareto optimal either. In short, the agency solution requires a trade-off between productive efficiency and risk-sharing efficiency.

Finally, it should be noted that the optimal agency employment contract is *ex ante* efficient, but not necessarily *ex post* efficient. After the agent has chosen his preventive maintenance level and the machine's sales output is realized, both individuals might be made better off by renegotiating the chosen payment schedule and monitoring system. But since the original agreement is assumed to be legally enforceable, they are prohibited from renegotiating. If the agent knew that they would renegotiate the employment contract after his action was implemented, his original action choice would no longer be optimal. Both individuals are made better off, *ex ante* by being prohibited from renegotiating the contract, *ex post*.

III.4 The Mathematical Formulation of the Basic Agency Model

The principal and agent must agree on a contract that is Pareto optimal as of the time that the firm is formed. Therefore the efficiency of any contract must be evaluated based on the information possessed by each at the time that the firm is formed. In addition, the efficiency of the contract is constrained by the fact that the level of preventive maintenance implemented will be the one that maximizes the agent's expected utility given the employment contract and his information.

Any Pareto optimal contract can be represented as one that maximizes one person's expected utility subject to the other person receiving no less than some specified level of expected utility.[13] Thus, an optimal contract for the preventive maintenance example is one that maximizes the principal's expected utility subject to the agent receiving at least some specified level of expected utility and also subject to the level of preventive maintenance activity being chosen so as to maximize the agent's expected utility given the chosen contract and his own informa-

---

[13] It is irrelevant whose utility is being maximized. By adjusting the minimum utility constraint for the other person, any Pareto optimal solution can be attained.

tion. In the agency literature it is usually assumed that the principal is the dominant bargainer and therefore that the agent's minimum specified level of expected utility is the expected utility he could receive by selling his services to the market, K.[14] The following is therefore the standard agency formulation of the preventive maintenance example and, more generally, of the basic agency problem:[16]

$$\max_{\substack{\eta \epsilon \Xi \\ I(\cdot) \epsilon I \\ \underline{e} \epsilon E}} \iint G(x-I(y))\phi(x,y|e,\eta)\, dxdy \tag{1}$$

Subject to:
$$\int U(I(y),e)\phi(y|e,\eta)dy \geq K \tag{2}$$

$$e \epsilon \, \underset{e' \epsilon E}{\text{Argmax}} \left[\int U(I(y),e')\phi(y|e',\eta)dy \right] \tag{3}$$

The only jointly observed information signal is y; therefore the monitoring signal y is the only argument on which the payment schedule, I(•), can be based.[16] Second, all individuals are assumed to have the same beliefs at the time that the firm is formed. They also share these same beliefs at the time that the preventive maintenance level is chosen. This is reflected in the mathematical formulation by having all individuals use the same probability distribution $\phi(\cdot)$.

The preceding mathematical program represents the principal's problem of choosing a Pareto optimal employment contract. His problem is to choose that employment contract that maximizes his own expected utility (Expression (1)) subject to the agent finding it in his own best interest to work for the firm (Expression (2)) and subject to the agent choosing that preventive maintenance activity that maximizes his own expected utility (Expression (3)). It will be easiest to explain the above mathematical formulation by explaining the meaning of each expression starting first with (3).

Expression (3), referred to as the agent's action self-selection constraint, represents the agent's preventive maintenance decision rule. It specifies that the agent will choose that preventive maintenance activity that maximizes his expected utility, taking the principal's choice of the payment schedule and monitoring system as given. The agent does not try to influence the principal's choice of

---

[14] This assumption merely restricts our attention to examining one particular Pareto optimal contract. Since K is exogenously given, there is no loss of generality in posing the problem this way.

[16] It is assumed that the preventive maintenance problem has a feasible solution. Therefore, since the principal's expected utility is being maximized, it is assumed that his maximal expected utility from devoting his capital to the firm is at least as great as what he would receive by selling it to the market, C. Therefore the constraint that the principal's maximal expected utility be at least C is dropped.

There are two formulations of the agency problem: the approach used by Mirrlees [1974] and Holmstrom [1979] (which is used here) and the Ross state-space approach [1973]. See [Amershi, 1980a] and [Ramakrishanan and Thakor, 1979] for syntheses of these two approaches and a demonstration of their equivalence.

[16] The principal is assumed to observe the firm's sales output, x, while the agent observes y which may be an imperfect monitor of x. Thus the basic agency model, as formulated here is an inappropriate model if one is interested in addressing the auditing problem in which the agent observes x but the principal does not. This survey does not discuss the auditing literature. For those interested in that literature, see [Evans, 1980] and [Ng and Stoekenius, 1979].

42

I(•) and η with threats (the Perfect Nash solution). It is Expression (3) that restricts the principal's attention to only the self-enforcing triples $(\eta, I(•), e)$. The agent bases his decision on his beliefs (represented by $\phi(y \mid e, \eta)$), which are the same as those held by the agent and principal at the time that the firm was formed. No new information is revealed between the time that the firm is formed and when the agent chooses e. If, at optimality, Expression (3) was not a binding constraint and therefore could be dropped,[17] then the cooperative solution would be attained since the problem of motivating the agent represented by Expression (3) could then be ignored.

The agent will not join the firm unless his expected utility from doing so is at least as great as his expected utility from selling his services in the labor market. Since the principal knows the agent's preferences and beliefs, the principal is able to evaluate each $(\eta, I(•))$ and *induced* e combination from the agent's point of view. The principal can then restrict his search to those self-enforcing triples $(\eta, I(•), e)$ for which the agent would agree to work for the firm. This restriction is reflected in Expression (2).

Expression (1) indicates that the monitoring system and payment schedule are chosen to maximize the principal's expected utility. Of course, the value to the principal of any monitoring system - payment schedule pair depends upon the level of preventive maintenance that it will induce the agent to take. Again, the principal is assumed to know the agent's preferences and information. Therefore, for each feasible employment contract the principal can solve the agent's choice problem (Expression (3)) in order to determine the preventive maintenance activity that the agent would be induced to provide given that contract. Thus the solution to Expression (3) is an argument in the principal's objective function, Expression (1). If the solution to Expression (3) for any given pair $(\eta, I(.))$ is unique, then that preventive maintenance activity which the agent is induced to provide by $(\eta, I(•))$ is used in Expression (1) to evaluate that pair $(\eta, I(•))$. Thus only self-enforcing triples $(\eta, I(•), e)$ are evaluated by the principal. If, however, for any given pair $(\eta, I(•))$ the solution to Expression (3) is not unique, it is assumed that the agent will pick from the set of maintenance levels that satisfies Expression (3) the maintenance level most preferred by the principal (as implied by the Pareto criterion). This accounts for the presence of the preventive maintenance activity as a decision variable in the principal's objective function.

III.5 Criticisms and Extensions of the Basic Agency Problem

The basic agency problem described earlier can be criticized along at least two dimensions. First, its assumptions would seem to limit its descriptive validity to a very small set of problems. Second, even if we accept the intrinsic interest of this small set of problems, the standard mathematical formulation of the basic agency problem can be criticized. Because most of the agency research has been based on the basic agency problem using the formulation as given above, it is

---

[17] This would occur if the monitoring system reported e and the principal could severely penalize the agent for not choosing the preventive maintenance level specified by the principal.

necessary to consider the severity of these two types of criticisms in order to evaluate the potential of the agency model as a foundation for a positive as well as normative theory of managerial accounting. The criticisms of the standard mathematical formulation are discussed first.

III.5.1 Some Criticism of the Basic Agency Formulation

(a) The Class of Payment Schedules

In Expression (1), the principal restricts his choice of payment schedules to the class of pure, nonrandomized payment schedules. This seems intuitively reasonable since the agent and (usually) the principal are risk averse and therefore introducing any additional uncertainty by means of randomized payment schedules could only reduce utility. Accordingly, almost all of the agency research starts by implicitly restricting the payment schedule to be nonrandomized. (Myerson [1979; 1980; 1981] is the exception). However, if the Pareto efficient frontier is not concave, then randomized payment schedules may be Pareto superior to nonrandomized ones (see [Raiffa, 1968] for a graphical illustration of this point.). The idea here is that if the Pareto surface is not concave it can be made concave by randomizing the payment schedule.

A problem therefore arises in that the results of much of the basic agency research may be based on suboptimal payment schedules. However, Gjesdal [1981] showed that a sufficient condition for the Pareto optimality of pure payment schedules is that the agent's utility in wealth and effort be additively separable (i.e., U(I, e) = H(I) - V(e)). But that is the assumed form of the agent's utility function in most of the extant agency literature. Further, the condition that the agent's utility function be additively separable is a sufficient condition, not a necessary condition. Therefore, the Pareto optimality of pure payment schedules *may* hold for an even larger class of utility functions, as well. Thus the severity of the criticism cannot be determined until the entire class of utility functions for which pure payment schedules are Pareto superior to randomized ones is established. This remains an open question.

(b) Formulation of the Agent's Problem

The formulation of the basic agency problem (Equations (1), (2), and (3)) allows for the situation in which the agent's optimal maintenance choice is not unique. However, the problem is almost always analyzed using a solution approach which requires that the optimal preventive maintenance level exist, that it be *unique*, and that it satisfy a *stronger* condition than Expression (3), namely the stationarity condition:

$$\frac{\partial}{\partial e'}\left[\int U(I(y),e')\phi(y\mid e',\eta)dy\right]_{e'=e} = 0 \qquad (3')$$

which is comparable to a first-order condition in the calculus.

The uniqueness of the optimal maintenance activity is required because the agency problem is usually formulated as an optimal control problem with η and $I(\bullet)$ as the decision variables and e as the state variable. In optimal control problems the path of the state variable must always be uniquely defined by the state equation (Expression (3) or (3')).

Expression (3') is more restrictive than Expression (3) in that Expression (3) is the necessary and sufficient condition for the agent's choice problem for *all* situations, while Expression (3') is the necessary and sufficient condition for optimality for only a subset of situations. Therefore, most of the basic agency results hold only for the class of problems for which, at the optimal $I(\bullet)$ and η, the agent's optimal preventive maintenance level exists, is unique and satisfies Expression (3'). Does such a class of problems exist? Can the class be characterized? These questions are addressed next.

Grossman and Hart [1980] found examples for which, at the optimal $I(\bullet)$ and η, the agent's optimal action choice was not unique. Mirrlees [1974] and Gjesdal [1976] found a class of problems for which the agent's optimal action did not exist. This latter class of problems, however, does not appear to be very large or interesting, since it essentially assumes that the principal can inflict arbitrarily large penalities on the agent.

Mirrlees [1979], however, found conditions under which the agent's optimal action choice exists and is unique and for which Expression (3') is a necessary and sufficient condition. The conditions found by Mirrlees [1979] do not appear to be overly restrictive and are consistent with Gjesdal's [1981] sufficient condition for the optimality of pure payment schedules. Further, by employing a formulation of the basic agency problem different from Expressions (1), (2), and (3'), Grossman and Hart [1980] were able to use a less restrictive solution approach than that used in previous agency research. Their formulation and solution approach allowed for the situation in which the agent's optimal maintenance level choice is not unique. Most of the results derived by Grossman and Hart [1980] were consistent with results derived from the more usual formulation (Expressions (1), (2), and (3')).

Thus Mirrlees [1979] showed that the class of problems for which the usual agency formulation (Expressions (1), (2), and (3')) is appropriate is both large and interesting. Further, Grossman and Hart [1980] showed that many of the results derived from the usual agency formulation also hold for classes of problems that cannot be so formulated.

In summary, the generality of the basic agency results seems to withstand both of these technical criticisms. The basic agency problem still analyzes a highly simplified organizational context, however. To what extent can the model be generalized? This issue is addressed below.

III.5.2 Extensions of the Basic Agency Problem

The basic agency problem includes a number of restrictive assumptions. In this section the implications of some of these assumptions are discussed. What will *not* be discussed in this section is whether the assumptions are realistic or not. Rather an instrumentalist approach [Friedman, 1953; Boland, 1979] will be taken; this approach judges a theory by its implications, not by its assumptions. From an instrumentalist veiwpoint the falsity of a theory's assumptions does not matter if its predictions are correct. This section studies the sensitivity of the results derived from the basic agency problem to changes in its underlying assumptions. Among the most restrictive assumptions imposed by the basic agency problem are: a single agent, exogenous labor markets, and a single period. Almost all of the results that will be discussed later were derived from models incorporating these three assumptions; therefore it is important to analyze the implications of these assumptions before discussing the results.

(a) Multiple Agents

While the agency problem as formulated can be expanded to the case of more than two people, most results are based on the two-person case. The results from a two-person analysis may not necessarily extend to a larger firm for several reasons. First, the subtle and difficult problems associated with coalition formation among the members in a firm of three or more persons are suppressed in a two-person firm. Allowing for collusive behavior among the firm's members may give rise to substantially different employment contracts and managerial accounting procedures than in a two-person firm. In addition, admitting coalitions implies that the self-enforcing notion discussed earlier must be broadened to incorporate coalition formation. That is, not only must the contract be such that each agent acting on his own finds it in his best interest to act as promised, but each agent acting in concert with any subset of the firm's members finds it in his own best interest to act as promised (see [Amershi and Butterworth, 1979] on this point). Second a two-person firm ignores the full hierarchical nature of the firm. Admitting multilevel firms may give rise to results that are also different from those to be presented later. Finally, in a firm with several agents, an agent could engage in a simultaneous play game against the other agents and therefore find it optimal to engage in randomized behavior.[18] In the basic agency problem, the agent plays a sequential-play game with the only other person involved (the principal), and therefore a pure action strategy is optimal.

The extent to which allowing for multiple agents will qualitatively change the two-person agency results or reduce the tractability of the agency model must await further research. However, there appear to be no *conceptual* problems in expanding the agency model to incorporate more people.

---

[18] Myerson's [1979; 1980; 1981] formulation does allow for randomized action rules by the agents. More often, the multiagent models assume away randomized action choice rules for the agents (see [Harris and Townsend, 1981], [Baiman and Demski, 1980b], and [Holmstrom, 1981a] for examples where this is done).

(b) Exogenous Labor Market

Because the agent's minimum expected utility is given and independent of the decisions taken by both the agent and the principal, the analysis of the basic agency problem is a partial equilibrium analysis. Interesting issues such as the effect of introducing new monitoring technologies on the labor market cannot be addressed within the model as formulated. Again, there appear to be no conceptual or technical problems in expanding the basic agency model to incorporate an endogenous labor market. In addition, the result should not be qualitatively different with this change since the effect is merely to enlarge the range of rewards and penalities that the agent can incur.

(c) Single Period

By limiting the model to a single period, many interesting issues are suppressed. Certain observed phenomena such as downward wage rigidity and the importance of trust and reputation in market exchanges are all meaningless in a single-period world but can be shown to be optimal responses in multiperiod settings. (See [Townsend, 1980], [Dye, 1980], [Holmstrom, 1981b], [Milgrom and Roberts, 1980] and the implicit contract theory literature separately surveyed by Azariadis [1980]). By expanding the basic agency model to multiple periods one may also be able to address rigorously the issue of short-run vs. long-run maximization by management (see [Lambert, 1981]). Further, combining a multiperiod model with an endogenous labor market constraint may greatly reduce the problem of moral hazard by increasing the cost to the agent of diverging from the cooperative action choice. Fama [1980] has argued that moral hazard will be completely eliminated in this case. Townsend [1980] and Radner [1980] found restrictive conditions under which moral hazard can be eliminated when one goes to an *infinite* period problem.

In addition, two weaknesses in the Perfect Nash solution concept arise when the agency model is expanded to include multiple periods and asymmetric information. First the rationality implied by the Perfect Nash solution concept may not be applicable at all decision points. Second the imcompleteness of information may not be dealt with satisfactorily by the Perfect Nash solution concept. As a result, within a multiperiod setting, the solution concept may lead to results that do not conform to a priori notions of optimality. (See [Kreps and Wilson, 1981]).

For a multiperiod setting, the defintion of a Perfect Nash solution needs to be stated more formally than it was earlier for a single-period setting. A strategy is Perfect Nash for a game if for every proper subgame, the strategy restricted to that subgame constitutes a Nash equilibrium for that subgame. Given this definition, two problems may arise. First, at any information set on the game tree, what is optimal behavior depends on one's beliefs as to which node within that information set one is occupying. But these beliefs may depend on which strategies were previously implemented. The Perfect Nash solution concept does not allow for the complete incorporation of this dependence within one's beliefs. Second, in a game with asymmetric information, not every decision node is the start of a proper subgame. Therefore, the Perfect Nash solution concept does not require its rationality assumption to hold at any decision node that is not the start of a proper subgame.

Kreps and Wilson [1981] overcome these problems by generalizing the Perfect Nash solution concept to what they call a sequential equilibrium solution concept. A sequential equilibrium requires that the decision taken by each player at *each* information set must be part of the equilibrium strategy from that point forward given his beliefs about the evolution of the game to that point. His beliefs must be consistent with Bayesian updating based on the hypothesis that the equilibrium strategy has been used to date and will be used in the future.

Thus, the Kreps and Wilson [1981] analysis provides the techniques with which to expand the basic agency problem to a multiperiod setting. The few results based on the analyses that have been done within the context of a finite-lived agency model are not qualitatively different from results based on a single-period model (see [Lambert, 1981] and [Townsend, 1980]).

In summary, then, it appears that the three basic agency problem assumptions discussed here can each be relaxed without raising major conceptual or technical problems. Whether relaxing one or more of these assumptions will result in qualitatively different findings must await further analysis. However, at this time, while it appears that relaxing the labor market and single-period assumptions will result in richer findings, it does not appear that such relaxations will result in findings that are qualitatively different from those derived from the basic agency problem. More analysis of multiagent problems is needed before we can determine the effect of relaxing the single-agent assumption.

This completes the preparatory explanation of the agency model, its objectives and assumptions. Given this previous discussion, we can next proceed to the survey and evaluate the results of the agency literature.

IV. SURVEY OF THE AGENCY LITERATURE

IV.1 Classification Scheme for the Survey

The agency theory literature is concerned with two interrelated issues: the *ex ante* value of information and how that information should be used in contracts. These issues are interrelated since the value of information depends upon its use. These issues are also crucial to the managerial accountant in his work. In designing the firm's managerial accounting system, the accountant must decide which information to collect regularly and which to collect on an *ad hoc* basis. In short, he must have a way of assessing the *ex ante* value of information. The managerial accountant is also concerned with the use of the information collected. For example, simultaneous with deciding whether and how to measure the cost of a maintenance department, the managerial accountant must decide how to use that information in evaluating the performance of the maintenance department as well as the production departments that use the services of the maintenance department.

Can agency theory help the managerial accountant to assess the *ex ante* value of information and to design procedures to use that information? The agency literature is surveyed here with this question in mind. The literature dealing with the *ex ante* value of information (section IV.2) is broken down into parts. The value of the public post-decision information system (the monitoring system) in the basic agency problem is studied first (section IV.2.1). Thereafter, the value of information in the presence of pre-contract information asymmetry (section IV.2.2) and in the presence of pre-decision information asymmetry (section IV.2.3) is studied. The discussion in sections IV.2.1 and IV.2.3 may be more technical than some readers require. Therefore, each of these parts starts with a summary of the issues addressed and the results derived by the literature surveyed in that section. Section IV.2 is concerned only with necessary and sufficient conditions for information to have *ex ante* positive value, assuming that the information is used optimally. The normative aspects of agency results (when *should* information be collected) are therefore stressed.

The literature dealing with the optimal use of information is surveyed in section IV.3. The concept of responsibility accounting is often used as a framework when designing managerial accounting information systems and procedures. The responsibility accounting concept is evaluated in light of recent agency results (section IV.3.1). The question of interest here is whether the results of agency research are consistent with the implications of responsibility accounting. The remainder of section IV.3 discusses agency theory results relevant to managerial accounting tools, such as budgets (section IV.3.2), conditional variance investigation policies (section IV.3.3), cost allocation procedures (section IV.3.4), participative budgeting (section IV.3.5), and standards (section IV.3.6). The focus in each of these sections is whether the observed use and form of each of these managerial accounting procedures is consistent with an agency view of the firm. Thus, discussion of the positive implications of agency results is stressed, in section IV.3.

As noted earlier, managerial accounting information is used for two purposes: belief revision and performance evaluation. Performance evaluation involves risk-sharing and motivation. These three uses of information are often in conflict. By using information to reduce the risk borne by the agent one may reduce his motivation. By providing pre-decision information to the agent for belief revision purposes one may make it less risky for the agent to shirk and thereby reduce his motivation. These examples suggest that with incomplete information, moral hazard and adverse selection problems (that is, motivational problems) are often mitigated by inefficient risk-sharing (relative to when motivation is not an issue). Therefore, to understand the value and uses of information fully, it is important to study it in situations in which both state uncertainty (and therefore, risk-sharing) and motivational issues are present. For this reason, this survey will concentrate on the literature in which both risk-sharing and motivational considerations are important to the value and use of information. Table 1 presents a classification of the agency literature based on the previous discussion.

Table 1. Classification of Agency Literature

		Motivational Issues (Moral Hazard and/or Adverse Selection)	
		Suppressed	Allowed
State Uncertainty	Suppressed		Alchian and Demsetz [1972], Holmstrom [1981[a]]
	Allowed *State Information Symmetry*	Arrow [1973], Raviv [1979], Demski [1976], Wilson [1968], Demski-Swieringa [1974]	Harris and Raviv [1979], Demski and Feltham [1978], Gjesdal [1976], Feltham [1977], Mirrlees [1974, 1975, 1979], Shavell [1979], Holmstrom [1979], Baiman and Demski [1980a, 1980b], Fama [1980], Lambert [1981], Lewis [1980], Radner [1980], Townsend [1980], Grossmann and Hart [1980]
	Pre-Contract State Information Asymmetry		Harris and Townsend [1981], Myerson [1979, 1980, 1981], Sappington [1979], Demski and Feltham [1978]
	Pre-Decision State Information Asymmetry		Harris and Raviv [1979], Christensen [1979; 1980a; 1980b], Holmstron [1979], Groves [1975], Groves and Loeb [1979], Loeb [1975], Magee [1980], Atkinson [1978; 1979], Baiman and Evans [1981] Kanodia [1980], Baron and Holmstrom [1980], Ramakrishnan [1980], Sappington [1979]
	Post-Decision Information Asymmetry	Townsend [1979][a]	Gjesdal [1981], Holmstrom [1981a], Evans [1980][a], Ng and Stockenius [1979][a]

[a]These papers concern auditing and will not be discussed in this survey.

IV.2 The Value of Information

The uses of information were discussed in the previous sections. This section addresses the determinants of the value of information. Given the basic agency model in which the only information system to be manipulated is the post-decision information system producing signal y (i.e., the monitoring system), what changes in that system can make both principal and agent unambiguously better off? The literature addressing this issue is surveyed first; the literature dealing with pre-contract information is addressed next; and that concerned with pre-decision information is addressed last.

IV.2.1 The Value of Post-Decision Information in the Basic Agency Problem

Should a division's income be measured on the basis of historical cost, price-level adjusted historical cost, or current cost? Should a divison's fixed assets be measured on the basis of historical gross book value, historical net book value, or current cost? These and comparable questions are addressed in the managerial accounting literature but have not yet been satisfactorily resolved [Solomons, 1965; Anthony and Dearden, 1976]. Each of these questions is asking for a preference ordering over a set of public post-decision information systems. These questions are specific examples of the more general issue concerning the conditions under which one public post-decision information system (i.e. monitoring system) is strictly Pareto superior to another, independent of the preferences and beliefs of the individuals involved. (All comparison with respect to information systems are comparisons between their *Pareto frontiers*: η_1 is Pareto superior to η means that the Pareto frontier of η_1 is everywhere to the right (northeast) of the Pareto frontier of η.). The fact that a preference ordering over information systems is independent of the preferences and beliefs of the individuals involved is important since it reduces the amount of information required to correctly apply the ordering.

In this section, the agency literature that addresses this general issue is surveyed. Any guidelines this literature can offer to help the managerial accountant assess the relative values of different public post-decision information systems should be of great benefit.

The most general result in this area is due to Holmstrom [1981a]. His analysis concerns the relative evaluation of any two costless[19] public post-decision information systems such that the signal produced by the second system is a deterministic transformation (independent of the state realization and the agents' actions) of the signal produced by the first system. An example of such a comparison would be between one monitoring system whose signal is (x,e) and a second system whose signal is (x). His result states that the first costless public post-decision information system is *strictly* Pareto superior to the second, regardless of the preferences and beliefs of the principal and agents, *if and only if* the signals of the first system convey more information about the actions chosen by the agents than do the signals of the second system. The idea of more information as used here is that implied by the concept of statistical insufficiency as defined in statistics and decision theory. While the *if* part of this result may seem intuitive or even tautological, recall that the measure of more information is a technical condition derived from a single-person setting in which there are no problems of

---

[19] All comparisons in this part are between costless information systems. Costs are ignored because any information system can be made to be preferred to any other merely by changing the costs of each. While the cost of an information system is important, the relative benefits of different information systems can be addressed without referring to the cost to implement and operate each.

risk-sharing or motivation. But yet Holmstrom's result shows that this measure is still useful in a multiperson setting in which risk-sharing and motivational considerations are important. The *only if* part of Holmstrom's result is important in its restrictiveness. In order to evaluate the usefulness of this result for managerial accounting, it is first necessary to determine which, if any, pairs of managerial accounting reporting systems satisfy the information system relationship assumed by Holmstrom [1981a]. That is, which pairs are such that the signal of one is a deterministic transformation of the signal of the other. If the traditional reporting alternatives are found to satisfy the relationship between the information systems assumed by Holmstrom [1981a] *and* are comparable on the basis of his informativeness condition, then the sufficiency (*if* part) of Holmstrom's [1981a] result provides the managerial accountant with a way of choosing among alternative public post-decision information systems independent of the beliefs and preferences of the principal and agent involved. If the traditional reporting systems can be paired such that the signal of the second system is a deterministic transformation of the signal of the first but the first signal does not convey more information than the second, Holmstrom's [1981a] result says that the ranking of the two monitoring systems *cannot* be done independent of which principal and agent are to use the system. Finally, if the alternative monitoring systems with which the managerial accountant is concerned are such that the signal of one is not a deterministic transformation of the signal of any of the others, then Holmstrom's [1981a] result is of no direct help. Analysis of which of these three situations describes the managerial accountant's choice problem has not yet been addressed. But at least Holmstrom's [1981a] result helps us to know what to look for first in analyzing the managerial accountant's monitoring system choice problem.

In the basic agency problem, on which the research to be surveyed is based, there is (i) homogeneity of opinions, (ii) symmetric pre-decision information, (iii) symmetric pre-contract information, (iv) a single agent, and (v) the post-decision information system alternatives are costless. Asymmetry of information arises only after the single agent chooses his preventive maintenance as a result of the principal privately observing the output, x. This part of the survey of the agency literature is concerned with the value of public post-decision information systems and is organized and discussed in order of increasing generality of the information system comparisons.

IV.2.1.1 Comparing a Nonnull Public Post-Decision Information System With a Null System

The least general comparison between public post-decision information systems is between one that produces a signal $y \in Y$ and one that produces no signal at all (the null system). When would receiving the costless public post-decision signal y, be strictly Pareto superior to receiving no public post-decision signal? In other words, when can any constant payment schedule[20] be strictly Pareto domi-

---

[20] The only possible nonrandomized payment schedule based on the null information system is a constant payment schedule.

nated by a payment schedule based on $y \in Y$?[21] Clearly it can never be Pareto inferior to observe y jointly and costlessly because both individuals can always agree on a payment schedule that ignores y. However, when can *strict* gains be made by jointly and costlessly observing y? Shavell [1979] showed that the principal and agent can both be made strictly better off (a strict Pareto improvement can be made) by installing a costless information system that publicly reports y = x. Gjesdal [1981] generalized Shavell's result by showing that as long as y is correlated with x,[22] a strict Pareto improvement can be made by installing the information system and using its signal as an argument in the payment schedule. The reasoning behind both results is that by jointly observing y versus no signal, a contract with improved motivational effects [Shavell, 1979] and/or improved risk-sharing effects [Gjesdal, 1981] can be achieved, resulting in a strict Pareto improvement.

IV.2.1.2 Comparing a Public Post-Decision Information System That Produces Signal y With One That Produces Signal y' = (y,e)

Assume that the principal and the agent have previously agreed on an employment contract that incorporates the costless public post-decision information system, η, whose signal is $y \in Y$. Under what conditions can a strict Pareto improvement be made by substituting a new costless post-decision information system, η', whose signal $y' \in Y'$ reports both the signal from the previous system η and the agent's actual preventive maintenance activity e, i.e., y' = (y,e)? Again this question can be restated as: When can any payment schedule based solely on $y \in Y$ be strictly Pareto dominated by a payment schedule based solely on y' = (y, e)?

---

[21] If every feasible payment schedule based on the signals of public post-decision information system η can be strictly Pareto dominated by at least one feasible payment schedule based on the signals of public post-decision information system η', then the Pareto frontier associated with η' is everywhere to the right (northeast) of the Pareto frontier associated with η, which implies that η' is strictly Pareto superior to η.

[22] More precisely, the principal's marginal utility for the machine's sales output and y must be correlated.

Clearly a necessary condition for η' to be strictly preferred to η is that the cooperative solution cannot *be achieved with a payment schedule based only on y. Otherwise, reporting the maintenance level can have no value. Demski and Feltham [1978] and more generally Harris and Raviv [1979] showed that neither party can be made better off by expanding the public post-decision information systems to η' (i.e. substituting a payment schedule based on y' for one based on y) if either:*

(i) y = x and the agent is risk neutral

or

(ii) y = (x,Θ)

That is, if either (i) or (ii) holds, the cooperative solution can be achieved with a payment schedule based only on y and hence there can be no value to publicly reporting the agent's chosen preventive maintenance level, e. In the first case, efficient risk sharing implies that the agent should bear all the risk by paying the principal a flat fee. (This assumes that the agent will not go bankrupt and be unable to pay the fee.). The agent bears all the cost of his maintenance decision, thereby eliminating the motivational (moral hazard) problem by internalizing it. In the second case, knowing Θ and x(e,Θ) allows the principal effectively to infer ex post the agent's maintenance decision. Since the principal is work indifferent, all he needs to know is whether, given the realized breakdown parameter (Θ), the payoff would have been generated by his desired e*, if it had been chosen. If we view (x(e,Θ),Θ) as an imperfect monitor of e we see that the probability of a Type II error (concluding that the agent chose e ≠ e* when, in fact, he chose e*) is zero. Thus the negation of (i) and (ii) provides a necessary condition for the cooperative solution to be unattainable with a payment schedule based only on signal y and hence provides a necessary condition for the managerial accountant to collect information on the agent's maintenance activity, such as by installing time clocks, or supervisory monitoring. This necessary condition is simple to apply and, thus, may be useful to the managerial accountant who is assessing the value of expanding his public post-decision information system.

Is the negation of (i) and (ii) also a sufficient condition for the strict Pareto superiority of publicly, costlessly, and perfectly monitoring the agent's maintenance activity? That is, does the negation of (i) and (ii) imply that any payment schedule based only on signal y can be strictly Pareto dominated by a payment schedule based on signal y' = (y,e)? Harris and Raviv [1979] assert that given that y = x, the negation of (i) and (ii) is a sufficient condition. If this analysis held under general conditions, it would represent a very useful result for the managerial accountant. The Harris and Raviv [1979] proof is based on the calculus of variations and therefore holds only for those situations for which the optimal payment schedule exists, is unbounded, and is differentiable. How, general, then, is their sufficiency condition?

Mirrlees [1974] provides an example in which no optimal solution exists when one allows for unbounded payment schedules or an unbounded utility function for the agent. In this case a contract based solely on x can approximate arbitrarily closely one based on x and e. Further, Gjesdal [1976] and Feltham [1977] point out a class of problems for which the optimal payment schedules do exist but are neither differentiable nor continuous. For example, if the firm's production function is such that the minimum possible firm payoff is increasing in e (i.e. $\frac{\partial}{\partial e} \left\{ \min_{\theta} x(e,\theta) \right\} > 0$) and there are sufficient penalties available, then the optimal sharing rule based on y = x will be discontinuous, and either the cooperative solution is attained or it can be approximated arbitrarily closely.[22] Therefore, in neither of these cases would the agent or principal pay to report the level of maintenance. Notice that the assumption which drives the Gjesdal [1976] and Feltham [1977] results is that the production function is such that by using x as an imperfect monitor of e, one can construct a monitoring system wiht a zero probability of a Type II error. Thus the restrictions underlying Harris and Raviv's [1979] sufficiency result reduces its generality and usefulness for managerial

---

[22] For example, assume the following problem: The firm's profit is characterized as x = e + δ where δ is uniformly distributed between 0 and 1. The principal is risk neutral. The agent is risk and work averse with a utility function represented by $\sqrt{I(\bullet)}$ - e²/100. The agent's minimum expected utility from other employment is .5. The first-best solution results in: I(•) ≈ 27.35 and e* ≈ 4.78. The following contract, based solely on x can achieve the cooperative solution:

accounting.

Noting these problems with the Harris and Ravis [1979] result, Holmstrom [1979] formulated the agency problem differently. He restricted the optimal payment schedule to be bounded but allowed it to be nondifferentiable. Holmstrom [1979] showed that if the set of x's (the set of sales values of the machine's output) which have a positive probability of occurring is independent of e,[24] if x is increasing in e, and if the agent is strictly work averse, then the cooperative solution is not attainable with a contract based solely on x. These conditions eliminate the situation in which x can be used as an imperfect monitor of e but one whose probability of a Type II error of zero, such as the production functions studied by Gjesdal [1976] and Feltham [1977]. Because the cooperative solution can be achieved with a contract based solely on y' = (x,e),[25] and because his assumptions do not appear overly restrictive, Holmstrom [1979] has defined a large class of problems in which both the principal and agent can be made strictly better off by expanding the accounting system to costlessly and perfectly monitor the agent's maintenance decision.

In summary, recent agency results provide the managerial accountant with conditions as to when a strict Pareto improvement can be achieved by expanding the public post-decision information system to costlessly and perfectly report the agent's preventive maintenance activity (e). Costlessly expanding the monitoring system to report e has *no* value if either (i) the agent is risk-neutral and x is already being reported or (ii) x and Θ are already being reported [Harris and Raviv, 1979; Demski and Feltham, 1978]. Under either of these two conditions the cooperative solution is achievable with a contract based only on x and (x,Θ), respectively. Therefore reporting the agent's preventive maintenance activity (e) cannot result in a strict Pareto improvement. Further if x is currently being reported, if the principal can inflict arbitrarily large penalties on the agent and if the firm's production function is such that using x as a monitor of e results in a zero probability of a Type II error (concluding that the agent chose $e \neq e^*$ when in fact he chose e^* for any $e^* \in E$), then again reporting e cannot result in a strict Pareto improvement [Gjesdal, 1976; Feltham, 1977]. Thus, the negation of the above conditions is a necessary condition for monitoring the agent's activity to have strictly positive value. Finally, Holmstrom [1979] found a *sufficient* condition for a strict Pareto improvement to result from costlessly expanding the monitoring system from one that reports x to one that reports x and e. This sufficient condition is essentially the previously mentioned necessary condition. This sufficient condition seems to be consistent with a large class of problems. A drawback of these necessary results and sufficiency results is that they relate to the issue of costlessly expanding the public post-decision information system to include the perfect reporting of the agent's preventive maintenance activity. However, this is

$$I(x) = \begin{cases} 5.23 & \text{if} \quad x \geq 4.78 \\ 0 & \text{if} \quad x < 4.78 \end{cases}$$

[24] This condition is violated in the example in footnote 23. Since δ is uniformly distributed between [0,1], changing e changes the set of x's which have a positive probability of occurring.

[25] The cooperative solution can be achieved with the following payment schedule based on y' = (x,e):

if $e = e^*$ let I(y') be the cooperative payment schedule.

if $e \neq e^*$ let I(y') be the smallest feasible payment.

an alternative that the managerial accountant rarely has available. More often the accountant must decide whether to expand the accounting system to include an *imperfect* monitor of the agent's activity. This type of information system comparison is discussed next.

IV.2.1.3 Comparing a Public Post-Decision Information System Which Produces Signal y With One that Produces Signal y′ = (y,z) Where z Is An Imperfect Monitor

The question now becomes: When can a strict Pareto improvement be made by costlessly expanding the public post-decision information system from reporting $y = x$ to reporting $y′ = (x,z)$, where z is an *imperfect* monitor of Θ and/or e?[26] The answer is not intuitively obvious. For even if there are gains to the *perfect* monitoring of e, this may not imply that a strict Pareto improvement can be achieved with *imperfect* monitoring of e. While the imperfect monitoring of e may reinforce the agent's work incentive, the additional uncertainty introduced by the imperfect monitor may decrease the welfare of the risk-averse principal and agent more than enough to compensate for the first effect.

---

[26] Even if z is independent of e but is an imperfect monitor of θ, observing both z and x may improve the principal's assessment of the agent's preventive maintenance activity. Therefore the distinction between whether z is an imperfect monitor of e or of θ is unimportant.

With this in mind Harris and Raviv [1979] found conditions under which any contract based solely on signals $y = x$ can be Pareto dominated by one based solely on signals $y' = (x,z)$. However, the criticisms made earlier of the Harris and Raviv [1979] analysis also hold here. Harris and Raviv [1979] restricted their analysis to public post-decision information systems such that $z = e + \delta$ where the distribution of δ is independent of e and θ and the range of δ is independent of e. With unbounded payment schedules and this type of monitoring system, one can use the Gjesdal [1976] analysis to show that one can either attain the cooperative solution or come arbitrarily close to it. Since such monitoring systems are therefore essentially perfect, they are of limited interest.

Gjesdal [1976] and to a greater extent Shavell [1979] and Holmstrom [1979] generalized the imperfect monitoring results of Harris and Raviv [1979]. Holmstrom [1979] defined a signal, $y' = (x,z)$ to be informative relative to the signal $y = x$, with respect to action e, if $y = x$ is not sufficient for $y' = (x,z)$ with respect to e, in the sense of statistical sufficiency. That is, the signal $y' = (x,z)$ is informative relative to the signal $y = x$ with respect to e if z conveys information about e not already conveyed by x alone. Assuming that both information systems are costless, Holmstrom [1979] proved that, regardless of the preferences and beliefs of the principal and agent, a payment scheduled based on signal $y = x$ can be strictly Pareto dominated by one based on signal $y' = (x,z)$ if and only if $y' = (x,z)$ is informative relative to $y = x$, with respect to action e. Note that since x is reported by both information systems compared by Holmstrom [1979] and the principal and agent have homogeneous opinions, this informativeness condition assigns no purely risk-sharing value to the additional signal z. The value of reporting z derives solely from its motivational influence on the agent.

The analyses of Holmstrom [1979], Gjesdal [1976], and Shavell [1979] differ in a number of assumptions. Holmstrom [1979] assumed that the agent's utility function is separable in money and effort. Gjesdal [1976] proved the sufficiency part of Holmstrom's [1979] result for the same utility assumption as Holmstrom [1979] but for signals that are independent of the realized breakdown parameter (the state). Shavell [1979] proved the sufficiency part for a more general agent's utility function, one that is increasing and concave in money and decreasing in effort but not separable. Shavell [1979] assumed that a pure payment schedule is Pareto superior to a randomized one (see earlier comments on this issue in the third section). Also Gjesdal [1976] and Shavell [1979] assumed that their problems were such that the cooperative solution could not be attained or approximated arbitrarily closely with a contract based only on x, whereas Holmstrom [1979] proved this. Finally, Holmstrom's [1979] result should be carefully applied since technically it holds only for those production function-information system pairs for which $\dfrac{\phi a(x,z|e)}{\phi(x,z|e)} = g(x|e)$ for either all e or no e. That is, he uses a global (for all e) definition of nonsufficiency. Those distributions $\phi(\bullet|\bullet)$ for which the above holds for some but not all preventive maintenance levels are excluded from Holstrom's [1979] analysis. The size of the class of distributions thus excluded has not yet been established.

In summary, even when the managerial accountant is faced with a decision of whether to expand costlessly his managerial accounting system from one that currently reports only the firm's sales output to one that *also* reports an imperfect monitor of the agent's activity, the results of agency theory provide the managerial accountant with a theoretically correct method of comparison. If and only if the imperfect monitor of the expanded system conveys information about the agent's activity, not conveyed by the sales output number (in the sense of statistical sufficiency), can a strict Pareto improvement be achieved by expanding to the second system, independent of the beliefs and preferences of the principal and the agent [Holmstrom, 1979]. This result represents a significant step toward understanding the role and value of information within a multiperson firm and provides the managerial accountant with a theoretically correct method of comparing monitoring systems in multiperson firms. However, the comparisons discussed in this section were between a finer information system (reporting $y' = (x,z)$) and a coarser system (reporting $y = x$). What can be said if neither of the systems to be compared is finer than the other?

IV.2.1.4 Comparing a Public Post-Decision Information System Producing Signal y With One Producing Signal y^T

The three types of public post-decision information system comparisons discussed so far have had one feature in common. In all cases, the comparisons were between two systems, one of which was finer than the other. That is, in all three cases, one information system reported all the data reported by the other *plus* an additional piece of data. Can agency theory provide a utility-free and belief-free way of ordering two public post-decision information systems where one is not finer than the other? The limited success that agency research has had in this endeavor is discussed now.

Gjesdal [1981] and Holmstrom [1981a] generalized their earlier analyses to make such comparisons. Let public post-decision information system η produce signal y, which need not include x as an element. Let the public post-decision information system $η^T$ produce signal $y^T = T(y)$; where T(•) is any function whose sole argument is the output of system η. Again, both systems are costless. Holmstrom [1981a] then showed that a necessary and sufficient condition for any payment schedule based on signal $y^T = T(y)$ to be strictly Pareto dominated by one based on signal y, independent of the preferences and beliefs of the principal and agent, is that $y^T = T(y)$ is not sufficient for y with respect to e in the sense of statistical sufficiency. I shall refer to this as Holmstrom's second informativeness condition. Holmstrom's earlier informativeness result [1979] is a special case of this more recent one, since he uses the same condition of statistical sufficiency in both but in Holmstrom [1981a] he applies it to a more inclusive set of information system comparisons. However, Holmstrom [1981a] assumed a risk-neutral principal while Holmstrom [1979] allowed for a risk-averse principal. Gjesdal [1981] proved only the sufficient part of this result for noisy (necessity for noiseless) signals but for a risk-averse principal. Finally, the sufficient part of Holmstrom's [1981a] informativeness result dealt only with production function-information system pairs that were either sufficient or insufficient at all levels of maintenance activity (the same caveat must be made for Holmstrom [1981a] as for Holmstrom [1979]), while Gjesdal's [1981] informativeness condition was required to hold only at the preventive maintenance level which was optimal for the payment schedule based on y^T.

All of the results surveyed so far have maintained the one principal-one agent assumption of the basic agency model and maintenance example. Baiman and Demski [1980b] and more generally Holmstrom [1981a] expanded the analysis to include multiple agents. Holmstrom [1981a] showed that his second informativeness condition was necessary and sufficient for one information system to be strictly Pareto superior to another in a multiagent setting as well.[27] However, the generality of this result is limited since Holmstrom's [1981a] analysis was based on the assumption that each agent's action choice was pure rather than randomized (see the previous discussion in the third section).

In summary, agency theory research has made significant progress in analyzing the value and role of public post-decision information systems and in pro-

---

[27] Baiman and Desmki's [1980] result was similar to the sufficiency part of Holmstrom's [1981a] result but required an additional assumption that Holmstrom showed to be superfluous.

viding normative rules for correctly choosing between costless public post-decision information systems in multiperson firms. Holmstrom [1981a] provides the most general conditions available for the belief-free and utility-free comparison of such systems. However this result is restricted to a comparison between two public post-decision information systems such that the signal of the second system is a deterministic transformation, independent of the state realization and the agents' action choices, of the signal produced by the first system. The first system strictly Pareto dominates the second system if and only if the signal produced by the second system is not sufficient relative to the signal produced by the first, with respect to the agents' action choices. This informativeness condition provides the managerial accountant with a theoretically correct and intuitive way of structuring this choices among a class of public post-decision information systems.

However, much more work remains to be done in this area of agency research. First, and foremost, while Holmstrom's [1981a] result is intuitive and easy to use, it does not apply to a large set of information system comparisons. It is necessary to determine whether we can enlarge the class of public post-decision information systems for which we can make theoretically correct utility-free and belief-free comparisons. Second, can Holmstrom's [1981a] results be generalized to multiperiod settings? Finally, one significant limitation of Holmstrom's [1981a] result is that it applies to public *post-decision* information systems; that is, to information systems whose only role is to supply information for performance evaluation purposes. However, as stressed earlier, information also has a belief revision role. Gjesdal [1981] showed that the preference ordering over information systems that are used strictly for performance evaluation purposes need not be the same as the preference ordering over the *same* information systems when they are used strictly for belief revision purposes. Managerial accounting information systems are used for *both purposes simultaneously* especially in a multiperiod setting. This dual use of the output of most managerial accounting information systems further limits the applicability of Holmstrom's [1981a] result to managerial accounting choice problems.

At this point the reader should be reminded that all of the results surveyed in this section were derived in the context of the basic agency problem. The assumptions of this problem included: no pre-contract information asymmetry, no pre-decision information asymmetry, and costless information. All of the results in this section dealt with comparisons between costless unconditional post-decision information systems. The costly post-decision information systems literature is surveyed as part of the discussion of the conditional variance investigation literature. The literature in which the other information symmetry assumptions are relaxed is discussed next.

IV.2.2 The Value of Information in the Presence of a Pre-Contract Information System

The problem of interest here is the same as the basic agency problem except that the agent or principal receives private state information (for example, about the machine's breakdown parameter Θ) — not received by the other party —

prior to contract negotiations. It is assumed that the uninformed individual knows the characteristics of the private pre-contract information system but not the specific signal generated.

Several interesting issues regarding the use of information arise when one allows for private pre-contract information. When the individuals agree on an employment contract they do so based on their utility functions and on their information. Therefore, the uninformed individual may be able to infer something about the informed individual's information from the latter's bargaining behavior. How can the uninformed extract this information in the way most useful to him? How should the informed individual bargain over the employment contract considering that his bargaining behavior may reveal some of his private information? The pre-contract information asymmetry creates problems of adverse selection that are dealt with by the design of the employment contract. (See the signalling and screening literature such as [Riley, 1979] and [Spence, 1973], where the issue of adverse selection is of central importance).

The managerial accountant's role is to design the firm's pre-decision and post-decision information systems. Thus, issues related to the value of being "better" or "worse" informed prior to the formation of the firm are outside the purview of managerial accounting. (A more fundamental issue is whether such a partial ordering over pre-contract information systems can even be established). Of considerable interest, however, is the role of pre-decision and post-decision information systems in overcoming the efficiency losses due to adverse selection problems caused by the presence of pre-contract information asymmetry. For example, does Holmstrom's [1981a] ordering rule for post-decision information systems hold even in the presence of pre-contract information asymmetry? Unfortunately, such issues that do have managerial accounting implications have not yet been addressed in the agency literature.

However, methodological results that make it easier to address these managerial accounting issues have been derived. Harris and Townsend [1981] and Myerson [1980; 1981] have established variants of the Revelation Principle for the situation in which the pre-contract information asymmetry exists. This principle states that any vector of expected utility points (one component for each individual) which can be achieved by a contract that induces the informed individuals to lie about their private information can also be achieved by a contract that induces them to tell the truth. Thus, in searching for a Pareto optimal contract for a situation in which there is pre-contract information asymmetry, one need only search over the set of contracts that induce the informed individuals to reveal their private information truthfully. This principle also holds for pre-decision information asymmetry. The Revelation Principle is a significant finding since it greatly simplifies the formulation of problems with information asymmetry. It will be discussed in more detail later.

IV.2.3 The Value of Information in the Presence of a Pre-Decision Information System

Can all the members of the firm be made better off *ex ante* if the managerial accountant improves the pre-decision information which is made publicly available? Can all members of the firm be made better off *ex ante* if the managerial accountant improves the *private* pre-decision information of one or more division managers? How should headquarters structure the capital budgeting and operations budgeting processes to reduce the budgetary slack (inefficiency) that arises when the managers of divisions have private pre-decision information? All of these issues confront the managerial accountant of a decentralized firm, because in decentralized firms information as well as decisions are decentralized. Answers to questions such as those raised above are crucial for the design of a decentralized firm, including its information system.

In this section the agency literature that addresses many of these issues is surveyed. In the literature to be surveyed, the problem of interest is the same as the basic agency problem except that now in addition to the public post-decision information system, there exists a pre-decision information system. This system produces a signal with information about the machine's realized breakdown parameter. It disseminates this signal prior to the agent's preventive maintenance decision but subsequent to the employment contract agreement. This additional information system may be: public, in which case both principal and agent directly observe its signal; or it may be private, in which case *only the agent* directly observes the signal. The latter case may arise as a result of the agent testing the machine before servicing it, but not telling the principal the results of the test. In the latter case, the principal knows the characteristics of the agent's private pre-decision information system (i.e. the characteristics of the test procedure) but not the signal that it produced.

The role and value of a pre-decision information system is more complex than that of a post-decision information system. Expanding a post-decision information system to report an additional piece of information will always result in at least a weak Pareto improvement,[28] since the principal and agent can always agree to a payment schedule that ignores the additional information. However, expanding a pre-decision information system to report an additional piece of information may not result in even a weak Pareto improvement.[29] The agent generally cannot commit himself to ignore the additional information, and therefore the optimal employment contract without the additional pre-decision information is no longer necessarily self-enforcing given the additional information. This is true whether the additional pre-decision information is privately reported or publicly reported.

When a private pre-decision information system is introduced, problems of adverse selection arise, as they did in the case of asymmetric pre-contract information. In the basic agency problem, the principal knows what the cooperative preventive maintenance level is. With a private pre-decision information system,[30] the principal no longer even knows which level of preventive maintenance is best, since he does not have all of the information possessed by the agent. In this case, the agent's role is not only to supply preventive maintenance but also to supply expert information. Thus, the private pre-decision information system has a belief

---

[28] *Ex ante* no one is made worse off and one or more individuals may be made strictly better off.

[29] *Ex ante* one or more individuals may be made worse off, as a result of expanding the pre-decision information system.

[30] Again the signals of a private pre-decision information system are directly received only by the agent.

61

revision role. The principal's problem is to *induce* the agent to use that private information to the principal's advantage.

With a private pre-decision information system, the principal and agent can always agree that the agent will communicate his private information to the principal and that this message will affect the agent's reward. Of course, the agent will choose his message strategy to maximize his expected utility. In this case, not only does the private pre-decision information system have a belief revision role, it also has a performance evaluation role.

In the expanded agency problem that includes a pre-decision information system, three questions arise concerning the value of information: (1) do the preference-ordering rules for post-decision information systems previously discussed still hold; (2) do comparable preference ordering rules over pre-decision information systems exist; (3) given a private pre-decision information system, when will communication between agent and principal result in a strict Pareto improvement? This section reviews results with respect to the first two issues. The last question concerning the value of communication is considered later within the discussion of the value of participative budgeting.

The results of the agency literature concerning the issues related to pre-decision information are not as well developed as those discussed in regard to post-decision information. This should not be surprising since research in this area is more recent and, as discussed, the role of information is more subtle. The literature surveyed in this section finds that, in the presence of a private pre-decision information system, Holmstrom's (1979) informativeness ordering over public post-decision information systems holds as a necessary condition but no longer as a sufficient condition. In addition, expanding the basic agency problem to include either a public or a private pre-decision information system does not *necessarily* result in a Pareto improvement. However, conditions under which a Pareto improvement would result have been derived.

IV.2.3.1 The Value of a Public Post-Decision Information System in the Presence of a Private Pre-Decision Information System

What results are available on the value of a public post-decision information system when the agent has access to a private pre-decision information system?

First, assume that there is no communication between agent and principal about the agent's private pre-decision information. Harris and Raviv [1979] addressed the situation in which the agent's utility function was additively separable in wealth and effort and his private pre-decision information system noiselessly reported the state (the realized machine breakdown parameter). They found that the necessary and sufficient conditions for the post-decision information system whose signal is $y' = (x,e)$ to be strictly Pareto superior to the one whose signal is $y = x$ were the same as their conditions in the case in which there was no private pre-decision information system. Holmstrom [1979] also extended his imperfect monitoring model to the private pre-decision information asymmetry context. His informativeness condition (Holmstrom [1979]) is still necessary for the post-decision information system whose signal is $y' = (x,z)$ to be strictly Pareto superior to the one whose signal is $y = x$ when there is private pre-decision information. However, because of technical issues the informativeness condition is no longer sufficient.

Christensen [1979] extended Holmstrom's [1979] model to allow for communication between the agent and the principal about the agent's private pre-decision signal, ξ. Of course the message, m, chosen by the agent is his utility maximizing message which is not necessarily truthful. Again, the question is when is any payment schedule based on (x,m) strictly Pareto dominated by a payment schedule based on (x,z,m) where z is an imperfect monitor of e and ξ? Christensen [1979] showed that a generalization of Holmstrom's [1979] informativeness condition is still a necessary condition. In particular, a necessary condition for a contract based on (x,m) to be strictly Pareto dominated by one based on (x,z,m) is that (x,ξ) is not sufficient relative to (x,z,ξ) with respect to $e(\xi)$. Now the agent's preventive-maintenance decision is a function of his private signal ξ. Again this generalized informativeness condition is not sufficient because of technical reasons. Further, it would seem relatively straightforward to extend the necessity part of Holmstrom's [1981a] second informativeness condition to the situation in which the agent has private pre-decision information regardless of whether communication is allowed.

As noted earlier, if communication is allowed in an agency context, the agent will choose his message strategy so as to maximize his expected utility. In choosing the employment contract the principal would have to consider its effect on the agent's message strategy. However, as previously discussed, the Revelation Principle considerably simplifies the problem formulation. The Revelation Principle states that any outcome (in terms of the expected utilities of the individuals) which can be achieved by an employment contract that does not induce the agent to reveal his private information truthfully can also be achieved by an employment contract that does. It does not say that only truth-inducing employment contracts are optimal, but that without loss of generality the researcher can restrict his search to the class of truth-inducing employment contracts. The reasoning is fairly straightforward. Assume that the optimal employment contract is nontruth inducing so that the agent's optimal message mapping is $m(\xi)$. The principal can always commit himself, under the assumed legal structure, to garble the agent's message the same way that the agent did and then use the same employment contract as before. If $m(.)$ were the agent's optimal message strategy before, his optimal strategy now must be truth-telling. Further, the agent and principal receive the same expected utility under the new system as the old. The Revelation Principle was derived in its many forms by Harris and Townsend [1981], Myerson [1979; 1980; 1981] and Christensen [1979]. Harris and Townsend [1980] derived their result based on a multiperiod, multiagent formulation in which the agents were restricted to pure strategies. Myerson's [1979; 1980; 1981] analysis was based on a single-period, multiagent analysis in which the agents were allowed to use mixed strategies. Christensen's [1979] analysis was based on a single-agent, single-period analysis.

In summary, our ability to order public post-decision information systems, independent of the preferences and beliefs of the individuals involved, is considerably reduced in situations in which the agent has private pre-decision information. Holmstrom's [1979] informativeness condition is still a necessary condition for a strict Pareto improvement to result from expanding the public post-decision information system to report an additional piece of data. However, that condition is no longer sufficient when the agent has private pre-decision information. A more subtle question however, is under what conditions can a strict Pareto improvement be achieved by allowing the agent to acquire his superior *private* pre-decision state information? This issue is addressed in the next section.

IV.2.3.2 The Value of Pre-Decision Information Systems

While a better private pre-decision information system may allow the agent to be better informed and capable of making better preventive maintenance decisions, it may also reduce his motivation by reducing the risk with respect to the uncertainty of the breakdown parameter that he must face. That is, improving the agent's private pre-decision information system may exacerbate the moral hazard problem. The net effect of the counteracting forces is not obvious. In fact, as long as the agent's information about the breakdown parameter is not effectively perfect, it is not even clear that installing a *public* pre-decision information system will result in a strict Pareto improvement. The agent may still be able to use the additional pre-decision information to shirk, possibly making the principal worse off. What agency results are there concerning the value of pre-decision information systems?

When the basic agency model is expanded to include a private pre-decision information system for the agent, the analysis and results depend upon whether communication between agent and principal is allowed. For the case in which communication is not allowed, Christensen [1979] constructed an example in which making the agent better informed results in the principal being made worse off. Atkinson [1978; 1979] and Baron and Holmstrom [1980] also addressed this issue. They each found that for the case in which the firm's output is jointly observed ex post (y = x), if only linear payment schedules are considered, then a Pareto improvement can be achieved by allowing the agent private access to a pre-decision information system. However, for the situations investigated by Atkinson [1978; 1979] and Baron and Holmstrom [1980], linear payment schedules are not optimal. Therefore, their results need not hold when optimal contracts are considered. Further, Atkinson's [1978; 1979] unambiguous results were based on a work-neutral agent and therefore the problem of the agent using the additional information to shirk was not considered.

If communication between agent and principal with respect to the agent's private pre-decision information is allowed, more definitive results are available. Christensen [1979] again provided an example in which the principal is made worse off by allowing the agent to receive private pre-decision information even when communication is allowed. However, Baiman and Evans [1981] found sufficient conditions under which expanding the basic agency problem to include a private pre-decision information system results in at least a weak Pareto improvement. Further, they offer an example satisfying their sufficiency condition in which a strict Pareto improvement is achieved. Unfortunately, the Baiman and Evans [1981] sufficiency condition is technical and without a satisfactory intuitive interpretation. Thus the extent to which this sufficiency condition is widely applicable has not yet been established.

Thus agency research has only limited help to offer to the owner of the machine in our simple example who is trying to decide whether to provide the agent with a private pre-decision information which will improve his information about the machine's breakdown parameter. Christensen's [1979] examples point out that the principal will not necessarily benefit, and may even suffer as a result of providing the information system to the agent. Baiman and Evans [1981] established sufficient conditions under which a weak Pareto improvement can be attained by providing the agent with the private pre-decision information system, but the generality of the condition is difficult to establish. Thus the available results in this area are at best suggestive. General guidelines for when a strict Pareto improvement can be achieved by acquiring a private pre-decision information system to whose signals only the agent will have access have yet to be established. Further, what results we do have with respect to private pre-decision systems deal only with comparisons between null and nonnull information systems. The question of the value of improving an already existing private pre-decision information system is more often at issue but has not been addressed at all in the agency literature. Thus a great deal more work is necessary before we can start to understand the effect of private pre-decision information systems on the efficiency of the firm.

IV.2.4 Summary of the Value of Information Literature

As an overall summary, the extant agency theory literature has, with varying degress of success, analyzed parts of the managerial accountant's choice problem rather than his problem in its entirety. For example, results have been obtained with respect to the ordering of information systems whose signals are used solely for performance evaluation purposes. More limited results have been obtained with respect to the ordering of information systems whose signals are used solely for belief revision purposes. But the signals produced by managerial accounting systems are often used for both purposes. Agency research has essentially no general results on how to order such dual-purpose information systems. However, given the short period of time that the agency method of analysis has been applied to the problem, this last remark should not give agency theorists or managerial accountants cause to despair. The results of agency research have clarified our thinking about the managerial accountant's choice problem and have given us additional insight into the implications of his choices. Each new result afforded by use of the agency model has allowed us to address more subtle issues or to generalize earlier results. Thus, the results of agency research to date seem to provide a convincing argument that the agency model has the potential to serve as the basis for a useful normative theory of managerial accounting.

IV.3 Evaluation of Specific Managerial Accounting Procedures from an Agency Perspective

This survey of agency research has so far focused on those results that prescribed how to rank alternative information systems; the emphasis was on the normative contribution of agency theory to managerial accounting. The objective was to see what guidelines and insight the agency model could offer to the managerial accountant with respect to *how he should* choose among alternative accounting systems.

In general the extent to which we can have confidence that our normative prescriptions for managerial accounting will result in the desired outcomes depends upon how much confidence we have that the accounting systems will be used in the way hypothesized. What is important here is not whether people think and make choices in the way hypothesized but whether their actions are consistent with those implied by the hypothesized model of choice behavior. Thus any normative theory of managerial accounting must be based on some predictive or positive model. Can the agency model, which includes a model of individual behavior within the firm, serve in both these roles and thus be a self-contained and complete model of managerial accounting? This section focuses on the agency model as a positive model of managerial accounting. In order to do so, the major question addressed is the extent to which the results of agency research with respect to the use of information are consistent with currently observed uses.

IV.3.1 Responsibility Accounting

When information is to be used for performance evaluation the concept of responsibility accounting has traditionally been relied upon to indicate how the information should be used or organized. Responsibility accounting states that a person should be evaluated only on the basis of those factors that he controls. This is *usually interpreted* to mean that a person should be evaluated only on the basis of those *outcomes* that he affects. This implies that the firm's public post-decision information should be organized in such a way that all costs, revenues, assets, and liabilities are traced to the individual who is primarily responsibile for them.

For a world of complete certainty, agency research agrees with the above interpretation of responsibility accounting. The agent is assigned a task, the principal can costlessly verify whether the agent has performed the task and pays the agent the agreed upon fee for doing so. However, if we admit *ex ante* state uncertainty while still allowing for perfect costless post-decision information ($y = (x,e)$), the results of agency research no longer agree with the implications of responsibility accounting. In this case, with a risk-averse principal, the Pareto optimal contract would call for risk sharing. Therefore, the agent's payment would be a function not only of his task performance (level of preventive maintenance supplied), for which he is totally responsible, but also of the state realization for which he has no responsibility (see, [Demski, 1976]). However, if the principal holds a diversified portfolio of investments or represents the interests of a large group of diversified shareholders, he should be effectively risk neutral and would not use the agent to share risk for other than motivational purposes. If this were the case, then agency theory and responsibility accounting would both reward the agent strictly on the observed preventive maintenance level (e).

When imperfect post-decision information is also allowed, the results of agency research and the implications of responsibility accounting differ further. From an agency perspective, an agent should *not* be evaluated only on those costs for which he is "primarily" responsible. Rather, all available information should be used to learn about the agent's action choice. For example, assume that in the preventive maintenance example the principal owns two machines and that he hires two agents. Each agent supplies preventive maintenance to a different machine. The only common factor between machines is the state occurrence. Therefore $x = x_1(e_1,\theta) + x_2(e_2,\theta)$. Agent 1(2) is responsible only for $x_1(x_2)$, and therefore responsibility accounting would be interpreted to mean that his payment should be a function only of $x_1(x_2)$. However, observing x_1 and x_2 may tell the principal more about the state outcome than observing each separately. This may allow the principal to infer each agent's choice more accurately than he could by observing each machine's output separately. Thus, for motivational purposes alone it may be Pareto optimal to base agent 1's (2's) payment on x_1 *and* x_2 even though he is responsible only for $x_1(x_2)$. Baiman and Demski [1980b] and Holmstrom [1981a] demonstrate this more generally.

This two-machine example and the results of Baiman and Demski [1980b] and Holmstrom [1981a] are not inconsistent with the objective of responsibility accounting, but rather with the way that it is usually interpreted. Agency theory and responsibility accounting differ when the goal of evaluating an individual only on the basis of those factors that he controls is interpreted by managerial accounting to mean evaluate the individual only on the basis of those *outcomes* over which he exercises control. Agency research concludes that this is too narrow an interpretation of responsibility accounting. In evaluating and rewarding an agent who controls only part of the firm's output, it may be optimal to evaluate the agent on the basis of the firm's entire output. The key is that even outputs over which the subordinate exercises no influence may contain information that can be used by the supervisor to improve his assessment of the subordinate's action choice.

IV.3.2 Budgets

Budgeting is a frequently used managerial accounting tool. Does the current agency literature find the use of managerial accounting data in budget-based schedules to be Pareto optimal? Demski and Feltham [1977, p. 337] defined a budget-based payment schedule as one which satisfies three criteria:

> 1. the worker's compensation is, in part, a function of some observable attribute(s) of the outcome resulting from his actions;
> 2. the contract specifies a budgeted (standard) outcome (attribute) level that partitions the set of possible outcomes into favorable and unfavorable subsets; and
> 3. the worker's compensation function consists of two or more functions, one defined over the favorable subset and the other defined over the unfavorable subset.

The third point implies that a budget-based contract cannot be everywhere differentiable in the observable attribute.

Demski [1976] and Wilson [1968] did not find budget-based contracts to be Pareto optimal in the situations they addressed. The use of budgets is usually associated with motivational problems, and the Demski [1976] and Wilson [1968] analyses were concerned solely with optimal risk sharing and side betting.

Demski and Feltham [1978] addressed the issue of the optimality of budget-based payment schedules but were not able to demonstrate sufficiency conditions. They did present numerical examples demonstrating the Pareto superiority of budget-based contracts over optimal linear contracts. Lewis [1980] generalized Demski and Feltham's [1978] numerical examples. Mirrless [1974], Gjesdal

[1976], Feltham [1977] and Harris and Raviv [1979] all found conditions under which budget-based contracts are not only optimal but also either induce the cooperative solution or come arbitrarily close to the cooperative solution.[31] While it is heartening to find results that do support the use of managerial accounting data in budget-based payment schedules, these latter results are limited in their positive implications since some rely on unbounded penalties and all produce the cooperative solution, neither of which is usually observed in practice. Thus, the question remains: are budget-based contracts ever Pareto optimal in second-best situations? Holmstrom [1979] provides an affirmative answer.

Holmstrom [1979] characterized the optimal payment schedule for a class of problems for which the cooperative solution was not achievable. In this class of problems, which is restricted to those problems in which the payment schedule is bounded, the optimal payment schedule will be budget-based for at least two situations:

(i) The optimal incentive function is not everywhere interior (i.e., for some monitoring signals either the maximum or minimum allowable payment to the agent will be made).

(ii) The agent's action affects what "state" a machine is in, but not the output given that it is in that "state."

The second condition can be illustrated in terms of the preventive maintenance example. If the agent's preventive maintenance activity affects the probability of whether the machine breaks down, but not when it will break down (after how much output has been produced), then the second condition will be satisfied. In particular if the principal is risk neutral, then the optimal payment schedule will be one constant if the machine breaks down *at any time* and a different constant if it does not break down. This payment schedule clearly satisfies the definition of a budget-based contract.

Thus Holmstrom's [1979] result is consistent with the use of managerial accounting data in budget-based contracts. But how general are the sufficiency conditions? Does the agency model predict the use of budget-based contracts for those situations in which they are actually observed and not in other situations? Research at this level of detail has not yet been attempted. The problem is that the second condition is not very general while the first is difficult to apply. In particular the first condition is with respect to the optimal contract itself rather than an exogenous variable. Therefore it is difficult to know, *a priori*, when the first condition will be satisfied. Thus, the agency model is consistent with the use of budget-based contracts. But a finer test of the agency model based on comparing the predicted and actual use of budgets awaits the development of easier-to-apply sufficient conditions.

---

[31] Harris and Raviv's [1978] result states that any continuously differentiable contract based on x and z can be dominated by what they call a dichotomous contract based on x and z. However, they restrict themselves to a class of post-decision information systems that have a movable support. Mirrlees [1974], Gjesdal [1976], and Feltham [1977] showed this type of system can be used to either attain a cooperative solution or get arbitrarily close to one.

IV.3.3 Conditional Variance Investigation Policies[32]

The research surveyed on the value of post-decision information dealt with the value of *costless unconditional* monitoring of the agent's maintenance activity. However, by ignoring the cost of monitoring one can never explain management's use of exception reporting, sequential (multistage) audits, and conditional variance investigation, all of which are commonly used control techniques in managerial accounting. By ignoring the cost of monitoring, the question of when to investigate is reduced to a choice between always and never.

Most of the conditional-variance investigation policies observed in practice are one- or two-tail policies: Investigate if $x \leq x_L$ and/or $x \geq x_U$. The rationale for such policies is based on the statistical quality control literature. The question of interest here is whether their use is optimal in a multiperson agency setting.

Dyckman [1969] and Kaplan [1969] among others (See Kaplan's [1975] survey article) have studied the issue of when to undertake a costly investigation. All of these studies base their analyses on nonagency models in which the possibility of investigation has no motivational effects. That is, they assume that the transition probabilities between exogenously defined in-control and out-of-control states for the object of investigation are invariant to the choice of the investigation policy. While this assumption may be reasonable when the object is an automated machine, it is not when the object is a person. The value of a variance-investigation policy is based not only on the undesirable behavior that is attempted and detected, but also on the undesirable behavior that is *not* attempted because of the chosen investigation policy.

Demski and Feltham [1978] studied conditional variance investigation by starting with the basic agency model in which the monitoring system reported y = x. However, in their model, after the principal observes x, he has the option of gathering additional (costly and imperfect) information about the agent's preventive maintenance activity. Any additional information gathered would be public and hence would be a potential argument in the payment schedule. Using examples, they compared the effect on the expected utilities of the principal and agent of using lower-tail investigation policies with an exogenously specified payment schedule, to allowing no variance investigation at all. They left unresolved the interesting questions of when such costly lower-tail conditional variance investigation policies are Pareto optimal and what the associated Pareto optimal payment schedule would be.

Baiman and Demski [1980a] used a model similar to that used by Demski and Feltham [1978] and demonstrated that the optimal variance

---

[32] This topic deals with the value of gathering *costly* post-decision public information and therefore would also fit in with the discussion of the value of post-decision information. However, because variance analysis is a well-known managerial accounting procedure which is both based on managerial accounting information and produces managerial accounting information, it is included here.

investigation policy was pure rather than mixed. That is, for each possible sales output (x), the principal would either order an investigation or not, but he would not use a randomized decision rule. Further, Baiman and Demski [1980a] showed that the optimal conditional variance investigation policy was not, in general, lower-tail. Because the conditional variance investigation policy has both motivational and risk-sharing implications, the optimal policy tends to be quite complex. In fact, the set of sales outputs which trigger an investigation is not, in general, a convex set.

In a subsequent paper, Baiman and Demski [1980b] identified relatively mild conditions that were sufficient for the Pareto optimality of the one-tail conditional variance investigation policy studied by Demski and Feltham [1978]. However, Baiman and Demski [1980b] showed that the payment schedule assumed by Demski and Feltham [1978] was not optimal. The Baiman and Demski [1980a, 1980b] results thus show that the use and form of a much observed managerial accounting tool is optimal within an agency context.

To put the Baiman and Demski [1980a, 1980b] results in perspective, it is important to understand how sensitive they are to the particular assumptions made. While randomized investigation policies are never optimal for the problem analyzed by Baiman and Demski [1980a, 1980b], they can be optimal for the problem analyzed by Kanodia [1980]. The major reason for the difference in results seems to be two different assumptions. Kanodia [1980] assumed that the agent observed the state realization before choosing his action and that the investigation system was perfect. Baiman and Demski [1980a, 1980b] assumed that when the agent chose his action he was no better informed than the principal and that the investigation system was imperfect.

One further point should be mentioned about both the Baiman and Demski [1980a, 1980b] and Kanodia [1980] formulations. For the solution to work, the principal must irrevocably commit himself to carry out the chosen investigation policy. Within the basic agency model formulation, the principal *knows with certainty* what action the agent actually took. Therefore, the principal does not need to consume resources for a conditional variance investigation in order to learn the agent's action choice. In fact, it is totally irrational to investigate the action choice *after the fact* in these models. However, if the principal does not irrevocably commit himself to adhere to the *ex ante* optimal investigation policy, the agent will change his action choice accordingly, making *both* worse off. Thus, we should be careful in condemning certain policies that appear *ex post* irrational, as they may be unavoidable ways of achieving *ex ante* efficiency. This point will be discussed later in the context of cost allocations.

The Baiman and Demski [1980a; 1980b] and Kanodia [1980] papers open up a new way of looking at the familiar tool of conditional-variance investigation. It still remains to be seen whether the use of the two-tail investigation policies, also observed in practice, is optimal within an agency context. Further, while these studies have rationalized different structures for conditional-variance investigation policies that are observed in practice, they certainly have not rationalized the particular parameter settings used in these policies. That is, why, if the optimal policies are a function of the production process and risk characteristics of the principal and agent, do we typically see investigation being triggered based upon simple 1σ, 2σ, or 3σ rules? An interesting study here would be to see how robust such heuristic decision rules are within a simulation study. This simulation study would allow the agent to be a rational utility-maximizing individual, while previous simulation and numerical analysis studies, such as [Magee, 1976] and [Dittman and Prakash, 1979], assumed the agent to be a machine.

One final point concerning cost variance investigation is that while there is value to *gathering the information* on which variances are computed within the agency model, there is no value to the *computation* of variances (see [Baiman and Demski, 1981b]). Any variance policy or payment schedule that is stated in terms of some deviation from a standard can be stated equally well in terms of only the observation. Thus, within the agency model there is no value to computing variances. The rationale for calculating variances must lie elsewhere, perhaps in the notion that variances serve as a conveneint, easily understood means of communicating.

IV.3.4 Cost Allocation

Probably the most often used and least understood managerial accounting procedure is joint and overhead cost allocation. Textbooks teach cost allocation procedures but then provide examples of the problems that arise when performance evaluations or operating decisions are based on allocated costs. Despite the textbooks examples, evaluation and decisionmaking based on allocated costs continue to be common practice.

Zimmerman [1979] and Demski [1981] have attempted to explain the use of cost allocation within an agency context. Zimmerman [1979] shows that varying the fixed component of an individual's payment schedule may affect his incentives. One can vary this fixed component through the cost that is allocated to the individual. However, Zimmerman, [1979] does not show whether such a payment schedule form is optimal, nor does he connect this fixed part of the payment schedule to cost allocation. One does not need the existence of overhead or joint costs in order to use his analysis. Therefore, it does not provide a convincing rationale for cost allocations.

Demski's [1981] analysis is similar to Zimmerman's [1979] in that his general discussion of the optimal performance evaluation system is never related to what one would call a cost allocation procedure, i.e., a fixed cost that gets split among a group of individuals. However, Demski [1981] does emphasize that whatever value comes from overhead allocation comes solely from measuring the variables of activity on which the allocations will be made. No value arises from the allocation itself.

I would like to suggest one *very* tentative agency scenario that might lead to the allocation of costs. Recall that conditional-variance investigation was shown to be an *ex post* irrational act that was required in order to maintain the *ex ante* optimal solution. It may be possible that cost allocation is a similar phenomenon in a multiperiod setting. For example, assume that a firm wants to buy a central computer. To decide on the appropriate size, it is necessary to know the true demands of each division manager, which is privately held information. Headquarters can guess at the total demand or it can try to induce the division managers to reveal their private information. Headquarters can influence these divisional demand messages and subsequent divisional computer use through its choice of an employment contract for the division managers and by the choice of the actual decision rule that it promises to use in going from divisional demand message to computer size purchase. One type of employment contract might include a payment schedule based on an allocation of the computer's fixed cost. It may turn out that such a contract is part of the *ex ante* optimal solution. If it were, it would be necessary for headquarters to commit itself to such *ex post* "irrational behavior" and its undesirable effects in order to achieve the *ex ante* optimal solution. This is only a conjecture but perhaps one worth pursuing since it may produce results within a rational multiperson context that are consistent with the observed use of a *seemingly* inefficient managerial accounting procedure.

IV.3.5 Participative Budgeting

The conjectured rationale for cost allocation was based on the desire of the principal to extract private information from the agent. This communication process is often observed as part of the capital budgeting process of the firm and results from the headquarters and divisions bargaining over the latter's capital budget. This bargaining or communication procedure is often observed in the operational budgeting processes of firms as well. The latter is often referred to as participative budgeting since the agent is allowed to participate in the setting of the standards (budgets) against which his performance will be evaluated. A particular form of this participative budgeting is Management by Objectives in which discussions between principal and agent are used to set goals for the agent for several different activities rather than for just the agent's operating cost or profit.

The behavioral literature dealing with participation has emphasized the benefits derived from the mere act of participation. (For an excellent survey of the participation literature see, Locke and Schweiger [1979]). It has stressed that those involved in a participative arrangement derive utility from the act of participating independent of how participation influences the productivity of the firm. Agency theory research has emphasized that the value of participative budgeting arises from the information transmission that takes place. This information focus in agency theory is achieved by expanding the basic agency problem to incorporate a pre-decision information system with signals available only to the agent.

72

Given that the agent has private pre-decision information about the machine's realized breakdown parameter, when can a strict Pareto improvement be achieved by allowing for communication between the agent and principal subsequent to the agent receiving his private signal but prior to the firm's output being revealed? With communication, the payment schedule can be a function of the agent's message as well as the signal produced by the monitoring system. Of course, depending on the employment contract, the agent's optimal message strategy may *not* be to tell the truth. However, it can never be Pareto inferior to allow for communication since the agent and prinicpal can agree on a payment schedule that ignores the agent's message.

Christensen [1979; 1980a; 1980b] first formulated this expanded basic agency model to allow for both the agent's private pre-decision information system and communication. However, he did not address the value of communication. Magee [1980] studied the value of participation (communication) but only in the context of an example. Ramakrishnan [1980] further analyzed Magee's example.[33]

Baiman and Evans [1981] used Christensen's [1979] formulation and found necessary and sufficient conditions for communication (participation) to be strictly valuable in the Pareto sense. If the agent's private pre-decision information is perfect, then communication has no value. Observing the firm's output in that case allows the principal to infer all he needs to know about the agent's private pre-decision information. However, if the agent's private pre-decision information is imperfect, a necessary and sufficient condition for communication to be strictly valuable is for the honest revelation of the agent's private pre-decision information to be strictly valuable. That is, if any value can be achieved with the information being honestly revealed *to all*, then a strictly positive part of that value can be achieved by giving the agent sole direct access to the information and letting him communicate in a manner that maximizes *his* expected utility. The Baiman and Evans [1981] results thus provide a rationale for participative budgeting that is an alternative to (but not inconsistent with) the rationale offered by the behavioral literature.

---

[33] Ramakrishnan's [1980] more general analysis is based on a model which implicitly assumes away normal hazard problems associated with the agent's action choice.

While the results in this section are interesting, as with all analytical results, it is necessary to understand how sensitive they are to the assumptions made. The models employed by both Christensen [1979; 1980a; 1980b] and Baiman and Evans [1981] represent the agency labor market constraint in the same way. In order for the agent to work for the firm, his employment contract must offer him expected utility at least as great as he could get in the labor market. Since he won't receive any private pre-decision information unless and until he joins the firm, his expected utility is based on his beliefs prior to receiving his private pre-decision information. Therefore, the models assume that the labor market is such that the agent cannot quit the firm after he has received his private pre-decision information but before he takes his action (provides preventive maintenance services). Once he joins the firm it is assumed that he can be legally forced to stay and work. In actual fact, labor contracts are not enforceable to that extent. It would therefore be interesting to see whether the Baiman and Evans [1981] results still hold if the firm had to offer a contract that not only induced the agent to join the firm, but also induced him to stay even after he received his private pre-decision information. This criticism is equally valid for the research dealing with the value of information in the presence of pre-decision information.

This entire area of decentralized private information giving rise to budget slack (inefficiency resulting from asymmetric pre-decision information), budget manipulation, and participative budgeting is central to our understanding of managerial accounting and management control, but one for which we have only the most rudimentary results. A great deal of future research is possible in this area alone. In this regard, I must agree with Horngren [1977] who states that:

> The personal goals of managers (personal income, size of staff, esteem, power) will often lead to the "bargained" budget, whereby managers intentionally create slack as a protective device. . . . This seeking of slack premeates all budgeting in every conceivable sort of organization. Little has been done to counteract it. . . . Despite these attempts at counteraction, slack remains one of the major unsolved problems in budgetary control.

IV.3.6 Standards

An important concept in managerial accounting, central to both variance investigation and budget-based contracts, is that of a standard. Standards are output or cost levels that signal whether investigation should take place; they indicate points at which the nondifferentiability of the budget-based payment schedule occur. The traditional managerial accounting literature talks about descriptions of standards such as: perfection, tight but attainable, and historical average, among others. What does the agency literature suggest concerning the correct choice of standards?

Demski and Feltham [1978] use examples to indicate that the optimal performance standards, given some nonoptimal employment contracts, could be less than or greater than expected performance. Unfortunately work in this area has not progressed much beyond Demski and Feltham's [1978] examples, except for those cases such as Mirrlees [1974], Gjesdal [1976], Feltham [1977] and Harris and Raviv [1979] in which the cooperative solution is achievable. Using Holmstrom's [1979] formulation (for which only a second-best solution is achievable) to characterize the optimal standards and their sensitivity to the particular parameters of the problem, even if only by stimulation, remains an unexplored area

74

that could provide some valuable insights into the budgeting process and the choice of standards used in that process.

IV.3.7 Summary of Literature with Implications for Managerial Accounting Procedures

The purpose of this section was to survey and develop the insights that agency research can offer with respect to some commonly used managerial accounting procedures and their underlying frameworks. In particular the objective was to assess the extent to which the implications of agency research are consistent with managerial accounting practice. The framework of responsibility accounting was found to be consistent with the results of agency research. However, from an agency perspective, responsibility accounting was found to be interpreted too narrowly by managerial accounting texts.

The use and form of conditional-variance investigation, budgets, and participative budgeting were all found to be consistent with the agency model of the firm. In addition, agency analysis suggested a possible rationale for the observed use of cost allocations.

Thus the agency model has been quite successful so far as a positive model of managerial accounting. Its results have been found to be consistent with a number of commonly used procedures, and it has provided much insight into the managerial accounting process. Most of the results discussed in this section were based on the basic agency problem with its single-period and single-agent assumptions. The question remains whether expanding the agency problem to incorporate multiple periods and multiple agents will increase or decrease the extent to which the results of agency research are consistent with observed practice.

V. SUMMARY AND CONCLUSION

The purpose of this essay was fourfold: (1) to survey and synthesize the agency literature; (2) to provide a basis for evaluating the agency model as the foundation for a normative theory of managerial accounting; (3) to develop some of the implications of agency research for commonly used managerial accounting procedures; and (4) to identify some unanswered managerial accounting questions which may be amenable to an agency-type analysis. This was accomplished by analyzing the agency model, its assumptions and limitations, and by surveying its results.

While a number of criticisms of the mathematical formulation of the agency model were made, they do not appear to cause major difficulties. It is premature to translate the results of agency research into normative guidelines for the choice and design of information systems within decentralized firms. However, agency research concerning the value of information can provide the managerial accountant with useful insights into the implications of his choice and design of these information systems. Agency results pertaining to budgets, variance investigation, and participative budgeting were found to support observed practice. Of course, these latter results were based on single-period, single-agent models that assumed an exogenous labor market. Whether similar results can be obtained when these and other assumptions are relaxed awaits further research. However, it does not appear that relaxing these assumptions will change the qualitative nature of the results and hence their positive implications. In summary, the initial results of agency research do support the assertion that the agency model will be a fruitful tool for future research in managerial accounting and may, indeed, provide a framework from which a useful theory of managerial accounting can be derived.

REFERENCES

Alchian, A. A. and H. Demsetz (1972), "Production, Information Costs, and Economic Organization," *American Economic Review* (December 1972), pp. 777-795.

Amershi, A. (1979), "A Theory of Firms under Uncertainty and Differential Information with Accounting Implications," Unpublished Working Paper, Stanford University (1979).

Amershi, A. (1980a), "Agency Theory: Clarifications, Consolidation and Extensions," Unpublished Working Paper, Stanford University (1980).

Amershi, A. (1980b), "Strategy-Information Core Contracts and the Social Value of Information in Security Markets," Unpublished Working Paper, Stanford University (1980).

Amershi, A. and J. E. Butterworth (1979), "The Theory of Agency—A Core Analysis," Unpublished Working Paper, SFU and Ceremade (1979).

Anthony, R. N. and J. Dearden (1976), *Management Control Systems: Text and Cases*, (R. D. Irwin, Inc., 1976).

Arrow, K. J. (1973), "Optimal Insurance and Generalized Deductibles," R-1108-OEO, The Rand Corporation (February 1973).

Atkinson, A. A. (1978), "Standard Setting in An Agency," *Management Science* (September 1978), pp. 1531-1361.

Atkinson, A. A. (1979), "Information Incentives in a Standard-Setting Model of Control," *Journal of Accounting Research* (Spring 1979), pp. 1-22.

Atkinson, A. A. and G. A. Feltham (1981), "Information in Capital Markets: An Agency Theory Perspective," Unpublished Working Paper, University of British Columbia, (January 1981).

Baiman, S. (1975), "The Evaluation and Choice of Internal Information Systems Within a Multi-person World," *Journal of Accounting Research* (Supplement 1975), pp. 1-15.

Baiman, S. (1981), "Comments on the Concept of Fairness in the Choice of Joint Cost Allocation Methods," in Moriarity, S. (ed.), *Proceedings of the University of Oklahoma Conference on Cost Allocation* (1981).

Baiman, S. and J. S. Demski (1980a), "Variance Analysis Procedures as Motivation Devices," *Management Science* (August 1980), pp. 840-848.

Baiman, S. and J. S. Demski (1980b), "Economically Optimal Performance Evaluation and Control Systems," *Journal of Accounting Research* (Supplement 1980b), pp. 184-220.

Baiman, S. and J. H. Evans III (1981), "Decentralization and Pre-Decision Information," Unpublished Working Paper, University of Pittsburgh (August 1981).

Baron, D. P. and B. Holmstrom (1980), "The Investment Banking Contract for New Issues Under Asymmetric Information: Delegation and the Incentives Problem" *Journal of Finance* (December 1980), pp. 1115-1138.

Boland, L. A. (1979), "A Critique of Friedman's Critics," *Journal of Economic Literature* (June 1979), pp. 503-522.

Christensen, J. (1979), "Communication and Coordination in Agencies: An Approach to Participative Budgeting," Unpublished Ph.D. Thesis, Stanford University (August 1979).

Christensen, J. (1980a), "Communication in Agencies," Unpublished Working Paper, Odense University (1980).

Christensen, J. (1979), "Participative Budgeting: An Agency Approach," Odense University (1980b).

Demski, J. S. (1967), "An Accounting System Structured on a Linear Program," *Accounting Review (October 1967)*, pp. 701-712.

Demski, J. (1976), "Uncertainty and Evaluation Based on Controllable Performance," *Journal of Accounting Research* (Autumn 1976), pp. 230-245.

Demski, J. S. (1981), "Cost Allocation Games" in Moriarity, S. (ed.), *Proceedings of the University of Oklahoma Conference on Cost Allocation* (1981).

Demski, J. S. and G. Feltham (1977), *Cost Determination: A Conceptual Approach* (Iowa State University Press, 1977).

Demski, J. S. and G. Feltham (1978), "Economic Incentives and Budgetary Control Systems," *Accounting Review* (April 1978), pp. 336-359.

Demski, J. S. and R. J. Swieringa (1974), "A Cooperative Formulation of the Audit Choice Problem" *Accounting Review* (July 1974), pp. 506-513.

Dittman, D. and P. Prakash (1979), "Cost Variance Investigation: Markovian Control Versus Optimal Control," *Accounting Review* (April 1979), pp. 358-373.

Dopuch, J., J. G. Birnberg and J. S. Demski (1967), "An Extension of a Standard Cost Variance Analysis," *Accounting Review* (July 1967), pp. 526-536.

Dyckman, T. R. (1969), "The Investigation of Cost Variances," *Journal of Accounting Research* (Autumn 1969), pp. 215-244.

Dye, R. A. (1980), "Optimal Contract Length," Unpublished Working Paper, Carnegie-Mellon University (April 1980).

Evans, J. H. III (1980), "Optimal Contracts with Costly Conditional Auditing," *Journal of Accounting Research* (Supplement 1980), pp. 108-128.

Fama, E. F. (1980), "Agency Problems and the Theory of the Firm," *Journal of Political Economy* (April 1980), pp. 288-307.

Feltham, G. (1968), "The Value of Information," *The Accounting Review* (October 1968), pp. 684-696.

Feltham, G. (1977), "Optimal Incentive Contracts: Penalties, Costly Information and Multiple Workers," Unpublished Working Paper Number 588, University of British Columbia (October 1977).

Friedman, M. (1953), "The Methodology of Positive Economics," in Friedman, S. (ed.), *Essays in Postive Economics* (University of Chicago Press, 1953).

Gjesdal, F. (1976), "Accounting in Agencies," Unpublished Working Paper, Stanford University (1976).

Gjesdal, F. (1981), "Accounting for Stewardship," *Journal of Accounting Research* (Spring 1981), pp. 208-231.

Gonedes, N. J. and N. Dopuch (1974), "Capital Market Equilibrium, Information Production, and Selecting Accounting Techniques: Theoretical Framework and Review of Empirical Work," *Journal of Accounting Research* (Supplement 1974), pp. 48-129.

Grossman, S. J. and O. D. Hart (1980), "An Analysis of the Principal-Agent Problem" Unpublished Working Paper, CARESS (July 1980).

Grossman, S. J. and J. Stiglitz (1976), "Information and Competitive Price Systems," *American Economic Review* (May 1976), pp. 246-253.

Groves, T. (1975), "Information, Incentives, and the Internalization of Production Externalities," in Lin, S. (ed.), *Theory and Measurement of Economic Externalities* (Academic Press, 1975).

Groves, T. and J. O. Ledyard (1976), "Some Limitations of Demand Revealing Processes," Unpublished Working Paper, Northwestern University (May 1976).

Groves, T. and J. O. Ledyard (1977), "Optimal Allocation of Public Goods: A Solution to the 'Free Rider' Problem," *Econometrica* (May 1977), pp. 373-809.

Groves, T. and M. Loeb (1975), "Incentives and Public Inputs," *Journal of Public Economics* (1975), pp. 211-226.

Groves, T. and M. Loeb (1979), "Incentives in Divisionalized Firms," *Management Science* (March 1979), pp. 221-230.

Hakansson, N. (1977), "Interim Disclosure and Public Forecasts: An Economic Analysis and a Framework for Choice," *Accounting Review* (April 1977), pp. 396-416.

Hamlen, S. S. (1980), "A Chance-Constrained Mixed Integer Programming Model for Internal Control Design," *Accounting Review* (October 1980), pp. 578-593.

Hamlen, S. S., Hamlen, W. A. and J. T. Tschirhart (1977), "The Use of Core Theory in Evaluating Joint Cost Allocation Schemes," *Accounting Review* (July 1977), pp. 616-627.

Harnett, D. and W. Hamner (1973), "The Value of Information in Bargaining," *Western Economic Journal* (March 1973), pp. 81-88.

Harris, M. and A. Raviv (1979), "Optimal Incentive Contracts with Imperfect Information," *Journal of Economic Theory* (Vol. 20, 1979), pp. 231-259.

Harris, M. and R. M. Townsend (1981), "Resource Allocation Under Asymmetric Information," *Econometrica (January 1981)*, pp. 33-64.

Hayes, D. C. (1977), "The Contingency Theory of Managerial Accounting," *Accounting Review* (January 1977), pp. 22-39.

Hirshleifer, J. (1971), "The Private and Social Value of Information and the Reward to Inventive Activity," *American Economic Review*, (September 1971), pp. 561-574.

Holmstrom, B. R. (1979), "Moral Hazard and Observability," *The Bell Journal of Economics* (Spring 1979), pp. 74-91.

Holmstrom, B. R. (1981a), "Moral Hazard in Teams," Unpublished Working Paper, Northwestern University (February 1981).

Holmstrom, B. R. (1981b), "Equilibrium Long-Term Labor Contracts," Unpublished Working Paper, Northwestern University (January 1981b).

Horngren, C. T. (1977), *Cost Accounting: A Managerial Emphasis*, 4th ed. (Prentice-Hall, Inc. 1977).

Jennergren, L. P. (1971), *Studies in the Mathematical Theory of Decentralized Resource-Allocation*, Unpublished Ph.D. Thesis, Graduate School of Business, Stanford University (1971).

Jensen, M. C. and W. H. Meckling (1976), "Theory of the Firm: Managerial Behavior, Agency Costs and Ownership Structure," *Journal of Financial Economics* (3, 1976), pp. 305-360.

Kanodia, C. (1980), "Optimal Monitoring and Moral Hazard," Unpublished Working Paper, U.B.C. and University of Chicago (November 1980).

Kaplan, R. S. (1969), "Optimal Investigation Strategies with Imperfect Information," *Journal of Accounting Research* (Spring 1969), pp. 32-43.

Kaplan, R. S. (1975), "The Significance and Investigation of Cost Variables: Survey and Extensions," *Journal of Accounting Research* (Autumn 1975), pp. 311-337.

Kreps, D. M. and R. B. Wilson (1981), "Sequential Equilibria," Unpublished Working Paper, Stanford University (May 1981).

Lambert, R. A. (1981), "Managerial Incentives and Short-Run vs Long-Run Optimization," Unpublished Working Paper, Stanford University (January 1981).

Lewis, T. R. (1980), "Bonuses and Penalties in Incentive Contracting," *Bell Journal of Economics* (Spring 1980), pp. 292-301.

Locke, E. A. and D. M. Schweiger (1979), "Participation in Decision-Making: One More Look," *Research in Organizational Behavior* (1979), pp. 265-339.

Loeb, M. (1975), "Coordination and Informational Incentive Problems in the Multidivisional Firm," Unpublished Ph.D. dissertation, Graduate School of Management, Northwestern University (May 1975).

Luce, R. D. and H. Raiffa (1957), *Games and Decisions* (John Wiley & Sons, Inc., 1957).

Magee, R. P. (1976), "Simulation Analysis of Alternative Cost Variance Models," *Accounting Review* (July 1976), pp. 529-544.

Magee, R. P. (1980), "Equilibria in Budget Participation," *Journal of Accounting Research* (Autumn 1980), pp. 551-573.

Marschak, J. and R. Radner (1972), *Economic Theory of Games*, Cowles Foundation Monogrpah 22 (Yale University Press, 1972).

Milgrom, P. and J. Roberts (1980), "Predation, Reputation and Entry Deterrence," Unpublished Working Paper, Northwestern University (June 1980).

Mirrlees, J. A. (1974), "Notes on Welfare Economics, Information, and Uncertainty," in Balch, M., McFadden, F. and S. Wau (eds.) *Essays in Economic Behavior Under Uncertainty* (North-Holland 1974).

Mirrlees, J. A. (1975), "The Theory of Moral Hazard and Unobservable Behavior- Part I," CARESS Working Paper #80-17, Nuffield College, Oxford, 1975).

Mirrlees, J. A. (1979), "The Implications of Moral Hazard for Optimal Insurance," Unpublished Working Paper, Nuffield College, Oxford University (April 1979).

Myerson, R. B. (1979), "Incentive Compatibility and the Bargaining Problem," *Econometrica*, Vol. 47 (January 1979), pp. 61-74.

Myerson, R. B. (1980), "Optimal Coordination Mechanisms in Principal-Agent Problems," Unpublished Working Paper, Northwestern University (June 1980).

Myerson, R. B. (1981), "Mechanisms Designed by an Informed Principal," Unpublished Working Paper, Northwestern University (June 1981).

Ng, D. S. (1975), "Information Accuracy and Social Welfare under Homogenous Beliefs," *Journal of Financial Economics* (March 1975), pp. 53-70.

Ng, D. S. and J. Stoekenius (1979), "Auditing, Incentives and Truthful Reporting," *Journal of Accounting Research* (Supplement 1979), pp. 1-34.

Papoulis, A. (1965), *Probability, Random Variables and Stochastic Processes* (McGraw-Hill Book Company, 1965).

Ponssard, J. P. and S. Zamir (1973),"Zero Sum Sequential Games With Incomplete Information," *International Journal of Game Theory* (Vol. II, Issue 2, 1973), pp. 98-107.

Radner, R. (1980), "Does Decentralization Promote Wasteful Conflict?" Unpublished Working Paper, Bell Laboratories (June 1980).

Raiffa, H. (1968), *Decision Analysis* (Addison-Wesley Publishing Company, 1968).

Ramakrishnan, R. T. (1980), "Performance Evaluation and Budgeting with Asymmetric Information," Unpublished Working Paper, M.I.T. (April 1980).

Ramakrishnan, R. and A. Thakor (1979, "The Economic Theory of Agency: Synthesis and Clarification," Unpublished Working Paper, Northwestern University (August 1979).

Raviv, A. (1979), "The Design of an Optimal Insurance Policy," *The American Economic Review* (March 1979), pp. 84-96.

Riley, J. (1979), "Noncooperative Equilibrium and Market Signalling," *American Economic Review* (May 1979), pp. 84-96.

Ronen, J. and J. L. Livingstone (1975), "An Expectancy Theory Approach to the Motivational Impacts of Budgets," *Accounting Review* (October 1975), pp. 671-605.

Ross, S. A. (1973), "The Economic Theory of Agency: The Principal's Problem," *American Economic Review* (May 1973), pp. 134-139.

Sappington, D. (1979), "The Non-Optimality of the First-Best Contract in the Principal-Agent Model with Asymmetric Information," Unpublished Working Paper, Princeton University (November 1979).

Schelling, T. C. (1960), *The Strategy of Conflict* (Harvard University Press, 1960).

Schelling, T. C. (1978), *Micromotives and Macrobehavior*, (W. W. Norton & Co., 1978).

Shavell, S. (1979), "Risk-Sharing and Incentives in the Principal-Agent Relationship," *The Bell Journal of Economics* (Spring 1979), pp. 55-73.

Simon, H. A., H. Guetzkow, G. Kozmetzky and G. Tyndall (1954), *Centralization vs. Decentralization in Organizing the Controller's Department* (Controllership Foundation, 1954).

Solomons, D. (1965), *Divisional Performance: Measurement and Control*, (R. D. Irwin & Co., 1965).

Spence, M. (1973), "Job Market Signalling," *Quarterly Journal of Economics* (August 1973), pp. 355-374.

Townsend, R. M. (1979), "Optimal Contracts and Competitive Markets with Costly State Verification," *Journal of Economic Theory* (October 1979), pp. 265-293.

Townsend, R. M. (1980), "Contract Length and the Gain from Enduring Relationships," Unpublished Working Paper, Carnegie-Mellon University (May 1980).

Williamson, D. E., Wachter, M. L. and J. E. Harris (1975), "Understanding the Employment Relation: The Analysis of Idiosyncratic Exchange," *The Bell Journal of Economics* (Spring 1975), pp. 250-278.

Wilson, R. B. (1968), "The Theory of Syndicates," *Econometrica* (January 1968), pp. 119-132.

Zimmerman, J. L. (1979), "The Costs and Benefits of Cost Allocation," *Accounting Review* (July 1979), pp. 504-521.

SELECTED
ANNOTATED BIBLIOGRAPHY

1. Baiman, S. and J. S. Demski "Economically Optimal Performance Evaluation and Control Systems," *Journal of Accounting Research* (Supplement 1980), pp. 184-220.

Baiman and Demski analyze, within the context of the agency model, some of the uses of information in the firm's performance evaluation and control system. They first derive sufficient conditions for the optimality of the familiar one-tail variance-investigation strategy. They also show that some of the implications of responsibility accounting are nonoptimal within a multiagent firm context. Finally, they point out that the value of variance investigation and cost allocation comes from the underlying disaggregation of data and not from the computation of variances and allocations.

2. Baiman, S. and J. H. Evans III, "Decentralization and Pre-Decision Information," Unpublished Working Paper, University of Pittsburgh (August 1981).

Baiman and Evans focus on two issues in this paper: (1) conditions under which participative budgeting between a principal and a better informed agent leads to a strict Pareto improvement and (2) conditions under which a Pareto improvement is achieved by the agent acquiring additional private pre-decision information given a participative budgeting system is already in place. They use the participative budgeting formulation introduced by Christensen [1979] to address these issues. The authors find that participative budgeting will result in a strict Pareto improvement if and only if the agent's private information is such that costless public revelation of it would lead to a strict Pareto improvement. The authors also find a sufficient condition for both individuals to be made at least weakly better off by improving the agent's private pre-decision information. This sufficiency condition is of a technical nature and has no simple interpretation.

3. Christensen, J. "Communication and Coordination in Agencies: An Approach to Participative Budgeting," Unpublished Ph.D. Thesis, Stanford University, (August 1979).

Christensen generalizes and expands the agency model to include communication and participation. He derives necessary and sufficient conditions for a public post-decision information system to have value in his expanded model. His conditions are analogous to Holmstrom's [1979] informativeness condition. The author also demonstrates that improving the agent's private pre-decision information can leave the agent better off but the principal worse off.

4. Demski, J. S., "Cost Allocation Games," in S. Moriarity (ed.) *Proceedings of the University of Oklahoma Conference on Cost Allocation* (1981).

Demski criticizes the recent game-theoretic cost allocation literature for first assuming the use of cost allocations and only then offering properties that the required allocation should possess. Demski suggests that a more fundamental question is why we allocate costs at all. Demski posits three possible reasons for allocating costs and derives economically valuable allocation mechanisms that are consistent with these reasons.

5. Gjesdal, F., "Accounting for Stewardship," *Journal of Accounting Research* (Spring 1981), pp. 208-231.

Gjesdal discusses the traditional stewardship literature in accounting and demonstrates the relevance of the agency model for clarifying and advancing that literature. The author generalizes earlier work of Shavell [1979] and Holmstrom [1979] on sufficient conditions for the strict positive value of public post-decision information. The author further divides the value of this information into its incentive value and insurance value. The author also demonstrates that the ordering of information systems for decisionmaking and for incentives purposes are, in general, not the same. Thus when evaluating an information system that will have both decision-making (belief-revision) and incentive effects a trade-off between these two purposes will have to be made. Finally, the author finds that a sufficient condition for the agent in a two-person agency model to choose only pure strategies is that he have an additively separable utility functon in wealth and effort.

6. Grossman, S. J. and O. D. Hart, "An Analysis of the Principal-Agent Problem," Unpublished Working Paper, CARESS (July 1980).

Grossman and Hart introduce a new formulation of the two-person symmetric information agency problem. They show that this new formulation avoids many of the mathematical (existence) problems inherent in previous formulations. In addition, using their problem formulation, the authors are able to re-derive and refine previous agency results as well as derive new results.

7. Holmstrom, B. "Moral Hazard in Teams," Unpublished Working Paper, Northwestern University (February 1981).

Holmstrom examines remedies to the moral hazard problem under both certainty and uncertainty. The author shows that, under certainty, moral hazard becomes a problem for a team only when one restricts one's choice of sharing rules to the set that always allocates the team payoff in its entirety to the team members. If one retains this "budget balancing" constraint, then monitors are required to mitigate the moral hazard problem under certainty. For the uncertainty case, Holmstrom generalizes his earlier informativeness result [Holmstrom, 1979] to multiple agents and to a wider class of information system comparisons. His result is that one can partially order public postdecision information systems in terms of their Pareto effects essentially using the notion of statistical sufficiency.

8. Myerson, R. B., "Optimal Coordination Mechanisms in Principal-Agent Problems," Unpublished Working Paper, Northwestern University, (June 1980).

Myerson formulates the principal-agent problem allowing for multiple agents, each with private pre-decision information, as well as allowing for randomized strategies. The author shows that, without loss of generality, the principal can restrict himself to employment contracts whereby: (1) the agents are induced to honestly report their private information, and , (2) the agents are induced to follow the decisions made by the principal based on the centralized information. This "Revelation Principle" greatly simplifies the analysis of agency problems with asymmetric information.

Behavioral Assumptions of Management Accounting

EDWIN H. CAPLAN
University of New Mexico

ACCOUNTING has been closely associated with the development of the modern business organization. Thus, we might expect accountants to show a strong interest in recent contributions to organization theory which increase our understanding of the business firm and how it functions. An examination of accounting literature, however, suggests that (despite the steadily increasing flow of accounting articles and texts incorporating the words "management" and "decisions" in their titles) accountants have been relatively unconcerned with current research in organization theory. Although the past few years have witnessed the beginnings of an effort to bridge this gap, much still remains to be done.[1] This paper attempts to demonstrate that an understanding of behavioral theory is relevant to the development of management accounting theory and practice.

The discussion to be presented here may be summarized as follows:

1. The management accounting function is essentially a behavioral function and the nature and scope of management accounting systems is materially influenced by the view of human behavior which is held by the accountants who design and operate these systems.

2. It is possible to identify a "traditional" management accounting model of the firm and to associate with this model certain fundamental assumptions about human behavior. These assumptions are presented in Table I on page 497.

3. It is also possible to postulate behavioral assumptions based on modern organization theory and to relate them to the objectives of management accounting. A tentative set of such assumptions appears in Table II on page 498.

4. Research directed at testing the nature and validity of accounting assumptions with respect to human behavior in business organizations can be useful in evaluating and, perhaps, improving the effectiveness of management accounting systems.

MANAGEMENT ACCOUNTING AS A BEHAVIORAL PROCESS

The management of a business enterprise is faced with an environment—both internal and external to the firm—that is in a perpetual state of change. Not only is this environment constantly changing, but it is changing in many dimensions. These include physical changes (climate, availability of raw materials, etc.), technological changes (new products and processes, etc.), social changes (attitudes of em-

---

[1] See, for example: Robert T. Golembiewski, "Accountancy as a Function of Organization Theory," THE ACCOUNTING REVIEW, April 1964, pp. 333–341; and John J. Willingham, "The Accounting Entity: A Conceptual Model," THE ACCOUNTING REVIEW, July 1964, pp. 543–552.

TABLE I

BEHAVIORAL ASSUMPTIONS OF "TRADITIONAL" MANAGEMENT ACCOUNTING MODEL OF THE FIRM

Assumptions with Respect to Organization Goals
A. The principal objective of business activity is profit maximization (economic theory).
B. This principal objective can be segmented into sub-goals to be distributed throughout the organization (principles of management).
C. Goals are additive—what is good for the parts of the business is also good for the whole (principles of management).

Assumptions with Respect to the Behavior of Participants
A. Organization participants are motivated primarily by economic forces (economic theory).
B. Work is essentially an unpleasant task which people will avoid whenever possible (economic theory).
C. Human beings are ordinarily inefficient and wasteful (scientific management).

Assumptions with Respect to the Behavior of Management
A. The role of the business manager is to maximize the profits of the firm (economic theory).
B. In order to perform this role, management must control the tendencies of employees to be lazy, wasteful, and inefficient (scientific management).
C. The essence of management control is authority. The ultimate authority of management stems from its ability to affect the economic reward structure (scientific management).
D. There must be a balance between the authority a person has and his responsibility for performance (principles of management).

Assumptions with Respect to the Role of Management Accounting
A. The primary function of management accounting is to aid management in the process of profit maximization (scientific management).
B. The accounting system is a "goal-allocation" device which permits management to select its operating objectives and to divide and distribute them throughout the firm, i.e., assign responsibilities for performance. This is commonly referred to as "planning" (principles of management).
C. The accounting system is a control device which permits management to identify and correct undesirable performance (scientific management).
D. There is sufficient certainty, rationality, and knowledge within the system to permit an accurate comparison of responsibility for performance and the ultimate benefits and costs of that performance (principles of management).
E. The accounting system is "neutral" in its evaluations—personal bias is eliminated by the objectivity of the system (principles of management).

ployees, customers, competitors, etc.), and financial changes (asset composition, availability of funds, etc.).

An important characteristic of "good" management is the ability to evaluate past changes, to react to current changes, and to predict future changes. This is consistent with the view that management is essentially a decision-making process and the view that accounting is an information system which acts as an integral part of this decision-making process. It is inconceivable, however, that any workable information system could provide data relative to all, or even a substantial portion, of the changes occurring inside and outside of the organization. There are several reasons for this. Many changes—particularly those that occur in the external environment—are simply not available to the information system of the firm. These changes represent "external unknowns" in a world of uncertainty and limited knowledge. Further, a substantial number of changes that occur within the firm itself may not be perceived by the information system. Thus, there exist "internal" as well as "external" unknowns.

Even if accountants were aware of all the changes which are taking place—of if they could be made aware of them—they still would not be able to reflect them all within their information system. There must be a selection process, explicit or implicit, which permits the gathering and processing of only the most critical information and facilitates the screening out of all other data. In the first place, many items of information would cost more to gather and process than the value of the benefits they would provide. Also, an excessive flow of data would "clog" the sys-

TABLE II

SOME BEHAVIORAL ASSUMPTIONS FROM MODERN ORGANIZATION THEORY

Assumptions with Respect to Organization Goals

A. Organizations are coalitions of individual participants. Strictly speaking, the organization itself, which is "mindless," cannot have goals—only the individuals can have goals.

B. Those objectives which are usually viewed as organizational goals are, in fact, the objectives of the dominant members of the coalition, subject to whatever constraints are imposed by the other participants and by the external environment of the organization.

C. Organization objectives tend to change in response to: (1) changes in the goals of the dominant participants; (2) changes in the relationships within the coalition; and (3) changes in the external environment of the organization.

D. In the modern complex business enterprise, there is no single universal organization goal such as profit maximization. To the extent that any truly over-all objective might be identified, that objective is probably organization survival.

E. Facing a highly complex and uncertain world and equipped with only limited rationality, members of an organization tend to focus on "local" (i.e., individual and departmental) goals. These local goals are often in conflict with each other. In addition, there appears to be no valid basis for the assumption that they are homogeneous and thus additive—what is good for the parts of the organization is not necessarily good for the whole.

Assumptions with Respect to the Behavior of Participants

A. Human behavior within an organization is essentially an adaptive, problem-solving, decision-making process.

B. Organization participants are motivated by a wide variety of psychological, social, and economic needs and drives. The relative strength of these diverse needs differs between individuals and within the same individual over time.

C. The decision of an individual to join an organization, and the separate decision to contribute his productive efforts once a member, are based on the individual's perception of the extent to which such action will further the achievement of his personal goals.

D. The efficiency and effectiveness of human behavior and decision making within organizations is constrained by: (1) the inability to concentrate on more than a few things at a time; (2) limited awareness of the environment; (3) limited knowledge of alternative courses of action and the consequences of such alternatives; (4) limited reasoning ability; and (5) incomplete and inconsistent preference systems. As a result of these limits on human rationality, individual and organizational behavior is usually directed at attempts to find satisfactory—rather than optimal—solutions.

Assumptions with Respect to the Behavior of Management

A. The primary role of the business manager is to maintain a favorable balance between (1) the contributions required from the participants and (2) the inducement (i.e., perceived need satisfactions) which must be offered to secure these contributions.

B. The management role is essentially a decision-making process subject to the limitations on human rationality and cognitive ability. The manager must make decisions himself and must effectively influence the decision premises of others so that their decisions will be favorable for the organization.

C. The essence of management control is the willingness of other participants to *accept* the authority of management. This willingness appears to be a non-stable function of the inducement-contribution balance.

D. Responsibility is assigned from "above" and authority is accepted from "below." It is, therefore, meaningless to speak of the balance between responsibility and authority as if both of these were "given" to the manager.

Assumptions with Respect to the Role of Accounting

A. The management accounting process is an information system whose major purposes are: (1) to provide the various levels of management with data which will facilitate the decision-making functions of planning and control; and (2) to serve as a communications medium within the organization.

B. The effective use of budgets and other accounting control techniques requires an understanding of the interaction between these techniques and the motivations and aspiration levels of the individuals to be controlled.

C. The objectivity of the management accounting process is largely a myth. Accountants have wide areas of discretion in the selection, processing, and reporting of data.

D. In performing their function within an organization, accountants can be expected to be influenced by their own personal and departmental goals in the same way as other participants are influenced.

tem and prevent the timely and efficient passage and evaluation of more important information.[2] Therefore, only a certain, very limited, set of data (i.e., observations about changes) can be selected for admission into the system. The essential point to be noted here is that decisions regarding what information is the most critical, how it should be processed, and who should receive it are almost always made by accountants. In addition, they are often directly involved, as participants, in the management decision-making process itself.

[2] This is the "capacity problem" discussed by Anton. See Hector R. Anton, *Some Aspects of Measurement and Accounting*, Working Paper No. 84 (Berkeley, Calif.: Center for Research in Management Science, University of Calif., 1963).

In carrying out these activities, accountants utilize a frame of reference that is, in effect, their view of the nature of the firm and its participation. The operation of their system requires them to be constantly abstracting a selected flow of information from the complex real world and using this selected data as the variables in their "model" of the firm. It seems clear that accountants exercise choice in the design of their systems and the selection of data for admission into them. It also seems clear that the entire management accounting process can be viewed from the standpoint of attempting to influence the behavior of others. It follows, therefore, that they must perform these functions with certain expectations with respect to the reactions of others to what they do. In other words, their model of the firm must involve some set of explicit or implicit assumptions about human behavior in organizations.

THE "TRADITIONAL" VIEW OF BEHAVIOR

Once it has been demonstrated that the management accounting function does by necessity involve assumptions about behavior, the next task is to identify these assumptions. Our investigation is complicated by the fact that nowhere in the literature of accounting is there a formal statement of the behavioral assumptions of the management accounting model of the firm. It is necessary, therefore, to attempt to construct such a statement. We begin with the premise that present-day management accounting theory and practice is the product of three related conceptual forces, namely, industrial engineering technology, classical organization theory, and the economic "theory of the firm." An examination of the literature of management accounting suggests that accountants may have avoided the necessity of developing a behavioral model of

their own by borrowing a set of assumptions from these other areas. If this thesis is valid, an appropriate point to begin the search for such assumptions is by an examination of the assumptions of these related models. Since much of the engineering view appears to be incorporated in the classical organization theory model,[3] it can probably be eliminated from this analysis without significant loss. Further, it appears that classical organization theory and economics do not represent two completely different views of human behavior, but rather that they share essentially a single view.

The following paragraphs will attempt to demonstrate that—with the exception of the modern organization theory concepts of recent years—there has been a single view of human behavior in business organizations from the period of the industrial revolution to the present and that management accounting has adopted this view without significant modification or serious question as to its validity.

The Economic Theory of the Firm

It has been suggested that, from the beginnings of recorded history, the traditional determinants of human behavior in organizations have been either custom or physical force.[4] As long as this was the case, there was no real need for an organization theory or economic theory to explain how and why human beings worked together cooperatively to accomplish common goals. However, the changing structure of society, which accompanied—and to an extent caused—the industrial revolution, destroyed much of the force of these traditional determinants of behavior. The new entrepreneurial class of

[3] One of the earliest, and perhaps the best, example of this consolidation can be found in the work of Taylor. See, Frederick W. Taylor, *Scientific Management* (New York: Harper & Brothers, 1911).
[4] Robert L. Heilbroner, *The Worldly Philosophers* (ed. rev.; New York: Simon and Schuster, 1961), pp. 7–8.

the 18th century sought not only a social philosophy to rationalize its actions, it also sought practical solutions to the immediate problems of motivating, coordinating, and controlling the members of its organizations. The second of these needs resulted in the development of the classical organization theories which will be discussed in the following section. The first need, i.e., the quest for a rationalization, ultimately led to the incorporation of the economic theory of the firm into the logic of the industrial society.

The economic theory of the firm can be summarized as follows. The entrepreneur is faced with a series of behavior alternatives. These alternatives are limited by the economic constraints of the market and the technological constraints of the production function. Within these constraints he will act in such a way as to maximize his economic profit. This behavior is facilitated by the personality characteristic of complete rationality and the information system characteristic of perfect knowledge. Finally, the individual so described is one who is entirely motivated by economic forces. A more subtle elaboration of this last point is the view that leisure has value and that a person will not work except in response to sufficient economic incentives. Thus, the classical economist specifically assumed that man was essentially "lazy" and preferred to minimize his work effort.[5]

Most modern economists would agree that the classical theory of the firm is based on several rather severe abstractions from the real world of business enterprise.[6] Nevertheless, despite these criticisms, there can be little doubt that it has had a substantial influence on the development of management philosophy and practice. The explanation of human behavior offered by economists—i.e., economic motivation and profit maximization—was incorporated into the patterns of thought of the merging industrial community where it

not only became established in its own right but also provided the philosophical and psychological foundations of the scientific management movement.

Classical Organization Theory

At the turn of the century, Fredrick W. Taylor began a major investigation into the functioning of business organizations which became known as the scientific management movement. Taylor's approach combined the basic behavioral assumptions of the economic theory of the firm with the viewpoint of the engineer seeking the most effective utilization of the physical resources at his disposal. He was concerned with men primarily as "adjuncts to machines" and was interested in maximizing the productivity of the worker through increased efficiency and reduced costs. Implicit in this approach was the belief that if men who might otherwise be wasteful and inefficient could be instructed in methods of achieving increased productivity and, at the same time, provided with adequate economic incentives and proper working conditions, they could be motivated to adopt the improvements, and the organization would benefit accordingly.[7]

March and Simon have noted that the ideas of the scientific management movement are based predominantly on a model of human behavior which assumes that "organization members, and particularly employees, are primarily *passive instruments*, capable of performing work and accepting directions, but not initiating

[5] This assumption is the basis for the "backward-bending" labor supply curve found in the literature of economics.

[6] See, for example, Andreas G. Papandreou, "Some Basic Problems in the Theory of the Firm," *A Survey of Contemporary Economics*, ed. Bernard F. Haley (Homewood, Ill.: Richard D. Irwin, Inc., 1952), Vol. II, pp. 183–219.

[7] James G. March and Herbert A. Simon, *Organizations* (New York: John Wiley & Sons, Inc., 1958), pp. 12ff.

action or exerting influence in any significant way."[8]

The scientific management movement flourished and rapidly became an important part of the business enterprise scene; in fact, for many years it virtually dominated this scene. Furthermore, even a brief glance at current management literature and practices should satisfy the reader that most of Taylor's views are still widely accepted today. Newer theories of management may have supplemented but they have never entirely replaced the scientific management approach.

About 1920, a second major pattern of organization theory, usually referred to as "principles of management" or "administrative management theory," began to develop. This body of doctrine adopted what was essentially a departmentalized approach to the problem of management. Its primary objective was the efficient assignment of organization activities to individual jobs and the grouping of these jobs by departments in such a way as to minimize the total cost of carrying on the activities of the firm. Writers of this school concerned themselves largely with the development of "principles of management" dealing with such subjects as lines of authority and responsibility, specialization, span of control, and unity of command.[9] This administrative management theory appears to have had a substantial and continuing influence on management theory and practice.

The work of Taylor and his scientific management successors led them into detailed studies of factory costs and provided an important stimulus for the development of modern cost and management accounting. Administrative management theory further contributed to this development through its emphasis on control and departmental responsibility and accountability. Finally, all of this occurred within the over-all setting provided by the economic theory of the firm. In summary, it seems clear that with respect to both its philosophy and techniques, much of contemporary management accounting is a product of, and is geared to, these classical theories. This is what is referred to here as the traditional management accounting model of the firm.

A Tentative Statement of the Behavioral Assumptions Underlying Present-Day Management Accounting

It should now be possible to draw together the several strands of the preceding discussion and attempt to postulate some of the fundamental behavioral assumptions that appear to underlie the traditional management accounting model. These assumptions were presented in Table I above. The parenthetical notations note the major conceptual sources of the assumptions. In some cases, there appears to be a considerable overlapping of sources; however, since this is not crucial to the present investigation, the notations have been limited to the primary or most significant area.

SOME BEHAVIORAL CONCEPTS OF MODERN ORGANIZATION THEORY

The preceding paragraphs were concerned with an effort to identify a set of behavioral assumptions which could be associated with current theory and practice in management accounting. We will now attempt to develop an alternative set of behavioral assumptions for management accounting—one that is based on concepts from modern organization theory.

Of the several different modern organization theory approaches, the "decision-making model" of the firm has been selected for use here. The basis for this choice is the close relationship which ap-

[8] Ibid., p. 6.
[9] Ibid., pp. 22ff.

pears to exist between the "decision-making model" and the "information-system" concept of management accounting discussed earlier. The decision-making approach to organization theory effectively began with the writings of Chester I. Barnard, particularly in *The Functions of the Executive*, and was further developed by Simon and others.[10] The model is primarily concerned with the organizational processes of communication and decision making. While drawing heavily on sociology and psychology, it is distinguished from these organization theory approaches by its emphasis on the decision as the basic element of organization.

Organizations are viewed as cooperative efforts or coalitions entered into by individuals in order to achieve personal objectives which cannot be realized without such cooperation. These individuals are motivated to join the organization and contribute to the accomplishment of its objectives because they believe that in this way they can satisfy their personal goals. It is important to note that these personal goals include social and psychological, as well as economic, considerations. Thus, the survival and success of the organization depends on the maintenance of a favorable balance between the contributions required of each participant and the opportunities to satisfy personal goals which must be offered as inducements to secure effective participation.

It is common practice to speak of organization goals; however, to be completely precise, it is the participants who have goals. The organization itself is mindless and, therefore, can have no goals, In the sense that it is used here, the term organization goals is intended to mean the goals of the dominant members of the coalition subject to those constraints which are imposed by other participants and by the external environment. This view implies an organizational goal struc-

ture which is in a constant state of change as the environment and the balances and relationships among the participants change. Under such circumstances, it seems meaningless to talk of a single universal goal such as profit maximization. To the extent that any long-run over-all objective might be identified, it appears that this objective would have to be stated in very broad and general terms such as the goal of organization survival.

The decision-making process is usually described as a sequence of three steps: (1) the evoking of alternative courses of action; (2) a consideration of the consequences of the evoked alternatives; and (3) the assignment of values to the various consequences.[11]

It has been suggested that any behavioral theory of rational choice must consider certain limits on the decision maker.[12] These include his (1) limited knowledge with respect to all possible alternatives and consequences; (2) limited cognitive ability; (3) constantly changing value structure; and (4) tendency to "satisfice" rather than maximize. Rational behavior, therefore, consists of searching among limited alternatives for a reasonable solution under conditions in which the consequences of action are uncertain.

The behavioral concepts which flow from the decision-making model have a number of interesting implications. For example, authority is viewed as something which is accepted from "below" rather than imposed from "above."[13] In other

[10] Chester I. Barnard, *The Functions of the Executive* (Cambridge: Harvard University Press, 1938); Herbert A. Simon, *Administrative Behavior* (New York: John Wiley & Sons, Inc., 1947); March and Simon, *Organizations;* and Richard M. Cyert and James G. March, *A Behavioral Theory of the Firm* (Englewood Cliffs, N. J.: Prentice-Hall, Inc., 1963). The preceding works represent the principal theoretical sources for the decision-making model discussed here.
[11] March and Simon, p. 82.
[12] Simon, pp. xxv–xxvi.
[13] Douglas McGregor, *The Human Side of Enterprise*

words, there must be a *decision to accept* authority before such authority can become effective. Further, human activity is considered to be essentially a process of problem-solving and adaptive behavior—a process in which goals, perception, and abilities are all interrelated and all continually changing.

To summarize the decision-making model, the basic element of organization study is the decision. The objective of managerial decision-making is to secure and coordinate effectively the contributions of other participants. This is accomplished by influencing, to the extent possible, their perception of alternatives and consequences of choice and their value structures, so that the resulting decisions are consistent with the current objectives of the dominant members of the organization.

While the theorists of the "decision-making" school have paid substantial attention to behavioral concepts, the literature does not appear to contain a detailed and complete statement of their underlying behavioral assumptions. Accordingly, it becomes necessary, as it was with the traditional accounting model, to abstract and formulate a set of assumptions. The modern organization theory assumptions presented in Table II represent an attempt by the present writer to identify and extend the behavioral assumptions of the decision-making model in terms of the management accounting function.

Basic Conflicts between the Behavioral Assumptions of Traditional Management Accounting and Modern Organization Theory

An examination of the two sets of behavioral assumptions developed above suggests a number of interesting questions. Answers to these questions, however, can only be found through extended empirical analysis. Thus, whatever value attaches to the foregoing discussion appears to relate to its possible contribution in providing a theoretical framework for future empirical research. This research might be designed to explore such questions as the following:

A. What behavioral model provides the most realistic view of human behavior in business organizations? (Accountants should, perhaps, be willing to accept the research findings of organization theorists regarding this question.)

B. Is it possible to draw any general conclusions about the view of behavior actually held by accountants (and managers) in practice?

C. What, if any, are the major differences in the behavioral assumptions of the views in A and B above?

D. What, if any, are the consequences for the organization and its participants of the differences in the behavioral assumptions of the views in A and B?

E. Is it possible to design management accounting systems which are based on a more realistic view of behavior, and would such systems produce better results than present systems?

Lacking empirical evidence, any attempt to investigate the implications of the differences between the two views of behavior discussed in this paper must be considered highly speculative. We might, however, examine briefly a few of the major differences in order to illustrate the nature of the problem. Let us assume for the moment that the decision-making model represents a more realistic view of human behavior than the traditional management accounting model. Let us further assume that the traditional model is a reasonably accurate summary of actual management accounting views in practice. Under these circumstances, what are some of the consequences for business organizations of the use of accounting systems based on the traditional management accounting model of behavior? The system of classification used in Tables I and II will also be adopted here. Thus, this analysis

(New York: McGraw-Hill Book Co., Inc., 1960), pp. 158–160.

will concentrate on four major areas: organization goals; behavior of participants; behavior of management; and the role of accounting.

Assumptions with Respect to Organization Goals

In comparing these two sets of assumptions, the most immediately apparent difference concerns the relative simplicity and brevity of the traditional accounting assumptions as contrasted to those of the organization theory model. This should not be particularly surprising since such a difference seems to be consistent with the general philosophies of the two models. There can be little doubt that the view of human behavior associated with the scientific management movement and classical economics is much less complicated than the behavioral outlooks of modern organization theory. In fact, the principal conflict between modern and classical organization theories appears to rest precisely on this issue. Since traditional management accounting is closely related to the classical models, it seems reasonable to expect that it will also tend toward a relatively simple and uncomplicated view of behavior. For example, with respect to organization goals, the behavioral assumptions of the accounting model focus on a single universal objective of business activity. The organization theory assumptions, on the other hand, suggest a much broader and rather imprecise structure of goals.

The traditional management accounting view of organization goals, which appears to be directly related to the theory of the firm of classical economics, may be summarized as follows: The principal objective of business activity is the maximization of the economic profits of the enterprise; the total responsibility for the accomplishment of that objective can be divided into smaller portions and distributed to sub-units throughout the organization; the maximization by each sub-unit of its particular portion of the profit responsibility will result in maximization of the total profits of the enterprise.

The entire structure of traditional management accounting appears to be built around this concept of profit maximization and the related (but quite different) idea of cost minimization. Management accountants have, for the most part, limited the scope of their systems to the selection, processing, and reporting of data concerning certain economic events, the effects of which can be reduced—without too many complications—to monetary terms. This approach is justifiable only if the particular class of events under consideration can be viewed as *the* critical variables affecting the organization. Thus, accountants have been able to rationalize the importance of the data flowing through their systems by relating this data and its use directly to the assumed goal of profit maximization. However, the classical economic view of profits as the universal motivating force of business enterprises has come under substantial attack in recent years. This attack has been based on two general issues. First, questions have been raised concerning the adequacy of economic profits as the sole significant explanation for what takes place within an organization. Second, it has been suggested that limitations on the decision-making process result in behavior which is best described as satisficing rather than maximizing.

It should be particularly emphasized that the recognition of a more complex goal structure does not mean that economic profits can be ignored. Obviously, business firms cannot survive for any extended period of time without some minimum level of profits. Nevertheless, the attempt to summarize the entire goal structure of a complex business entity through the use of one index may result in an overly simplified and unrealistic view of the organization. In short, profits may represent a necessary but not a sufficient definition of the goal structure of business organizations.

The view of organization goals, suggested by the behavioral assumptions of the decision-making model, has two major aspects. First, those objectives which are commonly referred to as goals of the organization are, in fact, the goals of the dominant group of participants. Secondly, it is suggested that these goals are the result of the interaction of a set of constantly changing forces. Thus, the goal-structure of an organization is not only rather imperfectly defined at any given point in time, but it is also in a continual process of change throughout time. In order to identify any truly universal goal, it may be necessary, as suggested earlier, to generalize to the very broad—and perhaps meaningless—level of an objective such as organization survival.

In view of the complex nature of organization goals, it is possible that the profit maximization assumption unduly restricts the role of management accounting to providing a limited and inadequate range of data for decision making. It is as if the accountant were viewing the firm through a narrow aperture which permits him to observe only a thin "slice" of the total organization activity. In emphasizing this narrow view, traditional management accounting appears to ignore many of the complexities and interrelationships that make up the very substance of an organization. What is the practical implication of these observations? How would management accounting change if accountants did not concentrate exclusively on profit maximization? It is likely that this, in itself, would not involve immediate operational changes but rather a change in underlying philosophy. As this philosophy

is modified, it should become apparent that a number of specific changes in procedures and systems are in order. Examples of such specific changes might be found in the departmental budgeting and accounting techniques discussed below.

The traditional accounting assumption with respect to the divisibility and additivity of the responsibility for the accomplishment of organization goals seems to warrant some additional comment. Research in organization theory has indicated that individual members of an organization tend to identify with their immediate group rather than with the organization itself. This tendency appears to encourage the development of strong sub-unit loyalties and a concentration on the goals of the sub-unit even when these goals are in conflict with the interests of the organization. The usual departmental budgeting and accounting techniques, by which management accountants endeavor to measure the success of the various sub-units within an organization in achieving certain goals, are based on the assumption that profit maximization or cost minimization at the departmental level will lead to a similar result for the firm as a whole. Thus, accounting reports tend to highlight supposed departmental efficiencies and inefficiencies. Reports of this type seem to encourage departmental activities aimed at "making a good showing" regardless of the effect on the entire organization. It appears to be common for departments within an organization to be in a state of competition with each other for funds, recognition, authority, and so forth. Under such circumstances, it is not very likely that the cooperative efforts necessary to the efficient functioning of the organization as a whole will be furthered by an accounting system which emphasizes and, perhaps, even fosters interdepartmental conflicts.

The tendency for intra-organizational conflict appears to be further compounded by some of the common management accounting techniques for the allocation and control of costs. For example, in some organizations with relatively rigid budgeting procedures, it appears to be a normal practice for departments to attempt deliberately to use up their entire budget for a given period in order to avoid a reduction in the budgets of succeeding periods. Another example is the emphasis often placed on the desirability of keeping costs below some predetermined amount. In such cases, it is likely that, even though a departmental expenditure would be extremely beneficial to an organization, it will not be undertaken if such action would cause the costs of that department to exceed the predetermined limit.

Assumptions with Respect to the Behavior of Participants

The view of the individual inherent in the behavioral assumptions associated with traditional management accounting is one which has been completely rejected by most of the behavioral scientists interested in modern organization theory. To what extent this traditional view is actually held by accountants in practice is a question which, as stated earlier, can only be answered by empirical investigation. Our own limited experience suggests that it is held by a sufficient number of management accountants to be considered at least a significant view within the profession.

It is possible that the failure of management accountants to consider the more complex motivating forces which organization theory recognizes in the individual contributes to the use of accounting systems and procedures which produce "side-effects" in the form of a variety of unanticipated and undesired responses from participants. For example, many management accounting techniques intended to control costs, such as budgeting and standard costing, may virtually defeat themselves because they help to create feelings of confusion, frustration, suspicion, and hostility. These techniques may not motivate effectively because they fail to consider the broad spectrum of needs and drives of the participants.[14]

Assumptions with Respect to the Behavior of Management

Modern organization theory encompasses a view of the management process which differs substantially from the "classical" view associated here with management accounting. It is interesting, however, that both models appear to take essentially the same position with respect to the basic purpose of managerial activity. This purpose relates to securing effective participation from the other members of the organization. One way of emphasizing the nature of the conflict between the two models in this regard is to examine the manner in which each attempts to accomplish this basic purpose.

According to the traditional accounting model, management must control the performance of others—the principal instrument of control being authority. This model assumes that participants must be continually prodded to perform and that this prodding is accomplished through the use of authority which is applied from above. Also, it places heavy reliance on the use of economic rewards and penalties as devices to implement authority and motivate effective participation.

The decision-making model, on the other hand, assumes that management must *influence* the behavior of others. Furthermore, this approach suggests that, unless individuals are willing to accept such influence, effective participation cannot be

[14] For a discussion of the behavioral implications of budgets, see Andrew C. Stedry, *Budget Control and Cost Behavior* (Englewood Cliffs, N. J.: Prentice-Hall, Inc., 1960).

assured regardless of the extent of the formal (classical) authority available to management. Viewed in this sense, meaningful authority cannot be imposed on a participant; rather it must be accepted by him. Finally, the decision-making model assumes that the willingness of participants to accept authority and to make effective contributions to the organization depends not only on economic considerations but also to a substantial extent on social and psychological factors.

There seems to be a very close relationship between the behavioral assumptions of traditional management accounting and those associated with the classical management view of the firm. This is evidenced not only in their historical development but also by the manner in which management and management accounting currently interact in the modern business organization. It appears reasonable to expect that the effect of this interaction is to strengthen a jointly shared philosophy with respect to human behavior and the role of management. Managers who tend toward the classical view of behavior are likely to find support from traditional accounting systems which provide the kinds of data that emphasize this view. This accounting emphasis in turn probably serves to focus the attention of management on issues and solutions which are consistent with the philosophy of the classical view. Thus, a "feedback loop" is established which appears to be an important factor in perpetuating this relatively narrow view of human behavior among both management and accountants.

Since the assumptions of the traditional accounting model are so close to classical organization theory and, in fact, appear to be a reasonably good description of the classical theory itself, it would be interesting to consider two questions. First, does the classical view of management provide an efficient solution to the problems of in-fluencing behavior within an organization? Second, if the principal function of management accounting is to furnish relevant data for managerial decision making, should the accountant be concerned with providing the kinds of information that management actually wants or the kinds of information that management should want?

With respect to the first question, this paper has attempted to demonstrate that the classical view may not be an efficient approach in motivating organizationally desirable behavior. This premise appears to be supported by a substantial amount of theoretical and empirical research in modern organization theory. In terms of the present discussion, the important point is that traditional management accounting procedures and attitudes cannot be justified solely on the basis that they are consistent with other common management practices because serious questions have been raised regarding the desirability of many of these practices themselves.

In reference to the second question posed above, it can be argued that it is the task of management accounting to provide the information desired by management and to provide it in a manner which is consistent with existing management philosophy. In other words, it is not the responsibility of the accountant to attempt to change the viewpoint of management but only to function within the framework established by this viewpoint. The difficulty with this argument is that it treats accounting as something separate from management. This paper, on the other hand, assumes that management accounting is an integral part of management. The adoption of a more realistic model of behavior by accountants could place them in the position of leading rather than passively following the changes in management philosophy which are bound to occur as a result of the impact of modern organization theory. Thus, it might be hoped that the development of more sophisticated management accounting systems would encourage the evolution of a much more sophisticated management viewpoint in general.

Assumptions with Respect to the Role of Accounting

Modern economic organizations are, of course, highly complex entities. Business managers must continually operate under conditions of uncertainty and limited rationality. In addition, management accountants are subject to the same kinds of drives and needs as are other members of the organization. All of this suggests that management accounting systems could not, even under the best of circumstances, achieve the degree of certainty, neutrality, and objectivity that is often attributed to them. To the extent that management accounting fails to live up to its image in this regard, it can be anticipated that problems will arise for the organization. For one thing, organization members are often subject to evaluations based on information produced by the accounting system. These individuals are likely to be seriously confused and disturbed by a flow of seemingly precise and exact accounting data which they cannot really understand or explain, but which nevertheless implies that they are (or are not) performing their tasks properly. The better education of organization participants regarding the limitations of accounting data, while worthwhile in its own right, does not represent an adequate solution. A much more important step would be a clearer understanding of these limitations by accountants themselves.

Also, as members of the organizations which they serve, management accountants can be expected to seek such psychological and social objectives as security, prestige, and power. In some instances,

they might also be expected—as suggested by the discussion of sub-unit goals—to view the success of the accounting department and the technical perfection of the accounting process as ends in themselves. Thus, it is possible that some management accountants tend to view their function as primarily one of criticizing the actions of others and of placing the responsibility for failures to achieve certain desired levels of performance. Where this tendency exists, it may be expected to have a significant effect on motivation and be a major source of difficulty within the organization.[15]

CONCLUSIONS

This paper has attempted to postulate a set of behavioral assumptions which could be associated with the theory and practice of "traditional" management accounting. The resulting set of fifteen assumptions represents an accounting adaptation of what might be termed the classical view of human behavior in business organizations. This view emphasizes such concepts as profit maximization, economic incentives, and the inherent laziness and inefficiency of organization participants. It is a model which is structured primarily in terms of the classical ideas of departmentalization, authority, responsibility, and control. The accounting process which has emerged in response to the needs presented by this classical model appears to treat human behavior and goals essentially as given. Further, the generally accepted measure of "good" accounting seems to be one of relevance and usefulness in the maximization of the money profits of the enterprise.

In addition, we have examined a set of behavioral assumptions based on research in modern organization theory. It seems

[15] Chris Argyris, *The Impact of Budgets on People* (Ithaca, N. Y.: Prepared for the Controllership Foundation, Inc., at Cornell University, 1952).

clear that a management accounting system structured around this second set of behavioral assumptions would differ in many respects from the accounting systems found in practice and described in the literature.

One should not infer that the traditional assumptions considered here are completely invalid. The very fact that they have endured for so long suggests that this is not the case. It should at least be recognized, however, that in many respects the extent of their validity may be subject to question. Also, it is not argued that all accountants limit themselves at all times to this traditional view. Rather, the two sets of behavioral assumptions discussed might be considered as extreme points on a scale of many possible views. The significance of the traditional point on such a scale appears to be twofold: (a) it is likely that the traditional model represents a view of behavior which is relatively common in practice; and (b) this view seems to underlie much of what is written and taught about accounting.

If the modern organization theory model does ultimately prove to be a more realistic view of human behavior in business organizations, there is little doubt that the scope of management accounting theory and practice will need to be expanded and broadened. In particular, accountants will have to develop an increased awareness and understanding of the complex social and psychological motivations and limitations of organization participants. What is urgently needed, and what we have had very little of in the past, is solid empirical research designed to measure the effectiveness with which management accounting systems do, in fact, perform their functions of motivating, explaining, and predicting human behavior.

An Integrated Approach to Control System Design*

SHAHID L. ANSARI
New York University

Abstract

Existing approaches to the problem of designing management control systems may be described as primarily *structural* or *behavioral*. The first approach is characteristic of the accounting literature. It takes a rational and mechanistic view of control and treats the control system design problem as one of designing an effective information structure. The behavioral approach, exemplified by the socio-psychological literature on performance, views control as a problem of designing social relationships which lead to high performance.

This paper presents evidence which shows that there is a close interaction between the information structure and the human and social relationships. Using an open systems approach, it argues for the adoption of a view of management control in which the two elements are considered jointly. The minimization of perceptual differences between managers and subordinates is proposed as an operational criterion which designers can use as a guide. Finally, some propositions for further research which emerge from this proposed perspective are also presented.

Researchers interested in the problem of management control system design have focused on it from two different perspectives. The first one, adopted by researchers in cybernetics, accounting, and management information systems (MIS) concentrates mainly on the information and communication aspects of a control system. It may be described as a *structural* view. The other, based upon studies of human behavior in organizations, regards control as a problem of getting subordinates to achieve performance goals. Because of its emphasis on the human and social aspects of control, this may be described as a *behavioral* view.

These perspectives have resulted in a fragmented approach in which designers attempt to optimize the structural or behavioral variables alone. In this paper I will argue that designing control systems requires a consideration of both these variables. With the help of existing evidence, it will be shown that information and human–social variables are really interacting subsystems. An operational criterion by which a designer can more effectively integrate these components will also be proposed.

The presentation is divided into five parts. The first part introduces the terminology and assumptions used in the analyses. This is followed by a discussion of the two existing approaches to control system design. The next part of the paper argues that the present sole emphasis on information or behavior is inappropriate because of the interrelationships between these components. A framework which recognizes their interaction and suggests an operational way to combine them in a control system is proposed in the subsequent part. The final section is devoted to a consideration of the research implications of the proposed framework.

SOME KEY ASSUMPTIONS

The term management control has been used in a variety of ways in the literature.[1] To avoid confusion, this paper will restrict its usage to only

---

* I am grateful to my colleagues Jack McDonough, Dick Mason, Burt Swanson and Jim Taylor and two unknown reviewers for their useful comments and criticisms on earlier drafts of this paper.

[1] For example, Anthony & Dearden (1976) distinguish between management control and operational control. The former they define as control managers exercise over other managers. The latter is control over lower echelon supervisors for the performance of specific tasks. No such distinction is made in this paper.

---

those situations in which the controlled variable is human performance. Thus inventory control systems, using operational research models, are excluded. No distinction, however, will be made between controlling performance of first line supervisors as opposed to higher managers. The design problems are assumed to be generic and common to all echelons of an organization.

The working of a control system will be assumed to require a set of *structural* arrangements which allows the human behavioral *process* to function. While this will facilitate earlier discussion it will later be shown that this assumption, which is similar to a socio-technical systems view, is the proper perspective for a designer.[2]

Given these assumptions, a control system, as used here, may be simply described as "those organizational *arrangements* and *actions* designed to facilitate its members to achieve higher performance with least unintended consequences".

EXISTING VIEWS ON MANAGEMENT CONTROL

Most writers agree that a management control system consists of two elements. The first one is an information network which prescribes the rules for the measurement, collection, processing and transmission of information. It facilitates communication of information about performance goals, actual outputs and deviations from plans to managers and subordinates. The network may be regarded as the structure of a control system.

The other element is the set of social relationships through which such systems achieve their goals. It may be regarded as the control process. It is convenient to group existing research into these two catagories according to the emphasis they place on the structural or human-social variables.

The structural approach

This view is best exemplified by the early work in cybernetics which has been strictly and narrowly interpreted in the control literature. It is a closed systems, highly mechanistic view, which defines control as a problem of designing optimal

information networks. For example, Beer (1964, p. 23) states that control systems to be effective should be designed as cybernetic systems, which he defines as "a tightly knit network of information". Control is defined as "a homeostatic machine for regulating itself".

The cybernetics approach treats control as synonymous with communication of information. Therefore, it analyzes the control problem in terms of communication theory concepts. For instance, Ashby (1965) states that control consists essentially of blocking information about disturbances from reaching controlled variables by interjecting a regulatory mechanism. For effective control, the regulator must have so-called "requisite variety" and "channel capacity", concepts based upon Shannon's work on the mathematical theory of information communication.[3]

In the extreme cybernetics view there is no difference between a mechanical regulator, such as a thermostat, and a human regulator or manager. The model treats the response of the regulator as flowing automatically from the nature of communicated information. It fails to recognize that managers do not respond mechanically since they process information based on their *personal* goals and not the organizational goals imbedded in a control system.

The cybernetic closed systems perspective has been incorporated in recent years in the research in management information systems (MIS). Discussions about the design of MIS are conducted in much the same terminology and with many of the same assumptions. Behavioral effects, such as differences in information perception and reaction between people, if recognized, are sometimes regarded as nuisances. For example, Davis (1974, p. 97) states: "In much the same way that a closed system is insulated from disturbances in the environment, a closed feedback loop is insulated from disturbances in the control loop. An open control loop is one with *random disturbances*, such as those associated with *human control elements*." (Emphasis added.)

Again, to regard human behavior as a random disturbance, as the above quotation does, is to deny a great part of purposeful goal-oriented

[2] Readers interested in getting a better understanding of the theoretical underpinnings of the socio-technical view of organizations should see Emery & Trist (1960).

[3] For a detailed description of these concepts see Ashby (1956, p. 201).

behavior of people in control systems. It is incorrect to deny this, and to assume that the problem of control can somehow be solved by providing management with "right" information. The fact that the behavioral climate within which this information is perceived may reduce its usefulness, or even distort it, should be recognized.

Much of the same perspective, with few exceptions, is also evident in discussions of control in the accounting literature. Anthony & Dearden (1976) suggest that this greater emphasis on information as compared to social variables, may be because the former are more amenable to a systematic description. Even while recognizing the importance of social interactions, they describe management control structure in terms of financial responsibility centers (cost, revenue, profit and investment), and the control process in terms of financial reporting activities (programming, budgeting, reporting and appraisal).

If a designer approaches control with a structural perspective, the following questions are likely to be the ones he will emphasize in his task.

(1) What are the controlled variables and how are they to be broken down and measured at different levels? This question focuses on the goals or performance standards setting within a system. It deals with how large heirarchical organizations break down controlled variables into smaller components to be controlled separately. For example, breakdown of profit into divisional profit, departmental revenues or costs, etc., and assignment to a managerial responsibility center. This process of disaggregating goals into subgoals serves to: (a) coordinate activities of organizational units; and (b) evaluate performance of the various managers involved.

(2) What disturbances should be recognized and measured? There are many causes which can reduce a system's effectiveness. Not all of these are worth tracking, however. Only those that reflect the presence of a problem need be identified. The choice of disturbances, therefore, reflects the criteria laid down for distinguishing between a system's stable and out-of-control behaviors.

(3) When and how often to communicate information on deviations to management? The first issue (when) deals with the interval between

performance and the preparation of reports. At the one extreme are *feedback* systems which wait for performance to occur before reporting deviations. At the other are *feedforward* systems which anticipate disturbances and enable corrective action to be taken before performance is affected. The second issue (how often) deals with the appropriate frequency of reporting.

(4) What and how many transformations are to be performed on the information as it moves through a network? That is, at what point does the information enter the network, and how many times is it summarized, integrated or changed?

(5) What and how often feedback reports should be provided to subordinates? This factor relates the choice available to designers with respect to the type and frequency of feedback reports to use in performance evaluation.

The behavioral approach

This approach emphasizes the human and social process by which an organization achieves its goals. Its perspective is well stated by Tannenbaum (1964, p. 229), who describes control in a social organization as, "any process in which a person (or group of persons or organization of persons) determines or intentionally affects what another person or group or organization will do".

In most organizational situations, the above description refers to the process of affecting subordinate behavior. Research in how best to do this has gone through three evolutionary phases. Because of lack of space, only the most salient aspects are discussed here.

(1) Traditional management phase. This first phase coincides with the scientific management and traditional organization theory period. Here the problem of control was analyzed in terms of power, authority relations and sanctions.[5] Management had power over subordinates because they controlled their economic rewards and could terminate their membership in an organization. The main problem of control was to provide direction by dividing tasks, responsibilities, etc. Compliance could be obtained by offering appropriate economic incentives and the threat to use sanctions.

---

[4] An important type of feedback system is what Ashby calls the *error controlled* regulator. This system allows room for errors, learns from them, and then takes corrective action. Most management control systems, such as budgetary systems, are designed as error controlled regulators.

[5] This view of control is exemplified by the works of Taylor (1911), Urwick (1944) and Weber (1947).

Formal power and economic sanctions were the most important source of influence in this phase. The former was treated as a finite quantity (Tannenbaum, 1964). Delegation of authority, which allowed subordinates more freedom to control their actions, was regarded as a reduction in the power of the superiors. The key for management was to find how much authority to delegate without impairing its own power. In short, it regarded superiors as directive and subordinates as passive.

(2) Human relations phase. The second phase of research on the influence process coincides with the birth of the human relations movement.[6] It began by recognizing that subordinates have social needs which are sometimes more important than economic needs in determining their performance. What workers sought from organizations were not merely economic rewards, but also a sense of psychological satisfaction. A manager could, therefore, increase his influence by providing rewards that increased worker satisfaction.

The reduced role of economic rewards was accompanied by a concurrent deemphasis on the use of formal power. Researchers, such as Blau (1974) and Simon (1957), pointed out that compliance obtained by power can ensure a minimum effort but cannot guarantee a maximum effort by subordinates. To obtain high performance, a manager has to seek the cooperation of his workers. Techniques of persuasion were thus added to sources of influence.

The role of formal power was not only reduced, it was no longer viewed as a fixed quantity. On the basis of his own and other people's research, Tannenbaum (1964) concluded that "the total amount of control ... can increase, and the various participants can each acquire a share of this augmented power". He noted that an individual's performance and satisfaction were likely to be affected by his perception of the amount of control exercised by him and over him. Such effects would differ across individuals due to personality differences.

The major impact of this phase may be summarized as a change in focus of the managerial function from direction to *leadership*. It was no longer sufficient for a manager to rely on the formal organizational relations to get the work done. He had to become a leader and provide the impetus necessary for increasing the performance and satisfaction of his subordinates.

(3) Contingency theory phase. Both the first and second phases described above had one thing in common. They attempted to isolate a one best way. In the first phase it was the best management style, and in the second phase it was the one best leadership style. The third, and current, phase in the thinking on control is characterized by a move away from the search for a one best way suitable for all circumstances, to a search for circumstances under which certain combinations of variables work best.

This new emphasis results from the application of the general systems paradigm to the organizational design problem. As Kast & Rosensweig (1973, p. 307) note: "Systems concepts emphasize that organizations are composed of many subsystems whose interrelationships have to be recognized ... There are so many relevant variables that it is impossible for a simplistic model to depict reality." The effort, therefore, is on discovering what works best in a given situation.

Contingency theory of organizations is one concrete expression of this philosophy.[7] Its approach to the problem of influencing subordinate behavior is to focus on those organizational variables and relationships whose combination results in high performance. A good example is Fielder's (1967) work on leadership styles. His theory of leadership effectiveness is based on a study of the match between different supervision styles, worker personalities, and types of tasks. Results showed that autocratic leaders are more effective in some task environments and employee-oriented leaders are more effective in others.

---

[6] The beginning of this movement is generally ascribed to the Hawthorne studies done by Homans and others at Harvard. A description of this approach, with later research findings, is contained in Homans (1950).

[7] A slightly different application of this philosophy is in the literature on socio-technical systems. While both socio-technical systems theory and contingency theory are applications of the general systems theory to organizational problems, the former, unlike the latter, is concerned with both technical and behavioral variables in a work situation. This concern has been translated into a broader emphasis on improving the quality of working life through organizational redesign.

The most comprehensive model of performance in organizations, based on the contingency philosophy, is the so-called *expectancy model.*[8] It includes, not only Fiedler's variables, but also considers the match between a subordinate's needs and goals and the rewards offered by an organization.

The model states that an individual is motivated to perform because he has certain goals which an organization can satisfy by providing extrinsic and intrinsic rewards. An individual, therefore, computes two "expectancies" which indicate to him the likelihood of a given level of (a) effort resulting in high performance; and (b) performance providing him with the desired rewards. The higher those likelihoods, the more he will be motivated to perform at a high level.

A designer's job is to make sure that a control system maximizes these expectancies for subordinates. He can do this by designing task structures, leadership styles and reward structures which strengthen linkages between effort, performance, and rewards.

This current phase of research, therefore, is more situational based. Also, unlike preceding phases, it focuses more on the broader issue of improving subordinate performance instead of a narrow conception of constraining their behavior. It is also a phase on which research continues and new ideas and evidence will be forthcoming.

To recapitulate, the three phases described above represent the so-called behavioral view of control systems. The difference between this and the structural approach is best stated by Drucker (1964, p. 287): "Instead of a mechanical system, the control system in a human social situation is a volitional system." It requires motivating people to make choices favorable to an organization.

Need for a broader view of control systems

The problem with these approaches is that they emphasize a single perspective — one which ignores the existence of the other. Existing evidence suggests that information and human-social variables interact with each other in a way which necessitates their joint consideration. The nature of this interaction and the supporting evidence is described below.

The problem with the structural approach is that it treats information collection and communication as an abstract and rational decision-oriented process in which emotional and psychological variables play a limited role. The fact is that an information structure essentially represents a designer's perceptions of the control process. These perceptions reflect his *assumptions* — explicit or implicit — about the behavior of those using it, his *knowledge* and *skills*, and his *values*. All of these may be influenced by prior experiences and cultural factors.

This thesis is supported by Lawler & Rhode (1976, p. 129) who, after examining relevant evidence, conclude that "the financial control system of a corporation is demonstrably not isolated from the personality of the CPAs or financial officers who design, maintain and use the system". In discussing his experiences at General Motors, Sloan (1964) also concurs by stating that the decentralized reporting system of the company was a reflection of top management philosophy.

Caplan's (1968) field study of the assumptions underlying management accounting systems in organizations is one of the very few empirical studies on this subject. Some indirect support is provided by Reedy (1970) and Schlesinger (1974). In discussing the decision-making system of U.S. presidents, they point out that Presidential use of information sources largely reflects personal attitudes and beliefs about how best to exercise control over the federal government.

Finally, at a more abstract level, Mason & Mitroff (1972) point out that most information structures contain an assumption about a decision maker's cognitive style. Present systems, according to them, are designed for so-called "thinking-sensation" types of information processors. They suggest more varied assumptions so that information systems can be better matched with cognitive styles.

While structuralists fail to recognize the impact of people on information structures, behavioral writers tend to ignore the effects of information on people. They assume that information is neutral, and that, only the way it is used matters. For example, a typical statement is like the one by Cammann & Nadler (1976, p. 66), who state: "If managers use information well, the system works. If they use it poorly, the system may produce unintended consequences."

Such a position, however, is unrealistic on two

---

[8] An excellent description and summary of the research on the expectancy model is contained in Cummings & Schwab (1973).

counts. First, studies in human cognition show that information must first be *perceived* before it can be used. One important factor which can alter a person's perception is the characteristics of the perceived object – in this case information. Hence managerial use of information depends upon the characteristics of the information structure.

Second, besides managers, subordinates also use information for self guidance and self-evaluation of performance. This process is independent of supervisory evaluation and its results may differ with those of the supervisor. How information is measured and communicated is thus likely to alter subordinate perceptions of such information also.

An examination of this literature shows that the following characteristics of information structures are particularly relevant for a designer: (1) Nature of measures; (2) source and order of presentation; (3) timing; (4) route for transmission; and (5) extent of shared information.

(1) *Nature of measures*. Lawler & Rhode (1976) point out that subordinate motivation is affected by three characteristics of performance measures. The first is *completeness* and refers to the extent to which all behaviors necessary for good performance are measured. The second is *objectivity* which determines the impartiality of a measure and thus affects the trust subordinates place in it. The last one is the extent to which a subordinate's behavior can *influence* a measure (e.g. profits do not respond to performance of lower echelon workers). According to them, the more complete, objective and influencable a measure, the more likely it is to motivate subordinates.

(2) *Source and order of presentation*. This characteristic was one of the earliest to be studied. In a series of experiments, Hovland *et al.* (1953) showed that the order in which information is communicated, and the source attributed to such communications, can change a recipient's perception of a message. Credible sources tend to be used more often and have a greater influence on a user. Because of the conflicting research evidence, the influence of order is somewhat less clear.[9] A variant of order, placement, may explain why people get different signals when transactions are disclosed in footnotes as opposed to the body of a financial statement.

(3) *Timing*. There are two aspects of information timing – *speed* and *frequency* of communication. Bruner *et al.* (1956) cite several studies which show that speed can change information processing strategies of recipients. Because information comes faster, users may be forced to respond quickly. To do so, however, they may have to abandon slow but safe information processing strategies in favor of quicker but riskier strategies. The resulting perceptions may well be different. Frequency, on the other hand, refers to the reporting interval. Too long an interval may mean a loss of interest and usefulness of information to a user. Too short an interval may not measure all the things that should be included in a measure.

(4) *Route*. The communication network or route that information takes from a sender to a receiver can also influence the latter's perceptions. Ference (1970) shows that network features such as, point of entry of information, and the steps at which it is summarized, can alter the character of information. The sender and the receiver, therefore, may not be sharing the same information.

(5) *Shared information*. Information structures differ on the extent to which they have opened widely shared communications. For example, Lawler & Rhode (1976) point out that some systems keep pay and performance of workers secret from their co-workers. Also, in decentralized companies, divisions are known not to share information in order to increase their trading advantages with other divisions. The more open the communications, the more information a subordinate has to assess his own performance and the fairness of superior evaluation of his performance.

Based upon the prior discussion, it is now possible to offer a summary of the interaction between information and people in a control system. This is shown in Fig. 1. It shows that information structures reflect what a designer perceives to be the needs and goals of subordinates and managers. The designer, in essence, anticipates the type of information desired at the next stage in this system – self and supervisory evaluation of performance. These evaluations provide subordinates with most of their desired extrinsic and

---

[9] Research studies have reported two types of order effects – primacy and recency – making it difficult to resolve which is more prevalent and when. For a review see Hovland *et al.* (1957).

102

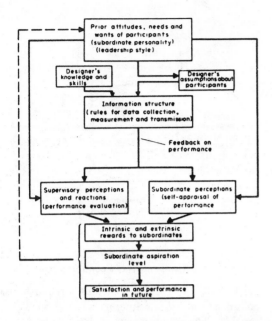

Fig. 1. Relationship between information and behavioral variables in a control system.

intrinsic rewards. Their satisfaction with such rewards determines their aspiration and motivation to perform in future.[10]

The above is a very brief overview of complex organizational relationships. It does make clear that it is inappropriate to talk of information for control without considering how people behave, or to talk of motivating behavior in control systems without considering the impact of information on it. This interaction is important not only from the practical standpoint of subordinate performance, but also provides a new conceptual way of analyzing control system problems.

A PROPOSED FRAMEWORK FOR CONTROL SYSTEM DESIGN

The need for a new way of thinking is especially important since even those who recognize the relationships between information and behavior still tend to treat control in a closed systems context. That is, they create closure or certainty by assuming one-way dependence relationships between these variables. For example, at one extreme, structuralists, including many who are aware of behavioral effects of information, treat technology and people as independent variables and information as dependent variable.[11]

What is needed, therefore, is a new paradigm which treats information, people and technology as *both* independent and dependent variables. This is a necessary precondition for a designer if he is to successfully address key design issues.

The *open systems concept* is proposed as a paradigm which is suitable for this purpose. It is consistent with the interactions shown in Fig. 1, and provides insights which allow dealing with design issues in a way which overcomes existing weaknesses.

The power of the open systems concept is best illustrated by socio-technical systems theory. Its use enabled those interested in the design of work systems to realize that: (1) technology was important in determining a system's efforts to achieve a steady state and, therefore, must be included in a system's boundaries along with the social system; and (2) technological and social systems were highly interactive components of a control system.

The concept of interaction, in particular, allowed designers to appreciate the relationship between these two components in a new way. They understood that technology dictates certain social inter-relations, and, in the absence of a one-to-one relationship between technological requirements and social systems, allows the use of alternative social systems with a given technology (see Emery & Trist, 1960). Interaction thus gave rise to the ideas of mutual influence and choice of technology and social systems.

In a similar way, the open systems view provides a conceptualization of control systems that allows designers to understand the unique

[10]For a comprehensive discussion of these relationships see Cummings & Schwab (1973). The expectancy model describes this process in terms of the impact of information on "effort–performance" and "performance–reward" probabilities.

[11]A good example of this is Lawler & Rhode (1976, Chapter 10). Even though they recognize the behavioral implications of information, their suggestions for designing control systems are one-way. That is, they recommend changes in information structures that are likely to produce better results for control purpose. What this approach ignores is that it may not be feasible or economical to change information alone. Old information habits die hard, and it may be easier to change social factors in some situations.

relationships between its parts. The following four insights are especially noteworthy. First, in an open system, all components which enable it to achieve a steady state or self-regulation in the face of environmental changes are included within its boundaries. Since both information and social relationships enable control systems to achieve regulation, they should be included as parts of this system. Second, interaction of information and human-social variables is not a superficial one-way impact. Rather, it means that there are (i) socially induced information structures; and (ii) informationally induced human-social interrelations. Third, a designer may combine alternative information structures and human-social variables. The one he chooses to treat as a given will reflect the constraining variable in a given situation.[12] Finally, the self-regulating view of control views the job of the regulatory mechanisms as elimination of disturbances. This means that managers as regulators exercise control over disturbances and not over people. A designer, therefore, should focus on those disturbance sources or interactions that are likely to affect system performance more than others.[13]

Given this perspective, it is now possible to answer the two key issues facing a control system designer. First, what are the components and how are they related? Second, how to combine these components effectively?

Components of a control system (boundaries)

Figure 2 shows the four major components of a control system. They center around a controlled variable or objective of the system. The controlled variable is sometimes very difficult to pin down as one moves to higher management levels. For example, while it is relatively easy to define task performance as the objective of control at lower levels, the controlled variable is more difficult to identify at higher management levels. Nevertheless, some sort of working definition is usually adopted. It should be noted that task performance,

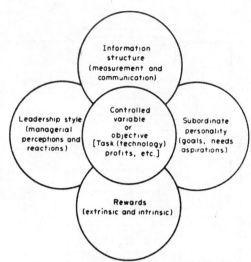

Fig. 2. Components of a control system.

particularly at lower echelons, requires the consideration of technology as a mediating variable. This requirement is less applicable to budgetary and profit oriented control systems.

These four components may be classed into three categories: Structural, Social and Support.

The *Structure* of the system is embodied in the information network. Measurement and communication of information are carried on through this network.

The *Social* side of the system revolves around the manager-subordinate interaction needed for goal accomplishment. It envisages two sets of psychological variables: (a) subordinate personality, which together with their needs, wants, and attitudes governs how they perceive and react to a control system; and (b) leadership style which essentially represents the personality and attitudes of managers and determines how they interact with subordinates.[14]

Support refers to the extrinsic and intrinsic rewards available to a subordinate. Only some of these rewards are controlled by an organization which uses them to facilitate the social interactions for goal achievement.

---

[12]In many organizations, especially bureaucracies, the available information, technology, rules and procedures of behavior, existing modes of thinking, etc. may actually make certain existing information as a constraint to be dealt with by a designer.

[13]This is similar to the concept of "key variances" used in socio-technical systems theory. It refers to the control of factors that are more significant in terms of affecting the outputs of a system than others.

[14]It should be noted that the terms manager and leader are used to refer to both individual as well as collective styles. For example, university faculties are usually evaluated by a committee of peers rather than any one person.

The overlap in these components, shown in Fig. 2, represents their interaction – that is, their mutual influence upon each other. Changes in any one component are thus likely to have system wide effects. Also, the choice of any one component cannot be made without considering its impact upon the others.

Criterion for effective integration

An effective combination of the components shown in Fig. 2 is one in which they are supportive of each other. In other words, there is a good match between them. The operational definition of a good match suggested here is the minimization of perceptual differences between managers and subordinates. That is, *a designer should choose those system elements which lower the possibility of cognitive conflict between the two*. The ultimate test of any design, of course, is the system's performance. It is, however, a post-design measure. What is needed is a predesign criterion because many components, once chosen, are difficult to change.

The above criterion is based on the concept of identifying the interactions critical to the success of a system (see page 107). In this case, the manager–subordinate interaction is viewed as the key to the effectiveness of a control system. Successful control requires leaders who can create conditions which motivate workers toward desired goals. For this to happen, subordinates must share, or at least must not reject, their manager's perceptions of what the goals are (ends), how they are to be met (means) and how well they were met (evaluation).

While managers and subordinates are likely to have different perceptions of all three – means, ends and evaluation – the greatest and potentially most harmful differences are likely to be at the evaluation stage. In fact, different perceptions of means and ends may well affect a subordinate's performance and thus show up in evaluation also. What turns their perceptual differences at this stage into a potentially disruptive conflict is that the outcomes (rewards) valued by subordinates are contingent on a favorable evaluation.

A brief digression on the nature of cognitive processes is needed to better understand the usefulness of the proposed criterion. Cognitive "consistency theories" – specially as set forth by Heider (1946), Osgood & Tannenbaum (1955), and Festinger (1957) – are particularly helpful. These theories predict that people as perceivers tend to organize their cognitions so as to achieve consonance (balance or congruity) between them. They find dissonant cognitions psychologically uncomfortable and undertake behaviors which remove them with least rearrangement of their existing beliefs.

The present problem can be analyzed with the help of Heider's (1946) "balance" framework which is the original formulation of the consistency theory. Figure 3 shows the cognitive systems of a subordinate and his supervisor. Figure 3a, in which the subordinate is the perceiver, has two cognitive units – his perception of his performance and his perception of his manager. The relations between these cognitions may be positive or negative. For example, if a subordinate feels positively about his manager, and he has a

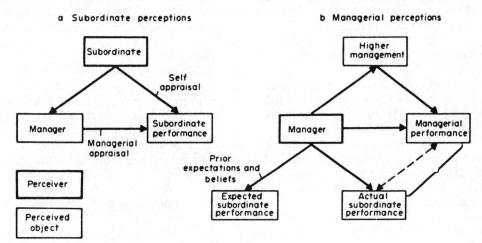

Fig. 3. Manager–subordinate perceptions in performance evaluation.

favorable self-appraisal of performance, then the arrows linking these cognitions are positive.

It should be noted that the sign of the manager–subordinate bond does not necessarily represent an affective like–dislike relationship. Rather, it represents an evaluation of the perceived fairness of a manager in his evaluative role. It thus depends on how he responds to subordinate performance. This last relationship, shown as the manager–performance bond, completes the triad shown in Fig. 3a. According to Heider, the three cognitions are in balance when the product of their relationship signs (+/−) is positive. Such a result is possible only if all relationships are positive or two are negative and one is positive. As summarized below, of the eight possible states for the triad, only half are balanced states.

Subordinate to performance	Manager to performance	Subordinate to manager	Resulting product
+	+	+	+ Balanced
+	+	−	−
+	−	+	−
+	−	−	+ Balanced
−	+	+	−
−	+	−	+ Balanced
−	−	+	+ Balanced
−	−	−	−

How a manager reacts to subordinate performance in Fig. 3a, depends upon how he organizes his own cognitions. Figure 3b shows that he has two sets of cognitions. In the first set, consisting of two units, he has to reconcile his prior expectations of subordinates with their actual performance. Again, these will be in balance when both are either positive or negative. In other words, a supervisor experiences no dissonance when a subordinate's performance confirms his expectations.

The second set, consisting of three units, relates a manager to his own superiors in a triadic relationship similar to Fig. 3a. It emphasizes that, like the subordinate, he too has to go through an evaluation process. His performance, however, may depend on the performance of his subordinates. This means that his perception of the latter may be influenced by his judgment of how his evaluation is affected by it.

This linkage between the higher and lower level performance evaluations is shown by the braces in Fig. 3b. The strength of this association will depend upon the measurement rules used by an organization. For example, in production situations it is not uncommon to use a simple additive rule in which a manager's performance is simply the sum of subordinate productivities. In others, a manager may be evaluated not so much on how well his subordinates perform, but rather, on how he *evaluates* them.[15] In both cases, managerial appraisal of subordinate performance is linked to his own appraisal in ways which increase the subjectivity of the evaluation process.

Returning to the design theme, the nature of the determinants of organizational performance suggests that a control system's regulatory effectiveness may be affected by the behaviors resulting from its participants efforts to deal with cognitive conflict. Since regulation depends upon subordinates willingly aspiring to perform, and leaders being able to motivate them to do so, behaviors which alter determinants such as aspiration levels and motivation are especially undesirable.

For example, a subordinate can reduce dissonance caused by differing self and managerial appraisals of performance by either agreeing or disagreeing with the manager. If agreeing means revising his own assessment downward, it is likely to reduce his satisfaction and aspiration. Findings which support this are reported in research on the expectancy model (see Cummings & Schwab, 1973). They show that self-appraisal is related to many intrinsic rewards such as a sense of accomplishment. These rewards determine how satisfied a subordinate is, and, how high he aspires in future. Reductions in aspiration level, tied to low past performance, causes subsequent reductions in performance.

If he chooses to disagree with his manager, it will have an impact on their relationship. The latter's ability to lead and motivate depends on acceptance by subordinates. If they feel that he is unfair in providing performance related rewards, they are likely to question his leadership. This may force managers to rely more on sanctions and less on persuasion — an outcome likely to reduce performance over time.

It is of course possible for the two to find a

---

[15]For example, in small public accounting firms, senior accountants are evaluated on how they evaluate a junior's performance on an audit.

compromise alternative which is consistent with their differing views. For example, they can discount the information (e.g. student ratings do not reflect teaching ability), or assign a special interpretation (e.g. this was just a bad week). The willingness to compromise will depend not only on a subordinate, but also on how uncomfortable it is for a manager to revise his prior expectations about subordinates, and how much pressure he faces from his own superiors.

In summary, a designer should combine components in a way which: (1) minimizes cognitive conflict; or (2) encourages behavior which can resolve such conflict with positive results for systems performance.

CONCLUDING REMARKS

The proposed framework presented here is potentially superior to existing approaches both conceptually and operationally. Conceptually, the use of the open systems logic allows a designer to deal with variables and relationships not considered previously. The most important contribution here is the appreciation for the key role cognitive processes play in a control system's efforts to achieve regulation. This latter, in turn, leads to an operational criterion which can serve as a design guide.

Because it is based on previously tested consistency models, the proposed criterion lends itself well to further research and testing. Clearly, the most important research issue is whether control system designs which lead to lower cognitive conflict (and/or encourage positive modes of conflict resolution), also lead to higher performance. It may be difficult to test this since there are many factors in an actual situation which affect performance. Separating their effects may be difficult.

A more feasible research strategy is to study the effects of supportive or non-supportive combinations of the various components of a control system. It is similar to the contingency theory approach which searches for good "fits" by *a priori* hypothesizing of the effects of certain combinations. A good example is Fiedler's work on leadership effectiveness in different task situations.

In the case of a control system, a number of interesting issues arise out of the information-human interaction. One of the primary ones is the notion of the kind of information structure which is best suited for a given type of behavioral climate. This latter being the social factors such as leadership and subordinate personality. There is some evidence to suggest that optimal information does not necessarily mean more and free communication. Ackoff (1970) cites a case in which free communication of information between parts of an organization actually led to greater disruption in the organization. Similarly, Ansari (1976) shows that autocratic leaders are able to function better when their subordinates have limited access to information. Clearly, one issue for further research is the amount of information which best supports a given leadership style.

A closely related research question is the quality of information needed to sustain certain social relationships. For instance, it is important to examine whether quality dimensions such as precision, objectivity, and completeness are always desirable no matter what the behavioral situation in a control system. The answer is not obvious since less controversy about information measures also reduces the likelihood of a compromise in which managers and subordinates can blame information instead of each other.[16]

The design of information structures usually follows the responsibility division outlined in an organization chart and is constrained only by available economic resources. This, in turn, impacts on the choice of structural characteristics such as the number of points at which information is transformed before reaching its destination, and the way in which information measures are integrated at various organization levels. Little research has been done on how these characteristics, which determine the amount of shared information between managers and subordinates about a given event, affect their relationship.

Finally, another important design issue that has been largely ignored is the relationship between reward and information structures. If rewards are too highly contingent on the outputs of an information structure, the greater is the likelihood that it (information) will become controversial. For instance, Hopwood (1972) found that the

[16]One effort designed to foster greater agreement between participants is the management-by-objectives (MBO) effort. It would be interesting to see if the amount and patterns of resolving cognitive conflict differ in MBO systems as compared to other managerial systems.

concern for and acceptance of accounting data by cost center heads is related to the emphasis placed upon it, as compared to other criteria, in performance evaluation. The research issue, therefore, is which rewards, and how closely, to tie them to the information structure.

The availability of computers has begun to revolutionize information structures used by organizations. Before these newer structures are implemented, it is imperative that control system designers consider the changes that will be necessary in the behavioral variables to fully reap their benefits. The proposal here, it is hoped, provides a beginning towards that goal.

BIBLIOGRAPHY

Ackoff, R. L., *A Concept of Corporate Planning* (New York: Wiley, 1970).

Ansari, S. L., Behavioral Factors in Variance Control, *Journal of Accounting Research* (Fall, 1976).

Anthony, R. N. & Dearden, J., *Management Control Systems* (Homewood, Ill.: Irwin, 1976).

Ashby, W. R., *An Introduction to Cybernetics* (London: Chapman & Hall, 1956).

Beer, S., *Cybernetics and Management* (New York: Wiley, 1964).

Blau, P. M., *On the Nature of Organization* (New York: Wiley, 1974).

Bruner, J. S., Goodnow, J. J. & Austin, G. A., *A Study of Thinking* (New York: Wiley, 1956).

Cammann, C. & Nadler, D. A., Fit Your Control System To Your Managerial Style, *Harvard Business Review* (Jan.–Feb., 1976), pp. 65–72.

Caplan, E. H., Behavioral Assumptions of Management Accounting – Report of a Field Study, *Accounting Review* (April, 1968), pp. 342–352.

Davis, G. B., *Management Information Systems* (New York: McGraw-Hill, 1974).

Drucker, P. M., Controls, Control and Management, in *Management Controls: New Directions In Basic Research*, C. P. Bonini, R. K. Jaedicke & H. M. Wagner, eds. (New York: McGraw-Hill, 1964).

Emery, F. E. & Trist, E. L., Socio-Technical Systems, in *Systems Thinking*, F. E. Emery, ed. (Harmondsworth, Middlesex: Penguin, 1969).

Ference, T. P., Organizational Communication System and the Decision Process, *Management Science* (Oct., 1970), pp. B285–293.

Festinger, L., *A Theory of Cognitive Dissonance* (Evanston, Ill.: Row, Petersen, 1957).

Fiedler, F. E., *A Theory of Leadership Effectiveness* (New York: McGraw-Hill, 1967).

Heider, F., Attitudes and Cognitive Organization, *Journal of Psychology*, 21, pp. 107–112.

Homans, G. C., *The Human Group* (New York: Harper & Row, 1950).

Hopwood, A. G., An Empirical Study of The Role of Accounting Data In Performance Evaluation *Journal of Accounting Research, Empirical Studies* (1972), pp. 156–182.

Hovland, C. I., Janis, I. & Kelley, H. H., *Communication and Persuasion* (New Haven: Yale University Press, 1953).

Hovland, C. I., Mandell, W., Campbell, E. H., Brock, C., Luchins, A. S., Cohen, A. R., McGuire, W. J., Janis, I. L., Feierabend, R. L. & Anderson, N. H., *The Order of Presentation in Persuasion* (New Haven: Yale University Press, 1957).

Kast, F. E. & Rosensweig, J. E., *Contingency Views of Organization and Management* (Chicago: Scientific Research Associates, 1973).

Lawler, E. E. III & Rhode, J. R., *Information and Control in Organizations* (Pacific Palisades, Ca.: Goodyear Publ., 1976).

Lawrence, P. R. & Lorsch, J. W., *Organization and Environment* (Boston: Division of Research, Graduate School of Business Administration, Harvard University, 1967).

Mason, R. O. & Mitroff, I. I., A Program for Research on Management Information Systems, *Management Science* (Jan., 1973), pp. 457–487.

Morse, J. J., Organizational Characteristics and Individual Motivation, in F. E. Kast & R. E. Rosenzweig, eds., *Contingency Views of Organization and Management* (Chicago: Scientific Research Associates, 1973).

Osgood, C. E. & Tannenbaum, P. H., The Principle of Congruity in the Prediction of Attitude Change, *Psychological Review*, 62, (1955), pp. 42–55.

Reedy, G. E., *The Twilight of the Presidency* (New York: New American Library, 1970).

Simon, H. A., *Administrative Behavior* (New York: Free Press, 1957).

Sloan, A. P., *My Years with General Motors* (New York: Doubleday, 1964).

Schlesinger, A.,M., Jr., *The Imperial Presidency* (Boston: Houghton Mifflin, 1973).

Tannenbaum, A. S., Control in Organizations: Individual Adjustment and Organizational Performance, in C. P. Bonini *et al.*, eds. *Management Controls* (New York: McGraw-Hill, 1964).

Taylor, F. W., *The Principle and Methods of Scientific Management* (New York: Harper & Row, 1911).

Urwick, L., *The Elements of Administration* (New York: Harper & Row, 1944).

Weber, M., *The Theory of Social and Economic Organization* (Glencoe, Ill.: Free Press, 1947).

PART II
BUDGETING CONTROL SYSTEMS

The articles in Section II look at budgeting from three different perspectives: technical cost-benefit, behavioral and integrated. Demski and Feltham's paper provides an agency theory (cost-benefit) explanation of why and how budgets should be employed for motivational purposes in an economic setting. It explains that budget-based incentive contracts arise because they provide the least costly information structure available on which to make labor allocation decisions. The authors are primarily interested in the types of employment contracts associated with equilibrium allocations in the labor market. They do not take into consideration any form of "non-pecuniary" benefits to workers; a topic of some concern to behavioral papers on the subject. The papers by Bruns and Waterhouse and by Schiff and Lewin present examples of how budgeting is viewed from a behavioral approach to control systems design. Issues such as participation, organization structure and the use of budget data in performance evaluation are treated as the control system design variables associated with performance outcomes.

Ansari's and Williams' articles treat budgeting from an integrated approach. The Ansari contribution criticizes traditional budgetary cost systems as representing a compartmentalized view of organizations. Ansari demonstrates that these systems fail to acknowledge the dynamic interaction and interdependencies among their parts. The author argues for an open-systems approach which recognizes, in part, that responsibility centers do not exist in isolation; rather they are in constant commerce with their environment. This environmental impact needs to be ackowledged in analyzing performance. Williams' article shows how a technical tool, zero-base budgeting, can be used to encourage the organization to respond effectively to changes in its environment. Zero-base budgeting can act as an important destabilizer. In its function as an early warning device, it can locate change signals, detect problems and conflicts in time, and counteract all standardized routines.

Economic Incentives in Budgetary Control Systems

JOEL S. DEMSKI
Stanford University

GERALD A. FELTHAM
University of British Columbia

ABSTRACT: This article explores conventional questions of why and how budgets should be employed for motivation purposes in an economic setting. The authors focus on the types of employment contracts that are associated with equilibrium allocations in the labor market. Market incompleteness is a necessary condition for use of budgets in the employment contract. Beyond this, issues of controllability, management by exception, and tightness of standards are observed to depend on the contracting environment faced by the individual agents.

THE use of standard costs and budgeted profits or costs in performance evaluation has long been advocated in management accounting. Comparison of actual results with some "norm," it is argued, provides a basis for motivating performance and for identifying situations requiring corrective action.

The purpose of this paper is to explore conditions that may induce the use of budgetary control systems in an economic setting. Basically, these conditions take the form of a market incompleteness [Radner, 1974]. Recognition of this incompleteness provides entry to explicit consideration of such questions as the type of standards that should be used, whether the evaluation should be confined to factors controllable by the subordinate, and the extent to which participation in setting the standards is desirable.

We begin with a general discussion of delegation in an incomplete market setting. Our basic model is then presented and analyzed. Exploration of pure moral hazard and adverse selection questions identifies conditions that may induce the use of budgetary control systems.

PRELIMINARY OBSERVATIONS

The basic question we explore is why we observe budgets and standards being used as motivation devices. They are often expensive to install and maintain, and the dysfunctional behaviors they may induce are well known.[1] Nevertheless, their use is both widespread and generally advocated by textbook literature.

We examine the use of these devices from both the employer's and employee's perspective. We translate our basic question into one of identifying factors that will induce an equilibrium in the demand and supply of labor such that contracting

We gratefully acknowledge the considerable help of John Dickhaut, an anonymous reviewer, and, especially, Lynn Marples and the financial help of the Canada Council and the Stanford Program in Professional Accounting (major contributors to which are: Arthur Andersen & Co.; Arthur Young & Company; Ernst & Ernst; Peat, Marwick, Mitchell & Co.; and Price Waterhouse & Co.).

[1] For example see Argyris [1952], Ridgeway [1956], Stedry [1960], Schiff and Lewin [1970], Hopwood [1972], Itami [1975], and Swieringa and Moncur [1975].

for (some) labor services is based on a standard of performance.

The basic feature of such contracting is that the compensation paid for labor services depends, in part, on the relationship between actual and standard performance. This payment may, of course, be somewhat indirect if we consider a multi-period setting with promotion contingent on current performance relative to standard. Compensation is a broad concept embracing direct cash payments, stock options, club memberships, pride, self-satisfaction, and so on.

In general, a standard may be expressed in terms of either the "quality" of the input provided or the outcome that results from its use. Contracts based on input quality are very common in the acquisition of physical goods such as wheat, beef steak, fabric and fertilizer, for which there are well developed quality "standards" expressed in terms of observable attributes of those goods. We term such contracting arrangements commodity contracts.

Commodity contracts may also be used in conjunction with labor services, the quality of which depends on both the worker's skill and the effort he expends. Skill may be assessed through examination (references and tests) while supervisory personnel may be used to assess effort. Thus, we observe contracts in which accountants are paid a fixed salary for specific tasks, and machine operators are paid a constant wage per hour of labor provided.

The costliness of precisely observing skill and effort levels, however, leads to other forms of contracts. For example, machine operators are sometimes compensated on a piece-rate basis; service station operators rent their facilities from oil companies, and salesmen have mixed contracts in which they receive a salary plus a bonus based on their total sales.

Of particular interest here are budget-based contracts in which worker compensation depends, at least in part, on the relationship between actual and budgeted performance where performance is expressed in terms of some observable attribute(s) of the outcome of worker actions.

More specifically, we define an employment contract as budget-based when

1. the worker's compensation is, in part, a function of some observable attribute(s) of the outcome resulting from his actions;
2. the contract specifies a budgeted (standard) outcome (attribute) level that partitions the set of possible outcomes into favorable and unfavorable subsets; and
3. the worker's compensation function consists of two functions, one defined over the favorable subset and the other over the unfavorable subset.[2]

An example is a contract in which a manager is paid a basic wage if some measure of profit (the outcome attribute) is below a specified budget and a higher wage (basic wage plus bonus) if profit is at or above the specified budget.

Contracting Incentives

Clearly, a necessary condition for budget-based contracts is that employers must be motivated to acquire labor services and workers must be motivated to sell their services. We briefly discuss these

[2] Obviously, we are not limited to a binary partition of the set of outcomes. Indeed, a budget-based contract is a contingent claims contract. and it can be contingent on more than just the outcome. It can depend, for example, on observed attributes of the worker's action or uncontrollable factors (state elements) that influence the outcome. The budgeted outcome may depend on these factors or they may only be observed if the outcome is unfavorable (or favorable). Flexible budgets and investigation of unfavorable variances are obvious examples.

motivations in terms of the "benefits" and "costs" associated with employment contracts, without, as yet, considering the specific type of contract into which the parties will enter.

Consider the extreme case of a sole proprietorship. The owner's benefit from acquiring labor services may take the form of increased income and, hence, increased consumption or increased work-related consumption. An increase in net income is likely if expansion permits the owner to use more effectively his capital and his own efforts. This may result from specialization, both in production in the narrow sense (Adam Smith's pin factory) and in decision-making. For example, information processing advantages may be available, as when a product-line manager acquires considerable local information. Also, specialization is likely to be particularly beneficial when workers possess complementary skills that can be matched to the tasks at hand.

The returns from expanding the firm's work force need not take the form of increased income to be desirable to the owner. He may choose to use such returns to obtain work-related consumption such as leisure, companionship, office decor, and so on (see Stafford and Cohen, 1974, and Jensen and Meckling, 1976). In our formal analysis later in the paper, we assume that the owner contracts for labor services so that he can obtain a return from his capital without expending any effort. (He achieves maximum leisure.)

The worker's benefit from selling his labor services may take the form of increased income or work-related consumption. His costs may include foregone self-employment opportunities and leisure. Additionally, some aspects of the job may be undesirable *per se*. Economies of scale from specialization, matching of complementary skills, and efficient use of

capital are likely to result in larger returns from the sale of labor services than from self-employment. The worker's return probably depends on his skill and the effort he expends. He cannot change his skill (at least in the short run), but effort is under his immediate control and he must trade off the return from additional effort and his personal cost from expending it.

Contracting in a Perfect and Complete Market Setting

The nature of the contracts induced by the owners' and workers' preferences is readily sketched in a setting of complete and perfect markets. Here, each conceivable commodity, including each conceivable type of labor service (skill and effort combination), is traded in an organized perfect market. Thus, in surveying the delegation opportunities, the sole proprietor has access to a specific known price for each possible employment task. The same holds for a worker. Assuming an expected utility representation of preferences for the "benefits" and "costs," each maximizes his subjective expected utility with respect to work-derived consumption goods and leisure. We arrive at the thoroughly classical result that, at equilibrium, marginal rates of substitution are equated and the allocation is Pareto optimal. Moreover, employment contracting is predicated on commodity contracts. No budget-based contracting is observed. Rather, we have an extreme case in which the worker is compensated only if the contracted labor services actually are supplied. Put another way, the worker supplies a specific commodity and is compensated accordingly. Implicitly, we assume that the type of labor service provided is costlessly verified and payment of contracts is costlessly enforced; otherwise such contracting may not be efficient.

Contracting in an Incomplete Market Setting

The situation changes drastically once we admit that some aspect of the above skill-task-effort dependent commodity contract is not observable by both parties. With such an information void, the parties cannot contract on the basis of these variables. For example, if only the worker knows his skill type or effort expended, contracting based on skill or effort is not available because of lack of enforceability. This, in turn, creates information production incentives. But if the cost is prohibitive, less than complete observation will be employed, and we arrive at the incomplete markets case. Certain types of trades, in other words, may be unavailable. It is here that we encounter incentives to use budget-based contracts.

Moral Hazard Issues[3] First consider the case in which it is too costly for the owner to observe worker effort, but where both can costlessly observe the worker's skill, the state (uncontrollable factors that influence the outcome) and the outcome. Non-observability of worker effort precludes a contract that directly pays a specific wage for a specific task involving a specified minimum effort level. However, the same contract can be indirectly constructed if, for a given state and skill, the task outcome is uniquely determined by the effort level. In particular, the wage would be paid if the observed outcome is at least as desirable to the owner as the outcome that would have resulted from the specified minimum effort level given the worker's skill and the state that occurred. In short, an *ex post*, standard (flexible budget) is used to obtain the allocation that would have been achieved with perfect and complete markets.

Though an admittedly extreme and simple case, this illustrates the basic idea of a budget-based contract: we employ the outcome to learn something about the worker's behavior. Indeed, the information available in this case is sufficient to learn precisely what effort was expended. In general, however, the requisite information is not costlessly available; various aspects of worker performance can be observed for a price and the fundamental question reduces to one of what information to obtain. Indeed, if the owner can observe the state or worker effort by providing some of the labor service himself, he may choose to forego some leisure and obtain this information by delegating less than the entire amount of labor services to hired workers.

Now, consider the opposite extreme in which the owner has no knowledge whatever of what state obtains or what effort the worker expends. (The cost of such knowledge is prohibitive.) Under these conditions, the two may "agree" upon a particular effort-price combination, but the worker has no incentive to honor such an agreement. The worker prefers less effort to more and random state occurrence will likely mask at least some shirking by the worker [Alchian and Demsetz, 1972 and Becker and Stigler, 1974]. Thus, pure wage contracts are unlikely in this case. One alternative, which avoids the shirking problem entirely, is a rental contract in which the owner rents his capital to the worker for a fixed fee. Under this contract the owner, obviously, is indifferent as to the worker's effort level and the

[3] In many contracted arrangements some actions that influence the outcome are not specified because observation of these actions is too costly. The moral hazard phenomenon arises in these contexts when the agent in question is personally motivated to take actions other than those that would have been specified in the contract if such specification had been possible. For example, the insured in a fire insurance contract is likely to expend less effort or money on safety precautions since the costs of those precautions fall directly on him, whereas the cost of a fire falls primarily on the insurer.

116

worker is induced to expend effort because he receives all returns in excess of the rental fee.

Despite the avoidance of shirking, a rental contract may be less desirable than a wage contract (with complete information) because a rental contract imposes risk on the worker whereas a wage contract does not. Of course, this risk does not present a problem if the worker is risk neutral or can offset it with insurance (or a diversified portfolio of investments). But risk neutrality is a limiting case and complete insurance will not be provided unless the state is observable.[4] Consequently, non-observability of the state and the worker's effort level (coupled with worker risk aversion) forces the owners and workers to agree to contracts which provide a balance between risk sharing and incentive effects.

One obvious means of balancing risk sharing and incentive effects is a mixed contract in which the worker pays a smaller rent than in the pure rental case and in turn gives the owner some portion of the output. In the extreme, the rent is zero, and we have, in effect, a piece-rate or pure profit-sharing contract.[5] In any event, with the worker risk averse and the owner risk neutral, use of mixed contracts in this case imposes some risk on the worker in order to provide an incentive for the worker to expend some agreed level of effort. We demonstrate later that a budget-based contract may induce more effort with less worker risk, and in such a manner that both parties are better off relative to the mixed contract. In one such contract, the worker is offered a fixed wage if the outcome is above some standard, but the mixed contract terms apply if the outcome is below standard. Thus, relative to the mixed contract, the budget-based contract provides the worker with partial insurance against state occurrence risk.

Also note that in this setting the owner is motivated to select information systems that balance the gains from improved contracting against the information costs. (See Arrow [1974], Stiglitz [1974] and [1975]. Williamson *et al.* [1975], and Jensen and Meckling [1976].) One system, familiar in accounting, is to use sequential analysis in which costly investigation is performed only if inexpensively monitored outcome statistics indicate that such activity is warranted. This is the familiar "when to investigate a variance" problem [Kaplan, 1975]. Another strategy is more clearly identified with organization design variables. Managers, or owners, may engage in some productive acts simply because crucial worker monitoring information is provided as a by-product of such activity [Alchian and Demsetz, 1972].

Finally, owners as well as workers may engage in shirking behavior. A contract calling for sequential investigation may, for example, not be honored by the owner. The incentive effects of a potential investigation are achieved prior to the investigation and if the owner believes the desired effort level has been induced he will choose to avoid the costs of investigation.[6]

Adverse Selection Issues[7] Another issue

[4] The absence of state observability raises the familiar moral hazard problem discussed in the insurance literature. See Spence and Zeckhauser [1971] and Kihlstrom and Pauly [1971].

[5] If the rent is negative we have a "wage plus profit share" type contract. See Stiglitz [1974] for an extensive analysis of mixed contracts.

[6] The incentive to investigate may arise if we explicitly introduce multiperiod considerations (or some form of external enforcement agency).

[7] Adverse selection is a phenomenon in which members of a population self-select in response to a contractual offer, resulting in a set of respondees critically different from the population at large. Perhaps only "lemons" are offered for sale in the used car market; the unhealthy may subscribe to health insurance that is actuarially fair for the population at large; an unskilled manager may knowingly represent himself as skilled; and so on.

in labor services contracting arises when the worker's skill type is not observable. Efficiency in a perfect and complete market setting requires contracts that are contingent on the worker's skill. If these skills are not observable, the owner is likely to hire lower skilled applicants who falsely claim the requisite skill level [Akerlof, 1970]. The applicants' strategy will be masked by the fact that poor performance can be blamed on the state, provided it, too, is unobservable.

Both the owner and higher skilled workers, therefore, may have an incentive to obtain or provide costly information that will distinguish among skill types. (See Spence's 1973 signaling work.) Alternatively, appropriately designed contracts may achieve the desired matching of skills and tasks by inducing the workers to self-select contracts that achieve that matching. For example, a budget-based contract that would be too risky for lower skilled workers to self-select may accomplish the desired screening (but at a cost of increased risk for the higher skilled workers). Varying deductibility provisions in insurance contracts provides a similar example.[8] In turn, sequential investigation strategies may be desirable. Ultimately, of course, we again balance the cost of information against gains from improved contracting arrangements.

The More General Case

A more general case arises when we simultaneously admit to moral hazard and adverse selection phenomena in a multi-period setting. This is particularly interesting for two reasons. First, admitting to both phenomena simultaneously raises the question of distinguishing between them. And in the context of a budget-based contract, this distinction may be provided by the information contained in different variances. In a simplis-tic setting, for example, labor efficiency variances may address the effort question and material variances the skill question. The important point, however, is the motivation for developing subanalyses within the overall budgetary framework. Indeed, if decision-making costs were also introduced into the setting, we would likely encounter the traditional planning and control dichotomy, or management by exception framework. This, in turn, would lead to more detailed variances.

Second, the multiperiod framework vastly enriches the strategies that the parties have available. Short-run production schedules, for example, may be designed in part to provide information as to the employee's skill (as well as state occurrence). And both parties may agree to an initial short-run contract designed to provide the desired information. Similarly, direct information questions become more varied. Current decisions may have future period effects and, by definition, these effects are not costlessly observable in the short run. Contracts based strictly on observable events may not be satisfactory and the parties may be motivated to contract on the basis of estimates of future effects. Manipulation of these estimates presents obvious problems, and provides an inducement to have them produced by independent third parties.

In summary, formal performance evaluation systems, including budget-based contracts, are widely advocated in our literature. Movement away from a classical setting—in which only commodity contracts are observed—is a necessary condition for use of budget-based contracts to be desirable. More specific analyses are developed in the remaining sections of this paper. For convenience,

---

[8] See Rothschild and Stiglitz [1976] for an extensive discussion of adverse selection contracting and self selection in an insurance setting.

we assume the owner fully delegates the labor input activities to a worker. This disregards questions of optimal delegation and joint production of information, but is rich enough to explore the basic issues we seek to address.

THE BASIC MODEL

To explore the issues sketched in the preceding section, we consider a simple economy consisting of J capital owners and I workers. A worker contracts to use an owner's capital (or some portion thereof) in return for some share of the output. In the most general setting addressed, his output, denoted x, will depend on his effort, denoted a, the amount of capital he is provided, denoted q, his skill type, denoted h, and random state factors beyond the control of either the owner or the worker, denoted s. We denote the outcome function by $x = p(s, a, q, h)$.

The contract between the owner and the worker will be conditioned only on those factors that are observed by both. Those observed factors are denoted y and we express them as a function of the state, worker effort, capital, and worker skill: $y = \eta(s, a, q, h)$. The worker's output share is denoted $x_w = \mathscr{I}(y)$ and the owner's share, denoted x_0, is the residual less any information costs, which we denote $x_\eta = C(s, a, q, h, \eta)$; that is $x_0 = x - x_w - x_\eta$.

Each individual's choice behavior is represented by the expected utility hypothesis. We assume the owner is only concerned with his residual outcome and denote his utility function $U_0(x_0)$.[9] The worker, on the other hand, is concerned with both his share of the outcome and his effort. Less effort is preferred to more effort. Consequently, we denote his utility function $U_w(x_w, a)$.[10]

The owners and the workers are assumed to have identical beliefs, encoded in the probability function $\phi(s)$.[11] The worker knows his own skill level, but the owner may be uncertain as to the skill of the worker who accepts his contract offer. The owner's beliefs are encoded in the probability function $\phi_0(h \mid \mathscr{C})$, where $\mathscr{C} = (q, \mathscr{I}, \eta)$ denotes the agreed contract.

The worker's expected utility is a function of the contract he signs, his skill and the effort he provides. In particular, for a worker of skill type h (and presuming suitable regularity) we have

$$E(U_{wh} \mid a, \mathscr{C})$$
$$= \int_S U_w(\mathscr{I}(\eta(s, a, q, h)), a)\phi(s)ds \quad (1a)$$

where S is the set of possible states. We let $a_h^*(\mathscr{C})$ denote his optimal effort given contract $\mathscr{C}$ and skill type h:[12]

$$E(U_{wh} \mid a_h^*(\mathscr{C}), \mathscr{C}) = \max_{a \in A} E(U_{wh} \mid a, \mathscr{C}) \quad (1b)$$

where A is the worker's set of feasible effort levels. The maximum of (1b) over the alternative contracts available provides the worker with his most preferred contract.

The owner's expected utility is a function of the contract he signs and his prediction of the worker effort it will induce. Assuming he predicts that a worker of skill type h will select effort $a_h^*(\mathscr{C})$, we have.[13]

[9] This could be the residual from more than one contract if he divides his capital among more than one worker. Also, other factors affecting his preferences may be viewed as implicit provided they are not influenced by the choices at hand. For example, the owner's effort level (possibly zero) is assumed constant across all contracting alternatives considered in this paper.

[10] The output share could come from more than one contract if he works for more than one owner.

[11] This implies that the worker is hired only for his skill and effort, and not for any specialized knowledge he may have about the state.

[12] Existence of a maximum is assumed.

[13] Again, if the owner contracts with more than one worker the outcome of interest will be the total from all his contracts. Vector interpretation of the effort and contract notation will accomplish this. Also, the notation

119

$$E(U_0 \mid a^*(\mathscr{C}), \mathscr{C}) = \int_H \int_S U_0(p(s, a_h^*(\mathscr{C}), q, h)$$
$$- \mathscr{I}(\eta(s, a_h^*(\mathscr{C}), q, h))$$
$$- C(s, a_h^*(\mathscr{C}), q, h, \eta))$$
$$\cdot \phi(s)ds \, \phi_0(h \mid \mathscr{C})dh \quad (2)$$

where H is the set of possible skill types. And, parallel to the worker, maximizing (2) over the set of alternative contracts provides the owner with his most preferred contract.

The element of interest in our analysis is the particular contract that is agreed upon between the owner and worker. That agreement will depend on the nature of the outcome and information cost functions as well as the worker's and owner's preferences and opportunities. We consider primarily the implications of different information cost functions.

In much of our analysis we assume that s, a, q, h, and x are scalars, with x measured in monetary units.[14] Furthermore, the outcome function is a stochastic constant returns to scale function of the form[15]

$$x = p(s, a, q, h) = g(s)\psi_h F(a, q)$$
$$= g(s)\psi_h f(a/q)q, \quad (3)$$

where $g(s)$ is the stochastic component, with $E(g(\cdot)) = 1$ and $\mathrm{Var}(g(\cdot)) > 0$ and finite. ψ_h is a positive scalar representing the skill level; $F(a, q)$ is homogeneous of degree one as well as an increasing concave (and differentiable) function with respect to any single component;[16] and $f(a)$ is the expected output from effort a by a worker with skill level $\psi = 1$ and one unit of capital (i.e., $f(a) = F(a, 1)$). Each worker can supply any non-negative amount of effort ($A = \{a \geq 0\}$), and each owner has one unit of capital.

We also assume that the worker's differentiable utility function is increasing with respect to money ($\partial U_w(\cdot)/\partial x_w > 0$) and that he may be either risk neutral

($\partial^2 U_w(\cdot)/\partial x_w^2 = 0$) or risk averse ($\partial^2 U_w(\cdot)/\partial x_w^2 < 0$). On the other hand, his utility function is decreasing and strictly concave with respect to effort ($\partial U_w(\cdot)/\partial a < 0$ and $\partial^2 U_w(\cdot)/\partial a^2 < 0$). The owner, on the other hand, is assumed to be risk neutral ($U_0(x_0) = x_0$) so that we may focus on incentive issues; risk is imposed on the worker only if it is necessary to efficiently induce effort or reveal his skill.[17]

MORAL HAZARD CONTRACTING

We now employ this basic model to examine contracting in a moral hazard setting. To limit the discussion to moral hazard effects, we assume in this section that all workers possess identical unit skill endowments, and since the skill does not vary, we suppress it in our notation. We also assume there are an equal number of owners and workers ($J = I$). This interpretation of the model in (1), (2), and (3) is termed the basic moral hazard model.

Table 1 provides the basic data of an example economy that will be used to obtain some specific results and to generate numerical examples.

The production function is a Cobb-Douglas function times a state that varies uniformly between 0 and 2. The worker's utility for money is a power function, as is his disutility for effort.

---

can be extended to reflect owner uncertainty as to the effort each type of worker will select upon agreement of a given contract.

[14] We can also interpret x as a single consumption good that is desired by both the owner and the worker.

[15] Excluding skill, this is the same form assumed by Stiglitz [1974] in his analysis of incentives and risk sharing.

[16] That is, $F(\lambda a, \lambda q) = \lambda F(a, q)$ for $\lambda > 0$, $F_i(a, q) > 0$ and $F_{ii}(a, q) < 0$ for $i = a, q$. For example, we use a Cobb-Douglas function in our illustrations: $F(a, q) = \xi a^k - q^{1-k}$ where $\xi > 0$ and $0 < k < 1$.

[17] If both the owner and worker are risk averse, then a Parato optimal contract will require that they both share in the risk. For example, see Wilson [1968] and Gjesdal [1976].

120

Costless Action or State Information

We begin with the case where the worker's action is costlessly observable. This corresponds to the neoclassical theory of the firm in which information costs are ignored and it is implicitly assumed that everyone can costlessly observe the relevant aspects of the commodities (including labor skill and effort) being demanded and supplied. In this case, the owner and worker will contract on the level of effort to be supplied. Furthermore, if there are a large number of identical owners and workers interacting in a perfect labor market, we may view the resulting contract as an equilibrium wage (W^*) per unit of labor effort: $C(s, a, q, \eta) = 0$, $\eta(s, a, q) = a$, and $\mathscr{I}(a) = aW^*$.

The equilibrium solution has, presuming existence and an interior effort solution, three well-known properties:

Proposition 1:[18]

In the basic moral hazard model, if the risk neutral owner can costlessly observe the worker's action and all workers have identical skills (with $I = J$), then the competitive equilibrium based on wage contracts will have the following properties:

(i) the wage rate is equal to the worker's expected marginal product: $W^* = f'(a^*(W^*))$;

(ii) the worker will select his effort so that the wage rate equals the marginal rate of substitution between income and effort:

$$W^* = -(\partial U_w(\cdot)/\partial a) \div (\partial U_w(\cdot)/\partial x_w);$$

and

(iii) the resulting allocation is Pareto optimal.

This allocation mechanism depends critically upon knowledge of the worker's effort. However, costless observation of of the state and capital is sufficient to produce the same allocation. In this case, the owner and worker can enter into a combined rental and insurance contract that will result in precisely the same allocation as in Proposition 1. More specifically, consider $\eta(s, a, q) = (s, q)$ and $\mathscr{I}(s, q) = x - Rq - I(s)$ where $I(s)$ is an insurance policy such that $E(I(s)) = 0$.[19] The worker will request

$$I(s) = (g(s) - 1)F(a, q).[20]$$

---

[18] (i) follows directly from the owner's first order conditions and (ii) follows directly from the worker's first order conditions, (iii) is obtained by focusing on one representative pair of individuals and maximizing the well-being of one while holding constant the well-being for the other:

$$\max_{x_w(\cdot), a} \left[\int_S U_w(x_w(s), a)\phi(s)ds \right] \text{ subject to } f(a)$$

$$- \int_S x_w(s)\phi(s)ds = \bar{U}_0.$$

First order conditions provide

$$f'(a^*) = - [\partial U_w(\cdot)/\partial a] \div [\partial U_w(\cdot)/\partial x_w].$$

[19] In this contract the worker receives the outcome x, but it is not an argument of $\mathscr{I}(\cdot)$ since the owner need not know the outcome—the worker operates the firm.

[20] This insurance policy guarantees the worker his expected profit. Note that the owner does not need to know or even infer the worker's effort; he need only be able to observe the state.

121

Denoting the equilibrium rent R^*, we then observe that the equilibrium solution is the same as in the effort observed case and therefore has the same properties. That is, again presuming existence and an interior effort solution, we have

Proposition 2:[21]

In the basic moral hazard model, if the risk neutral owner has sufficient wealth to provide insurance and both he and the worker can costlessly observe the state, then the competitive equilibrium based on rental and insurance contracts will have the following properties:

(i) the worker's average return per unit of effort is equal to his expected marginal product:

$$(f(a^*(R^*)) - R^*)/a^*(R^*) = f'(a^*(R^*));$$

(ii) the worker will select his effort so that his expected marginal product equals the marginal rate of substitution between income and effort:

$$f'(a^*(R^*)) = -(\partial U_w(\cdot)/\partial a)$$
$$\div (\partial U_w(\cdot)/\partial x_w);$$

and

(iii) the resulting allocation is Pareto optimal from a complete information perspective.

Table 2 presents a numerical example of the effort observed and state observed cases using the model formulated in Table 1.

In conclusion we note that there is no incentive to develop budget-based contracts if either the worker's effort or the state are costlessly observable. That is, under either case a Pareto optimal allocation of productive effort and return is achieved without the use of budget-based contracts. Consequently, we have

Proposition 3:[22,23]

TABLE 2

ILLUSTRATION OF EFFORT OBSERVED AND STATE OBSERVED CASES

Parameter Values:

$$k = .4, \xi = 200$$
$$\bar{x} = 400, \gamma = .5$$
$$\theta = 2, r = 2$$

Effort Observed Case

$$W^* = 106.7610$$

$E(U_w\|a^*(W^*), W^*) =$	20.8227

$$a^*(W^*) = .6182$$

$E(U_0\|a^*(W^*), W^*) =$	98.9995
$f(a^*(W^*)) =$	164.9991

State Observed Case

$$R^* = 98.9995$$

$E(U_w\|a^*(R^*), q^*(R^*), R^*) =$	20.8227

$$a^*(R^*) = .6182$$

$E(U_0\|q^*(R^*), R^*) =$	98.9995
$f(a^*(R^*)) =$	164.9991

---

[21] The owner, obviously, will supply one unit of capital if R is positive. The first order condition for the worker's maximization problem given a rental contract specifying q units of capital, is

$$\frac{\partial U_w(\cdot)}{\partial x_w} \frac{\partial F(\cdot)}{\partial a} + \frac{\partial U_w(\cdot)}{\partial a} = 0.$$

Similarly, the first order condition on the contract variable (capital) is

$$\frac{\partial U_w}{\partial x_w}\left(\frac{\partial F(\cdot)}{\partial q} - R\right) = 0.$$

And if we set $q = 1$ we obtain conditions (i) and (ii). These are equivalent to the conditions in Proposition 1 when we view $(f(a) - R)/a$ as the effective wage per unit of effort. (iii) follows as in Proposition 1.

[22] The basic argument here is that costless observation of effort or state leads—with wage or rental and insurance contracts—to allocative efficiency. Hence, we must remove this condition to rationalize use of other types of

A necessary condition for a budget-based contract to be Pareto superior to all alternative contracts in the basic moral hazard model is that it be costly to observe both the worker's effort and the state.

Effort and State Not Observed

We now consider the other extreme case in which observing either the effort or state is so costly that neither is observed. The outcome and capital, on the other hand, are costlessly observable. Consequently, the contract information is $\eta(s, a, q) = (q, p(s, a, q))$ and we are faced with determining the form of the outcome sharing function $\mathscr{I}(q, x)$.

Ideally, we would consider the set of all possible sharing functions and identify those that are, given the information assumption, Pareto optimal. However, identifying the set of efficient sharing functions is beyond our scope; and instead we take a more modest approach. (See Mirrlees [1976].) In particular, we compare linear sharing functions with two types of budget-based contracts and seek conditions under which the latter are Pareto superior to the former.[24]

Linear Sharing Functions Stiglitz [1974] provides fairly extensive analysis of incentives and linear sharing functions of the form $\mathscr{I}(q, x) = \alpha x - Rq$. This function represents a variety of contract forms, including a pure salary contract ($\alpha = 0$ and $R < 0$), a pure rental contract ($\alpha = 1$ and $R > 0$), a pure piece rate contract ($0 < \alpha < 1$ and $R = 0$) and a mixed contract ($0 < \alpha < 1$ and $R \neq 0$).

The pure salary contract can be quickly discarded from our consideration in that it provides no incentives. If such a contract were signed in our model, the worker would take his salary and select an effort level of zero. (To be sure, this is a rather extreme result, but it would occur to some extent even if we modify the worker's preference function to reflect social norms that induce him to provide some effort for his salary.)

The other contracts all provide some incentive effect in that the worker's outcome share is dependent on the outcome, which in turn depends on his effort. This incentive effect is strongest in the pure rental contract. However, this contract imposes all of the risk on the worker since the state is not observed and thus the worker cannot obtain insurance as he did in the state observed case.[25] On the other hand, this presents no difficulty if the worker is risk neutral. To see this, return to Proposition 2 and note that if the worker is risk neutral, no insurance is an optimal arrangement, and the state need not be observed to obtain an efficient allocation. Hence, we have

Proposition 4:[26]

A necessary condition for a budget-based contract to be Pareto superior to all alternative contracts in the basic moral hazard model is that the worker be risk averse.

---

contracts. This applies to rationalization of budget-based contracts, as discussed here, or costly action monitoring systems, as discussed in Harris and Raviv [1976].

[23] More precisely, it must be costly to observe the effort and either the state or the capital assigned. However, we treat the capital as costlessly observable throughout our analysis.

[24] Contract $\mathscr{C}$ is Pareto superior to $\mathscr{C}'$ if $E(U_w|a^*(\mathscr{C}), \mathscr{C}) \geq E(U_w|a^*(\mathscr{C}'), \mathscr{C}')$, $E(U_0|a^*(\mathscr{C}), \mathscr{C}) \geq E(U_0|a^*(\mathscr{C}'), \mathscr{C}')$ and strict inequality holds for either the worker or the owner.

[25] Insurance based on the outcome instead of the state would not be acceptable because of the moral hazard problem. Once insurance was obtained, the worker would be motivated to select a low effort level and then claim the resulting low outcome was due to a "bad" state.

[26] Again, as in Proposition 3, the argument is one of allocative efficiency. If the worker is also risk neutral a Pareto optimal allocation of productive effort and returns is available with a pure rental contract. Hence, we must drop the risk neutrality assumption to obtain Pareto superior contracts of any kind, including those based on superior information about the worker's behavior (as in Harris and Raviv [1976]).

123

As a basis for comparison in the case where the worker is risk averse, we focus on a linear contract (i) that is Pareto optimal with respect to all other linear contracts and (ii) that induces a demand for and a supply of capital equal to unity. This contract, denoted $\mathscr{C}^\ell = (q^* = 1, \alpha^*, R^*)$, represents an equilibrium contract that might be agreed upon if contracts were restricted to linear sharing functions.

Table 3 presents an equilibrium linear sharing function contract for the example formulated in Tables 1 and 2. Note that the worker's expected income per unit of effort is less than his marginal product. Also, his expected utility is lower than in the effort observed case, whereas the owner's expected profit is higher. The contract assigns over 80 percent of the outcome to the worker and thus imposes considerable risk on him. This is necessary in order to induce effort from him; even so, his effort is less than in the effort observed case.

TABLE 3

ILLUSTRATION OF LINEAR SHARING
FUNCTION CONTRACT

$\alpha^* = .827$

$R^* = 73.965 \quad E(U_w|a^*(\mathscr{C}^\ell), \mathscr{C}^\ell) = 20.6819$

$a^*(\mathscr{C}^\ell) = .53965 \quad E(U_0|a^*(\mathscr{C}^\ell), \mathscr{C}^\ell) = 101.0000$

$f(a^*(\mathscr{C}^\ell)) = 156.2697$

Expected Worker Income per Unit of Effort
$\quad = [\alpha^* f(a^*(\mathscr{C}^\ell)) - R^*]/a^*(\mathscr{C}^\ell) = 102.4184$
Expected Marginal Product
$\quad = f'(a^*(\mathscr{C}^\ell)) \qquad = 115.8304$

Budget-Based Contracts Consider use of budget-based contracts in this setting. Recall that the essential feature of such a contract is the use of an outcome standard to condition the manner in which payments are made. There are, of course, countless such contracts for any specific information system, varying in terms of the partitioning of the outcome into favorable and unfavorable categories and the form of the incentive function.[27] In the following discussion, the only non-outcome information is the capital, and it is assumed to be unity. Therefore, the budgeted outcome is a fixed amount, $\hat{x}$, and the outcome is favorable if it equals or exceeds this amount. We consider two forms of the incentive function, and explore whether such contracts can be Pareto superior to the linear contract $\mathscr{C}^\ell$.

In the first budget-based contract, the worker is paid a fixed wage if the outcome is above standard ($\mathscr{I}_1(x) = B_1$ for $x \geq \hat{x}$) and the amount he would have received under the linear contract $\mathscr{C}^\ell$ if below standard ($\mathscr{I}_2(x) = \alpha^* x - R^*$ for $x < \hat{x}$). This is termed a dichotomous contract and is denoted $\mathscr{C}^d = (q^* = 1, \alpha^*, R^*, \hat{x}, B_1)$.[28] Note that it in effect reduces the risk incurred by the worker for favorable outcomes ($x \geq \hat{x}$).

Since the worker is risk averse we might expect that there exists an $\hat{x}$ and B_1 such that the dichotomous contract $\mathscr{C}^d$ is Pareto superior to the linear contract $\mathscr{C}^\ell$. Observe, however, that unless we set B_1 sufficiently high, the dichotomous contract will induce a lower effort

---

[27] Recall that the outcome budget may be a function of other information. An extreme case occurs when the capital, state, and outcome are costlessly observed. Then the allocation in Proposition 1 can be achieved with the following budget based contract:

$$\mathscr{I}(q^*, s, x) = \begin{cases} a^*W^* & \text{if } x \geq \hat{x}(q^*, s) = sF(a^*, q^*) \\ 0 & \text{if } x < \hat{x}(q^*, s). \end{cases}$$

Furthermore, worker performance can be assessed as favorable or unfavorable on the basis of information other than the outcome. See Harris and Raviv [1976] for an exploration of such contracts.

[28] This is somewhat similar to the dichotomous contracts considered by Harris and Raviv [1976]. However, they divide the performance into favorable and unfavorable on the basis of imperfect action information (other than the outcome).

level than the linear contract. In turn, $\hat{x}$ cannot be too low; and because of this, in our example we were unsuccessful in finding a Pareto superior contract for values of $\hat{x}$ that were achievable with the action induced by the linear contract. However, Pareto superior contracts were found when, exploiting the boundedness of s, we set $\hat{x}$ at the maximum possible outcome from the linear contract effort $(2f(a^*(\mathscr{C}^\ell))$ and then set B_1 sufficiently high to induce a higher level of effort from the worker. This is illustrated in Table 4.

TABLE 4		
ILLUSTRATION OF A PARETO SUPERIOR DICHOTOMOUS SHARING FUNCTION		
$\alpha^* =$	.827	
$R^* =$	73.965	
$\hat{x} =$	312.539	$E(U_w\|a^*(\mathscr{C}^d), \mathscr{C}^d) =$ 20.6846
$B_1 =$	200	$E(U_0\|a^*(\mathscr{C}^d), \mathscr{C}^d) =$ 101.2442
$a^*(\mathscr{C}^d) =$	.56349	$f(a^*(\mathscr{C}^d)) =$ 158.9954

Of course, if B_1 is set too high the additional effort will be more expensive to the owner than it is worth.

The above type of Pareto superior contract is available in any context represented by the model formulated in Table 1 (in which the state is bounded). More formally we have

Proposition 5:[29]

For the model formulated in Table 1 and assuming interior effort solutions, there always exists a dichotomous contract that is Pareto superior to a linear contract in which $0 < \alpha < 1$.

The second budget-based contract we illustrate is one in which the worker is paid a high income if the outcome is favorable $(\mathscr{I}_1(x) = B_1$ for $x \geq \hat{x})$ and a lower income if the outcome is unfavorable $(\mathscr{I}_2(x) = B_2$ for $x < \hat{x})$. We term such a contract bang-bang and denote it $\mathscr{C}^b = (q = 1, \hat{x}, B_1, B_2)$. This contract is simple in its structure and has much the same appeal as the dichotomous contract.

We did manage to find a number of such contracts that are Pareto superior to the linear contract in Table 3. One such contract is presented in Table 5.

TABLE 5		
ILLUSTRATION OF A PARETO SUPERIOR BANG-BANG SHARING FUNCTION		
$\hat{x} =$ 250		
$B_1 =$ 193		
$B_2 =$ 20	$E(U_w\|a^*(\mathscr{C}^b), \mathscr{C}^b) =$	20.6842
	$E(U_0\|a^*(\mathscr{C}^b), \mathscr{C}^b) =$	101.8385
$a^*(\mathscr{C}^b) =$ .55282	$f(a^*(\mathscr{C}^b)) =$	157.7846

It is characterized by a rather high standard, and we were unsuccessful in finding Pareto superior contracts with "low" standards. If the standard is "low" the effort is "low" unless there is a large penalty $(B_1 - B_2)$ for not achieving the standard.[30] "High" standards have a strong incentive effect, but high incomes must be paid to offset the risk imposed on the worker.

[29] See appendix for proof.
[30] On the other hand, Mirrlees [1974] demonstrates that, with suitable regularity, employing a low $\hat{x}$ and an extreme penalty for not meeting the budget approximates the full information allocation. The only cost is an extreme penalty that falls on a small percentage of the workers (also see Harris and Raviv [1976]). (He also analyzes [1976] the case in which the full information equilibrium cannot be achieved.) In a similar vein, Gjesdal [1976] shows (assuming suitable regularity) that if the lower bound on the feasible outcome increases monotonically with effort then the full information contract can be approximated with a bang-bang contract. (In Table 1, for example, this would be available if $S = [\frac{1}{2}, \frac{3}{2}]$ instead of $S = [0, 2]$ and if the worker has a "large" initial wealth $\bar{x}$ that can be penalized, $B_2 = -\bar{x}$.)

Effort or State Observed at a Cost

We conclude this section with a brief examination of the intermediate case where the effort or state can be observed at some "reasonable" cost. The capital and outcome are again costlessly observable; and we assume that any decision to observe the effort (or, equivalently, the state) can be conditioned on the observed capital and outcome. That is, effort (or state) observation is in the form of an *ex post* investigation of the causes of the outcome.

Many investigation policies are possible, but we restrict our discussion to those in which an investigation is made only if the outcome is below some standard $\hat{x}$. That is,

$$\eta(s, a, q) = \begin{cases} (q, p(s, a, q)) & \text{if } p(s, a, q) \geq \hat{x} \\ (q, a, p(s, a, q)) & \text{if } p(s, a, q) < \hat{x}. \end{cases}$$

There are, of course, many incentive functions that could be considered in conjunction with this information system. We restrict our discussion, however, to bang-bang sharing functions in which a high income (B_1) is paid if the outcome is favorable or the observed effort is not below some standard effort ($\hat{a}$), and a low income (B_2) is paid if the observed effort is below the standard. That is, we have a budget-based conditional investigation contract in which $\mathscr{I}_1(x) = B_1$ for $x \geq \hat{x}$ and

$$\mathscr{I}_2(x, a) = \begin{cases} B_1 & \text{if } a \geq \hat{a} \\ B_2 & \text{if } a < \hat{a} \end{cases} \quad \text{for } x < \hat{x}.$$

We denote this contract $\mathscr{C}^i = (q = 1, \hat{x}, \hat{a}, B_1, B_2)$.

For discussion purposes, we assume the worker will agree to any contract that provides an expected utility of at least $\overline{U}_w$. The owner selects the personally preferred contract given that constraint. And to illustrate our discussion we use

our continuing example and let $\overline{U}_w = 20.6819$, the worker's utility from the linear contract in Table 3.

Note that if some standard action $\hat{a}$ is to be induced, the smallest possible worker income that will induce it and provide the worker with an expected utility of $\overline{U}_w$ is B_1^0, where

$$\overline{U}_w = U_w(B_1^0, \hat{a}).$$

(Implementing $\hat{a}$ guarantees, with conditional investigation, payment of B_1^0 to the worker.) Of course, $\hat{x}$ and B_2 must also be selected so that the worker prefers $\hat{a}$ to any lower effort. Obviously, the owner would like to select them so that he minimizes the expected cost of investigation. This is accomplished by first setting B_2 as small as possible and then letting $\hat{x}$ be as small as is consistent with inducing $\hat{a}$. The crucial question here is: How small can B_2 be?

Observe that if the worker selects $\hat{a}$, there is no chance he will receive B_2; therefore, it is irrelevant to him. Its lower bound must be determined either by the worker's wealth ($-B_2$ cannot exceed the amount collectible from the worker) or by institutional constraints (*e.g.*, negative wages may be illegal or minimum wage laws may be relevant).

To illustrate, we consider our example in Table 3 and let $\hat{a} = a^*(\mathscr{C}^\ell)$. Two minimum income levels are considered: (i) zero and (ii) minus the worker's wealth. The results are presented in Table 6. Observe that if the minimum income is zero, the probability of investigation is about .27 percent, and the owner would prefer this investigation contract to the linear contract if the investigation cost C is less than \$11.53. On the other hand, if the owner can collect all the worker's wealth if investigation reveals below standard effort, then the probability of investigation is only about .02 and the investigation contract is preferred if the

126

TABLE 6 ILLUSTRATION OF INVESTIGATION CONTRACTS	(i)	(ii)
$\hat{a} = a^*(\mathscr{C}^\ell)$	.53965	.53965
$B_1^0 = [\bar{U} + \theta \hat{a}^r]^{1/r} - \bar{x}$		
$= [20.6819 + 2(\hat{a})^2]^2 - 400 =$	52.17	52.17
B_2^0 -400.00	0	
$\hat{x}$	84	5
$\phi(x \le \hat{x} \mid \hat{a})$	.2688	.0160
$E(U_w \mid a^*(\mathscr{C}^i), \mathscr{C}^i)$	20.6819	20.6819
$E(U_0 \mid a^*(\mathscr{C}^i), \mathscr{C}^i)$	104.0997	104.0997
	$-.2688C$	$-.0160C$

investigation cost is less than $193.73.

Several additional comments are in order.[31] First note that in both contracts the standard is significantly below the expected performance. Its role is to trigger an investigation, thereby conditioning the worker's payment. There is no intrinsic reason for the standard to be close to or far from the expected performance.

Second, whether this type of contracting will be preferred is very dependent on the information cost. Comparing it with those in the effort and state unobserved case, we are adding to the information on which the contracting is based. Indeed, with a very high standard, we approach the effort observable case. Thus, we would expect this contracting to be superior to, say, the linear contract in the effort unobserved case—provided the information is not too expensive. This is precisely the case if the worker is risk averse.[32] At a minimum, he would pay some positive amount to guarantee selection of some particular $\hat{a}$ and thereby shift outcome risk entirely to the owner. More formally, we have

Proposition 6:[33]

In the basic moral hazard model, if the owner is risk neutral and the worker is risk averse, then there exists a budget-based conditional investigation contract $\mathscr{C}^i$ that is Pareto superior to the linear contract $\mathscr{C}^\ell$ (with $a^* > 0$ and $a^*(\mathscr{C}) > 0$) provided that the positive investigation cost is sufficiently small.

Third, as pointed out in the first section, the budget-based conditional investigation contract is not a Nash equilibrium without some external enforcement mechanism. The owner, but not the worker, has a unilateral incentive not to honor the agreement. Of course, with legal sanctions or a formal multiperiod structure this would not necessarily be the case.

[31] In the contracts we have considered $\hat{a} = a^*(\mathscr{C}^\ell)$. However, the owner can increase his expected utility to $105.0586 - C\phi(x \le \hat{x} \mid \hat{a})$ if he increases $\hat{a}$ to .6206. That is, under an investigation contract it will be optimal to induce a higher effort level than under the linear contract.

[32] See Harris and Raviv [1976] for an extensive discussion of conditions under which there are potential gains to observing the worker's effort. As in our analysis, such gains are not available if either the state is observed or the worker is risk neutral (assuming optimal contracting under those conditions). They demonstrate that there are potential gains to observing the effort if the worker is risk averse and the existing contract induces an effort in the interior of the set of possible effort levels. They do not directly consider conditional observation, but instead focus on unconditional observation (our full information case) and on contracts based on imperfect information about the effort.

Townsend [1976], on the other hand, considers observations that are conditional on outcomes known only by a single individual. This individual calls for an investigation if the outcome is in a specified region, and incentives are constructed such that it is in his best interest to honor such an agreement.

[33] Proof: Set B_1^0 such that

$$U_w(B_1^0, a^*(\mathscr{C}^\ell)) = E(U_w \mid a^*(\mathscr{C}^\ell), \mathscr{C}^\ell),$$

$B_2 = -R^*$, and $\hat{a} = a^*(\mathscr{C}^\ell)$. Then set

$$\hat{x} = \sup_{s \in S} \{p(s, \hat{a}, q)\}.$$

By construction $E(U_w \mid a^*(\mathscr{C}^i), \mathscr{C}^i) \ge E(U_w \mid a^*(\mathscr{C}^\ell), \mathscr{C}^\ell)$ and by Jensen's inequality $B_1^0 < \alpha^* f(a^*(\mathscr{C}^\ell)) - R^*$. Hence, the worker is, at worst, indifferent and the owner strictly prefers contract $\mathscr{C}^i$ provided that the cost is not too large.

127

ADVERSE SELECTION CONTRACTING

Consider a setting in which the worker's effort is costlessly observed but, in general, neither his skill nor the state are. If skill varies among the worker population, a full information equilibrium may entail capital and labor combinations that reflect the individual worker's skills (with more skillful workers paid higher wages). Without skill differentiation, however, the lower skilled may have the incentive and the opportunity to misrepresent themselves.

To explore this issue we return to our basic model in (1), (2) and (3) and now assume there are I_1 unskilled ($h=1$) workers and I_2 skilled ($h=2$) workers with $I_1=I_2=J$ and $\psi_1<\psi_2$. The owner can split his capital between the two types of workers so that the output from his capital is

$$p(s, a, q)=p(s, a_1, q_1, 1)+p(s, a_2, q_2, 2)$$

where $a=(a_1, a_2)$, a_h is the effort of the type h worker, $q=(q_1, q_2)$, and q_h is the capital assigned to the type h worker. This interpretation of the model is termed the basic adverse selection model. The example economy in Table 1 is again used to illustrate our analysis, but with $p(s, a_h, q_h, h)=s\psi_h\xi a_h^k q_h^{1-k}$.

Costless Skill or State Information

If the owner can costlessly observe the worker's skill and effort, we may view the parties as contracting at a market wage (W_h) per unit of effort for each skill type: $C(\cdot)=0$, $\eta(s, a_h, q_h, h)=(a_h, q_h, h)$, and $\mathscr{I}(a_h, h)=a_h W_h$. Equilibrium requires equality between the labor demanded and supplied for each skill type. And our assumptions guarantee that each owner will employ one worker of each skill type. Denoting the equilibrium wage vector $W^*=(W_1^*, W_2^*)$, we illustrate an equilibrium in Table 7 and, presuming

existence and interior effort solutions, summarize the essential properties with

Proposition 7:[34]

In the basic adverse selection model, if the risk neutral owner can costlessly observe each worker's skill and effort (with $I_1=I_2=J$), then the competitive equilibrium based on skill dependent wages will have the following properties:

(i) each wage rate is equal to the expected marginal product of the respective worker:

$$W_h^* = \psi_h\partial F(a_h^*(W^*), q_h^*(W^*))/\partial a_h;$$

(ii) each worker selects his effort so that his wage rate equals the marginal rate of substitution between income and effort:

$$W_h^*= -[\partial U_w(\cdot)/\partial a_h] \div [\partial U_w(\cdot)/\partial x_w];$$

(iii) the owner splits his capital between the skilled and unskilled workers so that the marginal rate of substitution is equal to the marginal rate of transformation (unity):

$$[\psi_1\partial F(\cdot)/\partial q_1] \div [\psi_2\partial F(\cdot)/\partial q_2]=1; \text{ and}$$

(iv) the resulting allocation is Pareto optimal.

As in the moral hazard case, costless observation of the capital and state will allow the same allocation. Again, the worker rents the capital from the owner and the owner also provides state insurance. That is,

$$C(\cdot)=0, \eta(s, a_h, q_h, h)=(s, q_h), \mathscr{I}(s, q_h)$$

---

[34] (i), (ii), and (iii) follow directly from the first order conditions for the workers and owner. (iv) follows, as in Proposition 1, from focusing on a representative trio of individuals and maximizing the well-being of one subject to constant well-being constraints for the other two.

TABLE 7

ILLUSTRATION OF ACTION AND SKILL OR STATE OBSERVED CASES

Parameter Values:

$$k = .4, \qquad \xi = 200$$

$$\bar{x} = 400, \qquad \gamma = .5$$

$$\theta = 2, \qquad r = 2$$

$$\psi_1 = .5, \qquad \psi_2 = 1$$

Skill Observed Case:

$W_1^* = 18.6333$	$W_2^* = 105.3727$	$E(U_{w1} \mid a_1^*(W^*), W^*) = 20.0271$
$a_1^*(W^*) = .1161$	$a_2^*(W^*) = .6113$	$E(U_{w2} \mid a_2^*(W^*), W^*) = 20.8029$
$q_1^*(W^*) = .0325$	$q_2^*(W^*) = .9675$	
$F(a_1^*(W^*), q_1^*(W^*)) = 5.41$		$E(U_0 \mid a^*(W^*), q^*(W^*), W^*) = 99.8664$
$F(a_2^*(W^*), q_2^*(W^*)) = 161.04$		

State Observed Case:

$R^* = 99.8562$		$E(U_{w1} \mid a_1^*(R^*), q_1^*(R^*), R^*) = 20.0271$
$q_1^*(R^*) = .0325$	$q_2^*(R^*) = .9675$	$E(U_{w2} \mid a_2^*(R^*), q_2^*(R^*), R^*) = 20.8029$
$a_1^*(R^*) = .1161$	$a_2^*(R^*) = .6113$	$E(U_0 \mid q^*(R^*), R^*) = 99.8664$

$$= x_h - Rq_h - I_h(s) \text{ and } E[I_h(s)] = 0.[35]$$

Thus, presuming existence of an equilibrium with interior effort solutions at rental rate R^* (which equates the demand and supply for capital), we have

Proposition 8:[36]

In the basic adverse selection model, if the risk neutral owner has sufficient wealth to provide insurance and both he and the workers can costlessly observe the state and capital, then the competitive equilibrium based on rental and insurance contracts will have the following properties:

(i) each worker's average return per normalized unit of effort equals his expected marginal product:

$$(\psi_h f(n) - R^*)/n = \psi_h f'(n),$$

where

$$n = a_h^*(R^*)/q_h^*(R^*);$$

(ii) each worker selects his effort and capital so that his expected marginal product equals the marginal rate of substitution between income and effort: $\psi_h f'(a_h^*(R^*)) = -[\partial U_w(\cdot)/\partial a_h] \div [\partial U_w(\cdot)/\partial x_w]$;

(iii) $[\psi_1 \partial F(\cdot)/\partial q_1] \div [\psi_2 \partial F(\cdot)/\partial q_2] = 1$

(iv) the resulting allocation is Pareto optimal from a complete information perspective.

Table 7 presents a numerical example.

Finally, we note that Pareto optimality

[35] Again the worker receives x_h because he operates his part of the firm; and it does not appear as an argument of $\mathscr{I}(\cdot)$ since it is not observed by the owner.

[36] (i), (ii), and (iii) follow from first order conditions and (iv) follows as in Proposition 7.

can be achieved without budget-based contracting in the two cases discussed above, and we therefore conclude

Proposition 9:

A necessary condition for a budget-based contract to be Pareto superior to all alternative contracts in the basic adverse selection model is that it be costly to observe both the workers' skills and state.

Skill and State Not Observed

Consider the case in which neither the worker's skill nor the state can be observed, except at prohibitive cost. Only the worker's effort, capital and outcome are (costlessly) observed: $\eta(s, a_h, q_h, h) = (a_h, q_h, p(s, a_h, q_h, h))$ and $C(\cdot) = 0$.

Determination of the sharing functions $\mathcal{I}(a_h, q_h, x_h)$ is important here because efficiency gains are generally available if the two worker classes can be distinguished, and some sharing functions may induce the workers to reveal their skill by their contract choices.

Initially, we consider the naive case in which a straightforward wage contract is offered, with $\mathcal{I}(\cdot) = a_i W$. With an inability to distinguish worker skill, the owner will split his capital between two workers. This contract clearly does not, in general, produce the allocation depicted in Propositions 7 and 8. See the illustration in Table 8 where we observe an incentive for the unskilled workers not to reveal their skill endowment.

The full information equilibrium can be achieved without skill or state information if the workers are risk neutral. This reduces to a special case of Proposition 8 in which the owner rents the capital to the workers but offers no insurance. Insurance is an indifferent proposition here, and not offering it obviates the need to observe the worker's state. Hence, (ignoring bankruptcy) we conclude

TABLE 8

ILLUSTRATION OF NONDIFFERENTIATION EQUILIBRIUM

$q_1^*(W^*) = q_2^*(W^*) = .500$

$$E(U_0 | a^*(W^*), q^*(W^*), W^*) = 83.0590$$

$a_1^*(W^*) = a_2^*(W^*) = .4091$

$$E(U_{wh} | a_h^*(W^*), W^*) = 20.3459$$

$$h = 1, 2$$

$W_1^* = W_2^* = W^* = 67.6761$

Expected Marginal Product:

unskilled	45.1174
skilled	90.2348

Proposition 10:

A necessary condition for a budget-based contract to be Pareto superior to all alternative contracts in the basic adverse selection model is that the workers be risk averse.

Consideration of budget-based contracts in this setting, then, is motivated by a desire to identify the worker's skills to assure production efficiency. Offering a pair of contracts such that the unskilled self-select one and the skilled self-select another is one way of distinguishing the workers. (Examination and ex post investigation are alternative mechanisms.) Budget-based contracts may be efficient in promoting this self-selection.

To explore this theme, we adopt the strategy employed in the moral hazard case and compare budget-based with linear contracts. Initially, we note that it is possible to distinguish the workers by offering a pair of linear contracts. One such pair for our example economy is presented in Table 9 (see Table 7 for parameter values).[37]

[37] We make no attempt here to determine a Pareto optimal or equilibrium pair of linear contracts. We merely illustrate that differentiation can be achieved. Also note that offering the two wage contracts in Table 7 will not achieve differentiation; all would select the higher wage alternative.

TABLE 9

ILLUSTRATION OF SKILL DIFFERENTIATING CONTRACTS

Contracts Preferred by

	Unskilled ($h=1$)		Skilled ($h=2$)
Linear Contracts	$(\mathscr{C}_1^\ell)$		$(\mathscr{C}_2^\ell)$
q_h	.0325		.9675
a_h	.1161		.6113
$\mathscr{I}_h(a_h, q_h, x_h)$[38]	2.1633		$x_h - 80$
$E(U_{w1}\,\vert\,a_1^*(\mathscr{C}_h^\ell), \mathscr{C}_h^\ell)$	20.0271		19.2316
$E(U_{w2}\,\vert\,a_2^*(\mathscr{C}_h^\ell), \mathscr{C}_h^\ell)$	20.0271		21.0805
$E(U_0\,\vert\,a^*(\mathscr{C}^\ell), \mathscr{C}^\ell)$		83.2450	
Dichotomous Contracts	$(\mathscr{C}_1^d = \mathscr{C}_1^\ell)$		$(\mathscr{C}_2^d)$
q_h	.0325		.9675
a_h	.1161		.6113
$\hat{x}_h$	—		161.0358
$\mathscr{I}_{h1}(a_h, q_h, x_h)$	2.1633		161.5536
$\mathscr{I}_{h2}(a_h, q_h, x_h)$	2.1633		$x_h - 80$
$E(U_{w1}\,\vert\,a_1^*(\mathscr{C}_h^d), \mathscr{C}_h^d)$	20.0271		19.2316
$E(U_{w2}\,\vert\,a_2^*(\mathscr{C}_h^d), \mathscr{C}_h^d)$	20.0271		21.0907
$E(U_0\,\vert\,a^*(\mathscr{C}^d), \mathscr{C}^d)$		83.2450	

The difficulty with separation via linear contracts, however, is their implicit cost. They are inherently risky and, with the risk neutral owner, we trade off risk sharing for separation effects. Under the assumptions of our example economy, budget-based contracts can generally accomplish the same separation but with less risk allocated to the worker. Quite simply, with $\psi_2 > \psi_1$, a bounded state, and $\alpha > 0$, partial insurance always can be offered to the skilled worker without affecting the separation and without encountering a moral hazard problem (because a_h is observed). More specifically, we have

Proposition 11:[39]

For the example economy formulated in Table 1 with two equal sized skill groups ($\psi_1 < \psi_2$) and with each work-er's action, capital, and outcome costlessly observed, there always exists a dichotomous contract $\mathscr{C}_2^d$ such that the pair of contracts $(\mathscr{C}_1^\ell, \mathscr{C}_2^d)$ is Pareto superior to the pair of skill differentiating contracts $(\mathscr{C}_1^\ell, \mathscr{C}_2^\ell)$ in which α_2, a_2, $q_2 > 0$.

[38] Payment is, of course, conditional on the observed effort level being at least the contracted level.

[39] We prove the proposition by illustrating a Pareto superior dichotomous contract. With $\psi_2 > \psi_1$, there exists a non-empty interval in the outcome space that, for any $0 < a, q$, will contain the skilled worker's outcome with nonzero probability but will contain the unskilled worker's outcome with probability zero; i.e., the interval $(2\psi_1 F(a, q), 2\psi_2 F(a, q))$. Let $\hat{x}_2 = 2\psi_1 F(a_2, q_2)$, $\mathscr{I}_{21}(a_2, q_2) = B_{21} = \alpha_2(\psi_2 + \psi_1) F(a_2, q_2) - R_2$, and $\mathscr{I}_{22}(a_2, q_2) = \alpha_2 x_2 - R_2$, where a_2, q_2, α_2, and R_2 are as specified in $\mathscr{C}_2^\ell$. The unskilled worker still prefers $\mathscr{C}_1^\ell$ and therefore is indifferent; the risk neutral owner's expected profit is unaffected and he, therefore, is indifferent; and Jensen's inequality guarantees that the skilled worker strictly prefers the dichotomous contract.

Table 9 provides an example of a Pareto superior dichotomous contract.

Skill or State Observed at a Cost

Finally, we briefly consider the case where the worker's skill or state can be observed at some "reasonable" cost. Each worker's effort, capital, and outcome are costlessly observable and observation activities can be conditioned on these variables.

As in the moral hazard case, the desirability of a conditional investigation contract will depend on the investigation costs and the type of sharing function employed. In general, however, investigation provides a strict increase in the amount of information on which the contracting is based and, thus, in general, we expect positive value to be associated with such a contract. Indeed, with the skilled worker forced into a risk position to gain separation from the unskilled worker, he will pay to shift that risk to the owner. Conditional investigation will accomplish this without dulling self-selection incentives. More formally, we have

Proposition 12:[40]

In the basic adverse selection model, if a risk neutral owner uses a pair of skill differentiating contracts (based on costless observation of the worker's effort, capital, and outcome) that impose risk on one of the two risk averse worker groups, then there is a pair of budget-based conditional investigation contracts that is Pareto superior to those existing contracts provided the positive investigation cost is sufficiently small.

As noted in the moral hazard case, however, conditional investigation contracts are not, in the absence of exogenous enforcement, Nash equilibria. Hence, we must expand our setting to fully rationalize such contracting procedures.

CONCLUDING REMARKS

Use of budget-based contracts, such as standard cost systems, can be analyzed in terms of conscious choice by both parties to the contract. We have demonstrated that market incompleteness (in terms of costly effort or skill observability) and risk aversion are necessary conditions for such contracting to be Pareto superior to other contracting alternatives. We have identified some conditions under which budget-based contracts are Pareto superior to linear contracts. Of course, our observations must be viewed as tentative in that they are based on a model of a simple economy. But it is clear that budget-based contracts can be rationalized in a market setting.

In concluding, we briefly relate our analysis to some of the debates in the accounting literature as to how budget-based contracts should be designed. (See Ronen and Livingstone [1975] for a recent review of this literature.) One continuing debate is whether the standard should be reasonably attainable. In our analysis attainability is not a direct issue. Furthermore, in the numerical cases examined, the standard is below expected performance when nonperformance triggers an investigation and above expected performance when no additional information is to be obtained. In each case, the budget-based contracts

[40] Let X^n be the set of possible outcomes for which one of the worker types incurs risk under the existing contracts. Investigating if $x \in X^n$, paying zero if the observed skill is not as represented but the conditional expected payment otherwise, provides a strictly superior budget-based conditional investigation contract. The owner is indifferent, the worker in question is strictly improved (by Jensen's inequality), and the remaining worker is unaffected. A similar contract can be constructed for the other worker, but there will be no improvement for him if X^n is null.

arise because of information voids, and when viewed in terms of the contracting arrangements that will be efficient, there is no reason to expect the standard to be reasonably attainable. Indeed, we are looking at market based allocations here and the contracting arrangements are jointly determined by the owners' and workers' tastes, beliefs, and opportunities.

To reinforce this point, recall the dichotomous contract with a high standard in Proposition 5. In this case the worker voluntarily increases his effort so as to have some chance of attaining the high standard because the compensation for doing so is sufficiently attractive. In many discussions of standards, the compensation aspects are largely ignored. Alternative standards will be associated with different compensation functions, and the preferences for one standard over another must reflect the changes in those functions. A *ceteris paribus* comparison is incomplete. On the other hand, discussions of standards often stress motivational aspects which we have ignored. In particular, we have ignored the possibility that the outcome relative to standard provides some form of non-pecuniary income to the worker.

A second issue in the design of budget-based systems is the degree of participation by the workers in establishing the standards. In our analysis, all aspects of a contract, including the standard, are unanimously agreed upon by both parties. But, of course, given our market setting, it is an equilibrium analysis interpreted in terms of the market forces that ultimately produce that agreement. More formal examination of participation in an economic model would require explicit recognition of contracting costs, information asymmetries, and internal labor markets.[41]

A third issue is the frequency or condi-tions under which management should investigate the causes of poor performance. In much of the accounting literature, that issue is explored in the context of simple analytical models that view the system as being either "in control" or "out of control." (See Kaplan [1975] for a review of this literature.) We provide a somewhat different view. In our analysis, system performance is not mechanistic, but is influenced by the worker; and the threat of investigation (and its consequences) is used to ensure that the worker provides the effort required by his wage contract. This "management by exception" may appear to be somewhat negative, but, in fact, the worker may benefit by obtaining a share of the larger returns such a system will provide if investigation costs are sufficiently small. (Note, however, that no non-pecuniary aspects of the owner-worker relationship were admitted in the analysis.)

A final issue is whether performance measures should encompass only that which is controllable by the worker. An affirmative answer is accepted dogma in much of the accounting literature (though risk sharing issues do arise). In the limiting case of costless information, that is what we observe in our analysis: the worker is responsible only for the effort he exerts with known skill. But recognition of information costs may result in contracts that leave the worker subject to the risks of factors beyond his control. In those cases, the worker would be worse off if he insisted on the controllability principle since the available returns with which to pay him would be smaller if the owner was forced to incur the in-

---

[41] See Doeringer and Piore [1971] for extensive development of the concept of internal labor markets. This concept gives formal recognition to the fact that while market forces are important at entry level positions, they are less important for many of the existing employees in a firm.

formation costs. On the other hand, the budget-based conditional investigation contract does effectively implement the controllability principle in the face of "reasonable" information costs.

In sum, budget-based contracts can be rationalized as labor allocation/employment devices when desirable information upon which to base the allocations is costly. This, in turn, adds insight into the nature and role of the standards and budgets that might be used.

Proof of Proposition 5

We set $\hat{x} = 2f(a^*(\mathscr{C}))$, where $\mathscr{C} = (1, \alpha, R)$ is the linear contract in question, and consider $B_1 \geq \alpha\hat{x} - R$.
Then

$$E(U_w | a^*(\mathscr{C}^d), \mathscr{C}^d) \geq E(U_w | a^*(\mathscr{C}), \mathscr{C}^d) = E(U_w | a^*(\mathscr{C}), \mathscr{C}).$$

And with $a^*(\mathscr{C}^d) \geq a^*(\mathscr{C})$, the optimal effort may be determined by differentiating the following:

$$E(U_w | a, \mathscr{C}^d) = [(\gamma + 1)\alpha 2\xi a^k]^{-1}\{[\alpha\hat{x} + \bar{x} - R]^{\gamma+1} - [\bar{x} - R]^{\gamma+1}\}$$
$$+ [\bar{x} + B_1]^\gamma (1 - \hat{x}/2\xi a^k) - \theta a^r$$

and setting it equal to zero. Let $a(B_1)$ denote the optimal effort:

$$a(B_1) = a^*(\mathscr{C}^d) = \left[\frac{k}{2\xi r\theta}\left([\bar{x} + B_1]^\gamma \hat{x} - \frac{[\alpha\hat{x} + \bar{x} - R]^{\gamma+1} - [\bar{x} - R]^{\gamma+1}}{(\gamma + 1)\alpha}\right)\right]^{1/(r+k)}$$

The owner's expected utility for the dichotomous contract is

$$E(U_0 | a(B_1), \mathscr{C}^d) = \xi[a(B_1)]^k - \alpha\xi[\alpha\xi[a(B_1)]^k\tfrac{1}{4}[\hat{s}(a(B_1))]^2 + R\tfrac{1}{2}\hat{s}(a(B_1))$$
$$- B_1(1 - \tfrac{1}{2}\hat{s}(a(B_1)))$$

where $\hat{s}(a) = \hat{x}/\xi a^k$ is the state that yields outcome $\hat{x}$ if effort a is selected.

We now differentiate the owner's expected utility with respect to B_1:

$$\frac{\partial E(U_0 | a(B_1), \mathscr{C}^d)}{\partial B_1} = \xi k[a(B_1)]^{k-1}a'(B_1) - \alpha\xi k[a(B_1)]^{k-1}a'(B_1)\tfrac{1}{4}[\hat{s}(a(B_1))]^2$$
$$- \alpha\xi\tfrac{1}{2}[a(B_1)]^k[\hat{s}(a(B_1))]\hat{s}'(a(B_1))a'(B_1) + R\tfrac{1}{2}\hat{s}'(a(B_1))a'(B_1)$$
$$- (1 - \tfrac{1}{2}\hat{s}(a(B_1))) + B_1\tfrac{1}{2}\hat{s}'(a(B_1))a'(B_1).$$

Evaluating this at $B_1 = \alpha\hat{x} - R$ and observing that $\hat{s}'(a) = -k\hat{x}/\xi a^{k+1}$ we obtain

$$\frac{\partial E(U_0 | \cdot)}{\partial B_1}\bigg|_{B_1 = \alpha\hat{x} - R} = a'(B_1)[a(B_1)]^{k-1}\{\xi k - \alpha k\hat{x}^2/4\xi[a(B_1)]^{2k}\} - (1 - \tfrac{1}{2}(\hat{x}/\xi[a(B_1)]^k)$$

And since $\hat{x} = 2f(a(B_1)) = 2\xi[a(B_1)]^k$ we have

$$\frac{\partial E(U_0 | \cdot)}{\partial B_1}\bigg|_{B_1 = \alpha\hat{x} - R} = a'(B_1)[a(B_1)]^{k-1}\xi k(1 - \alpha) > 0 \quad \text{if } \alpha < 1 \quad \text{and} \quad a'(B_1) > 0$$

134

But

$$a'(B_1) = \left[\frac{k}{2\xi r\theta}\left([\bar{x} + B_1]^\gamma \hat{x} - \frac{[\alpha\hat{x} + \bar{x} - R]^{\gamma+1} - [\bar{x} - R]^{\gamma+1}}{(\gamma+1)\alpha}\right)\right]^{1/(r+k)-1}$$

$$\cdot \frac{1}{r+k}\frac{k\hat{x}}{2\xi r\theta}[\bar{x} + B_1]^{\gamma-1}\gamma = [a(B_1)]^{1-r-k}\frac{1}{r+k}\frac{k\hat{x}\gamma}{2\xi r\theta}[\bar{x} + B_1]^{\gamma-1} > 0.$$

REFERENCES

Akerlof, G., "The Market for 'Lemons': Quality Uncertainty and the Market Mechanism," *Quarterly Journal of Economics* (August 1970), pp. 488–500.

Alchian, A. and H. Demsetz, "Production, Information Costs, and Economic Organization." *American Economic Review* (December 1972), pp. 777–795.

Argyris, C., *The Impact of Budgets on People* (Controllership Foundation, 1952).

Arrow, K. J., *The Limits of Organization* (Norton, 1974).

Becker, G. S. and G. J. Stigler, "Law Enforcement, Malfeasance, and Compensation of Enforcers." *Journal of Legal Studies* (January 1974).

Doeringer, P. and M. Piore, *Internal Labor Markets and Manpower Analysis* (Heath, 1971).

Gjesdal, Frøystein, "Accounting in Agencies" unpublished paper, Stanford University Graduate School of Business (1976).

Harris, M., and A. Raviv, "Optimal Incentive Contracts with Imperfect Information," unpublished working paper #70-75-76, GSIA, Carnegie-Mellon University (1976).

Hopwood, A. G., "An Empirical Study of the Role of Accounting Data in Performance Evaluation," *Journal of Accounting Research Supplement* (1972), pp. 156–193.

Itami, H., "Evaluation Measures and Goal Congruence under Uncertainty," *Journal of Accounting Research* (Spring 1975), pp. 73–96.

Jensen, M. C. and W. H. Meckling, "Theory of the Firm: Managerial Behavior, Agency Costs and Ownership Structure," *Journal of Financial Economics* (October 1976), pp. 305–360.

Kaplan, R., "The Significance and Investigation of Cost Variances: Survey and Extensions," *Journal of Accounting Research* (Fall, 1975), pp. 311–337.

Kihlstrom, R., and M. Pauly, "The Role of Insurance in the Allocation of Risk," *American Economic Review* (May 1971), pp. 371–379.

Mirrlees, J. A., "Notes on Welfare Economics, Information, and Uncertainty," in Balch, M., McFadden, D. and Wu, S. (eds.), *Essays on Economic Behavior Under Uncertainty* (North-Holland, 1974).

————, "The Optimal Structure of Incentives and Authority within an Organization," *Bell Journal of Economics* (Spring, 1976), pp. 105–131.

Radner, R., "Market Equilibrium and Uncertainty: Concepts and Problems," in M. D. Intriligator and D. A. Kendrick (eds.), *Frontiers of Quantitative Economics* Volume 2 (North-Holland, 1974).

Ridgeway, V. F., "Dysfunctional Consequences of Performance Measurement," *Administrative Science Quarterly* (September 1956), pp. 240–247.

Ronen, J. and J. L. Livingstone, "An Expectancy Theory Approach to the Motivational Impacts of Budgets," THE ACCOUNTING REVIEW (October 1975), pp. 671–685.

Rothschild, M. and J. Stiglitz, "Equilibrium in Competitive Insurance Markets: An Essay on the Economics of Imperfect Information," *Quarterly Journal of Economics* (November 1976), pp. 629–649.

Schiff, M. and A. Y. Lewin, "The Impact of People on Budgets," THE ACCOUNTING REVIEW (April 1970), pp. 259–268.

Spence, M., "Job Market Signaling," *Quarterly Journal of Economics* (August 1973), pp. 355–374.

Spence, M., and R. Zeckhauser, "Insurance, Information and Individual Action," *American Economic Review* (May 1971), pp. 380–391.

Stafford, F. P. and M. S. Cohen, "A Model of Work Effort and Productive Consumption," *Journal of Economic Theory* (March 1974), pp. 333–347.

Stedry, A. C., *Budget Control and Cost Behavior* (Prentice-Hall, 1960).

Stiglitz, J. E., "Risk Sharing and Incentives in Sharecropping," *Review of Economic Studies* (April 1974), pp. 219–255.

————, "Incentives, Risk, and Information: Notes Toward a Theory of Hierarchy," *Bell Journal of Economics* (Autumn 1975), pp. 552–579.

Swieringa, R. J. and R. H. Moncur, *Some Effects of Participative Budgeting on Managerial Behavior* (NAA, 1975).

Townsend, R. M., "Optimal Contracts and Competitive Markets with Costly State Verification," unpublished working paper, Graduate School of Industrial Administration, Carnegie-Mellon University (August 1976).

Williamson, O. E., M. L. Wachter, and J. E. Harris, "Understanding the Employment Relation: The Analysis of Idiosyncratic Exchange," *Bell Journal of Economics* (Spring 1975), pp. 250–278.

Wilson, R., "On the Theory of Syndicates," *Econometrica* (January 1968), pp. 119–132.

Budgetary Control
and Organization Structure

WILLIAM J. BRUNS, JR.
Harvard University

JOHN H. WATERHOUSE
University of Alberta

In spite of the widespread use of budgets for control of organization activities, relatively little is known about how budgets influence behavior. Furthermore, the interaction of budgets with other means of influencing human behavior has remained largely unexplored. This research explores the interaction and relationships of one source of control, organization structure, with another source of control, budgets. Data gathered from twenty-five organizations are analyzed to explore some of the interrelationships between organization structure and the use of budgets by managers. Data collected by mailed questionnaires were factor analyzed to provide measures of budget-related behavior that could be related to measures of organization structure and context that were collected in field interviews. The analysis of these data indicates clear relationships between organization structure and the use and effects of budgets and provides insight into several complex relationships suggested by other field and *a priori* research on control in organizations.

The findings of this study are consistent with those organizational studies which have concluded that the structure of organizations can be viewed as contingent upon environment and organization characteristics such as size, technology, and dependence (the extent to which an organization is autonomous in relationships with other organizations) (see Woodward [1965], Burns and Stalker [1961], Lawrence and Lorsch [1967], and Pugh, Hickson, Hinings, and Turner [1969]). Budget-related behavior is found to be contingent upon various aspects of organization structure such as centralization, autonomy, and the degree to which activities are structured. These findings lead to the conclusion that there must be alternative organizational control strategies in different kinds of organizations, and that prescriptions about how budgets should be used in organizational control should be written with care.

Some Theories of Organization and Budgetary Control

Budgets are potential means of influencing behavior. Control is the successful exercise of power to influence behavior available to an organization. Two other primary means to influence behavior are interpersonal contact, i.e., leadership, and organizational structure, i.e., the distribution of authority and work roles. This study focuses specifically on the relationship between formal properties of organizational structure and budgetary control. This is in contrast to other studies of budgeting which have examined the relationship between interpersonal variables and budgetary control (DeCoster and Fertakis [1968], Foran and DeCoster [1974], Hopwood [1974], Swieringa and Moncur [1972 and 1975]).

ORGANIZATION STRUCTURE AND CONTROL

Structure refers to internal patterns of organization relationships (Thompson [1967], p. 51).[1] Organization implies some ordering of work roles whereby the authority and resources for making decisions and performing tasks are distributed to defined positions within the organization. Much of the administrative systems literature, being concerned with economic efficiency, has focused on the means whereby organization activities and tasks can be rationally grouped by specialized function and subjected to standardized operating procedures (Barnard [1938], Weber [1947], and Chandler [1962]). To the extent that activities are specialized, standardized, and formalized, decision-making authority and tasks can be

---

[1] Research on organization structure is quite voluminous. A sample might include work cited below. Its diversity precludes more than recognition here that the structure of organizations has long fascinated many social scientists. The particular thread of research on organization structure to which our research most directly ties originates with Pugh, Hickson, Hinings, MacDonald, Turner, and Lupton (1963), who set out to devise measures of several dimensions of organization structures and to develop research techniques which could be standardized and repeated in different settings. This research, which we will refer to as the Aston approach, has led to a substantial body of related work on organization structure. (A sample should include Hickson (1966), Pugh, Hickson, Hinings, and Turner (1968) and (1969), and Child (1972a) and (1972b). Research on organization structure has often been linked with research on behavior of organization members. The effects of structure and environment on organizational behavior have been explored in classic studies such as those of Woodward (1965), Burns and Stalker (1968), and Lawrence and Lorsch (1967). In addition, social psychologists have considered the role of organization structure as an influence on individual behavior (see, for a sampling, Vroom [1960], McGregor [1960], Argyris [1960 and 1964], Fiedler [1967] and Child [1972b and 1973]).

controlled by decentralization and structuring of activities (the degree of formal regulation of intended activities of organization members). Child states the nature of control under decentralization with structuring in the following manner:

> . . . the locus of the decision-making authority on operational matters is decentralized down to the incumbents of official roles. These roles are structured by virtue of their specialized prescribed duties and particularly by a system of procedure and documentation designed to limit areas of discretion, as well as provide information on role performance (Child [1972b], p. 163).

This decentralized but structured approach comprises one strategy for organizational control.

An alternative strategy for control is to centralize decision-making authority at higher levels within the organization. Maintaining control by centralizing decision making reduces the need for organization, systems, procedures, and specialist personnel to operate administrative systems (Child [1973]). A number of empirical studies of organizations have found a negative correlation between centralization and the degree to which activities are structured (Blau and Schoenherr [1971], Inkson, Pugh and Hickson [1970], and Child [1972b]). Interpersonal relationships replace structured activities as primary means for maintaining control.

The choice between decentralization with structuring and centralization is limited to some extent by internal and external conditions faced by the organization. Several studies have shown that the size of the organization is positively associated with structuring of activities and negatively associated with centralization (see, for example, Pugh, Hickson, Hinings, and Turner [1969] and Child [1972b]). Technological sophistication may also be positively associated with structuring of activities (Child [1972a]). It appears that, as organizations become more closely tied to technology and means for standardized mass production, they formalize role definitions and decentralize decision-making authority (Perrow [1967]). Concurrently, these organizations develop means for maintaining control by utilizing procedures for defining and measuring role performance.

ORGANIZATION STRUCTURE AND PERCEIVED CONTROL

In a decentralized and structured organization, legitimate activities are clearly defined, areas of responsibility and authority are clearly delineated, and control is essentially impersonal. Since areas of authority are clearly defined, decision making can be delegated while organizational control is maintained. Individuals may feel they have a great degree of control within areas of defined authority. A decentralized and structured organization operating in a stable organizational environment seems particularly well suited to the use of budgetary control.

Centralization, where control of decisions is reserved to a small group at the top of an organization hierarchy, reduces perceived control by individuals at lower levels in the organization (Child [1973]). Whereas systems, procedures, and areas of authority are not or cannot be clearly defined, control by structuring may be replaced by interpersonal control. As a control strategy, centralization may allow control to be exerted and sanctioned not only from the organization *per se*, but also among individuals within the organization. Individuals can, and presumably do, build bases from which to exert influence and control within the organization. For example, Mechanic (1962) noted that, to the extent that subordinates can make supervisors dependent upon them, the subordinates have power. Crozier (1964) also has noted that when role performance is governed by rules and, therefore, is predictable, role incumbents find it difficult to build power bases. However, when organization structure does not clearly define areas of authority, a system of bargaining and power relationships may develop.

In those situations where work roles cannot be readily structured because either environment or technology is unstable, centralization may be adopted as a strategy for control. But these latter conditions may also create an opportunity for individuals to develop power bases, and a relatively high level of interpersonal bargaining and conflict might be expected. Budgets may be used as a means of control in either decentralized and structured or centralized organizations. However, the differences in structure may affect individual behavior in such a way that budget-related behavior will be different in organizations depending on the structural strategy an organization has adopted.

BUDGETARY CONTROL

Control systems based upon financial measures are widely used in economic organizations. The principal designs for assigning financial responsibility in organizations can be classified as follows: standard cost centers, revenue centers, discretionary expense centers, profit centers, and investment centers (Vancil [1973]). The order of this classification is from narrowest to broadest in terms of the decision-making discretion permitted or required of the manager. The manager of a standard cost center has control over fewer financial variables than the manager of an investment center. Vancil (1973) concluded that the choice of a design for assigning financial responsibility should be a function of the organizational structure, which he defined in terms of the delegation of authority and the specialization of effort, and organizational strategy.

Budgets are financial plans and provide a basis for directing and evaluating the performance of individuals or segments of organizations. Through budgets, activities of different parts of an organization can be coordinated and controlled. A control system typically incorporates measures and techniques which conform to the responsibilities delegated to managers under the organization's structure. As decision-making authority is decentralized and parts of an organization become more autonomous, managers will be responsible for more financial variables, and financial control systems will be more complex in the sense that they will incorporate more variables.

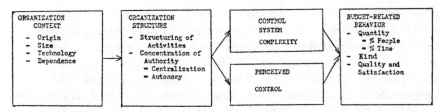

FIG. 1.—Research domain.

ORGANIZATION STRUCTURE AND BUDGET-RELATED BEHAVIOR

The research domain in which this study is based is shown in figure 1. Organization structure is viewed as being contingent on the context in which the organization operates, including such characteristics as its size, technology, and dependence (the extent to which an organization is autonomous in relationship with other organizations). Two variables, control system complexity and perceived control, are seen as intervening to affect budget-related behavior including the quantity of such behavior, the kind of behavior, and the quality and satisfaction in terms of the extent to which the budget is seen as effective in accomplishing organizational goals.

In this study budget-related behavior is defined as the activities, actions, and interactions of managers with each other and their tasks that relate either directly or indirectly to budget systems. Budget-related attitudes are defined as affective feelings of managers toward budgets and budget-related behaviors of themselves and others. Budgets are plans against which performance may be compared. To a large extent, the use of budgets for control purposes is thought to be dependent upon the ability to plan with a fairly high degree of certainty and to measure output or role performance with a relatively high degree of accuracy. A budget not only specifies a goal (i.e., X units of production at an expected total cost), but it may also specify the means for accomplishing the goal (i.e., material, labor, and other inputs at standard costs). In decision-making terms, the budget specifies both an objective function and decision alternatives. The budget may be seen as a means for decentralizing certain types of operation decisions. However, since the objective function and decision alternatives are specified, the decisions faced by budgetees are really very structured.

Since budgets tend to structure the decision-making environment, budgets would appear to be particularly well-suited as control devices under the same types of operating circumstances that are also prevalent in decentralized but structured organizations. Moreover, the use of budgets for control purposes and the structuring of activities may be mutually reinforcing. A relatively stable and predictable environment which will allow decentralization with structuring of activities produces conditions amenable to the use of budgets, and budgets further structure activities. Therefore, we hypothesize that the quantity of budget-related behavior will be high in organizations which are decentralized and structured. Because roles and rules are clearly defined in a decentralized but structured organization, structuring of activities and perceived control are expected to be positively related. The individual in a structured situation may perceive himself and others as having greater control in their areas of defined responsibility. For these reasons we hypothesize that budget-related behavior will tend to be administrative in character rather than interpersonal. Since subordinate managers have less authority and may perceive themselves as having less control in centralized organizations, any attempt to hold individuals responsible for directly meeting a budget is less likely to meet with much success and is likely to produce negative attitudes toward budgets. To the extent that budgets are used as control devices in centralized organizations, we hypothesize that they will be used in a more interpersonal manner than in decentralized but structured organizations. The hypothesized relationships between organization context structure and budget-related behavior are illustrated in figure 2.

Method and Data

Twenty-seven organizations were contacted to seek their participation in the study. Two criteria were utilized in selecting organizations: first, because we hoped our sample would include organizations with a wide variety of different structures, organizations of different sizes, operating in different environments, and with diverse technologies were contacted; second, since each organization would be visited as part of the research, the sample was geographically limited to the U.S. Midwest and Eastern regions and to Ontario in Canada to minimize interviewing costs. Organizations were defined, for purposes of this study, so that corporate divisions would comprise separate organizations. A letter was sent to the chief executive officer or another senior officer in each organization soliciting their cooperation in the project. The letter explained that we were engaged in a research project

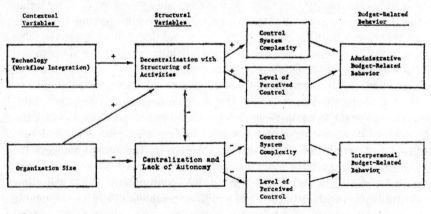

Fig. 2.—Expected relationships between organization context, structure, and budget-related behavior.

TABLE 1
Organizations Sampled

| Number of employees | N | Organizations | |
		Manufacturing	Service
0–249	7	Construction Products Building Materials	Research and Development Advertising Life Insurance (3)
250–999	6	Construction Products Utilities Vehicle Components Chemicals (2)	Sales
1,000–1,999	5	Food Products Newspaper Paper Products Electronic Equipment	Advertising
2,000 or greater	8	Paper Manufacturing Packaging Containers Vehicle Components (2) Steel	Life Insurance Facilities Maintenance

designed to learn something more about the effective use of budgets in organizations. Twenty-six organizations agreed to participate in the study. A profile of these organizations is provided in table 1. The research procedure included a two- to three-hour interview with the chief executive or a close associate in each organization. The interview time was spent in: (a) explaining the general nature of the study and why the cooperation of each executive was important; (b) administering questionnaires on organization structure and control systems according to the standard format of each (questionnaires will be described below) and in collecting necessary supporting documents (such as organization charts, etc.); and (c) identifying a sample of employees directly involved in preparing, using, or performing against a budget.

The identification of the employee sample usually occurred while the interviewee was explaining his organization chart. Our original plan to select a random sample from all employees in each organization proved unfeasible because organizations were reluctant or unable to make complete lists available to us. The number of employees identified varied from three to fifty depending on the size and nature of the organization. Budget-related behavior and perceived control questionnaires were mailed to each of the identified individuals, and their anonymous responses were returned by mail. Four hundred and twenty-nine questionnaires yielded two hundred and eighty-four usable responses for a response rate of sixty-six percent. The respondents had worked for their present employers an average of 14.8 years and in their current positions an average of 3.4 years. On the average they had worked for 22.3 years since leaving school. Respondents were experienced and held managerial positions.

In total, four different questionnaires were administered. Wherever possible, questionnaires which had been validated through previous research were sought for reasons of practicality and to provide comparisons to prior research. A description of the questionnaires follows.

Organization Structure and Context—Instruments developed by the Aston Group were used to operationalize the concepts of organization structure and context (Pugh, Hickson, Hinings and Turner [1968 and 1969]). The Aston Group identified from a review of the literature six primary dimensions of organization structure: specialization, standardization, formalization, centralization, configuration, and flexibility. Sixty-four scales were constructed to measure the first five of these variables. A factor analysis of the data from forty-six organizations disclosed four independent dimensions of structure: structuring of activities; concentration of authority; line of control of workflow; and relative size of supportive components. Subsequent research (Hinings and Lee [1971], Inkson, Pugh and Hickson [1970], and Child [1972b]) utilizing the Aston methodology has concentrated on the first two dimensions of structure: structuring of activities and concentration of authority.[2]

The dimension called structuring of activities concerns the degree of formal regulation of the intended activities of employees. The scales used to measure this dimension are: specialization, the number and kinds of specialists; standardization, the extent to which activities are subject to standard operating rules and procedures; and formalization, the degree to which rules and procedures are committed to writing. Concentration of authority is defined as the extent to which authority for making decisions lies at higher levels within the organization or outside the organization. Concentration of authority is measured by two scales: centralization, the extent to which formal authority for making decisions rests at higher levels of an organization; and lack of autonomy, the extent to which decisions cannot be made in the organization but are reserved for managers who are not part of it.

The abbreviated Aston schedule, with minor modifications, was used to collect data on organization structure and context.[3] Structuring of activities was measured on two of the three scales previously discussed—specialization and formalization—both of which are combined to create a single intraorganization measure. Whereas the abbreviated schedule measures organization autonomy by asking only if the formal authority for making a

---

[2] The Aston research has not gone on without some criticism. Some of this has concerned the scales and methods used in the research while other criticism has focused on the analysis and interpretation of findings. See, for example, Aldrich (1972).

[3] An abbreviated schedule was found to achieve results very similar to the original Aston schedule and requires substantially less time to complete. See Inkson, *et al.*, (1970).

TABLE 2
Summary of Measurements of Organization Context and Structure (N = 25)

	Means	Standard deviation	Observed range	Theoretical range
Size	2660	7051	70–36,000	N.A.
Dependence	4.8	2.04	0–9	0–9
Workflow Integration	6.72	3.67	0–11	0–12
Structuring of Activities	25.72	5.18	14–32	0–36
Lack of Autonomy	5.56	4.22	0–13	0–23
Centralization*	36.95	12.23	19–62	0–115

* N = 20 (data needed to measure centralization could not be obtained from five organizations).

number of decisions lies within or outside the organization, it was deemed desirable to also examine the degree to which these same decisions are centralized or decentralized within the organization. Consequently, the abbreviated schedule was modified to ask the respondent "which is the most junior level of job that has the authority to decide?" The resultant responses were scored according to the original unabbreviated Aston method. Three scales were used to measure organization context. Size of each organization was measured by the number of employees. Dependence was measured by scales which include relationships with owning or controlling organizations, if any, and other outside groups. Workflow integration was a measure of technology indicated by the degree of automated, continuous, fixed sequence operations.

The Aston questionnaire yielded data on three organization context variables (size, dependence, and workflow integration) and three structural variables (centralization, lack of autonomy, and structuring of activities). Table 2 presents the means, standard deviation, observed ranges, and theoretical ranges of these variables. In general, the organizations appear to be relatively autonomous and structured. A direct comparison of structural data from this study with other similar studies is difficult. However, general comparisons indicate close similarities between this sample and other samples on all variables.[4]

Complexity of Control Systems—A short questionnaire to measure the breadth or complexity of control systems was developed for this research. Since the questionnaire was to be administered at the same time and to the same persons as the structure and organization context questions, a format similar to the Aston questionnaire was used. Questions such as, "Is your division an Investment Center, a Profit Center, a Discretionary Cost Center, a Revenue Center, or a Standard Cost Center?" and, "At what

---

[4] For examples see Hickson, Hinings, McMillan, and Schwitter (1974) and Inkson, *et al.*, (1970). Table 2 shows our organization to be very similar to those reported in McMillan, Hickson, Hinings, and Schneck (1973).

level in the organization are performance standards established?" were asked. An *a priori* numerical scoring method was devised for the questions, with the numerical values in descending order from most to least complex. Also, each chief executive was asked to estimate the approximate number of employees involved in either planning or evaluation aspects of budgeting so that this number could be related to the total number of employees in the organization. The theoretical range of data from the complexity of control systems questionnaire was from four (simple) to twenty-one (complex) with a theoretical mid-point of 12.5. The observed range of scores was five to eighteen with an observed mean of 12.43. The mean percentage of estimates of the proportion of employees involved in making or using budgets was 10.8 percent, and the mean percentage of time reportedly spent by these employees on budget-related activities was 18.5 percent.

Budget Behavior Questionnaire—The questionnaire used to collect data on budget-related behavior was originally developed by Fertakis (1967) and has been substantially modified by Swieringa and Moncur (1975). In its original form, the questionnaire was designed to measure budget-induced pressure. It incorporates descriptions of budget-related activities and relationships to which a manager could relate his own budget situation. The original ninety-seven item questionnaire was reduced through factor analysis by Swieringa and Moncur to forty-four (shown in the Appendix). A continuous line response scale was used to measure frequency (how often does it take place?), normativeness (how often should it take place?), and the importance of each of the forty-four activities to the respondent. Each question was treated as a separate variable. The budget-related behavior data were reduced by factor analysis to uncover underlying patterns in the data. The factor analysis was conducted using the SPSS (*Special Programs for the Social Sciences*) statistical package (Nie, Bent, and Hull [1970]). A principal component analysis with iteration was conducted. The solution employed inferred factors, implying that any observed correlation between variables is due to common factors. Inferred factor techniques replace the main diagonal of the correlation matrix with communality estimates before factoring.[5] Thirteen factors were extracted with an eigenvalue greater than

---

[5] Swieringa and Moncur (1975) used a method of factor analysis which places unities in the diagonal of the correlation matrix. Only two of the factors in our analysis, FD_5 and FD_9 have an identical composition to factors reported by Swieringa and Moncur. Replacing the diagonal of our correlation matrix with unities did not change the composition of our factors substantially. Differences in factor composition may have arisen because of differences in sample size and/or sample composition. Swieringa and Moncur's sample size was 137 while ours was 284. Swieringa and Moncur sampled individuals from four companies which may have been selected because of similarities in industry, production methods, or markets. We purposely sampled from organizations from different industries, markets, and production methods. The fact that there are substantial differences between the factor results in the two studies lends support to the position that there are interorganizational differences in budget-related behavior.

one. These thirteen factors accounted for 62.4 percent of the variance, with the first factor accounting for 20.8 percent of the variance. The thirteen factors were rotated using the orthogonal varimax criteria. Variables with a loading of .40 or greater on a factor were selected as the factor's domain. Variables loading on each factor and factor loading coefficients were used to develop descriptive factor names. The factors and the variables were factorally pure (in that they loaded on only one factor). Six variables, 1, 16,

TABLE 3

Analysis of Budget-Related Behavior
Descriptive Factor Loadings (>.40) After Orthogonal Rotation, and Percentage
of Total Variance

Factor number and name	Variable number	Loading	Percentage of variance
FD_1	7	.700	20.8
Participation in planning	26	.633	
	8	.580	
	9	.560	
	5	.536	
	6	.483	
FD_2	24	.607	
Evaluation by the budget	25	.517	
	13	.417	5.9
	31	.416	
FD_3	41	.743	4.8
Enabling features of budgets	42	.643	
FD_4	38	.730	
Participation in budget systems	39	.648	4.1
	37	.476	
FD_5	34	.738	
Limiting features of budgets	35	.560	3.8
	33	.446	
FD_6	44	.760	3.4
Support from budget	43	.707	
FD_7	21	.596	3.3
Acceptance of methods	20	.573	
	23	.419	
FD_8	27	.637	
Required explanation of variances	19	.629	3.1
	32	.404	
FD_9	4	.651	2.9
Interaction with superior	18	.467	
FD_{10}	14	.544	
Difficulty in meeting budget	3	.451	2.8
	12	.422	
FD_{11}	15	.561	
Participation in feedback	36	.561	2.6
	16	.408	
FD_{12}	30	.600	2.5
	11	.417	
FD_{13}	2	.403	2.3

17, 22, 29, and 40, did not load on any factor at greater than .40. Factor scores were computed for each individual respondent.

Satisfaction scores were computed for each individual by taking the absolute value of the differences between (a) how often does it take place? and (b) how often should it take place? multiplied by the value for (c) how important is it to me? This scoring procedure is similar to that developed by Porter (1961) to measure job satisfaction except for our inclusion of an importance weighting. The rationale for this procedure is that discrepancies between what is perceived to be and what should be (i.e., equity) produce feelings of satisfaction or dissatisfaction (Vroom [1969], p. 206), and in the present context we were attempting to measure attitudes toward specific aspects of budgeting. The resultant satisfaction scores have a theoretical range of zero to twenty. Responses to all forty-four variables were skewed to the left with an observed overall mean of 2.7 and standard deviation of 1.7. These data indicate a generally high level of satisfaction with budget-related activities within the organizations sampled. Since no statistical inferences were directly made from the raw satisfaction scores, this skewness was not felt to be a serious problem.

The satisfaction scores were factor analyzed using the same technique that was used for the descriptive variables. If a subject failed to answer either parts a, b, or c on a given question, his responses were omitted from further analysis. This procedure yielded between 275 and 281 usable scores for each variable from the 284 questionnaires which were returned. Fifteen factors were extracted with an eigenvalue greater than one. Satisfaction factors and the variables which load on each are presented in table 4. All variables were factorally pure. Fourteen variables did not load on any factors (> .40). No variable loaded on Satisfaction Factor 15 (FS_{15}) (> .40). Factor scores were computed for each individual in the same manner as for the descriptive factors.

The factor scores for the thirteen descriptive factors and the fifteen satisfaction factors were averaged across each organization. These means were computed on samples of between four and thirty-one questionnaires per organization. Justification for this procedure is found in the argument that the variables were being studied as features of organizations, not as individuals within organizations:

Perceived Control—Tannenbaum's control graph questionnaire (Tannenbaum [1968]), was administered without modification with the budget behavior questionnaire. The Tannenbaum questionnaire yields data on the degree of perceived influence at six levels within the organization. Respondents are asked to indicate the amount of influence on what goes on in their organization they feel is exerted by top management, location managers, line department managers, line foremen, workers, and staff departments. A five-point Likert Scale was used to measure responses. Plotting the mean perceived control against the organization level yields a control graph for each organization. Perceived control can be represented by

TABLE 4

Analysis of Budget-Related Behavior
Satisfaction Factor Loadings (>.40) After Orthogonal Rotation, and Percentage
of Total Variance

Factor number and name	Variable number	Loading	Percentage of variance
FS$_1$	22	.726	14.9
Satisfaction with superior budget	25	.461	
behavior			
FS$_2$	9	.677	5.4
Satisfaction with participation in	8	.587	
planning	10	.548	
	6	.415	
	7	.408	
FS$_3$	43	.732	5.1
Satisfaction with usefulness of budgets	44	.698	
FS$_4$	42	.732	4.5
Satisfaction with flexibility permitted	41	.726	
by budgets			
FS$_5$	2	.519	3.6
Satisfaction with time-consuming	3	.507	
aspect of budgets			
FS$_6$	34	.633	3.5
Satisfaction with restrictive	35	.571	
features of budgets	33	.476	
FS$_7$	26	.732	3.4
Satisfaction with support from staff			
departments			
FS$_8$	40	.592	3.2
Satisfaction with outlets for discussing	23	.437	
budget matters			
FS$_9$	31	.673	3.1
Satisfaction with evaluative features	27	.406	
of budgets			
FS$_{10}$	37	.569	3.0
Satisfaction with participation in	38	.482	
budget systems			
FS$_{11}$	20	.523	2.6
Satisfaction with methods of reaching	21	.452	
the budget			
FS$_{12}$	30	.618	2.5
FS$_{13}$	16	.455	2.4
	18	.423	
FS$_{14}$	29	.455	2.3
	32	.423	

the shape of the curve (distribution of control) or the average height of the curve (the total amount of control). In this study attention was focused on total amount of perceived control. The range of these scores was from 4.27 to 1.83 with an observed mean of 2.91.

Results

Of the twenty-six organizations which agreed to participate in the study, one was excluded from the analysis because only one response to the budget behavior questionnaire was received. No imputation of causality should be made because our findings were derived through correlation analysis on cross-section data. In general our presentation of results is organized around the relationships specified in figures 1 and 2.

ORGANIZATION CONTEXT AND ORGANIZATION STRUCTURE

Table 5 represents the product moment correlation coefficients between structural and contextual variables. These are quite similar to the results obtained by previous studies employing comparable measures (McMillan, et al. [1973]) with the exception of the low significance of the negative correlation between workflow integration and lack of autonomy. Size emerged as a strong predictor of organization structure. Size and structuring of activities were strongly positively correlated ($r = .65, p < .001$), and there was a negative correlation ($r = -.39, p < .10$) between size and centralization. These results support the view that as organizations grow in size, economies of scale enable more specialists to fill role positions, and rules and procedures are developed to govern behavior. Also, size and workflow integration were correlated ($r = .46, p < .05$), and workflow integration was correlated with structuring of activities ($r = .41, p < .05$). These relationships imply that as organizations become more technologically

TABLE 5

Product Moment Correlations Between Organization Structure and Context
(N = 25)

| Variable | Depend-ence | Workflow integration | Concentration of authority | | Structuring of activities |
			Centralization*	Lack of autonomy	
Size**	−.02	.46****	−.39*****	−.03	.65***
Dependence		−.10	−.03	.35*****	.12
Workflow Integration			−.24	−.10	.41****
Concentration of Authority:					
Centralization				.76***	−.56****
Lack of Autonomy					−.12
Structuring of Activities					

* $N = 20$ (data needed to measure centralization could not be obtained from five organizations).
** Log of number of employees.
*** Significant at $p < .001$.
**** Significant at $p < .05$.
***** Significant at $p < .10$.

TABLE 6

Product Moment Correlations Between Organization Structure Variables and Selected Accounting Control Variables (N = 25)

	Structuring of activities	Concentration of authority	
		Centralization*	Lack of autonomy
Perceived Control	.39***	−.25	−.01
Control Systems Complexity	.04	−.70**	−.64**
Percentage of Employees Affected by the Budget****	.17	−.10	.16
Percentage of Time Spent on Budget Activities	.28	−.28	−.03

* $N = 20$ (data needed to measure centralization could not be obtained from five organizations).
** $p < .001$.
*** $p < .05$.
**** $N = 22$ (data needed to measure percentage of employees affected by the budget could not be obtained from three organizations).

sophisticated, they become larger and more structured.[6] Finally, structuring of activities was found to be negatively correlated with centralization ($r = -.56$, $p < .05$), supporting Child's (1972b) view that organizations exercise control either by centralizing decisions or by distributing decision-making authority but structuring roles and activities. The data appear consistent with classifying strategies for control into two extreme types: decentralized and structured organization as might be found in organizations with a more sophisticated technology, a larger number of employees, a larger number of functional specialists, and systems and procedures regulating performance; and centralization with responsibility centers dependent for decisions upon superiors and/or a parent organization.

ORGANIZATION STRUCTURE, PERCEIVED CONTROL, AND CONTROL SYSTEM COMPLEXITY

Table 6 presents the product moment correlation coefficients between perceived control, control systems complexity, mean percentage of time spent on budget-related activities, and percentage of total employees affected by the budget. Perceived control was hypothesized to be positively correlated with structuring of activities and negatively correlated with centralization and lack of autonomy. While the signs of correlation coefficients relating these variables are as predicted (see table 6), only the correlation between structuring of activities and perceived control is statistically significant ($r = .39$, $p < .05$). This finding says, in effect, that as an organization specializes, standardizes, and formalizes, the managers in our sample felt they, and others, had more control. In addition, both variables were cor-

---

[6] The causal relationships between size and technology, and structure are the subject of some debate. See for example Aldrich (1972) and Hilton (1972).

related with Descriptive Factor 1 (FD₁), participation in planning, as we will discuss below. Lack of autonomy was negatively correlated with control systems complexity ($r = -.64$, $p < .001$) as was centralization ($r = -.70$, $p < .001$). This implies that, as organizations become more independent and less centralized in terms of decision-making authority on administrative matters, the accounting system is likely to be based on broader measurements, permitting managers more discretion on how to achieve financial results.

TABLE 7
Product Moment Correlations Between Selected Organizational Variables and Thirteen Descriptive Budget Behavior Factors ($N = 25$)

Descriptive factors	Organization variables				
	Structuring of activities	Concentration of authority		Perceived control	Control systems complexity
		Centraliza-tion*	Lack of autonomy		
FD₁ Participation in Planning	.44***	.03	.09	.64**	−.10
FD₂ Evaluation by Superiors	.32	−.14	−.02	.24	.06
FD₃ Support for Innovation and Flexibility	−.35****	.11	.03	−.17	−.04
FD₄ Participation in Budget Systems	.25	−.25	.00	.12	.19
FD₅ Limiting Features of Budgets	.08	−.24	−.15	−.35****	.42***
FD₆ Support for Successful Management	−.15	.26	.02	.14	−.10
FD₇ Acceptance of Methods	−.03	−.39****	−.38****	.34****	.29
FD₈ Required Explanation of Variance	.14	.34	.39****	.03	−.28
FD₉ Interaction with Superior	−.25	−.06	−.38****	.16	.38****
FD₁₀ Difficulty in Meeting Budget	.22	.05	.16	−.03	.09
FD₁₁ Participation in Feedback	.09	−.13	−.13	.13	−.08
FD₁₂ Detail in Budgets	−.28	.34	.09	−.24	−.34****
FD₁₃ Fac. 13	.19	−.16	−.10	.30	.26

* $N = 20$ (data to measure centralization could not be obtained from five organizations).
** $p < .001$.
*** $p < .05$.
**** $p < .10$.

Tables 7 and 8 present the product moment correlation coefficients between the structural variables, the descriptive factors, and the satisfaction factors, respectively. Three aspects of budget-related behavior were examined: quantity, mode, and quality. The quantity of budget-oriented behavior was operationalized by two measures: the percentage of people in the organization involved in budget-related activities, and the percentage of a respondent's time spent on budget-related activities (involvement). Neither variable showed a significant ($p < .10$) relationship to the structure variables, although in each case the sign of the correlation was as predicted.

Structuring of Activities—Factor analysis of the budget-behavior questionnaire yielded thirteen descriptive factors which operationalized "kind of budget-related behavior." FD_1, participation in planning, was correlated with perceived control ($r = .64$, $p < .001$) and structuring of activities ($r = .44$, $p < .05$). We had hypothesized that structuring of activities would lead to higher levels of perceived control and more participation in budgeting. Holding the effects of perceived control constant yields a partial correlation of .26 between structuring of activities and participation. The reduction in the proportion of the common variance of structuring of activities and participation from 19.4% to 7.4% indicates that perceived control is an important intervening variable between structuring and participation. The argument that the direction of a causal link among these variables should be opposite, that is from participation to perceived control to structure, is not intuitively appealing. Therefore, it appears that a perceived participatory mode of budget administration is more typical of highly structured organizations partly because individuals within these organizations perceive themselves as exercising more control.

FD_3, support for innovation and flexibility, correlates negatively with structuring of activities, ($r = -.35$, $p < .10$). This is consistent with the idea that highly structured organizations are associated with routine, standardized activities. Controlling the effects of size yields a partial correlation between structuring of activities and FD_3 of $r = -.50$ ($p < .01$), which lends support to the argument that role formalization and specialization and not size decreases the extent to which the budget is seen as permitting flexibility and innovation. Contrary to expectations, there was no significant correlation between FD_6, support for successful management, and structuring of activities or any of the intervening variables.

Finally, additional evidence on the relationship between structuring of activities and budget-related behavior is found in the relationships between that variable and the satisfaction factors which were developed to operationalize "quality of budget-related behavior." Recall that the satisfaction scores were created by subtracting the normative value of a variable ("How often *should* I ask for assistance from staff departments. . . .?") from the descriptive value ("How often *do* I ask . . .?"), and multiplying the absolute

TABLE 8

Product Moment Correlations Between Selected Organization Variables and Fifteen
Budget Behavior Satisfaction Factors (N = 25)

Satisfaction factors	Organization variables				
	Structuring of activities	Concentration of authority		Perceived control	Control system complexity
		Centraliza-tion*	Lack of autonomy		
FS₁ Satisfaction with Superior-Subordinate Relationship	−.01	−.30	−.57***	−.09	.30
FS₂ Satisfaction with Participation in Planning	−.20	.02	−.30	−.22	.02
FS₃ Satisfaction with Usefulness of Budgets	.06	.36	.45***	−.18	−.16
FS₄ Satisfaction with Flexibility Permitted by Budgets	.21	.15	.40***	.40***	−.23
FS₅ Satisfaction with Time-Consuming Aspects of Budget	−.16	.21	.10	.03	.02
FS₆ Satisfaction with Restrictive Features of Budget	.27	−.26	−.21	.14	.31
FS₇ Satisfaction with Support from Staff Departments	−.43***	.14	−.21	−.25	.02
FS₈ Satisfaction with Outlets for Discussing Budget Matters	.13	−.02	−.26	−.03	.09
FS₉ Satisfaction with Evaluative Features of Budget	−.31	.23	.02	−.09	−.08
FS₁₀ Satisfaction with Participation in Budget Systems	.03	.00	.00	−.09	−.19
FS₁₁ Satisfaction with Methods of Reaching the Budget	−.12	.14	.09	.31	−.25
FS₁₂ Factor 12	.28	−.33	−.18	.30	.05
FS₁₃ Satisfaction with Participation in Budget Achievement	.33****	−.03	−.11	−.15	.11
FS₁₄ Factor 14	−.12	.24	−.12	−.06	−.31
FS₁₅ Factor 15	.09	.08	−.15	.03	−.01

* $N = 20$ (data to measure centralization could not be obtained from five organizations).

** $p < .001$.

*** $p < .05$.

**** $p < .10$.

154

value of the differences by the importance ("How important is this to me?"). Thus, a high score indicates greater dissatisfaction.

Structuring of activities was negatively correlated ($r = -.43, p < .05$) with Satisfaction Factor 7 (FS_7), satisfaction with support from staff departments, which implies that greater structure is associated with greater satisfaction in asking for assistance from staff departments. The positive relation of FS_{13}, satisfaction with participation in budget achievement, with structuring of activities ($r = .33, p < .10$) implies that, as activities become more structured, satisfaction with participation in budget achievement is diminished.

However, we further investigated these relationships using partial correlation analysis which allowed us to control the effect of size (remember, size is highly correlated with structuring of activities). The results were that the new correlation of FS_7 and structuring of activities became statistically not significant ($r = -.26, p > .10$), and the correlation of FS_{13}, satisfaction with participation in budget achievement, with structuring of activities also became statistically not significant ($r = .21, p > .10$). Thus, both of these relationships appear to be influenced by the size of the organization.

Concentration of Authority—In this report we have separated the dimension of concentration of authority into two parts based on the scale used to measure it: centralization, or the extent to which decisions are reserved to high levels in the organization; and lack of autonomy, or the extent to which decisions are made outside the organization under study. Each of these scales was found to be negatively correlated with the complexity of control systems (see table 5). This implies that the more decisions are centralized or removed from the purview of an organization the less complex the organization's control system is likely to be. But concentration of authority is also linked to budget-related behavior in other important ways, for we found significant correlations between centralization and lack of autonomy and FD_7, acceptance of methods, FD_8, required explanation of variances, and FD_9, interaction with superior.

FD_7, FD_8, and FD_9 describe superior-subordinate relationships in budgeting. FD_7, acceptance of methods, correlates negatively with centralization ($r = -.39, p < .10$) and lack of autonomy ($r = -.38 \ p < .10$) and positively with perceived control ($r = .34, p < .10$), indicating that, as the organization becomes more centralized and less autonomous, individuals perceive having less independence and more interference from superiors and subordinates on budgeting matters. This is consistent with responses to FD_8, required explanation of variances, which was correlated with lack of autonomy ($r = .39, p < .10$). Further, the relationship between superiors and subordinates is not participative or advisory as revealed by the negative correlation of FD_9, interaction with superior, with lack of autonomy ($r = -.38, p < .10$). These relationships are interrelated with the effects of control system complexity. Holding the effects of control system complexity constant by calculating partial correlations decreases the common variance between FD_7, FD_8, and FD_9 with lack of autonomy and centralization more than one-half. Taken collectively these results support a conclusion that concentration of authority, complexity of control systems, and mode of budget administration are intertwined in organizations which lack autonomy or are centralized.

Analysis of the relationship between lack of autonomy and satisfaction factor FS_1, satisfaction with superior-subordinate relationship, may shed additional light on the nature and effects of the superior-subordinate relationship. FS_1 is negatively correlated with lack of autonomy ($r = -.57$, $p < .05$), which would seem to imply that as an organization becomes less autonomous and fewer decisions are required of managers, those managers find themselves more satisfied with superior-subordinate contacts about budget variances and their efficiency. One interpretation of these relationships would be that, as lack of autonomy increases, managers spend less time working with superiors on budget planning (FD_9), and they are more satisfied by their superior-subordinate contacts concerning comparisons of budgets and results.[7] But to further complicate these relationships, both FS_3, satisfaction with the usefulness of budgets, and FS_4, satisfaction with flexibility permitted by the budget, are positively correlated with lack of autonomy ($r = .45$, $p < .05$; $r = .40$, $p < .05$). This implies that lack of autonomy increases dissatisfaction with the usefulness of budgets and perceptions of the flexibility and innovation they encourage.

Perceived Control and Control Systems Complexity—The linkage we hypothesized between structure and budget-related behavior included linkages through the financial (accounting) control system and the control perceived by organization members. Where appropriate, the interrelationships between these intervening variables, organization structure, and budget-related behavior have been discussed above. Nevertheless, our analysis reveals additional relationships, apparently independent from structural variables, which are worthy of mention. Perceived control was found to be negatively correlated with FD_5, limiting features of budgets ($r = -.35$, $p < .10$) and positively correlated with FD_7, acceptance of methods ($r = .34$, $p < .10$). Recalling the statistically significant relationship between perceived control and FD_1, participation in planning, the degree of perceived control appears to be related in important ways to budget-related behavior.

Furthermore, involvement was correlated with perceived control, ($r = .43$, $p < .05$). It appears as if the order implied by structuring of activities

---

[7] DeCoster and Fertakis (1968) reported that budget-induced pressure was positively correlated with both initiating structure and consideration as measured by the Ohio State Leadership Questionnaire. If FD_7, FD_8, and FD_9 are representative of initiating structure and if FS_1 is reflecting consideration by the leader, these results would suggest that DeCoster and Fertakis sampled predominantly centralized organizations lacking in autonomy.

reduces the uncertainties associated with centralized or external management, and people feel they are a part of their organization. This conclusion is consistent with our hypotheses.

Control system complexity was positively correlated with FD_5, limiting features of budgets ($r = .42$, $p < .05$), negatively correlated with FD_{12}, detail in budgets ($r = -.34$, $p < .10$), and, as was previously discussed, correlated with FD_9, interaction with superior ($r = .38$, $p < .10$). These relationships imply that complex control systems lead to perceptions that budgets limit activities, giving less attention to detail, and working more with superiors in preparing and achieving budgets. Other explanations of these interesting findings might be that complex systems are not as well understood and therefore are perceived as limiting activities, or are ignored, or require managers to seek help and approval from superiors.

Discussion

In reviewing the relationships between organization structure and budget-related behavior several complex relationships appear. While in general the structural and intervening variables explained only a portion of the variance in budget-related behavior, there are definite and important relationships which appear worthy of future investigation. The existence of these relationships points to some limitations in existing research on budgetary behavior. Since a portion of budget-related behavior is explained by organization structure, inferences from studies based on limited samples drawn from organizations of unknown structural properties must be made carefully. Moreover, universal policy prescriptions about how budgets should be prepared would be unwise.

The relationships between organization context, organization structure, and budget-related behavior are consistent with the view that organization control strategies may be dichotomized into two general categories, decentralized but structured, and centralized. Further, these general forms of organization control tend to elicit particular types of budget-related behavior. For discussion purposes we chose to label the set of variables associated with decentralized but structured organizations as the Administrative Control Strategy, and those variables associated with centralized organizations as the Interpersonal Control Strategy.

ADMINISTRATIVE CONTROL

Figure 3 summarizes the observed relationships among the variables which appear to be typical of an Administrative Control Strategy. This control strategy predominates in larger, more technologically sophisticated organizations. Formalized and standardized operating procedures predominate, and there tend to be more specialists. Work-related behavior is governed by rules, but managers tend to perceive themselves and others as having more control. Managers within these organizations perceive

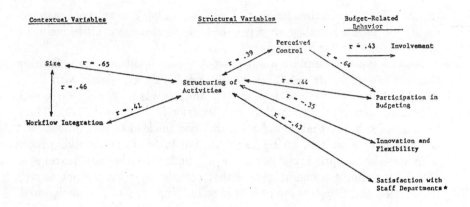

* For this factor, a low score indicates greater satisfaction.

FIG. 3.—The administrative control strategy.

themselves as participating in setting budgetary goals and spend more time on budgetary activities. Managers tend to see the budget as limiting innovation and flexibility in structured organizations.

One of the more interesting aspects of this scenario is the relationship of participation in budget planning with structuring of activities and perceived control. The accounting and related behavioral science literature contains conflicting admonitions with respect to the value of participatory approaches to budgeting. Argyris (1952), Hofstede (1967) and Becker and Green (1962) have emphasized the potential positive effects of participatory budgeting. On the other hand, Stedry (1960) suggested that in some cases it may be more beneficial for management to set the budget. Morse and Reimer (1956) reported results showing that nonparticipatory groups outperformed participatory groups. The present study showed a strong relationship between participation and perceived control and between perceived control and structuring of activities. Assuming that organizations "learn" management techniques which are suited to their needs, these findings may indicate that participatory approaches to budgeting are more suited to, and perhaps more effective in, structured organizations.

INTERPERSONAL CONTROL

Figure 4 summarizes the observed relationships among the variables associated with an Interpersonal Control Strategy. This strategy predominates in organizations which are small or dependent on other organizations. Typically, important decisions are either centralized within the organization or referred to outside authority. Financial control systems tend to be based on simple or narrowly defined measures (i.e., variances from standard cost). Budget-related behavior factors which correlated with lack

158

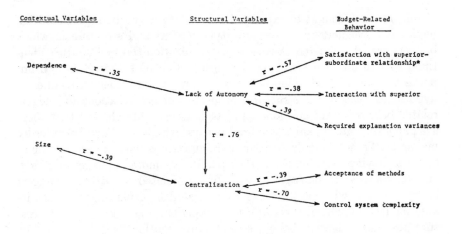

Fig. 4.—The interpersonal control strategy.

of autonomy and centralization centered mainly on the superior-subordinate relationship. Individuals perceive themselves as having more interaction with superiors and subordinates on budget-related matters, their methods of reaching the budget are not accepted, and they are required to explain budget variances. However, the individuals surveyed report being satisfied with their superior-subordinate relationship. These findings support the position that interpersonal control may predominate in organizations that are centralized and lack autonomy. Lack of autonomy is associated with possible pressure-inducing actions by superiors who do not accept methods used to reach budgeted performance and require explanation of variances. Lack of autonomy seems to be related to a reduction in interaction between superiors and subordinates during budget preparation and about means to achieve the budget, but this does not seem to be linked with dissatisfaction about superior-subordinate behavior regarding variances or subordinate efficiency.

The results seem to support the findings of Argyris (1952) in part. Budgets do seem a potential source of budget-related pressure in organizations which are centralized or lack autonomy, but they do not seem to lead to perceptions of dissatisfaction about the relationships of the subordinate to the superior. On the contrary, subordinates report being satisfied with their superiors' demands regarding discussion of variances and subordinate efficiency as revealed through budgets. Whether this results from recognition that in a centralized organization "the boss is the boss, and therefore, what he does is right," or that satisfaction is induced through the interpersonal relationships developed in the centralized organization cannot be determined from our data.

Summary and Conclusions

This research sought to explore the extent to which budget-related behavior is dependent on the organization context and structure in which budgets are administered. A review of organization theory literature identified structuring of activities and concentration of authority as two important means of controlling behavior within organizations. A number of hypotheses relating the structural properties of organizations to budget-related behavior were developed and tested. The data showed that there are important interorganizational differences in budget-related behavior by managers. Those in highly structured organizations tend to perceive themselves as having more influence, they participate more in budget planning, and they appear to be satisfied with budget-related activities. Managers in organizations where authority is concentrated are generally held accountable for fewer financial variables, they experience superior-initiated pressure, they see budgets as being less useful and limiting their flexibility, but they appear to be satisfied with the use of budgets by their superiors.

By seeking to relate structural measures to budget-related behavior, we have not sought to link contextual variables to budget-related behavior directly. But we cannot conclude this discussion without some comments about the practical managerial implications of doing so. Where a choice or change in organizational control system is indicated, change in the organization structure might be a means of enhancing the effectiveness of budgetary control. This research shows high participation and perceived control are associated with structuring of activities. Two contextual variables, size of organization and technology, are significantly, positively correlated with structuring activities. One possible implication of this is that large, process dominated, technological organizations may be not as inhumane as they have been pictured in some places. For increased size and advanced process technology lead to or are at least correlated with structuring of activities, and structuring implies distribution of authority and an increase in perceived control as well as increased participation in planning and feelings of involvement on the part of managers. Those who speak against large organizational units may be ignoring the countervailing tendency of size to lead to structuring of activities and greater job involvement.

APPENDIX

Budget Behavior Questionnaire (Variables)

1. I start preparing the budget for my unit before I am asked to.
2. I spend time outside of normal working hours preparing the budget for my unit.
3. I am not able to spend as much time as I would like preparing the budget for my unit.
4. I work with my superior in preparing the budget for my unit.
5. I work with my subordinates in preparing the budget for my unit.

6. I work with other unit heads in preparing the budget for my unit.
7. I work with financial staff people in preparing the budget for my unit.
8. I am consulted about special factors I would like to have included in the budget being prepared.
9. New budgets include changes I have suggested.
10. The budget is not finalized until I am satisfied with it.
11. Preparing the budget for my unit requires my attention to a great number of details.
12. I am reminded of the importance of meeting the budget for my unit.
13. I am evaluated on my ability to meet the budget for my unit.
14. I have difficulty meeting the budget for my unit.
15. I am shown comparisons of actual and budgeted performance for other units.
16. My explanation of budget variances is included in performance reports.
17. I investigate favorable as well as unfavorable budget variances for my unit.
18. I go to my superior for advice on how to achieve my budget.
19. I am required to prepare reports comparing actual results with budget.
20. My methods of reaching budgeted performance are accepted without question by my subordinates.
21. My methods of reaching budgeted performance are not accepted without question by my subordinates.
22. My superior calls me in to discuss variations from the budget.
23. My superior accepts my explanation of budget variations in my unit.
24. My superior expresses dissatisfaction to me about results in my unit when the budget has not been met.
25. My superior mentions budgets when talking to me about my efficiency as a manager.
26. I ask for assistance from staff departments concerned with budgeting.
27. I am required to submit an explanation in writing about causes of large budget variances.
28. I use the budget to plan activities in my unit.
29. I am required to trace the cause of budget variances to groups or individuals within my unit.
30. I personally investigate budget variances in my unit.
31. I evaluate my subordinates by means of the budget.
32. I am required to report actions I take to correct causes of budget variances.
33. I find it necessary to stop some activities in my unit when budgeted funds are used up.
34. I find it necessary to charge some activities to other accounts when budgeted funds for these activities have been used up.
35. I have to shift figures relating to operations to reduce budget variances.
36. Budget matters are mentioned in informal conversations.
37. I express my opinions on budget matters.
38. I offer suggestions for the improvement of budget systems.

39. The budgeting system is changed in accordance with my suggestions.
40. I discuss budget items when problems occur.
41. The budget enables me to be more flexible.
42. The budget enables me to be more innovative.
43. The budget enables me to keep track of my success as a manager.
44. The budget enables me to be a better manager.

REFERENCES

ALDRICH, H. E. "Technology and Organization Structure: A Re-examination of Findings of the Aston Group." *Administrative Science Quarterly* (March 1972): 26–43.

ARGYRIS, C. *The Impact of Budgets on People* (The Controllership Foundation, 1952).

——. *Personality and Organization; the Conflict Between Systems and the Individual* (Harper, 1957).

——. *Understanding Organizational Behavior* (Dorsey Press, 1960).

——. *Integrating the Individual and the Organization* (John Wiley and Sons, 1964).

BARNARD, C. I. *The Function of the Executive* (Harvard University Press, 1938).

BECKER, S. and D. GREEN, JR. "Budgeting and Employee Behavior." *The Journal of Business* (October 1962): 392–402.

BLAU, P. M. and R. M. SCHOENHERR. *The Structure of Organizations* (Basic Books, 1971).

BURNS, T. and G. M. STALKER. *The Management of Innovation* (Tavistock, 1968).

CHANDLER, A. D., JR. *Strategy and Structure* (M.I.T. Press, 1962).

CHILD, J. "Organizational Structure, Environment and Performance—The Role of Strategic Choice." *Sociology* (January 1972a): 1–22.

——. "Organization Structure and Strategies of Control: A Replication of the Aston Study." *Administrative Science Quarterly* (June 1972b): 163–77.

——. "Strategies of Control and Organizational Behavior." *Administrative Science Quarterly* (March 1973): 1–17.

CROZIER, M. *The Bureaucratic Phenomenon* (University of Chicago Press, 1964).

DeCOSTER, D. T. and J. P. FERTAKIS. "Budget-Induced Pressure and Its Relationship to Supervisory Behavior." *Journal of Accounting Research* 6 (Autumn 1968): 237–46.

FERTAKIS, J. P. "Budget-Induced Pressure and Its Relationship to Supervisory Behavior in Selected Organizations." Doctoral dissertation. University of Washington, 1967.

FIEDLER, F. W. *A Theory of Leadership Effectiveness* (McGraw-Hill, 1967).

FORAN, M. F. AND D. T. DeCOSTER. "An Experimental Study of the Effects of Participation, Authoritarianism, and Feedback on Cognitive Dissonance in a Standard Setting Situation." *The Accounting Review* (October 1974): 751–63.

GOULDNER, A. W. *Patterns of Industrial Bureaucracy* (Free Press, 1954).

HICKSON, D. "A Convergence in Organization Theory." *Administrative Science Quarterly* (September 1966): 244–37.

——, C. R. HININGS, C. J. McMILLAN, and J. P. SCHWITTER. "The Culture-Free Context of Organization Structure: A Tri-National Comparison." *Sociology* (January 1974): 59–80.

HILTON, G. "Causal Inference Analysis: A Seductive Process." *Administrative Science Quarterly* (March 1972): 44–57.

HININGS, C. R. and G. L. LEE. "Dimensions of Organization Structure and Their Context: A Replication." *Sociology* (January 1971): 83–93.

HOFSTEDE, G. H. *The Game of Budget Control* (Van Gorcum, 1967).

HOPWOOD, A. G. "An Empirical Study of the Role of Accounting Data in Performance Evaluation." *Empirical Research in Accounting: Selected Studies, 1972.* Supplement to *Journal of Accounting Research* 10: 156–82.

——. "Leadership Climate and the Use of Accounting Data in Performance Evaluation." *The Accounting Review* (July 1974): 485–95.

INKSON, J. H. K., D. S. PUGH, and D. J. HICKSON. "Organization Context and Structure: An Abbreviated Replication." *Administrative Science Quarterly* (September 1970): 318-29.

LAWRENCE, P. R. and J. W. LORSCH. *Organization and Environment* (Harvard University, 1967).

McGREGOR, D. *The Human Side of Enterprise* (McGraw-Hill, 1960).

McMILLAN, C. J., D. J. HICKSON, C. R. HININGS, and R. E. SCHNECK. "The Structure of Work Organizations Across Societies." *Academy of Management Journal* (December 1973): 555–69.

MECHANIC, D. "Source of Power of Lower Participants in Complex Organizations." *Administrative Science Quarterly* (December 1962): 349-64.

MORSE, N. C. and E. REIMER. "Experimental Change of a Major Organizational Variable." *Journal of Abnormal and Social Psychology* (1956): 120-29.

NIE, N., D. H. BENT, and C. H. HULL. *Statistical Package for the Social Sciences* (McGraw-Hill, 1970).

PERROW, C. "A Framework for the Comparative Analysis of Organizations." *American Sociological Review* (April 1967): 194–208.

PORTER, L. W. "A Study of Perceived Need Satisfaction in Bottom and Middle Management Jobs." *Journal of Applied Psychology* (1961): 8–10.

PUGH, D. S., D. J. HICKSON, and C. R. HININGS. "An Empirical Taxonomy of Structure of Work Organizations." *Administrative Science Quarterly* (March 1969): 115–26.

——, D. J. HICKSON, C. R. HININGS, K. M. MacDONALD, C. TURNER, and T. LUPTON. "A Conceptual Scheme for Organizational Analysis." *Administrative Science Quarterly* (December 1963): 289–315.

——, D. J. HICKSON, C. R. HININGS, and C. TURNER. "Dimensions of Organization Structure." *Administrative Science Quarterly* (June 1968): 65–105.

——, D. J. HICKSON, C. R. HININGS, and C. TURNER. "The Context of Organization Structures." *Administrative Science Quarterly* (March 1969): 91–114.

SEARFOSS, D. G. and R. M. MONCZKA. "Perceived Participation in the Budget Process and Motivation to Achieve the Budget." *Academy of Management Journal* (December 1973): 541-54.

STEDRY, A. C. *Budget Control and Cost Behavior* (Prentice-Hall, 1960).

——, and E. KAY. "The Effect of Goal Difficulty on Performance: A Field Experiment." *Behavioral Science* (November 1966): 451-70.

SWIERINGA, R. J. and R. H. MONCUR. "The Relationship Between Managers' Budget-Oriented Behavior and Selected Attitude, Position, Size, and Performance Measures." *Empirical Research in Accounting: Selected Studies, 1972.* Supplement to *Journal of Accounting Research* 10: 194–209.

——, and R. H. MONCUR. *Some Effects of Participative Budgeting on Managerial Behavior* (New York: National Association of Accountants, 1975).

TANNENBAUM, A. S. *Control in Organizations* (McGraw-Hill, 1968).

THOMPSON, J. D. *Organizations in Action* (McGraw-Hill, 1967).

VANCIL, R. F. "What Kind of Management Control Do You Need?" *Harvard Business Review* (March–April 1973): 75-86.

VROOM, V. H. "Industrial Social Psychology." *Handbook of Social Psychology*, Vol. 5. G. Lindsay and E. Aronson, Eds. (Addison-Wesley, 1969): 196–268.

——. *Some Personality Determinants of the Effects of Participation* (Prentice-Hall, 1960).

WEBER, M. *The Theory of Social and Economic Organizations* (Oxford University Press, 1947).

WOODWARD, J. *Industrial Organization: Theory and Practice* (Oxford University Press, 1965).

The Impact of People on Budgets

MICHAEL SCHIFF
New York University

ARIE Y. LEWIN
Duke University

IN THE past decade budgets have become widely accepted as the key element in the corporation's planning and control system. This is evident both from the extensive writings on the subject and from a random sampling of current textbooks in management in which the discussion of operational planning and control centers about the role and use of financial budgets.[1]

Financial budgets represent the firm's plans for the coming year summarized in projected financial statements. Because financial budgets are plans they become the criteria by which managerial performance is measured and therefore the basis of the control system. Indeed, whereas budgets have this dual role, of being plans and performance criteria, they are generally viewed as synonymous with control and not with planning.[2] Moreover, it is their use as control devices that has made budgets the focus of much criticism by behavioral scientists who view them as a coercive instrument used by top management to "enforce" its objectives on the participants of the organization.

It is the purpose of this article to review the role of financial budgets in the corporate planning and control process by reexamining the relationship between controller and the controlled.

THE TRADITIONAL ACCOUNTING MODEL OF THE FIRM

The most prevalent management accounting model of the firm is founded on classical economic theory of the corporation and the traditional Tayloristic model of the organization. The main features of this model are the emphasis on authority, accountability and control and the assumption that the organization members are passive participants. Indeed, most existing control practices assume the controlled to be passive elements within the controller-controlled relationship. As Caplan in his comparison of the behavioral decision-making model of organizations and the traditional model notes, the two models differ in their treatment of the role of humans in organizations.[3] In the behavioral model, humans are viewed as being goal directed, constrained by the cognitive limits on their rationality and possessing individual personalities. The emphasis is on the individual, his goals and aspirations and how he achieves them.[4]

[1] See for example the extensive bibliography presented in Y. Ijiri, J. C. Kinard, and F. B. Putney, "An Integrated Evaluation System for Budget Forecasting and Operating Performance with a Classified Budgeting Bibliography," *Journal of Accounting Research*, Vol. 6, No. 1, (Spring 1968), pp. 11–28.

[2] For an excellent summary and review on the applications of budgets, see G. H. Hofstede, *The Game of Budget Control*, (Van Gorcum and Comp. N. V. Assen, 1967), pp. 8–103.

[3] E. H. Caplan, "Behavioral Assumptions of Management Accounting," THE ACCOUNTING REVIEW, Vol. XLI, (July 1966), pp. 496–509.

[4] *Idem.*

The Tayloristic model of organizations has been further criticized by the participative advocates of organizations. These writers,[5] accept the view that organization members have aspirations and individual personalities, but firmly believe that organizations must provide the environment within which each individual can satisfy his needs as well as achieving the organization goals. According to the participative view, existing organizations are coercive systems along the lines of the Tayloristic model because of their insistence on accountability and control. Moreover in their view it is the use of imposed budgets which is instrumental to achievement of control and conformity.[6]

The emphasis on budgeting by the critics of traditional organizations derives from their equating control with coercion and from their belief that only in a participative environment is it possible to maximize organization effectiveness and individual satisfaction. As Leavitt points out, it is naive to describe organizations as "unhuman."[7] Indeed, many features of traditional organizations which are anathema to participative beliefs, such as division of labor, are necessary for the effective functioning of organizations.

It seems to us that the participative advocates of management, just as the traditionalists before them, fail to consider the goal-directed nature of human behavior. The Taylorists neglected humans altogether, whereas the participative practitioners believe that all humans in organizations should be able to self-actualize.

A More Pragmatic View
of Organizations

Clearly, as Leavitt has pointed out, organizations do not fit the Tayloristic model and cannot be identified as being either coercive or unhuman.[8] The main characteristic of real organizations is that they have to achieve complex tasks and objectives through the many efforts of their diverse participants. Indeed, Fayol was quite correct when he stated that:

The managerial function finds its only outlet through the members of the organization (body corporate). Whilst the other functions bring into play material and machines the managerial function operates only on the personnel.[9]

Dale in his discussion of management and the organization concludes that "Management is getting things done through other people."[10]

Whereas the organization may have specific objectives, activities and work flows which need to be achieved, it necessarily relies on humans who differ in their aspirations, perceptions, personalities, and capabilities to achieve them. Indeed, we need to understand why individuals join a particular organization, why they stay in or leave it, and what are the principle processes around which organizations revolve.

March and Simon have shown that the individual's decision to join, stay, or leave any organization depends on the interaction of a number of personal and situational variables.[11] Basically the individual seeks an organization which in his estimation will be instrumental to the achievement of his personal goals while he is furthering the organization goals. It is

[5] See for example the writings of H. A. Shepard, "Changing Interpersonal and Intergroup Relations in Organizations," in J. G. March, (ed) *Handbook of Organizations*, (Rand McNally & Co., 1967), pp. 1115–1144.
R. Likert, *The Human Organization: Its Management and Value*, (McGraw Hill, 1967).
D. McGregor, *The Human Side of Enterprise*, (McGraw Hill, 1961).
[6] This point is particularly emphasized by C. Argyris, *The Impact of Budgets on People*, (The Controllership Foundation, 1952), p. 25.
S. Becker and D. Green, "Budgeting and Employee Behavior," *Journal of Business*, Vol. 35, pp. 392–402.
[7] H. J. Leavitt, "Unhuman Organizations," *Harvard Business Review*, (July-August 1962), pp. 90–98.
[8] *Idem.*
[9] H. Fayol, *General and Industrial Management*, (Pitman, 1949), p. 19.
[10] E. Dale, *Management: Theory and Practice*, (McGraw-Hill, 1965), p. 4.
[11] J. G. March and H. A. Simon, *Organizations*, (Wiley, 1958), pp. 84–110.

clear that this does not imply a consistency between the individual's goals and the organization goals. Indeed, it suggests that some degree of latent conflict is always present within organizations. This conflict may occur between individuals and/or between sub-units of the organization and/or between individuals and their sub-units. These conflicts, as Cyert and March point out, revolve around the organization resource allocation processes, and are reflected in its continuing problem solving and decision making activities.[12]

Williamson has similarly observed that managers are motivated to achieve two sets of goals—the firm's goals and their personal goals. Personal goals, according to Williamson, are directly related to income (salary plus bonuses), size of staff, and discretionary control over allocation of resources. Williamson's conclusion was that managers can best achieve both their personal goals and the firm goals in a slack environment,[13] suggesting that managers will attempt to influence the budget process and obtain slack budgets.

The traditional budget and control system, however, operates on the principle of management by exception. Since budgets are the criteria for measuring performance, and management participates in their formulation, it clearly serves management's interests to influence the performance criteria incorporated in the budget. Lower level management, therefore, can be expected to strive for a budget which it feels is attainable and, at the same time, to meet top management's requirement for a desirable net income.

Thus, rather than viewing the organization as a coercive system, it is perforce quite participative, involving a dynamic interlevel bargaining process over goals, objectives and the means to these objectives (resource allocations). The budget preparation process satisfies the need for planning the operations of the firm, and the resulting budget serves as a mutually agreed upon control device for monitoring the activities of the various sub-units. Furthermore, the process of preparing the budget is highly instrumental in resolving the conflict among the various participants about organizational goals and resource allocation commitment and at the same time is precedent dependent.

Cyert and March defined organizational slack as the difference between the total resources available to the firm and the total necessary to maintain the organization coalition.[14] These slack resources arise from the imperfection of the resource allocation process and become available as additional payments to the organization participants. By comparison the resource allocation process of the firm in conventional economics allows for no slack under equilibrium conditions. Slack, furthermore, may be widely distributed or undistributed.[15] As the term implies, undistributed slack refers to resources which are recognizable and have not been distributed, such as idle cash and securities. Distributed slack refers to resources present in the firm in the form of "invisible" costs spread through the organization and hence not readily ascertained. In this paper we are concerned with the latter type of slack.

In a very real sense, then, every firm operates with slack resources which, in theory at least, are distributed in some way to all the participants of the organization. Thus, for example, shareholders may be paid dividends in excess of those required to keep them from selling their shares. Similarly workers may be paid excessive wages and executives may receive

[12] R. M. Cyert and J. G. March, *The Behavioral Theory of the Firm*, (Prentice Hall, 1963), pp. 26–127.
[13] O. E. Williamson, *The Economics of Discretionary Behavior: Managerial Objectives in a Theory of the Firm*, (Prentice Hall, 1964), pp. 28–37.
[14] Cyert and March, *op. cit.*, pp. 36–38.
[15] *Ibid.*, pp. 36–38, 279.

incentive compensation, services and luxuries beyond the minimum required to secure their continued participation in the organization.

Clearly, many more instances of distributed slack in the Cyert and March terms can be described. Our concern, however, is manager oriented. We have seen that slack exists and that managers possess the necessary motives to desire to operate in slack environment. For most corporations this environment is embodied in the budget document, and therefore it should not be surprising if managers attempted to influence the budget process and bargain for slack budgets. Stated differently, managers will create slack in budgets through a process of *understating revenues and overstating costs*. The last statement is an operational definition of slack.

A search of the literature, however, reveals that the problem of slack in budgets has not received much research attention although it is implicitly recognized throughout the budget literature. Stedry, on the basis of a laboratory experiment on levels of aspiration, suggests that the workers' aspirations affect their performance and that the budgetary process can be employed to impart to the worker higher aspirations resulting in a commitment to higher performance levels.[16] Lowe and Shaw report on downward bias introduced in sales forecasts by line managers aimed at assuring good performance where rewards were related to forecasts.[17] Dalton reports various examples of department managers who allocated resources to what they considered justifiable purposes which were not authorized in their budgets.[18] Shillinglaw notes that budgets can be extremely vulnerable when used to measure divisional performance because of the great control that division management exercises in the preparation of the budget and on the reporting of results.[19]

Williamson studied the slack content in

the budgets of three companies over a period of time in which the companies passed from profitable to significantly less profitable states. In his report he identifies the actions of top management (incumbent or new) in controlling and reducing costs. Based on his analysis there emerges a close correlation between the type of cost reductions undertaken and the expense categories in which slack would accumulate. Thus Williamson reports that the cost reduction programs would result in decreases in employment, decreases in overhead, decreases in corporate staffs, decreases in R&D expenditures, etc.[20]

Whereas the data reported by Williamson is clearly supportive of the occurrence of slack, it does not detail the role of managers in this process and does not relate it specifically to the annual budget process. A detailed description of how managers build slack into their budgets by understating revenues and overstating costs was reported by Schiff and Lewin[21] in their study of the budget process of three divisions, parts of multi-division companies. The study involved a two year budget sequence and detailed the process whereby managers satisfied personal aspirations through the use of slack in "good years" and reconverted slack into profits in bad years. Schiff and Lewin reported that division management generally created slack in their budgets by underestimating gross

[16] A. C. Stedry, *Budget Control and Cost Behavior*, (Prentice Hall, 1960).

[17] A. E. Lowe and R. W. Shaw, "An Analysis of Managerial Biasing: Evidence from a Company's Budgeting Process," *The Journal of Management Studies*, Vol. 5, No. 3, (October 1968) pp. 304–315.

[18] M. Dalton, *Men Who Manage*, (Wiley, 1959), pp. 36–38.

[19] G. Shillinglaw, "Divisional Performance Review: An Extension of Budgetary Control," In C. P. Bonini, R. K. Jaedicke, and H. M. Wagner, (eds) *Management Controls: New Directions in Basic Research*, (McGraw-Hill, 1964), pp. 149–163.

[20] Williamson, *op. cit.*, pp. 85–126.

[21] M. Schiff and A. Y. Lewin, "Where Traditional Budgeting Fails," *Financial Executive*, Vol. XXXVI, No. 5, pp. 51–62.

revenue, inclusion of discretionary increases in personnel requirements, establishment of marketing and sales budgets with internal limits on funds to be spent, use of manufacturing costs based on standard costs which do not reflect process improvements operationally available at the plant, and the inclusion of discretionary "special" projects.

Understating gross revenue was generally accomplished by understating potential unit sales and average expected unit prices. This normally was more than sufficient in accommodating expected top management requests for higher profits at budget review sessions.

Examples of discretionary budgetary allocations included increases in the budgeted personnel positions. These positions, however, were staffed progressively as the year's operating results met expectations. In other words, the additional personnel positions under adverse conditions would not be staffed and the savings in budgeted salaries would appear as increases in divisional net income. The same basic procedure was observed in regard to advertising budgets, promotional programs, sales meetings, training programs and allocations to special projects.

The observations that the introduction of operationally available process improvements in the manufacturing process was a discretionary managerial decision is quite significant. Based on the observations of Schiff and Lewin it would appear that standard manufacturing costs may include slack in terms of unincorporated process improvements. In the example cited by Schiff and Lewin such process improvements were introduced by management, again only under adverse conditions and were kept on the "shelf" otherwise.

The research reviewed here clearly raises the issue of the influence which various managerial levels have on the outcome of a company's financial budget, particularly

in terms of the slack which they strive to build into it. This slack may be quite significant and according to estimates by Schiff and Lewin may account for as much as 20–25 percent of a division's budgeted operating expenses. Similar estimates can be derived from the data reported by Williamson.

The Role of the Controller

The type of control system employed by the corporation may also be a factor in how slack is created within a division and how it is managed. For some time corporations have tended to decentralize their control system, partly in response to the participative critics of the traditional coercive organizations but mainly in the hope of improvements in the decision making process and in anticipation of tighter control over costs. The main feature of the decentralized control system is the creation of control positions on the division and subdivision level (sometimes down to the plant level) staffed with controllers who are directly responsible to the corporate controller.[22]

It appears, however, that in the decentralized companies the divisional controller, while formally responsible to the corporate controller, is in fact a key member of the division top management, and is closely involved in achieving division objectives. Thus Schiff and Lewin report that the divisional controller appears to have undertaken the task of creating and managing divisional slack and is most influential in the internal allocation of this slack.[23]

This apparently unexpected behavior may be due to a number of causes. Generally in the decentralized company the divisional controller and the division man-

[22] D. Solomons, *Divisional Performance: Measurement and Control*, (Financial Executives Research Foundation, 1965).
[23] Schiff and Lewin, *op. cit.*, pp. 51–62.

agement are spatially removed from corporate headquarters. This physical removal leads to infrequent interaction between the divisional controller and the corporate controller while it increases the interaction between the divisional controller and the division management. This increased interaction arises from the divisional controller's participation in the everyday problem-solving and decision-making activities of the division. As a result we find the formation of personal relationships, and more importantly the sharing of goals and objectives. Finally, it is clear that the achievement of the controller's personal goals depends on his active participation in the division's affairs and to a much smaller extent on his nominal superior, the corporate controller.

It is therefore not surprising that the divisional controller, with his intimate knowledge of the budget and its underlying elements, becomes the division's general manager's right-hand man in establishing division goals, presenting them to corporate management and overseeing their achievement. It is the achievement of the division plans which earns the controller both corporate and divisional recognition represented by his share of salary bonuses (normally tied to divisional earnings above plan), increased staff and discretionary control over allocation of slack resources.

Slack, however, occurs in a centralized company to the same extent as in the decentralized one. In a centralized company, however, slack created at the divisional level would exist in a less disguised form, primarily because the central controller is removed from the day-to-day problems of company divisions and personally not involved in creating budgetary slack. Indeed, in the centralized system, being part of corporate management requires the corporate controller to be mainly concerned with monitoring the implementation of plans and controlling costs.

The observations of Schiff and Lewin support this contention. In the two decentralized divisions, the controllers were intimately familiar with day-to-day operations and had very sophisticated procedures for managing division slack. In the case of the division operating within a group of divisions with control centralized at the group level, the group controller was uninformed about the extent of slack in the budgets of the various divisions in the group. Furthermore, within the group, division management lacked tight control over slack and, by comparison with controllers of the decentralized divisions, was rather unsophisticated in its efforts to manage slack. Indeed, lower levels of management of the centralized company including plant managers had significant influence in creating and appropriating this slack.

Thus it appears that *ceteris paribus*, the location and form of slack in the budget is also dependent on the type of control system employed. Specifically it appears that in a decentralized company, slack is concentrated at the divisional management level. Moreover, the divisional controller is intimately involved in the creation and "husbanding" of slack. Conversely, in a centralized company with a weaker control system, slack is diffused through all management levels of the division.

TOP CORPORATE MANAGEMENT AND SLACK

Top management role in the budgetary process is generally exercised in the divisional budget review sessions. Although top management has the formal power to accept or reject the budgets proposed, it is generally at a disadvantage, because it lacks the detailed information regarding makeup of items and underlying analyses which the divisional management has. Thus, while top management can be assumed to be aware of "padding" and "sandbagging" practices, it finds itself trying to guess at what a reasonable increase in profit requirements should be. Indeed, the fact that such higher profit targets are often achieved affirms the existence of slack. Yet slack can be a major problem for top management and can be viewed as representing lost opportunities to the firm and in the long run increasing its cost function.

The organization reward structure, by overreacting to under-achievement of objectives, is one of the causes of managerial desire for slack. This suggests that managers view slack as a means of avoiding the stigma normally attached to under-achievers. It may be that a reward structure based on an objective reporting system and which places equal emphasis on over-achieving as on under-achieving could lessen managerial uncertainty avoidance. However, as Birnberg and Nath point out, such a system has not been achieved yet, and to the best or our knowledge exists only as a hypothetical model.[24] Furthermore, we have noted that uncertainty avoidance is only one factor in management's motivation for slack. Managers we noted, possess personal goals and aspirations whose achievement depends on the existence of slack, under their control. Thus we feel that devising new objective reporting systems and restructuring the reward system, though important to the problem of assessing performance, will not by itself solve the problem of slack.

Indeed, as long as people are the corporation we must expect occurrence of dysfunctional behaviors such as the desire for and creation of slack. It would be feasible, however, for top management to influence the budget process in a constructive way, if it had the information base on which to make decisions.[25] Clearly top management cannot have any significant impact on a budget at the terminal review sessions, when it can only make aggregate demands for higher profits and improved return on investments. Similarly *ex post*

facto analyses like those proposed by Thiel[26] or internal audits would not get at the basic problems which revolves around the actual budget formulation process.

Theoretically it can be argued that if top management could evaluate and review the budget at key points during the budget preparation process it could also be more successful in countering the tendency toward the creation of slack. Stedry[27] has shown that imposed aspirations which exceed self-set aspirations often will be achieved and that their achievement depends on whether the subordinate accepts them as reasonable.

Thus, the problem for top management is first one of information—how to develop the information necessary to impose reasonable goals? Second, it is one of organization design—how to institutionalize top management's active participation in the budget process.

Some examples of pragmatic approaches to dealing with the problem of slack creation follow. It must be stressed that they are suggestive and would require further research before implementation.

INFLUENCING THE BUDGET: IN-DEPTH REVIEWS

As a first step, the evaluation and review of the budget would be shifted from the termination of the process to points *during* the process. This should not be confused with standard reviews of tentative or completed budgets or with budget audits which are performed *ex post facto*. Instead, top management should focus on examining the basic elements of the budget as they are quantified and assembled. Some of

[24] J. G. Birnberg and R. Nath, "Implications of Behavioral Science for Managerial Accounting," THE ACCOUNTING REVIEW, Vol. XLII, No. 3, pp. 468–479.
[25] A similar point is made by Lowe and Shaw, *op. cit.*, pp. 312–315.
[26] H. Theil, "How to Worry About Increased Expenditures," THE ACCOUNTING REVIEW, Vol. XLIV, No. 1, pp. 27–37.
[27] Stedry, *op. cit.*, pp. 61–90, 144–154.

these key elements occur in the formation of the following estimates:

1. Market shares
2. Sales
3. Unit selling prices
4. Standard costs
5. Marketing expenses
6. Personnel needs
7. Other expenses

To influence the budget process at its critical formative stages, top management must question the information base underlying the formulation of specific estimates. For example, sales projections can be reviewed by examining, among other variables, the inputs from marketing research, competitive intelligence, the economic environment and the company's own long range plans. Additionally, the critical reviews could involve staff and operating managers in manufacturing, engineering, marketing and administration and not merely the division president, his controller and their staffs. For example, when standard cost estimates are being reviewed, the factory cost accountant, the factory engineering staff concerned with process improvements and engineering studies, as well as the factory personnel manager could be involved. What should be stressed are questions of the "why" and "what if" variety along with the "how" type of questions.

The objective of top management is not to "second guess" divisional management or deny their decision-making prerogatives but rather to force them to *rethink* their previously unquestioned assumptions and long standing standard operating procedures. Such constant probing of basic assumptions will lead to a minimal slack environment and approach conditions of optimal performance.

The extensive reviews urged here should not be done in every division every year. Several divisions may be selected each

year and the effect of the review will carry over for a number of years. The characteristic of slack is that it builds up over cumulative successful operating periods and levels off in poor years. Furthermore, as slack builds up it becomes largely irretrievable in the long run. This suggests that the appropriate time to perform the in-depth budget reviews could be after a division has experienced a sequence of *successful* operating years. Whereas this recommendation seems to contradict the principles of management by exception it really augments it. Clearly top management must attend to problem divisions; however, successful divisions can be made even more effective.

INSTITUTIONALIZING IN-DEPTH REVIEWS

So far we have not dealt with the problem of implementing the proposed in-depth budget reviews. Clearly this is a task for top management. It is equally clear, however, that top management does not have the resources (time and personnel) to do the job. Since such in-depth reviews must be done periodically throughout the corporation and since it is important that different approaches be employed each time, it appears that special task groups directly reporting to the president might be best suited for this assignment. The staffing of these task groups is the determining factor in the success of these reviews and the following are three staffing strategies representing different approaches to the problem.

i) *Senior Managers*

Task groups composed of company senior managers—vice presidents of divisions and corporate staff members—probably would be top management's first choice for the review assignments. The senior managers are intimately familiar with company procedures and history. In the review process they often would be able to prescreen alternatives which have been tried in the past and failed. The same senior managers, however, are to a large extent prisoners of their own prior preconceptions derived from history and, therefore, may be reluctant to propose or accept new ideas. Furthermore, the reviews are likely to raise past issues in which they may have been personally involved, thus introducing personal biases which could clearly affect the outcome of the problem under review. Finally, the senior managers themselves may be the target of reviews at some other point in time, and this in itself could undermine the effectiveness of the periodic review procedures.

ii) Outside Consultants

Staffing the task groups with outside consultants clearly solves many of the disadvantages associated with the use of in-house senior managers teams. The outside consultants are not hampered by corporate precedents and history and would be inclined to approach the reviews with greater objectivity. They bring to the reviews broader backgrounds and interdisciplinary skills. Moreover, new groups of outside consultants can be used each time.

Corporations, however, can be expected to resist the use of outside consultants on budget reviews primarily because of a confidence gap. The budget, after all, reveals in detail the company short-term plan and the budget process itself may highlight various conflicts, all of which top management may prefer to keep in-house. Furthermore, the consultant takes what he has learned to his next job, thus increasing the likelihood of exposing confidential information.

iii) Whiz Kids

The "whiz kids" in this case would be recently hired top-flight MBA's. Like the outside consultants, they are free of corporate bias and will approach problems with greater objectivity. Unlike the consultants they have no broad prior background but instead are trained in the current state of the art of management, have an understanding of the behavioral aspects of management decision-making, are highly motivated to think creatively and are eager to question established standard operating procedures. Furthermore, the assignment to the budget review task groups provides them with a superb training period to learn about the company prior to their assignment within the company. Finally, unlike the consultant who takes what he has learned to his next job, the "whiz kids" approach has a carryover effect in terms of total organizational learning, on-the-job training of the "whiz kids" and in terms of accelerating the diffusion of innovative ideas in management decision making.

SUMMARY

In this paper we have reexamined the relationship between the controller and the controlled within the organization. We have argued that this relationship revolves around the budget process and that the "controlled" exercise significant influence on the outcome of their budgets. This influence manifests itself in the amount of slack which managers (and all other participants) can incorporate into their budgets.

The theoretical rationale for such dysfunctional behavior has been previously stated by a number of writers. However, except for the exploratory studies by Schiff and Lewin and Lowe and Shaw, there exist no observations or empirical evidence on how and why managers create slack. Decentralized control was expected to increase organization effectiveness due to the increased participation in decision making created on the local level and because the divisional controller was formally responsible to the corporate controller. Assuming, however, as we did, that financial budgets are no more than a mutually agreed upon control device, then the whole notion of control needs to be reexamined, particularly the role of the decentralized controller who appears to act as the divisional slack manager.

Finally, if managerial desire for slack and the attendant dysfunctional consequences must be taken as given then the implications for top management actions must be reconsidered. We have suggested a pragmatic approach aimed at increasing the participation of top management in the budget process on a selective basis. Specifically we have discussed the problem of how top management could impose reasonable goals[28] through constructive reviewing of the budget at critical points during the budget preparation process. We have also recognized that top management is severely limited in its ability to undertake on such a task. We have, therefore, proposed the creation of budget task groups, directly under the president, which will in effect participate in the budget preparation process. The success of these task groups clearly depends on their staffing and mode of operation within the organization. Whether the approach outlined here will work will require extensive further experimentation in the field.

[28] Lowe and Shaw, *op. cit.*, pp. 312–315.

Towards An Open Systems Approach to Budgeting*

SHAHID L. ANSARI
New York University

Abstract

The theory of open systems has been increasingly applied to the study of organizational planning and control systems. This is also true for the area of budgetary control. At present, however, there is a tendency for writers to treat the design problems as an either/or choice between an open or a closed system. This paper argues that the critical decision problem is where in a system closure can be most beneficially applied. It will show that the open systems view, with its emphasis upon the horizontal dimension in an organization, is better suited for designing effective budgetary control systems. The computation of budget variances is chosen as the key step at which the usefulness of this view can be fully appreciated. An alternative budget variances measurement scheme, based upon similar perspectives in the area of job design, is proposed. It is shown that variances computed under the proposed system more fully reflect the interacting nature of most organizations and provide better control information.

One feature which characterizes the past World War II period is the growth of new and more complex organizational forms. The growth in government, for instance has given rise to giant bureaucracies such as the Department of Defense (DOD) and the Department of Health, Education and Welfare (HEW). Similarly, new technologies have created their own organizational forms as evidenced by the National Aeronautics and Space Administration in the U.S. and EURATOM (a grouping of European countries for co-operation on atomic energy) in Europe. These newer organizational forms have changed the practice and philosophy of management. New concepts, designs and techniques of organizations and management have replaced their earlier counterparts.

One area of organizational design in which more fundamental change has been absent is in the design of management information systems (MIS). While recent technological advances have changed the structure of most MIS, the new structures are not necessarily in harmony with changes in other organizational and managerial variables. Elsewhere, I have argued that effective organizational design requires information structures which are consistent with the human-social, task and reward subsystems in organizations (Ansari, 1977). These arguments provide the central theme of this paper; that is: new developments in organizational forms and management systems require changes in the design of many MIS to make the functioning of the overall control system more effective.

This paper deals with this theme in the context of budget variance information. Budgets are selected because they are one of the most important and pervasive organizational control systems. The paper has a two fold purpose. First, it will be argued that while an "open" systems philosophy more closely reflects the nature of organizational changes; budget variances, as presently computed, reflect "closed" systems thinking. Second, the necessary changes will be outlined to make variance information consistent with this newer reality of organizational design.

The discussion is divided into four parts. The

*I gratefully acknowledge the help of Jan Oliver and Jack McDonough for their helpful comments on an earlier draft of this paper.

first part deals with changes in organizations which have necessitated a move from a closed systems view toward an open systems view. The next part of the paper argues that budgetary control systems are currently designed as closed systems. An open systems framework which is more consistent with the newer reality of organizations is presented in the subsequent part. The final section is devoted to a consideration of the relevance of the arguments presented earlier to changes in accounting systems.

ORGANIZATIONAL CHANGES — SOME BACKGROUND

Budgets operate within the context of other organizational variables such as technology, rewards and social systems. When that organizational context changes, it is now recognized that the changes must be reflected in the design of budgetary control systems. As recent studies of the contingent nature of management accounting systems have emphasized (Bruns & Waterhouse, 1975; Sathe, 1975; Waterhouse & Tiessen, 1978; Watson, 1975), budgetary control systems cannot be designed and operated in isolation of their organizational context.

Some of the changes in organizations which have necessitated a re-evaluation of budgeting in general and budget variances in particular will be discussed in this section. In doing so, a systems view of organizations will be adopted. There are two reasons for this. First, systems theory provides a useful metaphor because a lot of recent research on organizations uses its concepts and terminology. Second, and more important, the systems framework provides a powerful analytical model for the analysis of organizations because it allows designers to integrate the technical and social sides of an organization within a unified whole. It thus avoids a fragmented treatment of organizational problems.

Two views or approaches have been used in studying a phenomenon as a system. The first is a closed systems view which has its origins in classical physics and thermodynamics. The other is the open systems view which was first used in biology. Both of these approaches have been used in characterizing and studying organizations as systems.

Closed systems are characterized by *certainty, a static equilibrium*, and *little or no import or export of energy* from and to the environment.[1] Closure is designed to create a system whose future states are determined by its existing states. This, as Thompson (1967) observes, can happen only if the relationships are few and predictable.[2] Consequently, closed system approaches focus more on the internal organization and less on the relationships between a system and its environment.

In contrast, an open system is characterized by growth and *survival*. It achieves a *dynamic equilibrium* instead of a static equilibrium. The process of achieving it is marked by a constant *exchange (import and export) of energy* with the environment. Three other properties that mark an open system are: (i) *self-regulation* or use of negative feedback to take corrective action; (ii) *equifinality* or the ability to achieve the same final goal from different initial conditions: and (iii) *negative entropy* or the ability to store excess energy for use in counteracting later disturbances.[3]

As strategies for studying organizations closed and open systems' models differ in what they consider as playing a leading or independent role in explaining a system's behavior. In the closed system's model internal organizational structure plays a leading role; the open system's model ascribes a leading role to the environment. These differences are perhaps best captured by Gouldner (1959). He identified two models of organizations. The first, so-called "rational model", is a "mechanical" view of an organization as a structure of manipulable parts, subject to planned modification with a view to enhancing "the efficiency of the whole". The other is the "natural-system" model which stresses the interdependence of the parts of an "organismic" whole, in which the focus is on disruption of a homeostatically maintained organizational equilibrium rather ·than on "deviations from

---

[1] For a detailed discussion, see Emery & Trist (1969).

[2] Ashby (1956, p. 27) describes this as a one-to-one transformation in which fixing its (a determinate system's) "circumstances and the state it is at will determine i.e. make unique, the state it next moves to".

[3] A good description of open system properties is contained in Katz & Kahn (1966) and Thompson (1967).

rationality". Later writers, such as Thompson (1967), have interpreted Gouldner's "rational-model" as a closed system and his "natural-system" model as an open system. Using this analogy, their differences may be summarized as follows: the closed systems strategy is aimed more at the autonomous behavior of a system's components whereas the open systems strategy aims to study the ways in which these components are integrated and the behavior of the resulting whole.

The pyramid type of organization structure with its clear cut lines of authority and responsibility, best exemplifies the rational closed system's model. Here the design emphasizes vertical power and authority relationships that bind an organization together. Efficiency is achieved by successive factoring of organizational goals into compartmentalized subunits that are supposed to function more or less autonomously. As Sayles & Chandler (1971, p. 34) point out:

In traditional management thinking there is a clear line separating that which is delegated and that which is not, that which is in the jurisdiction of one manager and that which falls into the jurisdiction of an adjacent manager.

Such an emphasis on the achievement of certainty and efficiency by the use of organizational designs based on the delegation of authority and responsibility has not given attention to different organizational environments and the complex ways in which organizations depend on their environments (Katz & Kahn, 1966). Most of the newer organizational forms which have emerged can be best understood as responses to increasing complexity in both the internal and external organizational environment. The volatility of demand, the need to implement advanced technologies (as in space exploration), the complexity of tasks (as in HEW programs) are some of the many changes which have made it impractical to draw clear cut lines of authority and responsibility. This is due to considerable overlaps in the scope of problems and the differential distribution of technical abilities within an organization.

For instance, in their analysis of the impact of new high technology on organizational design, Sayles & Chandler (1971) note two major changes. First, advanced technology organizations, such as NASA are marked by greater interdependence of parts and are tied together horizontally as well as vertically. Second, project management (e.g. the Apollo Program) is replacing line management since most resources lie outside the domain of individual departments and often even the organization.[4] Projects borrow these resources for finite time periods for accomplishing specific goals. A similar emphasis on programs and missions is also true of large bureaucracies such as the DOD, HEW, etc. Sayles & Chandler (1971) conclude that one of the legacies of the Apollo Program is the innovation in organizational design which can be successfully transplanted to other organizations.

The organic or open systems model, with its emphasis upon interdependence between autonomous parts, is thus a better model for these newer organizational forms. There are at least two important implications of this model for management and hence management information systems. First, the absence of clear cut allocations of tasks and resources within any single unit requires the development of joint or shared systems of responsibility. In such systems, the regulation of the whole takes precedence over and is not synonymous with the regulation of its parts. Second, since no manager controls all of the resources, co-operation rather than competition becomes important. To encourage such behaviors performance evaluation becomes more an exercise in problem solving and less a method of assigning responsibility.

It should be noted that the prior discussion is not designed to suggest that closed and open systems are either/or choices. As Kast & Rosensweig (1973, p. 44) point out, "most social organizations and their subsystems are 'partially open' and 'partially closed'. Open and closed are a matter of degree". What needs to be recognized is that both are appropriate under certain circumstances. Thompson (1967) noted that the use of closed systems concepts is particularly needed at the technical core of any organization to reduce uncertainty and to create more effective performance at this level. The challenge is to avoid what Kremyanskiy (1958, p. 141) calls "conditionalism" or the tendency to ascribe an exclusive leading role to either the "inside" or the "outside" in explaining a system's behavior:

---

[4] For a discussion of the implications of this point see, S. Ansari & R. O. Mason, "Control System Design for Inter and Intra Organizational Performance", AIS Working Paper, Graduate School of Management, UCLA.

...it is profoundly mistaken to stress — only the augmentation of the organisms' "independence" from the environment. This occurs in association with a deepening and widening mediated dependence. But in the highest development of means of adaptation to the environment there also lay the need for the opposite process — the development of new ways and means for combating the environment.

The emphasis upon such a mediated-dependence means that the behavior of certain systems sometimes can be best studied by proceeding inside out or vice versa. Kremyanskiy illustrates this by using the brain as an example. As he points out, "The brain first developed as an organ of primarily internal interconnections, and then primarily as an organ of interconnections

with the environment". The following sections will show that in the development and analysis of budget information it is time to move away from placing primary emphasis on the "internal" toward placing more emphasis on "external" relationships.

BUDGETARY CONTROL AS A CLOSED SYSTEM

This section will demonstrate that existing budgetary cost control systems reflect the closed systems view of organizations and therefore create problems which make them unsuitable for the newer types of organizations. This conclusion can be supported by examining a typical budgeting

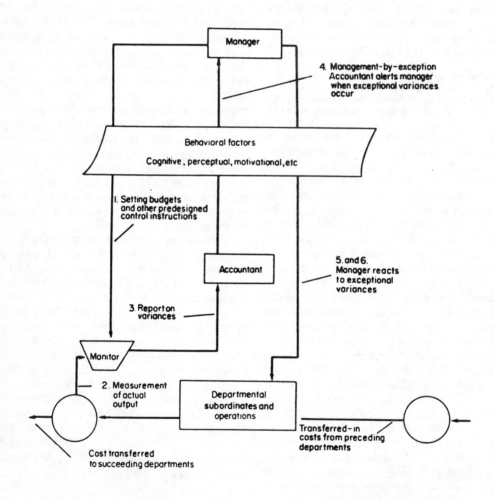

Fig. 1. A typical budgetary cost control system for an organizational unit.

178

system described in the cost accounting literature. Figure 1 describes such a system for an individual unit within an organization. The dynamics of this system can be described in six different stages.

1. *Specification of budget* represents the planning phase, in which the monitor is fed goals and other control instructions (e.g. measurement methods, frequency, etc.) agreed upon by managers and subordinates. The monitor may be a man or a machine or may have elements of both.

2. *Measurement of actual output* in which the monitor carries out the predesigned measurement instructions fed in step 1.

3. *Report on variances* involves the preparation of a variance report after comparing actual and budgeted outputs. The level of detail in the report will depend upon the level of management for whom the report is intended.[5]

4. *Problem identification* requires a cost accountant to use the output of the monitor (the variance report) to decide if an exceptional situation requiring managerial attention has arisen. If so, he brings such deviations to the attention of the manager.

5. *Search for causes* is undertaken by managers for all deviations of exceptional nature. The search may involve dealing with both subordinates or other managers (if cause is of external origin).

6. *Response* or the taking of appropriate corrective measures if manager discovers an out-of-control situation. If, however, a cause is uncontrollable, then the budgets for the following periods are adjusted to account for it.

Two additional features of this system should also be noted. First, all information passes through cognitive or perceptual filters, representing the socio-psychological dimensions of this system. This aspect, though important, is not the central concern of this paper.[6] Second, a cost center is part of a dynamic system of work-flows. It receives inputs from preceding departments and transforms them into outputs for succeeding departments.

An analysis of the budgetary system outlined in

Fig. 1 shows that both structurally and philosophically it reflects a closed systems view. Structurally, the system is analogous to a closed cybernetic control model known as the "error-controlled regulator".[7] This type of model works on the principle of feedback information on disturbances that affect a controlled variable. Regulatory action is taken only after some errors have occurred. That is, the system learns from small errors that it can tolerate and prevents more fatal errors.

This is precisely the principle on which budgetary control systems operate. Errors in this context are the budget variances. Two types of variances are computed from budgets. The first, which fall within some "normal" prespecified range, are called "nonsignificant" variances. The criterion for normality may be a rule of thumb, such as ±10 per cent of the budget, or it may utilize more refined statistical methods. If the latter are used, then nonsignificant are usually defined as random variances. The second type represent the so-called "exceptional" or non-random variances, and are investigated by managers for underlying causes. A report "explaining" such variances to higher level management is then prepared. This type of feedback is what allows management to control such systems and is the key to successful regulation.

Philosophically, the central notion underlying budgetary control systems is that of "responsibility accounting". Horngren (1977, p. 156) describes responsibility accounting systems as systems which "recognize various decision centers throughout an organization and trace costs (and revenues, assets and liabilities, where pertinent) to the individual managers who are primarily responsible for making decisions about the costs in question". All costs traced to decision centers are separated into two categories: controllable and uncontrollable. Only controllable costs are used for managerial performance evaluation because these are costs "that are directly influenced by a *manager* within a *given time span*". (Horngren, 1977, p. 160.)

---

[5] For instance Shillinglaw (1972) defines the so-called "basic plan" and "single plan" variance reporting systems. The former are less detailed and are designed for higher echelon managers, while the latter are more detailed and are intended for immediate superiors.

[6] For a discussion of the interaction between information and human-social variables and its implications for design of control systems, see Ansari (1977).

[7] For a complete discussion of "error controlled" and other types of regulation in cybernetic models, see Ashby (1956, Chapter 11).

Operationally, budgets are prepared by cost centers which generally coincide with the major decision centers in an organization. For example, in a typical functionally organized manufacturing firm, cost centers generally will be the various functional units such as production, marketing, finance, etc. Each of these may be further subdivided into other cost centers along the lines of the vertical chain of command specified by a firm's organization charts. Thus, cost centers generally reflect the distribution of responsibility, authority and power in an organization. The assumption is that control will work by assigning managers precisely defined tasks and time-tables and matching these with an adequate allocation of resources and authority.[8]

The responsibility view, therefore, is a compartmentalized view of organizations which fails to consider the dynamic interactions and interdependencies between its parts. It focuses only on the vertical (chain of command) dimension and ignores the horizontal (work flow) dimension. This, in turn, leads to the use of variances for fixing blame (or discovering heroes) rather than on managing the entire system. The internal structure and efficiency of cost centers dominates over their external and environmental relationships and dependencies. These, of course are the characteristics of a closed system approach described in the preceding section. They represent Gouldner's (1959) so-called "rational" model of organizations. Budgets based on this model, when applied to the newer types of interdependent organizations, can lead to at least three major problems.

First, as Shillinglaw (1972, p. 426) states: "No where does the responsibility accounting structure recognize organizational interdependence. It may even increase interdepartmental conflicts, as each manager seeks to improve his own record or protect himself from blame, without regard to what happens elsewhere". The accounting system is thus set up to reward *competition* and not *co-operation*. In many cases this leads to suboptimization.

Second, because the cost controllability criterion is interpreted in a jurisdictional sense, it ignores the fact that the underlying cause of a variance may be uncontrollable even though the cost itself is incurred within a cost center (e.g. a labor variance caused by improper workmanship in a prior department). That is, responsibility accounting defines controllability in terms of effects (outcomes) rather than causes. Much time and effort, therefore, is spent on unnecessary investigations on the part of higher managers, and defending, blame shifting, etc. on the part of lower managers. Given the fact that management-by-exception emphasizes negative performance more often than positive, these unnecessary investigations are likely to exacerbate a situation in which subordinates are conditioned to associate managers with a negative event. Lower morale and dysfunctional behavior aimed at "looking good" on measured variables thus are more likely to occur.[9]

Finally, the two-way variance classification places primary emphasis on performance evaluation and ignores the learning aspect of deviations. Managers do not have information about the underlying causes of system-wide variances. For example, a cause such as defective storage of raw materials may lead to cost variances in several departments, many of which are several stages away from the initial introduction of materials.[10] Its impact is not readily known to higher management since each department's variances are computed independent of others. Therefore, no system-wide learning takes place.

In this connection, it is interesting to note that a responsibility accounting system responds to the presence of interdependencies by attempting to create more artificial autonomy between parts and maintain the fiction of controllability. For example, it is not uncommon to charge inputs to departments at standard prices to protect them from cost fluctuations elsewhere. This only keeps management from focusing properly on the sources of disturbances because each manager pays attention to only those variances which have a sizeable impact in his department. Charging costs

---

[8] For a more general discussion of the behavioral assumptions underlying management accounting see Caplan (1966).

[9] For a complete discussion of some of the dysfunctional behaviors which can result in control systems see Lawler & Rhode (1976, Chapter 6).

[10] An illustration of this is paper manufacturing. If timber is improperly stored and gets exposed to weather, problems are created several stages later in the production process.

at standards thus ignores the larger problem of how problems in one area affect others.

To summarize, budgets, as part of responsibility accounting systems, are presently based upon a closed systems logic. One consequence of this is that the computation of budget variances fails to recognize the dynamic interacting nature of organizational units which may or may not correspond to established cost centers. Also, because the logic emphasizes rationality and efficiency, the existing two-way scheme of classifying variances is biased in favor of performance evaluation over learning. The system, therefore, reflects a "control over people" rather than a "control over system" view.

BUDGET VARIANCES – AN OPEN SYSTEMS APPROACH

The prior discussion shows that the deficiencies in budget information largely reflect the use of an organizational model which fails to capture the reality of many modern organizations. It also shows that for these organizations the open systems model is more suitable. This section explores the changes in budget variance information which are needed when organizations are viewed as open rather than closed systems.

The adoption of an open systems model requires a reorientation in the computation of variances along three dimensions.

First, in generating variances it should be recognized that a cost center does not exist in isolation. Rather it is characterized by an active exchange and adaptation to its environment. The impact of a cost center's environment on its performance needs to be recognized in generating variances. A recent empirical study by Hayes (1977) supports this conclusion. It shows that the performance of many organizational subunits is more contingent upon their interrelationships with other subunits (intra-organization environmental factors), and with environmental influences (inter-organizational environmental factors), than internal factors. Variances should inform managers about these interdependencies, and should also capture the likely system wide impacts of disturbances originating from any of these three contingencies.

Second, the open systems model views a manager as a "regulator" rather than as an authority figure. The concept of regulation, as used in the systems literature, accents the problem solving role of a manager over his evaluative role. This means that variances should aid managers in locating problems and bottlenecks and help them in neutralizing these sources of instability. It also means that the evaluative role of variances becomes less important.

Finally, since the management of the entire system takes precedence over the management of subunits, variances should help global problem solving rather than local problem solving. This is an important consideration since existing cost accounting literature either deals with standard costing for organizational subunits in which local optimization is emphasized, or with divisional performance measurement systems in which global optimization is more important. Currently, no systematic theory exists for the intermediate organizational level, which uses budget variance data as the primary control tool and requires both local and global optimization.

To implement this philosophy, two major changes must be made in the way in which variances are presently computed, reported and analysed. The first step is to develop a variance classification scheme which highlights the nature and origin of disturbances. Currently, as field studies done by the National Association of Accountants (NAA) (1974, p. 10) show, most companies compute variances by cost items (i.e. material, labor and overhead) for individual responsibility centers. That is, they use the same account classifications used for control and for inventory costing purposes. Control reports, therefore, provide little information to management on the underlying causes of these variances. The second step is to use this classification as a way of understanding the interaction between a cost center and its environment. This again is not available in current systems since they do not focus on the interdependencies within cost centers. Management can thus gain insights into the system wide impact of variances. These steps are described in more detail below.

Causal classification of variances

For purposes of control, management needs to know not only whether a variance is significant, but also the source or origin of the disturbances responsible for these variances. Without this knowledge, a lot of managerial effort may be expended in merely trying to discover where his efforts are most needed. The existing two-way

TABLE 1. A proposed classification scheme for variances

Nature \ Environmental origin	Internal (within a cost center)	External (from another cost center)	Exogenous (outside the organization)
Expected	11 e.g. Fluctuations in output caused by inexperienced workers	12 e.g. Defective raw materials purchased by stores agent	13 e.g. Change in prices of raw materials
Unexpected	21 e.g. Breakdown of machinery	22 e.g. Delay in receiving work from preceding department	23 e.g. Delay in shipment of materials due to strike

classification of variances is not very informative in this regard. An alternative scheme, shown in Table 1, is suggested as a replacement.

There are two dimensions to the proposed scheme. The first one focuses on the nature or significance of the variances. However, instead of random–nonrandom it uses the terms *expected* and *unexpected* variances. This is because random is a statistical concept which is more suited for statistical variance investigation decision models.[11] It implies that a standard or budget represents the mean of a probability distribution of *chance* causes.[12] In practice, managers may choose to include within a standard causes which are technically nonchance and thus controllable. This may be either an economic choice — because it is too costly to remove these causes — or a behavioral choice — it is desirable for motivational reasons to include some slack in budgets. In either case, expected variances are those that a manager judges to be insignificant.

The second dimension deals with the environmental source or origin of variances. Conceptually the environment of a cost center can be divided into three parts — *internal, external* and *exogenous.* Internal refers to those factors or disturbances which originate within a given cost or responsibility center. External highlights the interdependent nature of the cost centers and refers to those disturbances which originate in some other cost center. Exogenous disturbances are those which orginate outside an organization's boundaries and are within the environment of the total organizational system.

Each cell in Table 1, therefore, represents a combination of judged significance and environmental origin of a variance. It also shows typical examples of variances which will fall within each cell. For effective control, all variances should be assigned to one of the six cells of Table 1. This will generate a list in which all variances will be identified by a digital code number referencing their cell classification. For example, a variance caused by "breakdown of machinery" will be given a number 21.1. The first two digits, 21, will tell a manager that this is an "internal" and "unexpected" variance (cell 21 of Table 1); the last digit is a sequential listing within this class — i.e. this is the first variance assigned to cell 21. To illustrate this process, a list of variances from an NAA study have been classified in Table 2 on the basis of the above scheme.

The proposed variance classification in Table 2 serves an important role in highlighting which disturbance sources or cell are most critical to a units' operations. This can help individual managers better focus their energies. For example, if most of the disturbances in a cost center originate in cells 12 and 22 that is, external to the cost center, then its manager should spend most of

[11]The variance investigation decision is treated as a purely statistical problem in the literature. Hence the random–nonrandom scheme is used to decide which disturbances are worth investigating. For a review of these models see Kaplan (1975).

[12]An excellent example of this is the application of statistical quality control theory to investigation of cost variances. These models assume a constant cause system in which the standard is the expected value of a normal probability distribution. See Probst (1971).

TABLE 2. A sample list of departmental variances coded by the
proposed scheme*

	Month of			Year to date			
	Actual variance			Actual variance			
Reason for variance	Hours	Hours	Cost	Hours	Hours	Cost	Code†
No reason, variance less than 10 per cent							11.1
Estimated running time too high. Reported to Stds. Dept.							12.1
Estimated set-up time too high. Reported to Stds. Dept.							12.2
Men's effort and/or ability above average							21.1
New machine, standard has not been changed							21.2
Change in methods, standard has not been changed							21.3
New or improved tools, standard has not been changed							21.4
Used set-up from previous job							11.2
Time set for man operating one machine. Ran two							21.5
Time clock registers to 0.1 hours only							11.3
Work done under special supervision							21.6
Standard too low. Reported to Standards Dept.							22.1
First time job was made							11.4
Slow or obsolete machine used							21.7
Planning not correct. Was changed. Stds. Dept. notified							22.2
Could not follow oper. as planned, delivery requirements							23.1
Operations in previous departments not performed as planned							22.3
Time set for man operating two machines. One available							22.4
Quantity too small							13.1
Extra set-up result of machine breakdown							12.3
Extra work							13.2
Two men had to be assigned to jobs due to nature of job							21.8
Learner, apprentice, or student							11.5
Parts spoiled. Had to make additional parts							21.9
Tools not available at time job was started							23.2
Trying out new tools							13.3
Tools not correct when job was started. Had to be corrected							23.3
Broke tool. Time lost redressing and sharpening							21.10
Oversized material used							23.4
Castings warped, but are within Foundry tolerances							12.4
Castings not to dimensions. Time							

183

TABLE 2 (cont.)

Dept. No. . . . .

	Month of			Year to date			
	Actual variance				Actual variance		
Reason for variance	Hours	Hours	Cost	Hours	Hours	Cost	Code†
lost waiting for instructions							22.5
Material too hard. Frequent sharpening of tools required							23.5
Improper supervision							21.11
Illegible blue prints							22.6
Blowholes and porous castings							22.7
Sheet stock, secondary material or scrap ends used							13.4

* This Table is adapted from Exhibit 1, Part II (NAA, 1974), pp. 12–13.
† See Table 1 for interpretation of first two digits of code numbers. The assignment here represents my guess of which category a cause should be assigned to.

his time on managing external relationships. The scheme also serves a potentially greater and more valuable role in helping upper management understand a system's overall dynamics. That is, it can help management to better understand the inter-relationships between the various responsibility units in an organization and the relationships between an organization and its environment. This, however, requires the second change proposed from the current usage of variances. Information on six-way variance analysis from individual cost centers now must be combined into a single organizational matrix to be used for inter cost center variance analysis.

Inter cost center variance analysis

The purpose of this step is to combine the causal information on variance (shown in Table 2) from individual cost centers into an overall organizational matrix. Such a matrix arranges all cost centers in a sequential order representing the organization's work flow. It then arrays all variance causes against their respective cost centers to isolate what are termed as "key causes".[13] These are defined as those causes which impact on several cost centers and thus may be causing bottlenecks within the overall work flow system. Table 3 shows such a matrix of key causes for a simple manufacturing organization in which work flows sequentially from *production* to *assembly* to *packaging* – the three cost centers in this organization.

The matrix in Table 3 is a partial representation of what is likely to be a large matrix for most real situations. For illustrative purposes it is assumed that only 15 actual causes have been identified for the period under review. The first four (from top to bottom) of these causes resulted in variances in the production department; the next six caused variances in the assembly department; and the last four caused variances in the packaging department. Using the classification scheme of Table 1, all of these causes have been assigned to one of its six cells and sequentially numbered within each cell. It should be noted that the causes shown are not differentiated by traditional categories such as materials, labor or overhead. The emphasis at this stage is on the total performance of a cost center. However, if needed, the matrix and classification scheme can be easily expanded to include an identification of causes by cost elements.

To identify "key causes", a manager has to assess both the direct and indirect impact of a cause on costs. Direct impacts are measured by variances in the cost centers in which a cause is first isolated. Existing responsibility accounting reports currently provide such information and

---

[13]The idea of a matrix of key causes is borrowed from the area of job design. In structuring and formulating jobs, designers use what is known as a matrix of "Key variances" (not accounting variances). These variances help them identify the *most important* technical requirements which impact upon the successful completion of a job. For details see Englestad (1972).

184

TABLE 3. A sample matrix of key causes

	Production				Assembly					Packaging					
Production															11.1 – No detectable reason – variance less than 10%
															13.3 – Increase in material prices
															21.4 – Slow or obsolete machine used
															23.1 – Oversized materials used
Assembly															11.3 – No detectable reason – variance less than 10%
															11.3 – Men's effort and/or ability above average
															12.2 – Time set for man operating two machines – one available
		X													22.5 – Parts spoiled due to defects originating in production
															22.3 – Tools not available at time job started
															23.4 – Materials too hard and/or oversized
Packaging															11.1 – No detectable reason variance less than 10%
									X						12.2 – Castings not to dimensions – had to be sent back
									X						21.4 – Broken tool – time lost in repairing it
		X					X	X							22.3 – Delay in receiving assembled parts
															23.5 – Shortage of materials due to strike

Table 3 incorporates it in the matrix. The indirect impact is assessed by analysing past data to see whether a cause resulted in variances in other cost centers. In Table 3, this is indicated by a cross (X) in an appropriate cell. For instance, under the column for the cause "slow or obsolete machine used", there are two crosses. The first cross is in the row "parts spoiled" in Assembly and the second is in "delay in receiving assembled parts" in Packaging. This means that the use of an obsolete machine causes spoiled parts in Assembly and causes delays in sending parts from Assembly to Packaging. Similarly, when the Assembly Department uses "hard materials" it causes Packaging to "send back castings" and "break tools". This information is obtained by reading those rows in Table 3 in which the crosses appear.

The total variance attributable to a cause can be computed by adding the crosses down the columns of Table 3. In the example cited above, the total variance attributable to the Production department cause "slow or obsolete machine used" is the sum of the variance resulting from this cause in Production and the variance in assembly and packaging due to "spoiled parts" and "delay in receiving parts" respectively. It shows that the total cost of an obsolete machine is larger than the amount shown in the Production Department. In fact, it is possible that the indirect costs may be much greater than the direct costs. Thus causes which might have been ignored in a typical responsibility accounting system may be key causes when both the costs are added. This type of information is not available in existing responsibility accounting structures and is extremely useful if budgetary control is to move toward the system regulation view discussed earlier. It helps to pinpoint those areas in which co-operation is needed more than competition. Also, for a designer this type of information is very useful. For instance, if most variances in packaging originate in assembly, then it may be useful to combine these two cost centers into one or to better co-ordinate their activities.

CONCLUDING REMARKS

The central theme of this paper is that the development of new and more complex organizational forms has led to a new view of organizations and management. This new view, which is best captured by an open systems model, emphasizes the vast commerce between an organization and its environment in explaining behavior. Most management and accounting information systems, how-

185

ever, continue to reflect a closed systems view of organizations. Thus, they currently constrain organizational development since the information provided fails to capture the impact of a system's environment on its performance.

The consequences of operating in a closed systems mode in a dynamic environment impacts on both the external and internal accounting functions. Externally, financial accounting systems have failed to meet the demands placed on them by a dynamically changed environment. Hence the frustration of the profession at being held accountable for things that the accounting system is ill equipped to handle. Internally, budgetary control reflects the same problem. Budgets are currently used for *ad hoc* problem solving rather than for developing systematic notions of accountability. A bottom line mentality prevails and budget variances are the key to this bottom line mentality. This is why the focus of this paper has been on budget variances. It shows that budget variances, as currently reported, lead to at least three major problems in organizations.

First, valuable managerial time and resources are expended on investigating causes that are not controllable within given cost centers. This is because current variance reporting does not recognize organizational interdependencies. Therefore, it also causes dysfunctional behaviors such as blame shifting, manipulation of data, etc. Second, managers are encouraged toward local rather than global problem solving. Again, this is due to lack of information on organizational interdependencies. Finally, variance information is designed to encourage competition rather than co-operation. This is inappropriate since a great deal of dependence between organizational parts exists. Knowing when to encourage co-operative behavior between parts is a major need of a manager.

To solve these problems, an alternative scheme for computing budget variances is proposed here. It supplements information from a traditional responsibility accounting system with information on variances in a cost center caused by its external interactions. The attempt is to discover and recognize those key causes whose impact extends well beyond the boundaries of a single cost center. These key causes can be instrumental in shifting management toward global system regulation. It can also replace the existing control over people with a control over system view.

In closing, it should be noted that what is proposed here is a change in *both* the philosophy and structure of computing budget variances. Thus, the new scheme for computing variances is good only if managers are willing to buy into the philosophy which underlies it. Managers who think in responsibility accounting terms rather than in terms of regulation or problem solving will not recognize the need for or use this type of information. Without expanding one's view of organization and management, information is unlikely to be very effective in controlling organizations.

BIBLIOGRAPHY

Ansari, S., An Integrated Approach to Control System Design, *Accounting Organization & Society* (1977), pp. 101–112.

Ashby, R., *An Introduction to Cybernetics* (London: Chapman & Hall, 1956).

Bruns, W. H. & J. H. Waterhouse, Budgetary Control and Organization Structure, *Journal of Accounting Research* (Autumn, 1975), pp. 177–203.

Caplan, E. H., Behavioral Assumptions of Management Accounting – Report of A Field Study, *Accounting Review* (April 1968), pp. 342–352.

Englestad, P. H., Socio-Technical Approach to Problems of Process Control in L. E. Davis and J. C. Taylor (eds.), *Design of Jobs* (Penguin Books, 1972).

Emery, F. E. & Trist, E. L., Socio-Technical Systems. In F. E. Emery (ed.) *Systems Thinking* (Harmondsworth, U.K.: Penguin Books, 1969).

Gouldner, A. W., Organizational Analysis. In Robert K. Merton, Leonard Broom, Leonard S. Cottrell, Jr. (eds.), *Sociology Today* (New York: Basic Books, 1959).

Hayes, D. C., The Contingency Theory of Managerial Accounting, *Accounting Review* (January 1977), pp. 22–39.

Horngren, C. T., *Cost Accounting: A Managerial Emphasis* (Englewood Cliffs, N.J.: Prentice-Hall, 1977).

Kaplan, R. S., The Significance and Investigation of Cost Variances, *Journal of Accounting Research* (Autumn 1975), pp. 311–337.

Kast, F. E. & Rosensweig, J. E., *Contingency Views of Organization and Management* (Pala Alto, CA: Scientific Research Associates, Inc., 1973).

Katz, D. & Kahn, R. L., *The Social Psychology of Organizations* (New York: John Wiley, 1966).

Kremyanskiy, V. I., Certain Peculiarities of Organisms As a System From the Point of View of Physics, Cybernetics and Biology. In F. E. Emery (ed.), *Systems Thinking.*

Lawler, E. E. & Rhode, J. P., *Information and Control in Organizations* (Pacific Palisades, CA: Goodyear Publishing Co., 1976).

National Association of Accountants, *Standard Costs and Variance Analysis* (New York: NAA, 1974).

Probst, F. R., Probabilistic Cost Controls: A Behavioral Dimension, *The Accounting Review* (January 1971), pp. 113–118.

Sathe, V., Contingency Theory of Organization Structure, In J. L. Livingstone (ed.), *Managerial Accounting: The Behavioural Foundations* (Grid, 1975).

Sayles, L. R. & Chandler, M. K., *Managing Large Systems: Organizations For The Future* (New York: Harper & Row, 1971).

Shillinglaw, G., *Cost Accounting: Analysis and Control* (Homewood, Illinois: Irwin-Dorsey, 1972).

Thompson, J. D., *Organizations In Action* (New York: McGraw Hill, 1967).

Waterhouse, J. H. & Tiessen, P., A Contingency Framework for Management Accounting Systems Research, *Accounting, Organizations and Society* (August, 1978), pp. 65–76.

Watson, D. J. H., Contingency Formulations of Organizational Structure: Implications for Managerial Accounting. In J. L. Livingstone (ed.), *Managerial Accounting: The Behavioural Foundations* (Grid, 1975).

Zero-Base Budgeting: Prospects for Developing a Semi-Confusing Budgeting Information System

JOHN J. WILLIAMS
University of Alberta

Abstract

This paper argues for the recognition that zero-base budgeting (ZBB) is a destabilizing process which may co-exist in the future with traditional budgeting systems (TBS) to form a semi-confusing information system. The stabilizing and destabilizing features of a semi-confusing information system are explored first. The characteristics of ZBB as a formal budgeting process are examined next to provide a comparative profile of its destabilizing features in a changing environment. Analytically, ZBB characteristics match with the destabilizing properties of a semi-confusing information system and this insight has substantial implications for the future use of ZBB.

Since its advent approximately a decade ago, the phrase "zero-base budgeting" (ZBB) has been echoed in many public and private organizations. During this short tenure, an impressive list of claims and benefits has been amassed in the literature by zealous supporters of ZBB. Assertions have been advanced, for example, that ZBB leads to better decision making, more effective use of resources, and yields many behavioral advantages such as improved communication, participation, and motivation (Bergeron, 1979; Knight, 1979a; Roehm & Castellano, 1977). These sources and others, suggest ZBB is superior to its historical precedent, traditional budgeting. In the process, the traditional budgeting system (TBS) has been criticized using empirical observations while ZBB, in contrast, has been favored by normatively based arguments. Thus, there are logical inconsistencies in the supportive arguments for ZBB.

Equally obvious in the literature, are antagonists who have condemned ZBB in the same method and manner. For example, critics point to ZBB as fraudulent, due to its apparent inability to deliver a complete review of expenditures; unrealistic, because the ZBB methodology cannot work; unmanageable, because of the large amount of paper work, and more (Anthony, 1977; Lipstein, 1977). The essence of the antagonists' mission has been to discredit ZBB empirically, and

reinforce the entrenched TBS. Yet despite the praise and criticism, real or alleged, the number of converts to ZBB may be small, but are growing (Stonich, 1977).

The motivating forces contributing to the growth of interest in ZBB are open to debate. Its emergence and early use can be traced to innovative management at Texas Instruments, Inc. (Phyrr, 1970); it has been used to support political images in government elections (Pattillo, 1977) and to resolve budget crises (MacFarlane, 1976). A fundamental contemporary reason however, is the increasing inability of managers to cope with discretionary costs which are "strangling" budget planning and resource allocation in the public sector and "squeezing" profits in the private sector.

There are several indications that developments in the economy are straining the traditional budgeting mechanism in its attempt to control discretionary expenditures. Public administrators appear to be very perplexed over the growing number and magnitude of new funding requests combined with higher expenditures necessary to maintain incumbent projects. In many instances, a significant portion of annual expenditures are discretionary in nature and involve judgments about social values which are not readily assessed using quantitative, rational "scientific" evaluations

(Ogden, 1978; Wildavsky, 1978).

The impact of discretionary costs has been manifested in several respects throughout the economy. In the private sector, the last several decades have produced a technological shift in the direction of increased service support systems within the organization. The service industry itself has experienced rapid growth. In wages alone, discretionary costs represent over 80 per cent of Canada's total payroll (Macintosh, 1980). Even within the traditional manufacturing sector of the economy, there has been, and continues to be at the firm level, a shifting emphasis toward service-oriented support systems. These areas include more sophisticated and complex maintenance systems, computer systems, ecological and pollution control systems, and a score of other ancillary staff functions. Not only has this trend drastically altered the structure of many organizations, but it has also magnified the importance of controlling discretionary costs. Needless to say, inflation has not eased the concern of managers and public administrators over spiralling discretionary costs in the budget.

If the environment is inducing so much havoc in the budgeting process, and if traditional budgeting is an anachronistic mechanism for controlling discretionary costs, why cannot ZBB and TBS co-exist? Co-existent budgeting systems is not a novel thought; Stedry (1960), and later Hofstede (1967), advocated multiple budgeting systems where separate budgets were prescribed for different purposes. Even most of the ZBB critics acknowledge some kind of zero-base review roughly every five years on the grounds that annual ZBB is expensive, time consuming, and adds little insight into annual government programs. Of course, proponents of ZBB envisage it as more than a mere periodic review process; to them, it is a competitive alternative, not a supplementary contribution to an organization's budgeting system (Williams, in press). However, it is very unlikely that they can argue convincingly for the claim that ZBB has all the virtues of TBS and one less defect. If this is such a foreboding task, why not then, maintain the merits and defects of the traditional budgeting process in its present evolutionary state and add ZBB as a separate, parallel process for controlling discretionary costs? Novel, maybe, but absurd? — no. My intent in outlining the characteristics of a semi-confusing information system is to reveal the potential virtues of two budgeting processes co-existing within a *single* information system.

CHARACTERISTICS OF SEMI-CONFUSING INFORMATION SYSTEMS

In part, organizations interact with their environments through formalized information systems implemented by human behavior. Like organizations, information systems can stagnate because design imbalances prevent them from processing and responding effectively to changes in their environments. In benevolent, stable environments, stabilizers keep behavior and information processes consistent over time through standardizing procedures and by reinforcing success with repeated use (March & Simon, 1958; Hedburg & Jönsson, 1978). Stabilizing processes tend to build-in desired rigidity and inflexibility, clarify roles and procedures, drive out ambiguity of purpose, filter away inconsistencies and duplication, and strive for zero redundancy and no overlap (Hedburg et al., 1976; Hedburg & Jönsson, 1978; Landau, 1973). Stabilizers thus breed insensitivity to change signals through routinization and bureaucratic rigidity (Cyert & March, 1963) and introduce serious response delays into organizations' decision systems which can threaten survival (Hedburg, 1975; 1978). As a consequence, gradual environmental changes are not recognized, old information processes evolve into sanctioned organization ideologies, communication is displaced by executive planning, and effectiveness is measured in terms of conformity to the past (Hedburg, 1975; Hedburg & Jönsson, 1978; Thompson, 1974).

However, when the environment is hostile and fluctuating, previously programmed experience and repertoires of behavior prevent new responses from taking place and dampen, if not destroy, initiatives to behave differently. This inhibits organizations' adaptability and leads instead to organizational inertia. To counteract the inertia induced by stabilizing processes, organizations require information systems that enable them to adapt and tune into changing environments. Specifically, they need destabilizing processes which are the antitheses of stabilizing processes. Destabilizers act as early warning devices to locate change signals, detect problems and conflicts in time, and to counteract old standardized routines. The critical intent is to design information systems that can dialectically destabilize organizations by using planned confusion (Hedburg, 1978; Hedburg & Jönsson, 1978) to combat modern information system designs which tend to thwart organizational search, and which filter away relevant uncertainty, diversity, and change signals (Marshowitz, 1976). Hence, an ideal semi-confusing information system would contain balancing destabilizing elements and stabilizing elements.

Finding the right balance though, is not an easy task because of the highly interactive processes that dominate organizations, the decision makers in them, the formalized information systems, and changing environments. Both Nystrom *et al.* (1976) and Hedburg & Jönsson (1978) agree however, that the dialectical process of learning, unlearning, and relearning is a major design issue. Moreover, not only are the complexities of cognitive structure important in this regard, but also, semi-confusing information systems must have built-in mechanisms for dealing with contingencies related to the state of the organization–environment interface.

Hedburg & Jönsson (1978) outline cognitive and emotional phases which characterize the cyclical behavior pattern of organization states over time. During the cognitive phase, organizations develop inertia through stabilizing processes which brings on a crisis situation as problems accumulate but go unnoticed. The crisis in turn, generates enthusiasm for a solution-in-principle, initiates experimental behavior and new action, which then leads to the replacement of old theories (myths) with new ones. Thus, design features should foster experimental behavior, emphasize evaluations, and be easy to rearrange. On the other hand, changing environments may well challenge design issues not only of existing models but also the assumptions of future user needs and systems and the very way in which information is collected. In short, different environments demand different decision processes, and in turn, different information systems (Hedburg & Jönsson, 1978).

Implicit in the concept of a semi-confusing information system is a "duality" of processes which envelop both stabilizing and destabilizing characteristics. Current accounting systems, inclusive of the budgeting process, in both the public and private sector, are thought to be stabilizing processes (Hedburg & Jönsson, 1978; Nystrom *et al.*, 1976; Wildavsky, 1972; 1978). Alternatively, Hedburg & Jönsson (1978) imply

that accounting information systems can be destabilizing processes, but no concrete solution-in-principle is offered.

The challenge is pending: the remainder of this paper examines ZBB from a formal systems perspective in an effort to identify its destabilizing characteristics. The rationale for pursuing this effort rests on a simple paradox: in order for a stabilizing process to reach or maintain equilibrium *vis à vis* a hostile environment, a destabilizing process is actually required. This is contrary to most traditional thinking which suggests that a stabilizing process *by itself* is necessary *and* sufficient for the attainment of equilibrium. This view is not advocated here however; instead, the destabilizing process is perceived as a stabilizing element in striving toward equilibrium. Since TBS cannot be both stabilizing and destabilizing simultaneously, and since any discontinuity in its use is highly remote, there is a need to identify a destabilizing budgetary process (ZBB) that can simultaneously co-exist with TBS as a single, planned semi-confusing budgeting system. Such a marriage of ZBB and TBS would preclude unnecessary disparaging remarks revolving around the choice of one process or the other; instead they could co-evolve in the limit of equilibrium as one budgetary system.

SYSTEMS CHARACTERISTICS OF ZBB

In a formal context, any planning and control system can be represented schematically as shown in Fig. 1. The substantive content or core of a process delimits its domain (data base) and defines the elements (dimensions) which the information system should measure (Dill, 1958; Thompson, 1967). The processing stage generally includes a program for axiomatic manipulation and calculation together with cognitive inferences about desired goals, ascertaining the magnitude of elements deemed necessary to reach those goals, and finally, format procedures for arranging the output. The output of the system is usually designed to convey the intended relationships of the data formulated in the processing stage. The *ex ante*, or planning phase of a budgeting system in particular, considers the data set in a future context while the *ex post* phase of control,

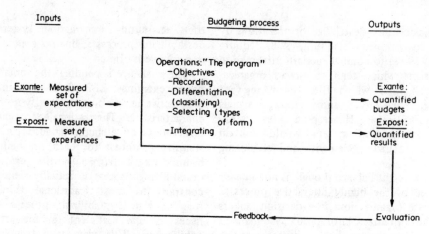

Fig. 1. A formal budgeting system.

evaluation, and feedback, compares the expectations with experience. Externalities and management preferences usually dictate the relevant time dimension.

The above systems framework provides a basis for analyzing the theoretical features of ZBB. In so doing, it becomes possible to delineate and describe the semi-confusing information system characteristics of ZBB.

The data set

ZBB deals exclusively with discretionary cost activity; state-oriented elements such as assets, liabilities, and equities, as well as revenue activities are outside its domain (Phyrr, 1970; MacIntosh, 1980). A subtle feature of discretionary cost is that it is meaningful only when considered jointly from an economic and behavioral perspective. Economic analysis assumes that total cost can be decomposed into a variable component which is functionally related to discrete units of output over a relevant range of activity, and a fixed component which is related to long-run capacity. On the other hand, behavioral analysis partitions total cost into the categories of controllable and non-controllable according to the authority structure of the organization. This approach recognizes "people" rather than output as the activity variable. The resultant combinations are illustrated in Fig. 2.

Relative to the economic dimension of Fig. 2, only fixed cost is common to ZBB. Phyrr (1973), the pioneering authority in ZBB, makes this distinction clear by eliminating all those costs

Fig. 2. Behavioral and economic data set for cost control.

which are conducive to "standard-setting". Budgeting literature clearly links standard cost to variable cost, and not fixed cost (Horngren, 1977). On the behavioral side, the apposed classes of controllable/non-controllable cost are not usually recognized in the ZBB literature, *per se*, but Phyrr (1970, p. 112) specifically uses the referent "activities where the manager has discretion to choose" which is synonymous with controllable cost. In short, then, the data set of ZBB consists of those cost activities which have the joint attributes of cell C_1, notwithstanding the conventional references to proposal, project, function, discrete activity, or any other description.

Viewed in this manner, the word "zero-base", or starting from "scratch" each period which is a popular description of the ZBB method, assumes significance. A moment's reflection will quickly reveal that, by definition, all discretionary costs are initiated afresh each budget period. Hence, the assertions in the literature that ZBB deals with nondirect expenses such as pure overhead (Stonich, 1977); that an agency makes no reference to the level of previous appropriations (Merewitz & Sosnick, 1971); and all projected levels of expenditure must be justified in total with no level taken for granted (Suver & Brown, 1977), are all suspect and erroneous generalizations about the substantive data base of ZBB.

The data base of ZBB exemplifies several semi-confusing information system characteristics, one of which is redundancy. Redundancy operates through such factors as duplication and overlap. These are important because they lead to error suppression and enhance the adaptiveness and flexibility of organizations facing changing environments. Pragmatically, duplication requires a system composed of independent and separate parts such that the failure of any part will not induce or directly impair the functioning of other parts (Landau, 1969). Furthermore, the system must have diagnostic capabilities, adjustment mechanisms to minimize the impact of errors (malfunctions), and the ability to correct faulty parts. These properties of overlap are typically manifested in parallel networks and not those wired together in a long linked series (Von Neumann, 1956; Landau, 1969). Typical examples of duplication and overlap are to be found in the design of safety features for aircraft and dual braking systems for automobiles.

How does ZBB contribute to redundancy? In the first place, ZBB duplicates part of the domain of traditional budgeting since both processes deal explicitly with a data set comprising discretionary cost. But more interesting, is the manner in which the respective data sets are created in the budgetary process. The logic of TBS calls for the extrapolation of past levels of discretionary cost spending by account classification, each classification to articulate with the total master budget, to produce a current level of discretionary spending for each account classification. In essence, the data is arranged serially; additions or deletions to any particular account necessarily impact *all* of the associated activities across the entire organization. ZBB, on the other hand, overlaps the discretionary cost domain of TBS and it accomplishes this through a mutually exclusive process. Instead of a serial linkage for each discretionary cost classifica-

tion in the budget process, ZBB creates separate and independent units of activity which not only parallel one another across the organization, but which in aggregate, parallel the traditional budgeting process in dealing with discretionary cost. Hence, there is no interdependence in the process of arriving at current budgeted discretionary costs under the two processes. At the fundamental data level, then, ZBB has potential redundancy factors; the destabilizing implications will be more completely examined in conjunction with its methodology.

For the present though, it is important to realize that the impact of top management policy associated with the concept of discretionary expenditures is analogous to the behavioral dimension of Fig. 2. For example, the distribution of controllable cost within the organizational hierarchy is directly related to the dispersion of authority by the top echelon. This leaves considerable latitude for experimental behavior since the choice of discretionary activities can span various subsegments of the total planned activities of the organization depending on the needs of management. In fact Knight (1979a, b) and Phyrr (1973) fully endorse this possibility. It follows that the choice of data base becomes easy to rearrange and contributes to increased flexibility. The organization can adapt to a changing organizational–environmental interface without severe pressures of rigidity and constraint.

Moreover, the potential use of ZBB at discontinuous time intervals has also been condoned by the literature. This simply means that ZBB would be activated, say every second or third year. Its cycle would thus be inconsistent and not particularly congruent to the facilitation of planning if predictability is the key criterion. But flexibility would be enhanced, most likely at the expense of increased ambiguity of both roles and purpose. Indeed, such destabilizing characteristics are the very cornerstone of a semi-confusing information system.

ZBB methodology

As a budgeting process, ZBB is a planning and control mechanism and includes the elements of objective setting, operational decision making, and evaluation. Its method is generally characterized as a bottom-to-top communication process involving two basic steps (Pattillo, 1977; Phyrr, 1977). The first step is one of differentiation; discrete activities (of a discretionary cost nature) for decision units are analyzed and developed in the form of decision packages within the context of a minimum level of effort (usually below the current level of expenditure). Also, any additional activity for a decision unit can be formulated in an independent series of incremental decision packages, each one having a specified dollar cost. In addition to the requested dollar funding, all of the narrative explaining why the expenditure is necessary, consequences of not performing an activity, alternative procedures for accomplishing the goals, cross-impact analysis with other decision units, and cost/benefit analysis are included in the decision package documentation. There is no theoretical limit to the number of decision units identified or the number of decision packages developed within each decision unit (Phyrr, 1973).

The second step is one of integration; all decision packages are ranked, first within each decision unit, and then vertically across all decision units in the organizational hierarchy. The ranking procedure can be accomplished through cost/benefit analysis or subjective evaluation (Phyrr, 1970) but empirically, the former approach has been the most generally accepted (Farney, 1977; Knight, 1979a, b).

Redundancy factors, an essential feature of semi-confusing information systems, also characterize the methodology of ZBB because there is duplication of purpose and planning relative to TBS. Internal to its own boundaries, ZBB accommodates more than modest amounts of pluralism in objectives, diversity of perspectives, and incompatibility of measurement. In addition to the mere allocation of resources and operational decision processes, Phyrr (1970) stressed the objective setting and evaluation capabilities of ZBB *vis à vis* organizational states and changing environments. In attempting to fulfil these idealistic purposes, ZBB must penetrate several different decision levels in an organization. However, Dirsmith & Jablonsky (1979) effectively challenge the potential ability of ZBB to co-mingle the decision strategies required at the technical, managerial, and institutional levels. In doing so, they refer to the contentions of Parson (1960) that quantitative and qualitative shifts in the decision process are required as one progresses through these three levels. This creates ambiguity and distorts the clarity of roles under the ZBB process and means that ZBB cannot be uniformly applied, interpreted, and used across diverse sectors.

Planning discretionary expenditures becomes ambiguous because of the economic dimension alluded to earlier (see Fig. 2). ZBB deals with fixed costs, and *a priori*, management does not know what the proper level of fixed costs should be for any budget period. Paradoxically, the decision on the appropriate level of fixed costs is shifted to lower levels in the organization via the behavioral dimension. The traditional role of top management's objective setting process is now reversed, but subjective judgment is still required at these lower levels. Regardless of the authority level involved, appropriations cannot be justified, *per se*; there is no basis for determining whether the allocation of funds could be improved, and no way of ascertaining the efficiency associated with any given allocation and expenditure (Merewitz & Sosnick, 1971). Yet there is the expectation in the ZBB process, that lower level management is capable of and motivated toward the identification of legitimate output goals within their respective decision units, searching out alternative courses of action, quantifying them, and ranking them accordingly. No doubt this engenders some degree of experimental behavior, co-existent with a transition of roles for lower level management. More will be said on the evaluative implications of ZBB in a subsequent section.

The method of calculation in the ZBB methodology raises other possible ambiguities and displays other characteristics of semi-confusing information systems. Unlike the incremental calculation of line-item dollar magnitudes inherent in TBS, Wildavsky (1978) has called the method of ZBB calculation comprehensive. This feature directly relates to several destabilizing qualities since ZBB calculation envelops the process of evaluation in an *a priori* sense, and impacts error recognition and correction. Evaluation becomes non-trivial and complex under ZBB because each independent decision package is presumed to focus on outputs of the system as they relate to strategic objectives. Operationally, however, cost/benefit analysis can only quantify the costs (inputs). There is ample room therefore, for extremes of bias in the evaluation process which further contribute to ambiguity. Moreover, the evaluation process is ahistorical; there is no retention by definition because all discretionary expenditures for the current budget period are reviewed from "scratch". Hence, from one time period to the next, the consistency and continuity of decision packages are non-existent. The result is induced amnesia and the presence of such a state in the budgetary process prompted Wildavsky to conclude that "both calculation and conflict increase exponentially, the former worsening selection, and the latter, correction of error" (1978; p. 501).

In a different, but not contradictory sense, the overlapping qualities of ZBB can inhibit errors and lead to a more reliable information system. Here, it must be remembered that not only are decision units viewed as separate entities, but each decision package developed within any decision unit is assumed to be serially independent and allowed to stand on its own merit. Therefore, in addition to potential diagnostic capabilities manifested in the cost/benefit evaluation, the impact of errors or malfunctions (in an *ex post* sense) can be handled in isolation. Marginal adjustments to the organization are thus possible because of the parallel network of mutually exclusive decision packages.

Von Neumann (1956) demonstrated that increased reliability in an information system is exponentially related to increases in redundancy factors such as overlapping and duplication. Internally, ZBB exhibits overlapping calculations by virtue of "cross-impact analysis" which is inherently part of the cost/benefit evaluation (Knight, 1979a, b). It is precisely such redundancies that allow for the delicate process of mutual adjustment, of self-regulation, and permit the whole system to absorb severe localized disturbances and still function creditably (Landau, 1969).

Adaptability is further enhanced by ZBB because behavior can be strictly changed in accordance with changed stimuli that have a specific decision package effect, unlike the serially-linked line-items of TBS which transcend the entire hierarchy. Obviously there arises a trade-off between cost and reliability but the latter can be increased geometrically with only arithmetic increases in redundancy (Von Neumann, 1956). In short, ZBB calculation appears to provide for flexibility in objectives while simultaneously removing the threat of a single change effecting the entire organization.

In a somewhat different context, the calculation of cost/benefit decision packages illuminates other semi-confusing information system characteristics. As Wildavsky observes "for purposes of resource allocation, which is what budgeting is about, ranking objectives without consideration of resources is irrational" (1978; p. 506). Yet, this is the central core of the ZBB

procedural mechanism: decision packages are prepared without explicit knowledge of the amount of fundings, or even whether any of the decision packages within a decision unit will be funded. When such "systems" logic is combined with non-quantifiable outputs, it is clear that ZBB does not avoid filtering away inconsistencies and incompatible information. This increases the noxiety proportion of the decision base but renders potential problems more visible (Streufert; 1973).

The ranking process, distinct from calculation, harbors additional destabilizing design features which arise from two fundamental issues. First, the specific level in the hierarchy at which to consolidate decision packages must be decided; and second, the basis for ranking must be determined. Phyrr (1970) acknowledged the two theoretical extremes in response to the former issue; one ranking for the entire organization or a set of rankings for each of the lowest decision unit levels in the organization. One ranking not only poses severe logistics problems of circumscribing a "manageable task" for any reasonable sized organization, but it also effectively negates the role of middle management in the budgeting process. The other extreme appears to nullify the "rational calculus" of ZBB and effectively presents inter-decision unit trade-offs from a total organizational perspective. It is not surprising to find both of these theoretical ranking extremes rejected in the normative ZBB literature.

Instead, consolidated rankings are advocated for each progressively higher authority level in the organization structure. Phyrr (1970) suggests that the optimum arrangement will ultimately depend on factors such as the number of decision packages involved, time and effort associated with reviewing these decision packages, the ability and willingness of lower level managers to rank unfamiliar activities, and the need for an extensive organizational review. In a dynamic environment, it is most unlikely that standardized procedures or elements of consistency would ensue. Even more interesting is that Phyrr advocates either a consolidated multi-level ranking process conforming to the "formal" authority hierarchy or one based on groupings of similar activities that transcend normal authority boundaries. Either situation yields flexibility and emphasizes evaluation; however the latter clearly would induce increased role ambiguity and conflict, not to mention the increased complexity of *ex post facto* performance

195

evaluation. On the other hand, the multi-level approach to ranking would encompass more review, increase the search process, and increase the sensitivity of the organization to change signals reflected in proposed discretionary expenditures.

The basis of ranking at each consolidation level amplifies ambiguity in the ZBB process in additional ways. Phyrr (1970) originally advocated a committee type of voting mechanism. For example, decision unit managers from the same level of authority would form a group chaired by the next higher ranking manager. This scheme would continue to the top of the organization until all decision packages were ranked. More recently, weighted voting schemes, the development of a value matrix, and methods relying on bargaining and negotiation, have been advanced as alternative bases (Knight, 1979a, b). Regardless of choice, all of these techniques manifest a high degree of arbitrariness and political sensitivity because the output goals representing each funding request are ambiguous and ill-defined. A similar anomaly occurs with *ex post facto* evaluation. The rationale underlying these assessment problems will be examined more fully in a following section. In the final analysis, it appears to be elements of power, authority, and bargaining prowess by lower level managers that would dominate any chosen technique.

In summary, the ranking process of ZBB has the potential to permeate the organization, individual decision makers, and change signals reaching not only the organization itself, but also different management levels. It can foster the type of experimental behavior and variety in communication envisaged and endorsed by Burns & Stalker (1961), Hedburg *et al.* (1976), Landau (1973), and Wildavsky (1972). Focusing on individual decision makers, the ranking process envelops a variety of perception and evaluation techniques by mixing and integrating cognitive styles (Mason & Mitroff; 1973), learning styles (Kolb; 1974), and multiple performance criteria (Ridgeway; 1956). Finally, it counteracts the stabilizing process by which changes in budgeted discretionary expenditures (signals) are normally brought about. The search process of establishing decision packages, adding, deleting, or rearranging the rankings as the process transcends the hierarchy *en route* to the ultimate ranking at the top, is fundamentally different from the incremental stabilizing approach of TBS. All in all, this indicates a comprehensive set of semi-confusing information system characteristics being demonstrated by ZBB.

The output

The output from the ZBB system is a vector of ranked decision packages identified in order of decreasing benefit to the organization (Phyrr, 1970). At this point, only one decision remains for top management: resources are simply allocated to decision units by funding all decision packages up to the cut-off point which then exhausts the resources available for the current budgeting period.

It is perhaps expedient at this stage of inquiry to caution that ZBB is a product of logic and not historical evolution. Its purposes and procedures represent a set of postulated propositions. However, the design of its output format is surely as artistic (versus scientific) as that found in any other discipline and may be more so. The literature is replete with how-to-do-it formats for decision package design. They can be simple or complex, detailed or vague, easily re-arranged, and stimulate as much creativity as management is willing to put forth. Currently available tutorial and seminar material substantiates the immense flexibility and possibilities for experimental behavior induced by ZBB format design.

In principle, the output of the ZBB process has a built-in contingency mechanism. To the extent that changes occur in the level of available funding during the budget cycle, the priority of the final ranking may be easily reviewed and re-arranged such that discarded decision packages are re-activated. Of course, changes in the environment may not affect the level of funding which is available *per se*, but rather it may create a need to "priorize" decision packages in a different order at some interim point during the budget cycle. The output vector of rankings in this case allows for easy review and permits "localized" changes if necessary, without jeopardizing the assumed benefits of all the remaining decision packages.

Control and evaluation

The formalized features of ZBB abruptly end with the systems features outlined above. Budgeted discretionary cost data would normally be fed into the chart of accounts contained in an organization's accounting system and *ex post facto* monitoring would ensue. Alternatively, decision packages could be monitored for accountability and effectiveness (Cheek, 1977; Knight, 1979a, b).

However, one of the reasons for carefully delineating the joint attributes (i.e., fixed and controllable) of discretionary cost is to facilitate the identification of the type of assessment which is appropriate for measuring the systemic relevance of ZBB. Thompson (1967) provides a convenient two-dimensional matrix for analyzing this problem. Along one dimension in Fig. 3, beliefs about cause–effect relationships are classified at the extremes of complete and incomplete, while the other dimension dichotomizes goal relevance into the categories crystallized and ambiguous.

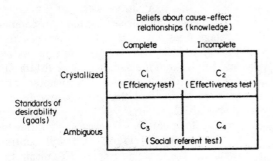

Fig. 3. Assessing knowledge and goals.

In cell C_1, measures of efficiency are appropriate because input–output relationships can be accurately defined and operationalized on a relative basis. Cell C_2 calls for the instrumental test of determining whether the desired goal is achieved and is typically referred to in accounting as a measure of effectiveness. Efficiency tests are not appropriate here because there is no way of assessing the causal action. If standards of desirability are ambiguous, cells C_3 and C_4 must be assessed by social reference groups.

The evaluative concepts germane to ZBB are compatible with the framework established by Thompson (1967). *A priori*, there are no scientific standards available for discretionary costs because the optimal relationship between results (output) and resource requirements (input) is not known. Results from specific discretionary activities such as research and development nearly defy identification, never mind quantification. Thus, efficiency and effectiveness tests are inappropriate. This leaves social reference tests as constituting an integral part of ZBB evaluation and assessment (MacIntosh, 1980). Peer group rankings, value matrices, and bargaining all reflect just this kind of test.

For purposes of *ex post facto* monitoring, established amounts of discretionary cost spending for each decision package and/or unit can be viewed as crystallized in the absence of no changes. However, knowledge of cause–effect relationships for discretionary cost spending still remains less than scientific. Under such circumstances, accountants traditionally resort to effectiveness measures over the budget cycle. Such assessments are appropriate for ZBB as well.

In summary, the above sub-sections have focused on the critical elements of ZBB from a systems perspective. The domain, methodology, output, and evaluation aspects of ZBB each reveal a sub-set of destabilizing properties. Admittedly, there is not complete uniformity of these properties across each element in the system. In aggregate though, it is appropriate to suggest that all of the combined destabilizing properties of ZBB yield a destabilizing process. It should be recalled that this distinguishing feature provides a critical linkage in the design of a semi-confusing information system. Viewing ZBB in this manner would appear to have implications for the planned, simultaneous use of ZBB and traditional budgeting.

IMPLICATIONS

The notion of co-existing budgeting systems, with ZBB as the destabilizing component, is not advocated by the ZBB literature. ZBB is usually cast in a competitive role with TBS and the complementary aspects of ZBB, especially from a semi-confusing design aspect, have been ignored. Instead, a lot of effort has been expended in attempting to convince managers that ZBB is "better than" TBS, or conversely, that ZBB is patently "inferior" to TBS. Perhaps the difficulty is that management, and postulated management practice, are conditioned by an historical precedent which says that there can only be one budgetary process at a time. Admittedly, Cheek (1977), Knight (1979a, b), Phyrr (1973), and others speak of "phasing-in" routines for ZBB; and Fogarty & Turnbull (1977) explore the concept of rotating ZBB. Still, one cannot help but deduce that management is restricted to the choice of either TBS or ZBB on a trial basis, rather than the prospect of consolidating both into an integrated, permanent semi-confusing budgeting design.

Since TBS is currently such an engrained

budget philosophy, it is not unreasonable to conclude that a majority of managers would prefer precedent over innovation, rigidity over flexibility, consistency and rationality rather than inconsistency and ambiguity, and easy, incremental calculation to complex, comprehensive calculation. This preference prevails despite the fact that for many organizations, discretionary activity does exist; the environment is hostile in terms of technological, social, and regulatory changes, and each of these impact a discretionary cost base which is unmanageable because it contains a primary unpredictable element. At present, it is in vogue to use only one budgeting process at a time; but as Landau cautions

managements may do this in the interest of economy and control, but the economy will be false and the control a ritual – for we are acting, and organizing, as if we "know" when we do not (1969; p. 355).

Future problems, unforeseen, may well arise and lead to greater, unforeseen costs.

It should be observed however, that this singularity of thinking is not a consequence of the theoretical merits of any budgeting schemes. Rather, singularity is due to an historical preference based on tradition. Alternatively, Hedburg & Jönsson (1978) argue that the attitudes of top management, conditioned by the cognitive and emotional complexity of the organizational environment, dictate the adaptability of a particular information structure. Texas Instruments Inc. is a prime illustration. It has been repeatedly referred to as a leader in innovation and creative management which accounts for the successful co-existence of ZBB and TBS within that organization. This behavior is largely predicated by the fact that proactive inspirational and experimental behavior is an *a priori* expectation at Texas Instruments Inc. (Millar & Friesen, 1978).

But attitudes can be equally reactive to organization–environment relationships such as those conditioned by a crisis situation. MacFarlane (1976) describes a university faced with an oppressive budget deficit. The traditional budgeting approach induced fears of across-the-board cuts such that some departments would only be marginally affected while others would have their ability to perform severely impaired. ZBB was activated to highlight essential areas and activities which had to be maintained relative to those of lesser importance. Their traditional budgeting system was not shelved however, and the opportunity for TBS and ZBB to co-exist was realized. The salient message here however, is that TBS and ZBB should be employed simultaneously on a continuing basis, not to *manage* crises situations, but to *avoid* them.

While ZBB might thrive for reasons of management attitudes, there is potential for failure for the same reasons. In an interesting analysis of the environmental context of the United States Federal government, Dirsmith & Jablonsky conclude "that an atmosphere of environmental benevolence conducive to the development of strategy does not exist in the federal government" (1979, p. 563). Hence, the strategic, innovative, and inspiration-directed aspects of future ZBB use are jeopardized because "a wholly different attitude is required than is presently discernible" (Dirsmith & Jablonsky, 1979, p. 564). They are careful to point out however, that the tactical (operational) aspects of ZBB will continue to dominate the strategic aspects. This means that the potential for ZBB existing simultaneously within a single system with TBS is positive, but will encounter attitudinal restrictions in the implementation process.

A similar view is shared by Herzlinger who reviewed ZBB in the Public Health Service and concluded that "procedure and purpose became inverted in importance; ZBB drove out the analysis and substituted the mechanics" (1979, p. 10). The reasons were actually political and not the result of the ZBB process, but this inference may be reason enough to dampen the tolerance for more extensive ZBB exposure to federal government agencies in the future.

CONCLUSIONS

The theoretical framework of ZBB manifests virtually all of the destabilizing semi-confusing information system characteristics tentatively suggested by Hedburg & Jönsson (1978). Inherent in the ZBB process are ambiguity, inconsistency, redundancy, multiple perspectives, flexibility, and impermanency. It has the capability to locate change signals in discretionary cost activities and counteract old routines. Furthermore, the basic philosophy of ZBB promotes innovative and experimental behavior, encourages evaluation of strategic, managerial, and operational decision making, and stresses proaction in a changing environment. In short, ZBB is an ideal example of a destabilizing budgeting process which is sorely needed in contemporary management information systems.

There is no presumption in this exploratory inquiry that all of the destabilizing properties of ZBB have been exhausted, nor for that matter, that all of the properties of a semi-confusing information system in general have been identified – it is only an ambitious beginning. Hedburg & Jönsson (1978) have taken the first step by formulating the semi-confusing framework while the thoughts expressed here are a second step by delineating those destabilizing properties of ZBB which conform to that framework. It remains for future studies to research the implications of a semi-confusing budgeting system as it relates to co-ordination, performance measurement issues, and behavioral consequences. More immediate though, is the need to re-assess the use of ZBB in particular organization–environment situations, notably along the lines pursued by Dirsmith & Jablonsky (1979).

Until now, attitudinal and implementation problems have cast a shadow on the potential merits of ZBB but the clouds are moving. The environment is constantly changing for most organizations, public administrations of many types are expanding, the private sector is experiencing a growing service industry, and manufacturing industries are increasingly being deluged by necessary ancillary support functions. Discretionary activities permeate all of this and demand management attention. In turn, discretionary cost becomes a perpetual phenomenon; it simply will not disappear.

Thus, managers must abandon the idea that a single stabilizing budgetary process will promote organizational equilibrium in a changing, hostile environment. They must reshape their cognitive processes to include the planned co-existence of both destabilizing processes (ZBB) and stabilizing processes (TBS) within a single system – a semi-confusing budgeting information system.

BIBLIOGRAPHY

Anthony, R. N., Zero-Base Budgeting is a Fraud, *Wall Street Journal* (April 27, 1977).

Bergeron, P., Zero-Base Budgeting: A Methodology for Linking Action Plans to Program Goals, *Cost and Management* (March–April, 1979), pp. 11–17.

Burns, T. & Stalker, G. M., *The Management of Information* (London: Tavistock, 1961).

Cheek, Logan M., *Zero-Base Budgeting Comes of Age* (New York: AMACON, 1977).

Cyert, R. M. & March, J. G., *A Behavioral Theory of the Firm* (Englewood Cliffs, NJ: Prentice-Hall, 1963).

Dill, William R., Environment as an Influence on Managerial Autonomy, *Administrative Science Quarterly* (March, 1958), pp. 409–443.

Dirsmith, Mark W. & Jablonsky, Stephen F., Zero-Base Budgeting as a Management Technique and Political Strategy, *Academy of Management Review* (1979), pp. 555–565.

Farney, D., Birth Pains: Zero-Base Budgeting, A Pet Carter Project, is off to a Slow Start, *Wall Street Journal* (December 19, 1977).

Fogarty, Andrew B. & Turnbull, Augustus B., Ill., Legislative Oversight Through a Rotating Zero-Base Budget, *State and Local Government Review* (January 1977), pp. 18–22.

Hedburg, Bo, Growth Stagnation as a Managerial Discontinuity, in *Proceedings of the Insead Seminar on Management Under Discontinuity* (Brussels: European Institute for Advanced Studies in Management, 1975), pp. 34–59.

Hedburg, Bo, How Organizations Learn and Unlearn, in Paul C. Nystrom and William H. Starbuck, eds., *Handbook of Organizational Design, Vol. 1* (Oxford, Oxford University Press, 1981).

Hedburg, Bo & Jönsson, Sten, Designing Semi-Confusing Information Systems for Organizations in Changing Environments, *Accounting, Organizations and Society* (1978), pp. 47–64.

Hedburg, Bo, Nystrom, Paul C. & Starbuck, William H., Camping on Seesaws: Prescriptions for a Self-Designing Organization, *Administrative Science Quarterly* (March 1976), pp. 41–65.

Herzlinger, Regina E., Zero-Base Budgeting in the Federal Government: A Case Study, *Sloan Management Review* (Winter, 1979), pp. 3–14.

Hofstede, G. H., *The Game of Budget Control* (Van Garcum, 1967).

Horngren, Charles T., *Cost Accounting: A Managerial Emphasis* (Englewood Cliffs, NJ: Prentice-Hall, 1977).

PART III
INFORMATION ISSUES IN CONTROL SYSTEMS

Section three contains articles on typical information issues in planning and control systems; e.g., transfer pricing, direct versus absorption costing, and cost-volume-profit analysis and variance investigation decisions. Most of these articles treat the technical aspects of these information issues, either from a cost-benefit approach (Kaplan, Jaedicke & Robichek) or a "flexible" approach, and give a representative overview of the development of the discipline. The paper by Watson and Baumler did pioneering work on the need for an integrated approach to control systems design. Their paper demonstrates that firms face differing amounts of uncertainty because of technological and environmental factors. Watson & Baumler suggest that uncertainty leads to differentiation and the use of particular organizational structures. They see transfer prices as one control system variable that can be used to re-integrate the interdependent subcomponents of the organization. The criticism by Ansari and Tsuji and the recommendations of Watson and Baumler are the beginning of a new way of looking at technical information system issues.

Cost-Volume-Profit Analysis
Under Conditions of Uncertainty

ROBERT K. JAEDICKE
Stanford University

ALEXANDER A. ROBICHEK †

Traditional cost-volume-profit analysis is frequently used to make choices among alternative courses of action. The usefulness of this analysis is limited because the relative risk of various alternatives is not explicitly accounted for. When risk is introduced into the model, the resulting statement of probabilities with respect to various levels of profits and losses for each alternative should aid the decision maker, once his attitude toward risk has been defined. Illustrations are presented.

Cost-volume-profit analysis is frequently used by management as a basis for choosing among alternatives such decisions as: (1) the sales volume required to attain a given level of profits, and (2) the most profitable combination of products to produce and sell. However, the fact that traditional C-V-P analysis does not include adjustments for risk and uncertainty may, in any given instance, severely limit its usefulness. Some of the limitations can be seen from the following example.

Assume that the firm is considering the introduction of two new products, either of which can be produced by using present facilities. Both products require an increase in annual fixed cost of the same amount, say $400,000. Each product has the same selling price and variable cost per unit, say, $10 and $8, respectively, and each requires the same amount of capacity. Using these data, the break-even point of either product is 200,000 units. C-V-P analysis helps to establish the break-even volume of each product, but this analysis does not distinguish the relative desirability of the two products for at least two reasons.

The first piece of missing information is the *expected* sales volume of each product. Obviously, if the annual sales of A are expected to be 300,000 units and of B are expected to be 350,000 units, then B is clearly preferred to A so far as the sales expectation is concerned.

However, assume that the expected annual sales of each product is the same— say, 300,000 units. Is it right to conclude that management should be indifferent as far as a choice between A and B is concerned? The answer is *no, unless* each sales expectation is certain. If both sales estimates are subject to uncertainty, the decision process will be improved if the relative risk associated with each product can somehow be brought into the analysis. The discussion which follows suggests some changes which might be made in traditional C-V-P analysis so as to make it a more useful tool in analyzing decision problems under uncertainty.

Reprinted from The Accounting Review, October 1964 by permission of the publisher. © Copyright 1964 by the American Accounting Association. All rights reserved.

In the previous section, it was pointed out that *expected* volume of the annual sales is an important decision variable. Some concepts of probability will be discussed using the example posed earlier.

The four fundamental relationships used in the example were: (1) the selling price per unit; (2) the variable cost per unit; (3) the total fixed cost; and (4) the expected sales volume of each product. In any given decision problem, all four of these factors can be uncertain. However, it may be that, *relative to* the expected sales quantity, the costs and selling prices are quite certain. That is, for analytical purposes, the decision maker may be justified in treating several factors as certainty equivalents. Such a procedure simplifies the analysis and will be followed here as a first approximation. In this section of the paper, sales volume will be treated as the only uncertain quantity. Later, all decision factors in the above example will be treated under conditions of uncertainty.

In the example, sales volume is treated as a *random variable*. A random variable can be thought of as an *unknown quantity*. In this case, the best decision hinges on the value of the random variable, sales volume of each product. One decision approach which allows for uncertainty is to estimate, for each random variable, the likelihood that the random variable will take on various possible values. Such an estimate is called a subjective probability distribution. The decision would then be made by choosing that course of action which has the highest *expected monetary value*. This approach is illustrated in Table 1.

The expected value of the random variables, sales demand for each product, is calculated by weighting the possible conditional values by their respective probabilities. In other words, the expected value is a weighted average. The calculation is given in Table 2.

Based on an expected value approach, the firm should select product B rather than A. The expected profits of each possible action are as follows:

TABLE 1. Probability distribution for products A and B

Events (Units Demanded)	Probability Distribution— (Product A)	Probability Distribution— (Product B)
50,000	—	.1
100,000	.1	.1
200,000	.2	.1
300,000	.4	.2
400,000	.2	.4
500,000	.1	.1
	1.00	1.00

TABLE 2. Expected value of sales demand for products A and B

(1) Event	(2) P(A)	(1 X 2)	(3) P(B)	(1 X 3)
50,000	—	—	.1	5,000
100,000	.1	10,000	.1	10,000
200,000	.2	40,000	.1	20,000
300,000	.4	120,000	.2	60,000
400,000	.2	80,000	.4	160,000
500,000	.1	50,000	.1	50,000
	1.00		1.00	
Expected Value		300,000 units		305,000 units

TABLE 3.

Demand	P(A)	E.V.(A)	P(B)	E.V.(B)
100,000 units	.1	10,000	—	—
200,000 units	.2	40,000	—	—
300,000 units	.4	120,000	1.00	300,000
400,000 units	.2	80,000	—	—
500,000 units	.1	50,000	—	—
	1.00		1.00	
Expected Sales Demand		300,000		300,000

Product A:

$$\$2(300,000 \text{ units}) - \$400,000 = \$200,000$$

Product B:

$$\$2(305,000 \text{ units}) - \$400,000 = \$210,000$$

Several observations are appropriate at this point. First, the respective probabilities for each product, used in Table 1, add to 1.00. Furthermore, the possible demand levels (events) are assumed to be mutually exclusive and also exhaustive. That is, the listing is done in such a way that no two events can happen simultaneously and any events *not* listed are assumed to have a zero probability of occurring. Herein are three important (basic) concepts of probability analyses.

Secondly, the probability distributions may have been assigned by using historical demand data on similar products, or the weights may be purely subjective in the sense that there is no historical data available. Even if the probability distributions are entirely subjective, this approach still has merit. It allows the estimator to express his uncertainty about the sales estimate. An estimate of sales is necessary to make a decision. Hence, the question is *not* whether an estimate must be made, but simply [what is] the best way to make and express the estimate.

Now, suppose that the expected value of sales for each product is 300,000, as shown in Table 3. In this example, it is easy to see that the firm would *not* be indifferent between products A and B, even though the expected value of sales is 300,000 units in both cases. In the case of product A, for example, there is a .1 chance that sales will be only 100,000 units, and in that case, a loss of $200,000 would be incurred (i.e., $2 X 100,000 units - $400,000). On the other hand, there is a .3 chance that sales will be above 300,000 units, and if this is the case, higher profits are possible with product A than with product B. Hence, the firm's attitude toward risk becomes important. The expected value (or the mean of the distribution) is important, but so is the "spread" in the distribution. Typically, the greater the "spread," the greater the risk involved. A quantitative measure of the spread is available in the form of standard deviation of the distribution, and this concept and its application will be refined later in the paper.

THE NORMAL PROBABILITY DISTRIBUTION

The preceding examples were highly simplified and yet the calculations are relatively long and cumbersome. The possible sales volumes were few in number and the probability distribution was discrete, that is, a sales volume of 205,762 units was considered an impossible event. The use of a continuous probability distribution is desirable not only because the calculation will usually be simplified but because the distribution may also be a more realistic description of the uncertainty aspects of the situation. The normal probability distribution will be introduced and used in the following analysis which illustrates the methodology involved. This distribution, although widely used, is not appropriate in all situations. The appropriate distribution depends on the decisions problem and should, of course, be selected accordingly.

The normal probability distribution is a smooth, symmetric, continuous, bell-shaped curve as shown in Figure 1. The area under the curve sums to 1. The curve reaches a maximum at the mean of the distribution, and one-half the area lies on either side of the mean.

On the horizontal axis are plotted the values of the appropriate unknown quantity or random variable; in the examples used here, the unknown quantity is the sales for the coming periods.

A particular normal probability distribution can be completely determined if its mean and its standard deviation, σ, are known. The standard deviation is a measure of the dispersion of the distribution about its mean. The area under any normal distribution is 1, but one distribution may be "spread out" more than another distribution. For example, in Figure 2, both normal distributions have the same area and the same mean. However, in one case the σ is 1 and in the other case the σ is greater than 1. The larger the σ, the more spread out is the distribution. It should be noted that the standard deviation is not an area but is a measure of the dispersion of the individual observations about the mean of all the observations—it is a distance.

Since the normal probability distribution is continuous rather than discrete, the probability of an event cannot be read directly from the graph. The unknown quantity must be thought of as being in an interval. Assume, for example, that the mean sales for the coming period is estimated to be 10,000 units and the normal distribution appears as in Figure 3. Given Figure 3, certain probability statements can be made. For example:

1. The probability of the actual sales being between 10,000 and 11,000 units is .20. This is shown by area C. Because of the symmetry of the curve, the probability of the sales being between 9,000 and 10,000 is also .20. This is shown by shaded area B. These probabilities can be given a frequency interpretation. That is, area C indicates that the actual sales will be between 10,000 and 11,000 units in about 20 per cent of the cases.

2. The probability of the actual sales being greater than 11,000 units is .30 as shown by area D.

3. The probability of the sales being greater than 9,000 units is .70, the sum of areas B, C, and D.

Given a specific normal distribution, it is possible to read probabilities of the type described above directly from a normal probability table.

Another important characteristic of any normal distribution is that approximately .50 of the area lies within ±.67 standard deviations of the mean; about .68 of the area lies within ±1.0 standard deviations of the mean; .95 of the area lies within ±1.96 standard deviations of the mean.

As was mentioned above, normal probabilities can be read from a normal probability table. A partial table of normal probabilities is given in Table 4. This table is the "right tail" of the distribution; that is, probabilities of the unknown quantity being greater than X standard deviations from the mean are given in the table. For example, the probability of the unknown quantity being greater than the mean plus .35σ is .3632. The distribution tabulated is a normal distribution with mean zero and

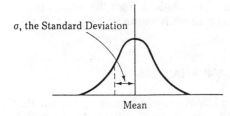

σ, the Standard Deviation

Mean

FIGURE 1. The normal probability distribution

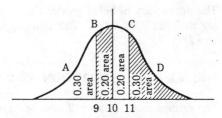

B   C

A   0.30 area   0.20 area   0.20 area   0.30 area   D

9 10 11

Units of Sales (Thousands)

FIGURE 3.

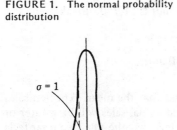

σ = 1

Mean

σ > 1

Mean

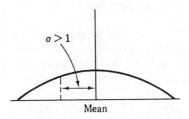

FIGURE 2. Normal probability distributions with different standard deviations

TABLE 4. Area under the normal probability function

X	0.00	0.05
.1	.4602	.4404
.3	.3821	.3632
.5	.3085	.2912
.6	.2743	.2578
.7	.2420	.2266
.8	.2119	.1977
.9	.1841	.1711
1.0	.1587	.1469
1.1	.1357	.1251
1.5	.0668	.0606
2.0	.0228	.0202

standard deviation of 1. Such a distribution is known as a standard normal distribution. However, any normal distribution can be standardized and hence, with proper adjustment, Table 4 will serve for any normal distribution.

For example, consider the earlier case where the mean of the distribution is 10,000 units. The distribution was constructed so that the standard deviation is about 2,000 units.[1] To standardize the distribution, use the following formula, where X is the number of standard deviations from the mean:

$$X = \frac{\text{Actual sales} - \text{mean sales}}{\text{Standard deviation of the distribution}}$$

To calculate the probability of the sales being greater than 11,000 units, first standardize the distribution and then use the table.

$$X = \frac{11,000 - 10,000}{2,000}$$

$$= .50 \text{ standard deviations.}$$

[1]To see why this normal distribution has a standard deviation of 2,000 units, remember that the probability of sales being greater than 11,000 units is .30. Now examine Table 4, and it can be seen that the probability of a random variable being greater than .5 standard deviations from the mean is .3085. Hence, 1,000 units is about the same as $\frac{1}{2}$ standard deviations. So, 2,000 units is about 1 standard deviation.

209

The probability of being greater than .50 standard deviations from the mean, according to Table 4, is .3085. This same approximate result is shown by Figure 3, that is, area D is .30.

THE NORMAL DISTRIBUTION USED IN C-V-P ANALYSIS

The normal distribution will now be used in a C-V-P analysis problem, assuming that sales quantity is a random variable. Assume that the per-unit selling price is $3,000, the fixed cost is $5,800,000, and the variable cost per unit is $1,750. Break-even sales (in units) is calculated as follows:

$$S_B = \frac{\$5,800,000}{\$3,000 - \$1,750} = 4,640 \text{ units.}$$

Furthermore, suppose that the sales manager estimates that the mean expected sales volume is 5,000 units and that it is equally likely that actual sales will be greater or less than the mean of 5,000 units. Furthermore, assume that the sales manager feels that there is roughly a 2/3 (i.e., .667) chance that the actual sales will be within 400 units of the mean. These subjective estimates can be expressed by using a normal distribution with mean $E(Q) = 5,000$ units and standard deviation $\sigma_q = 400$ units. The reason that σ_q is about 400 units is that, as mentioned earlier, about 2/3 of the area under the normal curve (actually .68) lies within 1 standard deviation of the mean. The probability distribution is shown in Figure 4.

The horizontal axis of Figure 4 denotes sales quantity. The probability of an actual sales even taking place is given by the area under the probability distribution. For example, the probability that the sales quantity will exceed 4,640 units (the break-even point) is the shaded area under the probability distribution (the probability of actual sales exceeding 4,640 units).

The probability distribution of Figure 4 can be superimposed on the profit portion of the traditional C-V-P; this is done in Figure 5. The values for price, fixed costs, and variable costs are presumed to be known with certainty. Expected profit is given by:

$$E(Z) = E(Q)(P\text{-}V) - F$$

$$= \$450,000$$

$$E(Z) = \text{Expected Profit}$$

$$E(Q) = \text{Expected Sales}$$

$$P = \text{Price}$$

$$V = \text{Variable Cost}$$

$$F = \text{Fixed Cost.}$$

The standard deviation of the profit (σ_z) is:

$$\sigma_z = \sigma_q \times \$1,250 \text{ contribution per unit}$$

$$= 400 \text{ units} \times \$1,250 = \$500,000.$$

Since profits are directly related to the volume of sales, and since it is the level of profits which is often the concern of management, it may be desirable to separate

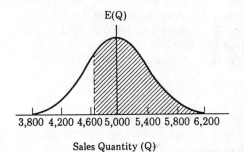

E(Q)

3,800 4,200 4,600 5,000 5,400 5,800 6,200

Sales Quantity (Q)

FIGURE 4.

the information in Figure 5 which relates to profit. Figure 6 is a graphical illustration of the relationship between profit level and the probability distribution of the profit level. A number of important relationships can now be obtained in probabilistic terms. Since the probability distribution of sales quantity is normal with a mean of 5,000 units and a standard deviation of 400 units, the probability distribution of profits will also be normal with a mean, as shown earlier, of $450,000 and a standard deviation of $500,000.

Using the probability distribution shown in Figure 6, the following probabilities can be calculated (using Table 4).

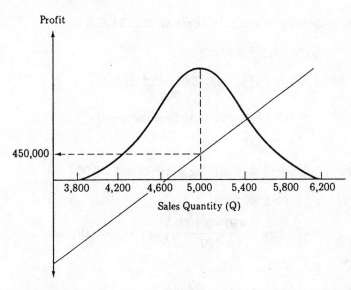

Profit

450,000

3,800   4,200   4,600   5,000   5,400   5,800   6,200

Sales Quantity (Q)

FIGURE 5.

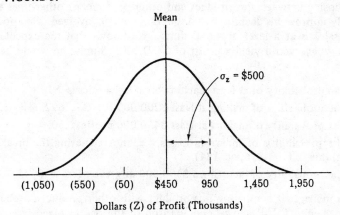

Mean

$\sigma_z = \$500$

(1,050)   (550)   (50) $450   950   1,450   1,950

Dollars (Z) of Profit (Thousands)

FIGURE 6.

211

1. The probability of at least breaking even: This is the probability of profits being greater than zero and can be calculated by summing the area under the distribution to the right of zero profits. This probability can be calculated as 1–(the probability of profits being less than zero). Since the distribution is symmetric, Table 4 can be used to read left tail as well as right tail probabilities. Zero profits fall .9 standard deviations to the left of the mean

$$\left(\text{ie.,} \frac{\$450 - 0}{\$500} = .9 \right)$$

Hence the probability of profits being less than zero is:

$$P(\text{Profits} < .9\sigma \text{ from the mean}) = .184.$$

Therefore

$$P(\text{Profits} > 0) = 1 - .184 = .816.$$

2. The probability of profits being greater than $200,000.

$$P(\text{Profits} > \$200,000)$$

$$= 1 - P\left(\text{Profits} < \frac{450 - 200}{500} \, \sigma \text{ from the mean} \right)$$

$$= 1 - P(\text{Profits} < .5\sigma \text{ from the mean})$$

$$= 1 - .3085 = .692.$$

3. The probability of the loss being greater than $300,000.

$$P(\text{Loss} > \$300,000)$$

$$= P\left(\text{Loss} > \frac{450 - (-300)}{500}, \right) \text{ or } 1.5\sigma \text{ from the mean}$$

$$P = .067.$$

The question of how the above information can be used now arises. The manager, in choosing between this product and other products or other lines of activity, can probably improve his decision by considering the risk involved. He knows that the break-even sales is at a level of 4,640 units. He knows that the expected sales are 5,000 units which would yield a profit of $450,000. Surely, he would benefit from knowing that:

1. The probability of at least reaching break-even sales is .816.
2. The probability of making at least $200,000 profit is .692.
3. The probability of making at least $450,000 profit is .50.
4. The probability of incurring losses, i.e., not achieving the break-even sales volume, is (1 - .816, or .184).
5. The probability of incurring a $300,000 or greater loss is .067.

If the manager is comparing this product with other products, probability analysis combined with C-V-P allows a comparison of the risk involved in each product, as well as a comparison of relative break-even points and expected profits. Given the firm's attitude toward and willingness to assume risk (of losses as well as high profits), the decision of choosing among alternatives should be facilitated by the above analysis.

SEVERAL RELEVANT FACTORS PROBABILISTIC

It is evident from the above discussion that profit, Z, is a function of the quantity of sales in units (Q); the unit selling price (P); the fixed cost (F); and the variable cost (V). Up to this point P, F, and V were considered only as given constants, so that profit was variable only as a function of changes in sales quantity. In the following discussion, P, F, and V will be treated in a manner similar to Q, i.e., as random variables whose probability distribution is known.[2] Continuing the example from the preceding section, let

Variable

    Sales Quantity (Q)
    Selling Price (P)
    Fixed Costs (F)
    Variable Costs (V)

Expectation (Mean)

$$E(Q') = 5,000 \text{ units}$$
$$E(P') = \$3,000^2$$
$$E(F') = \$5,800,000^2$$
$$E(V') = \$1,750^2$$

Standard Deviation

$$\sigma_{Q'} = 400 \text{ units}$$
$$\sigma_{P'} = \$50^2$$
$$\sigma_{F'} = \$100,000^2$$
$$\sigma_{V'} = \$75^2$$

For purposes of illustration, the random variables will be assumed to be independent, so that no correlation exists between events of the different random variables.[3] In this case, the expected profit $E(Z')$ and the related standard deviation $\sigma_{Z'}$ can be calculated as follows[4]:

---

[2] The mean and standard deviation for P, F, and V can be established by using the same method described earlier. That is, the sales manager may estimate a mean selling price of $3,000 per unit and, given the above information, he should feel that there is roughly a 2/3 probability that the actual sales price per unit will be within $50 of this mean estimate.

[3] This assumption is made to facilitate computation in the example. Where correlation among variables is present the computational procedure must take into account the values of the respective covariances.

[4] For the case of independent variables given here, $\sigma_{Z'}$ is the solution value in the equation:

$$\sigma_Z = \sqrt{[\sigma_{Q^2}(\sigma_{P^2} + \sigma_{V^2}) + E(Q')^2(\sigma_{P^2} + \sigma_{V^2}) + [E(P') - E(V')]^2 \sigma_{Q^2} + \sigma_{F^2}]}$$

$$E(Z') = E(Q')[E(P' - E(V')] - E(F')$$
$$= \$450{,}000.$$
$$\sigma_{z'} = \$681{,}500.$$

Note that when factors other than sales are treated as random variables, the expected profit is still $450,000 as in the previous cases. However, the profit's risk as measured by the standard deviation is increased from $500,000 to $681,500. The reason for this is that the variability in all of the components (i.e., sales price, cost, etc.) will add to the variability in the profit. Is this change in the standard deviation significant? The significance of the change is a value judgment based on a comparison of various probabilistic measures and on the firm's attitude toward risk. Using a normal distribution, Table 5 compares expected profits, standard deviations of profits, and select probabilistic measures for three hypothetical products.

In all three situations, the proposed products have the same break-even quantity—4,640 units. The first case is the first example discussed where sales quantity is the only random variable. The second case is the one just discussed; that is, all factors are probabilistic. In the third case, the assumed product has the same expected values for selling price, variable cost, fixed cost, and sales volume, but the standard deviations on each of these random variables have been increased to $\sigma_{Q''} = 600$ (instead of 400 units); $\sigma_{P''} = \$125$ (instead of $50); $\sigma_{F''} = \$200{,}000$ (instead of $100,000); and $\sigma_{V''} = \$150$ (instead of $75).

Table 5 shows the relative "risk" involved in the three new products which have been proposed. The chances of at least breaking even are greatest with product 1. However, even though the standard deviation of the profit on product 3 is over twice that of product 1, the probability of breaking even on product 3 is only .17 lower than product 1. Likewise, the probability of earning at least $250,000 profit is higher for product 1 (which has the lowest σ) than for the other two products.

However, note that the probability of earning profits above the expected value of $450,000 (for each product) is *greater* for products 2 and 3 than for 1. If the firm is willing to assume some risk, the chances of high profits are improved with product 3, rather than with 2 and 1. To offset this, however, the chance of loss is also greatest with product 3. This is to be expected, since product 3 has the highest standard deviation (variability) as far as profit is concerned.

The best alternative cannot be chosen without some statement of the firm's attitude toward risk. However, given a certain attitude, the proper choice should be facilitated by using probability information of the type given in Table 5. As an example, suppose that the firm's position is such that any loss at all may have an adverse

TABLE 5. Comparison of expected profits, standard deviations of profits, and probabilistic measures*

	Products		
	(1)	*(2)*	*(3)*
Expected profit	$450,000	$450,000	$ 450,000
Standard deviation of profit	$500,000	$681,500	$1,253,000
The probability of:			
(a) at least breaking even	.816	.745	.641
(b) profit at least + $250,000	.655	.615	.564
(c) profit at least + $600,000	.382	.413	.456
(d) loss greater than $300,000	.067	.136	.274

*Note: The above probabilities, in some cases, cannot be read from Table 4. However, all probabilities come from a more complete version of Table 4.

effect on its ability to stay in business. Some probability criteria can, perhaps, be established in order to screen proposals for new products. If, for example, top management feels that any project which is acceptable must have no greater than a .30 probability of incurring a loss, then projects 1 or 2 would be acceptable but project 3 would not.

On the other hand, the firm's attitude toward risk may be such that the possibility of high profit is attractive, provided the probability of losses can be reasonably controlled. In this case, it may be possible to set a range within which acceptable projects must fall. For example, suppose that the firm is willing to accept projects where the probability of profits being greater than $600,000 is at least .40, provided that the probability of loss being greater than $300,000 does not exceed .15. In this case, project 2 would be acceptable, but project 3 would not. Given statements of attitude toward risk of this nature, it seems that a probability dimension added to C-V-P analysis would be useful.

SUMMARY AND CONCLUSION

In many cases, the choice among alternatives is facilitated greatly by C-V-P analysis. However, traditional C-V-P analysis does not take account of the relative risk of various alternatives. The interaction of costs, selling prices, and volume is important in summarizing the effect of various alternatives on the profits of the firm. The techniques discussed in this paper preserve the traditional analysis but also add another dimension—that is, risk is brought in as another important decision factor. The statement of probabilities with respect to various levels of profits and losses for each alternative should aid the decision maker once his attitude toward risk has been defined.

The Direct Costing Controversy— An Identification of Issues

JAMES M. FREMGEN
Naval Postgraduate School

WHATEVER one's views of direct costing may be, it is impossible to deny that it has become one of the most prominent current issues in the continuing discussion that surrounds the evolution of accounting theory and practice. Direct costing has been considered and reconsidered by both its advocates and its opponents from just about every conceivable point of view for more than a quarter of a century. Hence, it is appropriate at this time to review some of the arguments for and against the concept and to attempt to identify the principal issues in the controversy. My purpose here is to examine these issues critically and dispassionately —recognizing my own limitations as a partisan in the dispute. This presentation is in the nature of an interim report, with primary attention focused upon the development and present status of direct costing but with some consideration of the prospects for the future also. My objective is to crystallize issues, not to resolve them. It is possible that, given the present status of the accountant's art, they are irresolvable.

Concern with external reports only. Direct costing has undoubtedly attained the status of an accepted technique of internal reporting to management. (This does not mean, of course, that it is used in all firms or even in a majority of them.) In the area of external reports to stockholders, creditors, and other interested outside parties, however, the controversy is in full bloom. The discussion in this paper will be confined to the implications of direct costing in external reports. There are two reasons for this. First, as already indicated, it is in external reporting that the real controversy lies today. Second, the basic criterion guiding the selection of internal reporting practices is utility to management. What is useful to management is good management accounting. In external reporting, the criterion of utility is still present; but it is more difficult to define. The market for external reports is much broader than that for internal reports, and the needs and interests of the various users of the former are more diverse than those of a single firm's management. Thus, in practice, the criterion of utility as applied to external reports has come to be interpreted as general acceptance. As we all know, general acceptance is actually predicated upon quite a variety of premises, ranging from the matching concept to the Internal Revenue Code. Ideally, however, general acceptance ought to be based upon economic realities and logic. However subjective and tenuous this ideal may be, it is a worthy goal; and we should attempt to evaluate direct costing within a framework wherein economic facts and relationships are paramount.

Historical cost assumption. A second constraint within which the discussion must proceed is the current generally accepted practice of valuing inventories at historical cost, however measured. At a time when increasing attention is being given in the accounting literature to alternative bases of inventory valuation, this may appear to be an overly restrictive framework for discussion. But direct costing is an historical cost method. The abandonment of the historical cost basis would render direct costing just as obsolete as the alternative full costing.

A note on terminology. As a final note before beginning a critical examination of the issues, it is appropriate to consider the terminologies of the alternative costing methods. No matter how entrenched the term "direct costing" may be, it really is not suitable. The distinction at the heart of the method is that between variable and fixed costs, not between direct and indirect costs. The British term, "marginal costing," is not desirable either in view of the very specific meaning of the term "marginal cost" in micro-economic analysis. Particularly in view of the increasing popularity of the concept, general adoption of the term "variable costing" is highly desirable; and that term shall be used consistently throughout the remainder of this paper.

On the other side of the controversy, the alternative concept is best described as "full costing" to indicate the inclusion in inventory of all production costs. "Absorption costing" is not really objectionable, but it is less descriptive. Finally, I have a very positive dislike for the term "conventional costing." This is not at all descriptive and makes about as much sense as it would to call the incumbent party the "conventional party" in American politics.

SOME EARLY ARGUMENTS IN THE CONTROVERSY

Most of the early arguments in the controversy over variable costing were discussed within the framework of internal reporting. They are, however, generally relevant to external reporting as well; and most of them have been extended to this area at one time or another. For present purposes, it will be sufficient to consider three of these early arguments on each side of the controversy.[1]

Early arguments in favor of variable costing. 1. *Variable costing involves the separate reporting of variable and fixed costs.* The separation of variable and fixed costs has generally been conceded to be useful to management.[2] Whether it is equally useful to stockholders, creditors, and other outside parties is problematic. In any case, there is no reason why variable and fixed costs cannot be recorded and reported separately under full costing as well as variable costing. As a practical matter, they seldom are. Nevertheless, the separation of fixed and variable costs should be regarded as a benefit from variable costing in current practice and not as an inherent advantage.

2. *Variable costing facilitates incremental profit analyses.*[3] This alleged advantage of variable costing follows from the previous one, and the same counter-argument is applicable. There is no theoretical reason why the same information (i.e. variable profit) should not be available in full costing reports. Once again, too, there is the question as to whether such information is relevant to the users of external reports.

---

[1] The discussion here is not intended to be exhaustive. Rather, it is designed to indicate the types of arguments raised for and against variable costing. These "early" arguments, incidentally, are by no means extinct; they continue to appear in the current literature. For a more complete discussion of these early pros and cons of variable costing, see *Current Application of Direct Costing,* NAA Research Report 37 (New York: National Association of Accountants, 1961) and "Direct Costing," *NACA Bulletin,* Vol. 34 (April 1953), Section 3.

[2] *Current Application of Direct Costing, op. cit.,* pp. 5–7.

[3] *Current Application of Direct Costing, op. cit.,* pp. 22–40, and "Direct Costing," *op. cit.,* p. 1127.

We shall return to this question later in the paper.

3. *Variable costing removes from income the effect of inventory changes.*[4] This is one of the arguments most frequently advanced for variable costing. Under full costing in a period of declining sales, net income may not reflect the decline in sales volume because production volume has been maintained and a substantial portion of the fixed production costs of the period has been deferred in inventory. Under variable costing, these fixed costs would be treated as current expenses, not chargeable to inventory. Thus, in variable costing, net income is more directly a function of sales volume than in full costing and is unaffected by production volume.

This particular argument is deficient in that it presumes there is something wrong with the volume of production as well as the volume of sales influencing income. In other words, underlying this contention is the more basic one that fixed production costs are not properly chargeable to the product. Thus, the argument concerning the impact of inventory changes on income is a corollary to the more fundamental argument as to whether fixed manufacturing costs are product costs or period costs. This question will be considered shortly.

Early arguments against variable costing.
1. *It is difficult in practice to separate variable and fixed costs.*[5] This contention is, of course, valid from the viewpoint of practical application; but it is not a damning flaw of the variable costing concept. It is a problem of measurement, not of theory. To be sure, measurement problems are very real and very important ones; but they often can be solved. In view of current practices, apparently a substantial number of industrial firms believe that this particular measurement problem can be solved effectively.[6]

2. *Variable costing tends to ignore or understate the importance of fixed costs.* Probably the most familiar example of this argument is the contention that pricing decisions based upon variable costs may result in prices that fail to cover all costs.[7] This contention has always struck me as being particularly weak, however. To begin with, it seems to ignore the role of the market in price setting decisions. Further it appears to presume that business managers are not very bright; and this hardly seems to be a valid generalization.

3. *Variable costing understates inventory values.*[8] This argument presumes the validity of the product cost treatment of fixed manufacturing costs. Considered in light of current practice, variable costing quite clearly understates inventory values. Current practice, of course, is subject to change and, in this particular connection, has come under heavy attack in recent years. Unless valid theoretical arguments can be raised in support of the product cost treatment, the inclusion of fixed costs inventory is merely a practice—albeit one of long standing—based upon unsupported judgments.

Conclusions on Early Arguments. It may appear that I have endeavored to disparage all of these early arguments raised here; and, indeed, such was my intention. The objection to these arguments is not that they are necessarily invalid but that they are superficial. They fail to attack the basic premises underlying the variable costing and full costing techniques. Recently these basic premises have been ex-

---

[4] *Current Application of Direct Costing, op. cit.,* pp. 81–4, and "Direct Costing," *op. cit.,* p. 1127.

[5] "Direct Costing," *op. cit.,* pp. 1127–8.

[6] "Separating and Using Costs as Fixed and Variable," *NAA Bulletin,* Vol. 41 (June 1960), Section 3.

[7] Adolph Matz, Othel J. Curry, and George W. Frank, *Cost Accounting,* 3rd Edition (Cincinnati: South-Western Publishing Company, 1962), pp. 798–9, and John J. W. Neuner, *Cost Accounting,* 6th Edition (Homewood: Richard D. Irwin, Inc., 1962), pp. 783–4. It should be noted that, while these writers discuss this argument, they do not necessarily accept it.

[8] "Direct Costing," *op. cit.,* p. 1128.

posed and subjected to careful scrutiny. The result has been a vigorous and stimulating controversy over the relative theoretic merits of full and variable costing.

INCOME MEASUREMENT: THE PERIOD/PRODUCT COST QUESTION

Probably the most fundamental point of controversy between variable and full costing is the question of whether fixed manufacturing costs are costs of the product produced or of the period in which they are incurred. Traditionally, accounting reports have treated them, substantially at least, as product costs. Variable costing would treat them wholly as period costs. Logically, treatment should follow from the nature of the costs; and there is a very clear dispute regarding the nature of fixed production costs.

The period cost concept. The concept of a period cost, or capacity cost, has been explained by many writers. One good explanation of this concept was offered by Charles T. Horngren and George H. Sorter.

Proponents of variable costing maintain that fixed factory overhead provides capacity to produce. Whether that capacity is used to the fullest extent or not used at all is usually irrelevant insofar as the expiration of fixed costs is concerned. . . . As the clock ticks, fixed costs expire, to be replenished by new bundles of fixed costs that will enable production to continue in succeeding periods.[9]

The period cost concept, in its essence, states that there are certain costs which, by their nature, expire with the passage of time, regardless of production activity. They are incurred for the benefit of operations during a given period of time. The benefit is unchanged by the actual level of operations, if any, during that period; and it expires at the end of the period in any event.

The period cost concept clearly conflicts with the traditional accounting view that costs attach to production. Paton and Littleton, for example, averred that all costs attach to goods or services sold and that "time periods are a convenience, a substitute"[10] for the product in the process of matching costs with revenues. To my knowledge, only one advocate of variable costing has taken specific issue with this traditional view of the time period. David Green, Jr., raised the question of the time period versus the product very pointedly.

Again there is a suggestion of choice of orientation—to the product or to time interval. Why choose the product?

In large part, the work of the accountant is related to the time interval. Indeed, the income statement becomes meaningful only when the time period is known.[11]

He went on to argue that it is the process of dividing the life of an enterprise into relatively short time periods, such as a year, that distinguishes the accountant from the historian.[12] Whether one agrees or disagrees with Green's conclusion regarding the product/time period question, his direct identification of the issue is a significant contribution to a clear understanding of the variable costing controversy.

The product cost concept. Two of the most vigorous proponents of the product cost concept in the recent literature have been William L. Ferrara and Philip E. Fess.[13]

[9] Charles T. Horngren and George H. Sorter, " 'Direct' Costing for External Reporting," THE ACCOUNTING REVIEW, Vol. 36 (January 1961), p. 88.

[10] W. A. Paton and A. C. Littleton, *An Introduction to Corporate Accounting Standards* (Urbana: American Accounting Association, 1949), p. 15.

[11] David Green, Jr., "A Moral to the Direct-Costing Controversy?" *The Journal of Business*, Vol. 33 (July 1960), p. 221.

[12] *Ibid.*

[13] See, for examples, William L. Ferrara, "Idle Capacity as a Loss—Fact or Fiction," THE ACCOUNTING REVIEW, Vol. 35 (July 1960), pp. 490–6; Ferrara, "The Importance of Idle Capacity Costs—A Rejoinder," *ibid.*, Vol. 36 (July 1961), pp. 422–4; Philip E. Fess, "The Theory of Manufacturing Costs," *ibid.*, Vol. 36 (July 1961), pp. 446–53; and Fess and Ferrara, "The Period Cost Concept for Income Measurement—Can It Be Defended?" *ibid.*, Vol. 36 (October 1961), pp. 598–602.

Basically, they have argued that all manufacturing costs are costs of the product and that there is no such thing as a manufacturing cost of the period. Ferrara, writing alone, contended that, logically, all so-called fixed production costs should be amortized by a unit-of-output method, which would make them variable costs.[14] Time period amortization is acceptable only as a practical convenience, the need for which derives from uncertainty as to future operations. Writing jointly, Fess and Ferrara supported a value-added approach to revenue recognition but accepted the deferral of revenue recognition to the point of sale on grounds that measurement is more objective at that point. The deferral of revenue recognition, they contended, must then be paralleled by the deferral of all production costs, regardless of their behavior with respect to changes in volume.[15]

At another time, when I was not attempting to be dispassionate in my point of view, I took what might be regarded as the extreme position in support of the product cost concept. I contended that

. . . in theory, there is no such thing as a true period cost. All costs incurred by a firm, including non-manufacturing costs, are costs of the product. For the product of a firm is not merely a physical commodity from a production line; it is a bundle of economic utilities, which include time and place as well as form. Thus, in theory, distribution and administrative costs are just as much costs of the product as are factory costs. The product is not complete until it is in a form and place and at a time desired by the customer; and this product completion involves distribution just as essentially as it does manufacturing.[16]

This position might be restated as follows: An enterprise is not interested in capacity as such but in production and the consequent revenue. Capacity is merely a means to production and should be regarded as part of the cost thereof in the same way as materials and labor. To quote Fess, ". . . a plant is not purchased for the sake of owning masonry but for the services it will provide."[17]

According to the product cost approach, fixed costs are assigned to the product rather than to the period because it is the product that generates revenue. The time period is viewed as a passive factor, purely incidental to the operations of the firm. Revenue derives from the sale of the product (or, at least, is ordinarily recognized when the sale takes place), no matter when that sale occurs; and *all* production costs are matched with the revenue in the period of sale.

ASSET MEASUREMENT: THE NATURE
OF SERVICE-POTENTIAL

Fundamental to any decision as to what constitutes the value of an inventory is a definition of the concept of an asset. The familiar definition of the Committee on Accounting Concepts and Standards of the American Accounting Association is that assets are "aggregates of service-potentials available for or beneficial to expected operations."[18] Recently Robert T. Sprouse and Maurice Moonitz asserted that "assets represent expected future economic benefits."[19] These definitions may be taken as

---

[14] Ferrara, "Idle Capacity as a Loss—Fact or Fiction," *op. cit.*, p. 490. I believe there is a need for much more study of the nature of fixed costs. Many costs are fixed by definition—notably depreciation. Unit-of-output depreciation, as contrasted with the more commonly used time-based methods, renders depreciation a variable cost (as recommended by Ferrara). If there is an important distinction between fixed and variable costs—and variable costing most certainly presumes there is—it is disquieting to observe that so significant a cost item as depreciation may be either variable or fixed, depending upon a managerial decision between equally acceptable alternative accounting procedures.

[15] Fess and Ferrara, *op. cit.*, p. 600.

[16] James M. Fremgen, "Variable Costing for External Reporting—A Reconsideration," THE ACCOUNTING REVIEW, Vol. 37 (January 1962), p. 78.

[17] Fess, *op. cit.*, p. 448.

[18] *Accounting and Reporting Standards for Corporate Financial Statements and Preceding Statements and Supplements* (Columbus: American Accounting Association, 1957), p. 4.

[19] Robert T. Sprouse and Maurice Moonitz, *A Tentative Set of Broad Accounting Principles for Business Enterprises*, Accounting Research Study No. 3 (New

essentially identical. This concept of service-potential, or future benefit, has played an important role in the controversy over variable costing.

Cost obviation concept of service-potential. One interpretation of the service-potential notion has been that assets have service-potential to the extent that they avert the necessity for incurring costs in the future. Robert B. Wetnight contended that variable costing meets the test of future benefit better than full costing.

> If this test of future benefit is applied to the two methods of costing under discussion, it can be seen that direct costing most closely fits the requirements. In the first place, there is a future benefit from the incurrence of variable costs. These costs will not need to be incurred in a future period. However, in the case of the fixed costs, no future benefit exists, since these costs will be incurred during the future period, no matter what the level of operations.[20]

David Green coined the term "cost obviation" and posited the concept as the basis for the measurement of all assets excepting financial claims, such as cash and receivables. He suggested that the measurement of an asset is the costs that will be obviated in the future as a result of cost incurrence in the past. And he pointed out that the past incurrence of fixed production costs does not avoid the reincurrence of the same costs in the future.[21]

The most expansive discussions of the cost obviation notion have been by Horngren and Sorter. In their first article on the subject, they offered it as support for variable costing. They stated there that

> ... a cost has service potential, in the traditional accounting sense, if its incurrence now will result in future cost avoidance in the ordinary course of business ...
>
> Expressed another way, if the total future costs of an enterprise will be decreased because of the presence of a given cost, that cost is relevant to the future and is an asset; if not, that cost is irrelevant and is expired.[22]

This position might be restated as follows: The production of goods for inventory in one period enables a firm to realize some revenue in a subsequent period without reincurring the variable costs of producing that inventory. But the availability of inventory completed in one period does not forestall the incurrence of any fixed costs in a subsequent period. Hence, the variable costs are relevant to future periods but the fixed costs are not.

In a second article, Horngren and Sorter pursued the cost obviation concept further and refined it somewhat. To begin with, they made it clear that they would include opportunity costs within the scope of cost obviation. Specifically, the loss of future revenues is a cost to be avoided.[23] More significantly, they sought to disassociate their position from variable costing. They propounded a theory of "relevant costing" in which only such costs as will obviate future costs or loss revenues are relevant and, hence, properly chargeable to inventory. Under this theory, fixed production costs might be relevant under certain conditions. Specifically, fixed costs would be included in inventory when future sales demand would exceed existing productive capacity, when future sales would be lost forever because of a shortage of inventory, or when variable manufacturing costs are expected to rise in the future.[24] One practical problem apparent in relevant costing is the burden placed upon the accountant (or someone) of determining whether a given inventory is actually necessary to meet future needs or whether it is exces-

York: American Institute of Certified Public Accountants, 1962), p. 20.

[20] Robert B. Wetnight, "Direct Costing Passes the 'Future Benefit' Test," *NAA Bulletin*, Vol. 39 (August 1958), p. 84.

[21] Green, *op. cit.*, p. 223.

[22] Horngren and Sorter, *op. cit.*, p. 86.

[23] George H. Sorter and Charles T. Horngren, "Asset Recognition and Economic Attributes—The Relevant Costing Approach," THE ACCOUNTING REVIEW, Vol. 37 (July 1962), p. 394.

[24] *Ibid.*, p. 399.

sive. (Note that, if inventories were generally viewed as necessary at their existing levels in order to avoid losing future orders, the practical effect of relevant costing would be equivalent to that of full costing.) Horngren and Sorter have recognized this problem, and they concede that relevant costing would be more difficult to apply than either full or strict variable costing. Nevertheless, they believe their position is conceptually sound.

There is, to be sure, a distinction between variable costing and relevant costing as described above. There are also certain similarities between them which admit of their being considered jointly in contrast to full costing. Specifically, both variable and relevant costing accept the possible treatment of fixed manufacturing costs as costs of the period rather than of the product. Variable costing goes one step further and insists upon such treatment in all instances. In correspondence, Horngren and Sorter have argued that any linking of relevant costing to variable costing misses the fundamental point of their theory, namely, that it is future oriented. It is not concerned with the time-period expiration of fixed costs but with future benefits. It would seem, however, that, while one may wish to emphasize that only variable costs are inventoried because only they will obviate future costs, he must also recognize the concomitant expensing of fixed costs in the period of incurrence. The latter fact may not be viewed simply as a secondary side effect; it must be justified in itself if relevant costing is to stand. This is not to say that relevant costing cannot stand, of course. If one accepts the cost obviation approach to asset valuation, then the time-period expiration of fixed costs as called for in relevant costing is correct. In other words, the future orientation of relevant costing may not and need not overlook the resultant current expensing of fixed costs. Both

implications of the method are consistent with its basic premise.

Revenue production concept of service-potential. The cost obviation interpretation of service-potential is relatively recent. Others have interpreted the service-potential of an asset to mean its capacity to contribute to the production of revenue in the future.[25] This revenue production approach distinguishes between unexpired and expired costs, respectively, according to whether their incurrence will or will not contribute to the realization of revenue in the future. Under this theory, any cost essential to the production of a product that may reasonably be expected to be sold and, thus, generate revenue is a cost of obtaining such revenue and should be deferred in inventory so that it may be matched with the revenue in the determination of income for the period of sale.

Conclusions on alternative interpretations of service-potential. At the risk of oversimplification, I believe it is correct to say that the cost obviation concept of service-potential necessarily presumes the validity of the period cost treatment of fixed costs. Similarly, the revenue production concept as outlined above is inextricably linked with the product cost position. These are the conflicting points of view, and there is no supreme principle of accounting upon which we can call to resolve the conflict. Both positions are internally consistent. Any selection between the two must be primarily intuitive. Inasmuch as intuition is not a standardized commodity, it is probable that the fate of variable costing and/or relevant costing in external reports

---

[25] See, for example, Fremgen, *op. cit.*, p. 77. One member of the Committee on Accounting Concepts and Standards that drafted the 1957 American Accounting Association statement has indicated to me that, at the time that statement was prepared, he understood service-potential to mean revenue production, especially in the case of inventories.

will be determined ultimately on grounds of utility.[26]

INVENTORY COSTING AND DECISION MAKING

The basic justification for the preparation of financial reports at all is that they are useful to someone. Logically, therefore, the standards of financial reporting should be designed to further this objective of usefulness. While variable costing has been generally conceded to be useful in reports to management, is it useful also in reports to stockholders, creditors, and other outside parties? Green[27] and Horngren and Sorter[28] believe that it is. I am not prepared to answer this question at this time. Frankly, I have no information that would suggest a preference on the parts of the users of external financial reports for either full costing or variable costing. However, it is relevant to consider the distinctions between variable and full costing reports. The principal distinctive features of the variable costing income statement are (1) that it shows directly relationships between costs and volume and (2) that it makes net income a function of sales volume to the exclusion of production volume. With regard to the first feature, we must remember that management has some degree of control over costs and/or volume. Normally the users of external reports have none. The latter group's decisions are on a different plane.[29] The question then is this: On that plane, are cost-volume relationships as significant as they are to management? With respect to the second feature of the variable costing income statement, this is either misleading or correct depending upon whether production volume should or should not influence income. Again we face the product/period cost question.

This discussion suggests that whether variable costing ever achieves general acceptance will depend primarily upon whether it comes to be regarded generally as useful in external reports (and, to be realistic, upon its acceptance for federal income tax reports also). Thus, it is important that we investigate the relative utilities of variable and full costing in external reports to the extent that these can be ascertained.

THE FUTURE OF VARIABLE COSTING

After a quarter of a century of development, variable costing is being considered more and more frequently as an acceptable technique of inventory measurement in external as well as internal financial reports. If variable costing is accepted, it may be taken either as an alternative to or as a replacement for full costing. Certainly, there would be nothing unique about two different methods of measuring one quantity being acceptable in accounting practice—particularly where inventories are concerned. Nevertheless, I feel that the conceptual differences between variable and full costing are so great that their concurrent general acceptance would not be in the best interests of financial statement readers or of the accounting profession. Financial statements are, after all, media of communication; and it is difficult to see how communication can be effective where two fundamentally conflicting methods of reporting the same information are considered equally correct.

Inventory valuation at net realizable value. As a final note, it is possible that the con-

[26] In 1953 a research study by the National Association of Accountants concluded that the costing method to be employed in profit measurement should be selected on the basis of utility. However, it stated further that each company must decide for itself in this matter. (See "Direct Costing," *op. cit.*, p. 1119.) I cannot agree that this extremely important aspect of utility in external reports may be left to the discretion of the individual firm.

[27] Green, *op. cit.*, p. 222.

[28] Horngren and Sorter, " 'Direct' Costing for External Reporting," *op. cit.*, p. 91.

[29] Fremgen, *op. cit.*, p. 80.

troversy over variable costing may be discarded in lieu of being resolved. Some attention is being given in the current accounting literature to the proposal that inventories be valued at net realizable values.[30] If this were to become the generally accepted practice, both variable and full costing would be irrelevant and both might be laid to indeterminate graves. In light of the history of the development of accounting principles, however, and in view of the general tenor of the reactions from accounting practitioners to Sprouse and Moonitz' recommendation of net realizable value in inventory,[31] it is reasonable to anticipate that any change so basic as the abandonment of the historical cost basis will not come about quickly. Hence, it is probable that the direct costing controversy will be with us for some time yet and that the issues considered here will have to be faced. Whether the controversy will ever be resolved—let alone what the resolution will be—is an unanswerable question at the present.

---

[30] Sprouse and Moonitz, *op. cit.*, pp. 27–30.
[31] "Comments on 'A Tentative Set of Broad Accounting Principles for Business Enterprises'," *The Journal of Accountancy*, Vol. 115 (April 1963), pp. 36–48.

Transfer Pricing—A Synthesis

A. RASHAD ABDEL-KHALIK
University of Alberta

EDWARD J. LUSK
University of Pennsylvania

TRANSFER pricing systems attempt to generate prices for internally produced and consumed commodities. The purpose of this paper is to appraise the nature and scope of some major transfer pricing models. This synthesis will attempt to provide insights into the situational orientation of several transfer pricing approaches. The analysis considers the development of transfer pricing models in the following categories: (I) the economic theory of the firm, (II) mathematical programming approaches, and (III) other analytic approaches.

THE MOTIVATION FOR INTERNAL PRICING

An internal pricing mechanism is of interest whenever (1) the transfer commodity's cost is a material component of the final product and (2) when profitability is an important consideration in evaluating divisional performance. In these cases, inaccurate transfer prices may impede rather than stimulate the efficient allocation of resources. For example, if a transfer price is established at an arbitrarily low level, divisions that purchase the transfer good may appear to be more profitable and thereby command a disproportionately large allocation of scarce resources.

The rationale for an internal pricing system is motivated by the presumed behavioral advantage of operating autonomous units in a decentralized firm in the absence of externally determined market prices for the internally exchanged commodities. The emphasis on autonomy arises out of organizational attempts to establish internal pricing systems which motivate, coordinate, and control the allocation of economic resources and factors of production so that the over-all organizational goals can be achieved. It was this initial pragmatic emphasis that stimulated academic research into the study of the techniques of transfer pricing.[1] In conceptualizing the transfer pricing problem, it was argued that a rationally conceived and systematically applied transfer pricing system would enable divisions to maintain their autonomy while making decisions that benefit the entire organization.[2] A

The authors would like to thank Nicholas Dopuch, V. Jaikumar, and Gordon Shillinglaw for reading earlier drafts of this paper and providing helpful comments. A referee has made some very good comments which improved the overall discussion of the paper.

[1] J. Dean, "Decentralization and Intra-Company Pricing," *Harvard Business Review*, Vol. 33, No. 4 (September–October 1955), and J. Dearden, "The Case of Disputing Divisions," *Harvard Business Review* (July–August 1964), p. 174.

[2] W. E. Stone, "Intercompany Pricing," THE ACCOUNTING REVIEW, Vol. XXXI, No. 4 (October 1956), p. 627, and Jack Hirschleifer, "On the Economics of Transfer Pricing," *Journal of Business* (July 1956), p. 182.

requirement of transfer pricing systems then is that individual divisions must be allowed to pursue divisional goals that are coincident with the global organizational goals. However, this "goal coincidence" may be difficult to operationalize. For example, it was agreed by executives participating in a study conducted by the Industrial Conference Board that, in the presence of conflict, corporate interests must take precedence over divisional interest even though their personal incomes depend upon divisional performance.[3]

Although academicians may share the executives' opinion, they view the implied conflict of goals differently. They maintain that a conflict between the objectives of each division and the organization comprising the divisions will not exist if a proper model is implemented. Hence, academic interest has centered on presenting a set of rules that integrate the complex elements of the organization in order to allow for divisional autonomy while recognizing global organizational goals.

This paper will examine the ability of various transfer pricing models to deal with the issues of decentralization and organizational optimization.

I. THE THEORY OF THE FIRM APPROACH

Traditional economic theory states that a properly functioning economic system should allow the entrepreneur, through price relationships of the production factors and final products, to make the necessary cost-profit calculations and select a product mix which maximizes the organization's profitability. If this classical economic perspective is to be used as *the* mechanism to facilitate effective decentralization, it must allow divisional managers independently to: (1) obtain ex post evaluation information by indicating the economic value generated through resources allocated to the divisions, (2) ascertain factor interactions as they gener-

ate production, and (3) price intermediate commodities based upon their economic value. As Menge indicates:

> Market prices, it should be noted, are guides to the rational allocation of resources and are the principal determinants of the direction of the flow of goods and services. Customers note the price before they buy. They do not buy and then decide on the price. Yet, the latter procedure is substantially how many internal transfer price systems function today. This provides little basis for the best use of resource within the firm or the economy, regardless of the possible, but improbable, "perfectness" of the predetermined internal transfer price.[4]

The assumptions characterizing the structure of the economic modeling approach to transfer pricing may be summarized as follows:

Operational Assumptions —Hirschleifer System

1. The firm, whose pricing decisions are under consideration, comprises two profit centers. The first is referred to as the selling division and the latter as the buying division. The material input of the buying division is the output of the selling division.

[3] The National Industrial Conference Board, *Interdivisional Transfer Pricing* (Business Policy Study No. 122, New York: Industrial Conference Board, 1967), p. 1. A similar thought was expressed by Hayek in an earlier publication as he writes:
"As decentralization has become necessary because nobody can consciously balance all the considerations bearing on the decisions of so many individuals, the coordination can clearly not be affected by "conscious control," but only by arrangements which convey to each agent the information he must possess in order effectively to adjust his decisions to those of others. And because all the details of the changes constantly affecting the conditions of demand and supply of the different commodities can never be fully known, or quickly enough be collected and disseminated, by any one centre, what is required is some apparatus of registration which automatically records all the relevant effects of individual actions, and whose indications are at the same time the resultant of, and the guide for, all the individual decisions."
See F. A. Hayek, *The Road to Serfdom* (University of Chicago Press, 1944), pp. 49–50.
[4] J. A. Menge, "The Backward Art of Interdivisional Transfer Pricing," *Journal of Industrial Economics* (July 1961), p. 216.

2. Each division produces only one product.

3. Operating costs of either division are independent of the operating costs of the other; i.e., technological independence.

4. The products of both divisions have external markets.

5. The external market's demand for each division's product is independent of the other's, i.e., demand independence.

6. Marginal costs of each product are readily determinable.

7. The management of each center is autonomous.

8. The revenue functions are concave and the cost functions are convex; also that at least one function be strictly concave (convex).

Given these operational assumptions, the initial presentation of the transfer pricing systems rationale was made by Hirschleifer. His initial analysis made the following structural assumptions: (a) the demand for the intermediate commodity is perfectly competitive, (b) there is an externally determined price for the intermediate commodity, and (c) the final good is sold in an imperfect market. These structural assumptions are best presented graphically as shown in Figure 1.

In Figure 1, the selling division should produce q_s which, under marginal cost pricing, will be priced at $P(t)$. The marginal revenue of the internal consumer will be denoted $MR(f)$. At the intersection of the total cost $(MC(b)+P(t))$ with $MR(f)$, the buying division will determine the output of the final product, q_b.

From Perfect to Imperfect Competition

Let us now relax the assumption of perfect competition in the market for the intermediate product. We shall assume that selling and processing divisions may interact with external markets, but this interaction does not affect the external market

price. Therefore, the imperfect aspect is with respect to the cost of buying and selling the intermediate product. As Gould[5] points out, in these circumstances there may be three prices for the intermediate good: (1) the internal price $P(t)$ which exists at the intersection of the net marginal revenue of the seller $(NMR(s) = MR(f) - MC(b))$ with the marginal cost of the seller $MC(s)$; (2) the gross purchase price $P(b)$; and (3) the net selling price $P(s)$. The exchange quantities, however, depend on the relative structure of the three prices. Gould indicates two transfer pricing situations which are to be contrasted with the internal transfer price $P(t)$.

CASE 1:

$$P(b) > P(s) > P(t)$$

This case is represented in Figure 2a. The transfer price will be $P(s)$, and the difference $P(b) - P(s)$ represents the cost of buying and selling in external markets. The processing division will require q_2; while the selling division will produce q_1. The quantity $q_1 - q_2$, will be marketed externally.

In this case the $NMR(s)$ is discontinuous at A and extends a long $P(s)$ to B. The production rule is to produce until the NMR equals $P(s)$. However, as Gould points out:

The transfer price rule which insures these out-puts is that central management should instruct the transferee to supply the quantity that the processing division demands at $P(s)$. Subject to this constraint, autonomous profit-maximizing behavior on the part of the individual divisions will lead to the optimum for the firm. . . . it should be noted that at $P(s)$ the transferee has no incentive to supply the processing division rather than outside customers. Thus it must be

[5] J. R. Gould, "Economic Price Determination," *Journal of Business* (January 1964), pp. 61-7.

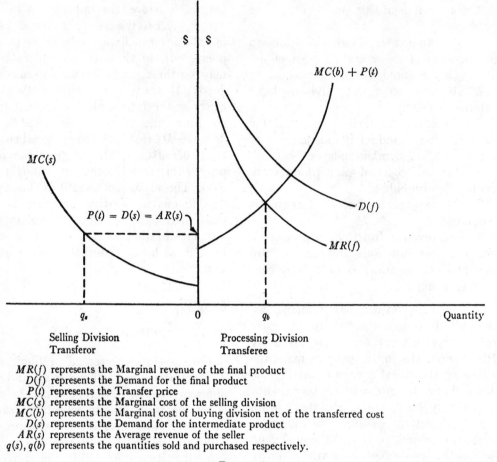

$$MR(f) \text{ represents the Marginal revenue of the final product}$$

MR(f) represents the Marginal revenue of the final product
 D(f) represents the Demand for the final product
 P(t) represents the Transfer price
MC(s) represents the Marginal cost of the selling division
MC(b) represents the Marginal cost of buying division net of the transferred cost
 D(s) represents the Demand for the intermediate product
 AR(s) represents the Average revenue of the seller
q(s), q(b) represents the quantities sold and purchased respectively.

FIGURE 1

PRICE DETERMINATION FOR THE SELLING·DIVISION AND EFFECT ON THE OPTIMUM
OUTPUT OF THE BUYING DIVISION

instructed to supply all the processing divisions requirements at $P(s)$.[6]

CASE 2:

$$P(t) > P(b) > P(s)$$

This case is represented by Figure 2b. In this case the net marginal revenue is discontinuous at A' extending along $P(s)$ to B'; while the marginal cost curve is discontinuous at C' extending along $P(b)$ to D'. The profit maximizing output for the firm is q_1 where $P(b)$ (now the marginal cost curve) intersects $NMR(s)$. However, the processing division should produce q_2 where marginal costs intersect $P(b)$. The balance $q_1 - q_2$ is purchased externally. As Gould notes:

In contrast to the previous case, the rule now is that the processing division must accept the quantity that the selling division wishes to supply at $P(b)$. *Mutates mutandis*, the discussion of the necessity for the constraint in the previous case applies here as well.[7]

In general, then, the net selling price

[6] *Ibid.*, p. 63.
[7] *Ibid.*, p. 64. A third case where $P(b) > P(t) > P(s)$ finds the profit maximizing output at the same point where there is no external trade (i.e. Hirschleifer's analysis), since there are no economies for external dealings.

230

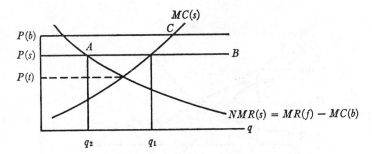

FIGURE 2a

must be used if there are external sales, and the gross purchase cost is used if there are external purchases.

There are two reasonable ways to deal with the organizational coordination problems evidenced in the above situations. One solution relegates the responsibility for the accuracy and efficiency of inputs to the decentralized divisional managers.[8] That is, even though the transfer price and the level of output to be transferred are centrally determined, the division's management may still retain the authority to determine the production mix, suppliers, terms of purchase, and other factor inputs. Another possible solution is for the central management to levy taxes or grant bounties to profit centers for the opportunity costs foregone.

From Imperfect Competition to a Discriminating Monopoly

Relaxing the imperfect competition structural assumption, Hirschleifer considers the case of the seller as a price-discriminating-monopolist. This case is shown in Figure 3. In this situation, where the seller intentionally separates the markets, the optimum output of the intermediate commodity is q_1, while q_2 is transferred to the buying division and $q_3 = (q_1 - q_2)$ is sold externally. The relationship between the transfer price $P(t)$ and external price $P(0)$ will remain valid only if the buying division is restricted

[8] N. Dopuch and D. Drake, "Accounting Implications of a Mathematical Programming Approach to the Transfer Pricing Problem," *Journal of Accounting Research* (Spring 1964), p. 16.

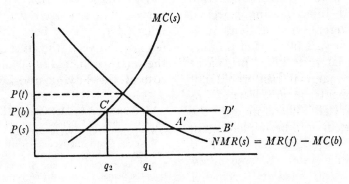

FIGURE 2b

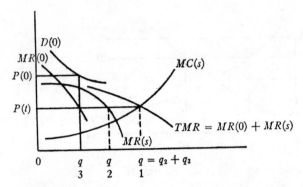

$MR(0)$, $D(0)$ represent the external marginal revenue and demand

$MR(s)$ represents the seller's marginal revenue

$MC(s)$ represents the marginal cost of the selling division, and

TMR represents the total marginal revenue (horizontally added):

$TMR = MR(0) + MR(s)$

FIGURE 3

PRICE DISCRIMINATION OF THE INTERMEDIATE PRODUCT

from reselling the intermediate commodity. This is a necessary assumption (although not explicitly stated by Hirshleifer) since resale of the intermediate product by the buying division would reduce the external price $P(0)$, thereby reducing the firm's profits.

In summary, Hirschleifer suggests as a transfer pricing rule: price along the marginal cost curve. Hirschleifer has used the term "marginal cost" in the context of economic theory, i.e., the additional cost of producing an additional unit where cost includes returns to all factors of production including capital. In accounting, marginal cost has a different connotation; it is equated with the variable cost of producing one additional unit. Thus, pricing at the accounting marginal cost would not recover investments in fixed assets or returns to capital. Therefore, if the Hirschleifer system is to be implemented, modifications to the information generated by the accounting system become necessary. The analyses provided by Hirschleifer and Gould demonstrate the existence of a

transfer price, but fail to suggest an operational method of implementation.

In extending Hirschleifer's system, Ronen and McKinney suggest a system for channeling information between divisions and headquarters so that Hirschleifer's system may be implemented while maintaining divisional autonomy.[9] In keeping with the economic theory of the firm, they suggest that the selling division price the intermediate product along its average revenue curve, while continuing to determine the optimum quantity of output at the intersection with its marginal curve.[10] The average revenue curve of the seller $(AR(s))$ may be derived as the difference between the average revenue of the final product $AR(f)$ and the average cost of the buying division, i.e., $AR(f)$

[9] J. Ronen and G. McKinney, III, "Transfer Pricing for Divisional Autonomy," *Journal of Accounting Research* (Spring 1970), pp. 99–113.

[10] Notice that in perfect competition, the elasticity of demand (E) is infinity and average revenue equals price as well as marginal revenue. But in imperfect competition, the demand is inelastic $(E$ is less than one) and the marginal revenue is equal to price $(1 - 1/E)$, which is less than the price or average revenue.

$-AC(b)=AR(s)=P(s)$. However, the buying division faces the average cost curve of the selling division as its supply curve. Thus, pricing the transfer good of the buying division is determined by this supply curve for the given transferred quantity. According to this derivation, the price of the selling division $P(s)$ and of the buying division $P(b)$ probably will not be the same since $AR(s)$ does not have to equal $AC(s)$. In this situation, Ronen and McKinney suggest that the divisions will submit this information to headquarters so that the central management may credit the selling division by an amount equal to $P(s)-P(b)$ per unit. Since this subsidy is centrally administered, it is not clear that the divisional managers would accept the "routinely produced" accounting reports as the measure of autonomous divisional interaction.[11] For similar reasons, the suggestion that this divisional contribution be used regarding abandonment or continuance of divisional activity may be difficult to implement. Moreover, the average revenue curve of the selling division was suggested to be deduced as the variable difference between the demand for the final product and the average cost of the buying division, $D(f) -AC(b)$. In this situation the inefficiencies incorporated in $AC(b)$ will in effect be passed on to the selling division in terms of a lower average revenue, price, and profits. Under this procedure, it will not be surprising if the selling division asks for the right to "audit" the cost records of the buying division or, alternatively, both divisions may agree that headquarters would control the cost of the buying divisions in order to watch for any "inflation" of the $AC(b)$ due to inefficiency. Accordingly, any claim as to maintaining autonomous divisional units is suspect.

In reviewing these economic models, the following doubts arise as to the validity of the underlying assumptions and to the adequacy of the prescribed procedures:

(a) These models are static, presuming temporal stability. Thus, pricing policies— e.g., price discrimination—are concerned with market segmentation only at one point in time. Cost relationships are assumed to continue over a period of time long enough to be covered by pricing policies. Therefore, the possibility of having a dynamic model which considers time as a dimension is not entertained. For example, price discrimination may take place in the same market but over different time periods.

(b) In general, the independence of demand (and of technology) may be difficult to justify. This limitation was recognized by Hirschleifer as he notes: "Where demand dependence exists, the analysis is rather complex. Generally speaking, the solution falls between market price and marginal cost."[12] Accepting the proposition that the demand for the intermediate product is primarily a derived demand entails two main issues as pointed out by Friedman.[13] First, and most important, a solution that is based on derived demands is consistent only at the point of equilibrium (a problem that also exists in using shadow prices as will be shown later). Second, the elasticity of derived demand becomes an important issue if the external market of the intermediate product is not perfectly competitive. As Friedman points out,[14] the elasticity of derived demand will be a function of several variables: the extent of vertical integration of the production process, the elasticity of demand for the final product, and the elasticity of supply of the intermediate product. To the extent of these elasticities and their

[11] *Ibid.*, p. 110.
[12] Hirschleifer, p. 183.
[13] M. Friedman, *Price Theory: A Provisional Text* (Aldine Publishing Co., 1962), pp. 150–3.
[14] *Ibid.*, p. 153.

relationships, the assumption of demand independence will be difficult to ascertain.[15]

(c) If the services of each of the buying and selling divisions are considered inputs to the final product, then all the models presented above assume a linear production function with constant proportions. A linear production function, however, may not exist in the real world at all levels of output. It is not possible, therefore, to consider these models for implementation without specifying the form of the production function.

(d) Marginal cost pricing might induce dysfunctional behavior of divisional managers. In this regard, Gould mentions the possibility of "sabotaging" the accuracy of cost information submitted by divisional managers for the purpose of transfer price calculations.[16] In a recent study, Jennergren refers to the manipulation of data by divisional managers who attempt to suboptimize as "optimal cheating."[17] Under these circumstances, total optimization will not be attainable.

(e) As was previously mentioned, inefficiencies incurred in one division may be passed on to other divisions in the form of higher prices. Therefore divisions may seek some control procedure to confine inefficiencies to originating division. These control procedures may impair divisional autonomy.

(f) These models do not incorporate cost-benefit criteria which compare the benefits derived from establishing marginal-cost pricing systems with the cost involved in providing the relevant information. It should not be assumed that the benefits outweigh the costs.

(g) Finally, the case was presented only for two divisions. No solution has been offered for the multidivisional situation, which leads us to the mathematical programming approach.

II. THE MATHEMATICAL PROGRAMMING APPROACH

The failure of the marginal cost pricing models to deal with pricing of transfer goods in a multidivision, multiproduct, decentralized organization prompted the introduction of other models to determine transfer prices that will achieve efficient allocation of resources while maintaining autonomy. According to the mathematical programming approach, transfer prices should be set at the opportunity cost of producing the intermediate product. In the absence of an external market price for the transfer goods, measuring opportunity cost requires an assessment of alternative uses of these goods. This measure is provided for by the use of mathematical programming techniques.

(A) *The Linear Program*

The initial research regarding the use of linear programming for the allocation of resources was primarily concerned with planning and control. Transfer pricing considerations were a by-product of using programming techniques. In considering the use of a linear programming model for establishing transfer prices, Dopuch and Drake have identified three different market orientations:[18]

(1) *Internal Monopsony* Whenever there is one buying division, the internal market resembles a monopsonist's market. Supplying divisions compete to sell the intermediate goods to the monopsonist. They in effect have no control over the sale price. For this reason, Dopuch and

[15] One possible approach to check on demand dependence is the measurement of cross elasticity between the demand for the transfer commodity and the price of the final product *or* between demand for the transfer commodity and the external demand for it.

[16] Gould, p. 66.

[17] P. Jennergren, "Studies in the Mathematical Theory of Decentralized Resource Allocation," Unpublished Ph.D. Dissertation, Graduate School of Business, Stanford University, 1971.

[18] Dopuch and Drake, pp. 14–5.

Drake consider marginal cost to be a preferred basis in setting transfer prices. Thus, selling divisions will compete on the basis of internal efficiency.

(2) *Internal Monopoly* Whenever there is more than one buying division facing one internal selling division, the internal exchange resembles a seller's monopoly market. In this situation, the monopolist occupies a dominant position similar to that of a central management, possibly impairing the degree of decentralization.

(3) *Monopolistic Competition* Whenever there is more than one buying and selling division, the internal market resembles a monopolistically competitive market. In this situation, unless transfer prices are set according to some allocation model, they will in effect be negotiated. Divisional profits therefore may reflect the ability to negotiate rather than effectively to utilize resources.[19] It is this third case of monopolistic competition with several participants which initially motivated the use of linear programming to generate transfer prices.

The construct underlying the transfer pricing rationale is the use of shadow prices as they provide a measure for the internal opportunity cost.

Addressing the opportunity cost pricing dimension Onsi[20] considered a situation of a single selling division which produces two independent products X_1 and X_2, where only one of them (say, X_2) has an outside market price. The other product (say, X_1) is used by the buying division to produce good Y. In this case, the opportunity cost of X_2 is its market price, while the opportunity cost of X_1 is its shadow price. Therefore, a high contribution margin for X_2 will result in a high shadow price for X_1 which means that the division's optimal plan may lead to production of only X_2. But this may prove to be suboptimal for the organization since the buying division would have to purchase X_1 externally in

order to produce the final product Y. Onsi's suggested system utilizes a linear decomposition which algorithmically provides for joint optimization. (The decomposition aspects of transfer pricing are examined in the next section.)

Producing X_1 and X_2 as indicated by the joint optimization may be less profitable for the selling division in comparison to its individually derived plan. If the seller is paid the difference between its individually derived profits and the profits derived jointly, the seller would be indifferent as to its production plan. The question is how to motivate the selling division to take the "optimal" action? Onsi's solution is to require the seller to produce at a volume which would facilitate the organizational optimum and transfer this production at a price equal to its variable cost. Onsi suggests that crediting the selling division with the profits lost by the shift of its operations and pricing from the suboptimal plan to the jointly optimal plan would permit the selling division to operate as a profit center. To this extent, he blended opportunity and marginal costs in a transfer pricing framework.

With regard to the use of shadow prices in determining transfer prices in linear systems, the following should be noted:

(a) If the specifications of inputs, output, and shadow prices are centrally determined by a linear program, the need for decentralization in the form of profit centers is questionable. In such a case, a persuasive argument for centralization can be made based upon the economics of communications.

(b) Imposing a transfer price by headquarters as determined by shadow prices may create adverse effects on morale similar to that of imposing any standard.

[19] *Ibid.*, p. 16.
[20] Mohamed Onsi, "A Transfer Pricing System Based on Opportunity Cost," THE ACCOUNTING REVIEW (July 1970), pp. 535–43.

(c) As Bernhard[21] indicates, shadow prices are accurate measures of opportunity costs as long as two conditions prevail: (a) the product mix does not change, and (b) resources are efficiently utilized. Any deviation from the optimal solution will render the optimally determined shadow prices invalid for pricing the transfer goods.

(d) Jennergren showed that an algorithmically derived transfer price does not exist in a linear system, except in certain degenerate cases.[22] He suggests that instead of setting constant (shadow) prices on corporate resources, headquarters should announce a set of perturbated prices which would increase prices by a nonconstant margin whenever a division demands more corporate resources.[23] His algorithm leads to a set of quadradic divisional subprograms that will simultaneously achieve optimization.

(e) The linearity assumption simplifies the measurement process in parameterizing the model, but only at the expense of restricting the model's applicability in nonlinear situations. Specifically, the linearity assumption excludes the consideration of externalities. Some of the decomposition models attempt to deal with this problem.

(B) *The Decomposition Principle*

As the previous comments indicate, a system based on a linear programming solution has definite centralizing overtones, and it therefore violates the *raison d'être* of the transfer pricing system—decentralization. To deal with this organizational incongruity, the decomposition of mathematical programs was utilized. The study by Jennergren mentioned above is one application of this principle. Other models were developed by Baumol and Fabian, Charnes, Clower and Kortanek, and Hass. These will be considered in the following section.

Baumol and Fabian suggest utilization of the Dantzig-Wolfe decomposition procedure in divisional pricing whenever the linear program cannot be used (for motivational reasons) to derive the optimal solution.[24] The Baumol and Fabian decomposition procedure may be stated as follows:

(1) The headquarters sends prices to the divisions.

(2) Divisions determine their optimal solutions and report results and resources required.

(3) Headquarters uses divisional results to determine new prices and resubmit the altered prices to the divisions (if the prices have changed). Repeat step two until prices have not changed.

(4) If prices have not changed, headquarters tells the divisions what to do, i.e., prices are not required at the final iteration.

Baumol and Fabian recognize two limitations of their suggested solution system:

(a) *The problem of motivation* "It is to be emphasized that now division managers *must be told by the company* (headquarters) what weights they are to employ, i.e., what combination of their proposals the company desires them to produce. There is no automatic motivation mechanism which will lead division managers to arrive at such a combination of output of their own volition. In this way, the decentralization permitted by decomposition breaks down completely at this point."[25]

(b) *The degree of decentralization* "We

[21] R. I. Bernhard, "Some Problems in Applying Mathematical Programming to Opportunity Costing," *Journal of Accounting Research* (Spring 1968), pp. 143–8.

[22] Jennergren, p. 38.

[23] P. Jennergren, "Decentralization on the Basis of Price Schedules in Linear Decomposable Resource-Allocation Problems," *Journal of Financial and Quantitative Analysis* (January 1972), pp. 1407–15.

[24] W. J. Baumol and T. Fabian, "Decomposition, Pricing for Decentralization and External Economies," *Management Science* (September 1964), pp. 1–31.

[25] *Ibid.*, p. 14.

must, however, be careful not to overstate the degree of autonomy of the divisional decision-maker in the decomposition process. True, the calculation process is sufficiently localized that central management does not have to know *anything* about the internal technological arrangements of the divisions. But in the final analysis the output decisions are made and enforced by the central planner (headquarters)."[26]

To address these difficulties, Charnes, Clower and Kortanek[27] developed a decomposition system based upon the setting of goal priorities, which they termed as "preemptive goals." Goals are preemptive if (1) they are ordered into a well-ordered set, and (2) they are assigned priorities according to the relative importance of individual goal fulfillment. Their basic thesis is that decentralization by prices alone is inadequate. For decentralization to be effective, it must be coupled by a set of preemptive goals. This unique organizational structure is termed "coherent decentralization." In the coherent system, preemptive goals may be incorporated into the functional or the constraint set. The system of coherent decentralization does not explicitly consider transfer pricing. It serves as an extension of the Baumol and Fabian analysis and a basis for the quadratic decomposition suggested by Hass[28] which explicitly addresses interdivisional transfers. We wish to describe the decentralization system suggested by Hass to facilitate a discussion of its transfer pricing implications.

The Hass decomposition model is based upon a quadratic program with an objective function adjustment derived from the dual variables on the corporate constraints (constraints for resources shared by the divisions). The transfer good relationships are explicitly introduced with the following constraint:

$$\sum_k C_k X_j{}^i \leqq X_1{}^m; \qquad \text{for some } (i,j)_k$$

where division m transfers product $X_1{}^m$ to division i to produce goods $X_j{}^i, \forall_j$.

The decomposition is effected through a linear adjustment of the divisional demand curves. In the two-division case, the demand curve adjustment will be:

	Original Divisional Demand Curve	Adjustment
Division 1	$P + \Phi_1 \overline{X}^1$	$-C'_1 \bar{\lambda} + 2\Phi_3 \hat{X}^2$
Division 2	$Q + \Phi_2 \overline{X}^2$	$-C'_2 \bar{\lambda} + 2\Phi_3 \hat{X}^1$

where

$\overline{X}^1, \overline{X}^2$ are the divisional product sets.

C_1, C_2 represent the respective corporate technological coefficients for divisions 1 and 2.

$\bar{\lambda}$ is a vector of dual variables (shadowprices) from the solution of the headquarters program.

Φ_3 represents the matrix of externalities.

$\hat{X}^1, \hat{X}^2$ represent the respective previous solutions 1 and 2.

P, Q, Φ_1, Φ_2 represent the parameters of the individual demand curves.

Since $(P + \Phi_1 \overline{X}^1)\overline{X}^1$ and $(Q + \Phi_2 \overline{X}^2)\overline{X}^2$ are the objective functions of divisions 1 and 2 respectively, the remaining terms may be considered as the functional adjustments. (See Jennergren[29] for a complete discussion of functional adjustment models). Therefore, let us examine the adjustment factors $C_1'\bar{\lambda}$ and $2\Phi_3\hat{X}^2$ for division 1 (a similar analysis applies to division 2).

$C_1'\bar{\lambda}$ is a functional adjustment which prices the divisionally shared resources (corporate resources) at $\bar{\lambda}$ per unit. $2\Phi_3\hat{X}^2$ is a functional adjustment representing the tax or bounty for producing or using an additional unit of $\overline{X}^2$ given the last feasible solution. These adjustments (for both divisions) enable any interior solution point to be located and the divi-

[26] *Ibid.*, p. 2.
[27] A. Charnes, R. W. Clower and K. O. Kortanek, "Effective Control Through Coherent Decentralization with Preemptive Goals," *Econometrica* (April 1967), pp. 294-320.
[28] J. E. Hass, "Transfer Pricing in a Decentralized Firm," *Management Science* (February 1968), pp. B310-B33.
[29] Jennergren, Ph.D. Dissertation, p. 106.

sions to share corporate resources based upon relative divisional profitability.

Initially the program does not proceed from a trivial solution but rather as Hass suggests from a "guesstimate" of the prices generated by headquarters, a situation similar to the Baumol and Fabian decomposition. This is important because in many cases headquarters knows the ranges of the optimal solution, and if the algorithm is started with a solution from this range, then the costs and time required to make unnecessary iterations will be saved. Also, the algorithm must be considered a real-time, continuously iterative process and, therefore, whenever internal or external market conditions change, the iterative process is started up again by using the last optimal solution to initialize the algorithm. Hass pointed out the danger here as follows:

The only fear is that the production plans generated more than a few iterations prior are no longer feasible. Hence, they should simply be dropped as variables from the corporate problem. If the changes are not extreme at any point, the algorithm should still track the optimal transfer prices and, therefore, the optimal solution quite well.[30]

Consequently, aside from major shifts in economic conditions within which a company operates, the algorithm requires relatively small operating costs since the original formulation need only be revised and not completely reformulated with each change in the underlying problem.[31]

Now that the essential elements of the Hass decomposition model have been stated, we wish to consider its transfer pricing dimension. Our discussion will examine pricing of the transfer goods and the related issue of divisional autonomy.

Pricing of Transfer Goods

In the solution of the Hass model, the marginal contribution coefficient of the transfer goods with no external market is zero. This zero coefficient indicates that the transfer product is assumed to generate no profit, i.e., pricing under monopsony or monopoly would be eliminated. (Hass assumes Φ_1, Φ_2 to be nonzero excluding perfect competition for those markets.) It should be recalled from the model that transfer goods are treated as corporate resources and therefore may be priced at opportunity cost.[32] We previously discussed the control and evaluation problems which may be evidenced when the intermediate product is priced at the opportunity cost derived from a mathematical program.

When the transfer good does not form a binding constraint, the dual variable (opportunity cost) is zero. In this case, the transfer price may be set at accounting cost. However, considering the long run, the seller would not be able to generate sufficient funds to replenish its technology, unless future technological requirements are recognized in establishing the definition of cost. Given the problems in establishing the adjustments of accounting costs for future technological requirements, headquarters may be required to intervene as a negotiator between the buyer and seller or establish a system of bounties and taxes to guide the negotiation process.

Division Autonomy

Even if it is assumed that a reasonable transfer price is generated from this intervention, the fact of the intervention may dissipate the level of divisional autonomy. Although the model does not allow complete divisional autonomy, it does minimize the need for centralized control to the extent that the divisional management can be evaluated on the utilization

[30] Hass, pp. B310–B25.
[31] *Ibid.*, p. B328.
[32] The same accountability considerations arise here owing to the fact that high contribution margins generate high value for dual variables.

238

of its resources. The fact that corporate management must know the individual elements of P, Q, Φ, and C does not dissipate the accountability of the divisions because division managers may independently determine output levels and prices from the optimal demand and supply relationships for each of their products.[33] (Recall the argument advanced by Dopuch and Drake.)

A system's complication effected by the decomposition is that the accounting system must be modified to accommodate information flows between autonomous units. Essentially, divisions send information to headquarters in order to formulate the corporate profit maximization problem, have it solved and receive back information enabling them to set up their divisional optimization. The role of the division manager in such a system is to make sure that data are transmitted when required, accept the optimal transfer price, and use the set of relationships that have been communicated by headquarters to set the production levels.[34] Even though divisions solve their quadratic programs to determine the output level, the fact remains that the divisions do not *independently* formulate the entire problem. It is doubtful that divisional decision-makers will perceive these communication manipulations as representing decentralized decision-making.

Economic Model Approach Contrasted with Mathematical Program Routine

Given the discussion of the transfer pricing in a classical economic framework and mathematical program format, the following points of comparison emerge:

(a) The pricing rule of the economic model centers on marginal cost; the mathematical program approaches pricing from an opportunity cost perspective. These measures are not necessarily the same. As the firm moves toward a stable equili-

brium marginal cost equals opportunity cost.

(b) The economist's system is determined only for two divisions at a time; the mathematical programming approach deals with a multidivisional problem.

(c) The economist's approach deals with one transfer good at a time; the mathematical programming deals with multiple transfer products.

(d) The economist's solution results in internalizing externalities;[35] the mathematical programming solution explicitly deals with external economies and diseconomies between divisions.

(e) Both approaches have common shortcomings: the need for perfect information, the possibility of sabotage, and cheating.

III. OTHER ANALYTIC APPROACHES

The National Association of Accountants reports on the practice of transfer pricing using manufacturing cost, full-cost, full-cost plus, or variable-cost-plus as some of the major practical approaches to pricing transfer goods in the absence of competitive prices.[36] Full-cost-plus is found to be the most accepted approach under the following conditions: (a) absence of competitive prices, (b) interest in saving the cost of negotiating prices, and (c) need

[33] The decomposition algorithm uses the Dantzig-Wolfe algorithm and therefore assumes that headquarters knows the corporate constraints. However, similar algorithms have been developed in which headquarters knows only the right-hand side of the corporate constraints. The divisions are required to report their projected profits and the corporate resource requirements after each price vector they receive. For example, see A. M. Geoffrion, "Generalized Benders Decomposition," *Journal of Optimization Theory and Application* (October 1972), pp. 237–66. Also see Jennergren, Dissertation, pp. 41–8, 54–69.

[34] A. Whinston, "Price Guides in Decentralized Organizations," *New Perspective in Organizational Research*, eds. W. W. Cooper, H. J. Leavitt, and M. W. Shelly, Vol. II (Wiley, 1964), p. 439.

[35] O. A. Davis, and Andrew Whinston, "Externalities, Welfare, and the Theory of Games," *The Journal of Political Economy*, Vol. LXX, No. 3 (1962).

[36] The National Association of Accountants, *Accounting for Intra-Company Transfers*. Research Report No. 30 (1954), p. 34.

to implement a policy of pricing final products.[37]

Recently, Gordon has suggested a cost-plus transfer pricing model which, although developed for a socialist economy, is applicable to diversified company in a capitalist system.[38] The objective of the model is to establish a "transfer price system that is considered a feasible and efficient instrument of control in the administration of a socialist economy."[39] Gordon makes three general limiting assumptions: (1) each firm produces only one product; (2) each product is produced by one firm; and (3) there are no externalities.

The price of the intermediate product in period (t) is determined as:

$$\overline{P}(t) = \overline{C}(t) + (\overline{F}(t) + \overline{Y}(t))/\overline{X}(t)$$

where

> $\overline{C}(t)$ is the standard variable cost per unit.
> $\overline{F}(t)$ is the standard fixed cost.
> $\overline{Y}(t)$ is the standard profit.
> $\overline{X}(t)$ is the standard output.

Besides the limitations inherent in the implementation of the model,[40] it is subject to the general limitations of the full-cost-plus approach to pricing transfer goods. In brief, these limitations may be summarized as follows:

(1) The allocation of joint and fixed costs to products is necessarily arbitrary. It is true that in some situations, such as those assumed by Gordon, there are no joint costs; but even then the transfer price will vary according to volume. As a matter of fact, even under Gordon's assumptions, joint costs exist—e.g., the cost of the central administration.

(2) Pricing at full-cost-plus implies willingness to incorporate inefficiencies that may be passed on to the consumer—a function of consumer demand inelasticity. This "pass it on" perspective may negate the operational controls used to evaluate divisional performance.

(3) The method assumes that opportunity cost is not different from average cost-plus or, alternatively, opportunity costs are ignored.

(4) In the absence of opportunity cost concepts, the mark-up could be determined by the dictates of the central management. Accordingly, this will disregard responses of demand elasticity to different rates.

(5) Finally, an important critique of cost-plus is advanced by Shubik.[41] To him, cost-plus pricing of transfer goods might impede search for technological progress by the manufacturing division. For example, assume p is the price of final product; k is cost of processing and selling incurred by the second (internally buying) division; C is the full cost of producing a unit of the intermediate product in the selling division; q is the quantity of output of the final product; and j is the mark-up on the selling center's cost. Accordingly, the transfer price at cost plus is $((1+j)C)$. The profit of the buying division is defined as $PR_1 = (p - k - C(1+j))q$; the profit of the selling division is defined as $PR_2 = Cjq$. Now, if the selling division achieved some technological break-through such that the cost of producing the intermediate product is cut into halves—i.e., becomes $C/2$—then the profits of the selling division will also be cut by one half:

$$PR_b = \left(p - k - \frac{C}{2}(1+j)\right)q \quad \text{and}$$

$$PR_s = (Cjq)/2$$

[37] Ibid., pp. 31–36.
[38] M. Gordon, "Pricing for a Socialist Economy," THE ACCOUNTING REVIEW (July 1970), pp. 427–43.
[39] Ibid., p. 442.
[40] A. R. Abdel-khalik, "On Gordon's Model of Transfer-Pricing System," THE ACCOUNTING REVIEW (October 1972), pp. 783–8. See also Gordon's reply in the same issue.
[41] M. Shubik, "Incentives, Decentralized Control: The Assignment of Joint Costs and Internal Pricing," Man-

Hence, the selling division is penalized for taking innovative action. This, of course, will produce adverse motivational effects. Accordingly, the mark-up (j) should be changed or the two divisions must share this additional profit. But we do not think this will solve the problem since the determination of j may be subject to the manipulation and dictates of headquarters.

In view of these difficulties, Solomons[42] rejects full cost as a basis for transfer pricing with the sole exception of contract pricing. His reason is simply that fixed costs are not relevant in the short run. In this regard, he implies that the opportunity cost of capacity is in fact zero. This, however, need not be the case unless the equipment is very specialized so that alternative uses do not exist.

A Behavioral Dimension: Negotiation

Cyert and March view the organization as a coalition of interests. The elements of this coalition comprise production, inventory, sales, market share, and profit. The coalition's goals are determined by a bargaining process. Generally, internal allocation of resources involves such a bargaining process. Further, transfer pricing is part of that general problem of allocation of resources. In this process of negotiation, it appears that the efficiency of a division or a subunit is comprised. Cyert and March have suggested that "transfer payment rules result primarily from a long-run bargaining process rather than problem-solving."[43] It is a result of "long-run" negotiation because the initial solution is subject to modification because of the learning and search processes incurred by the firm's subunits. Negotiation and renegotiation of transfer pricing may be expected to create conflict among the subunits constituting the coalition. Empirical evidence in support of negotiated price does not seem to offer conclusive evidence.

The NAA report suggests that negotiation of intercompany prices occurred "sometimes."

In a more recent study, some additional empirical evidence is supplied by Whinston.[44] In one company, conflict took place because of centrally setting prices at what competitive prices ought to be. Whinston called this type of conflict a test of the managerial innovating ability of the affected official and his staff. In another situation, the selling division appealed to central management for a price higher than that charged by the external competitor. The appeal was based on differences in volume—essentially a "comparable economies of scale" argument. Accordingly, Whinston indicated that this practice is in conflict with the ordinary budget procedures, for it considers a division responsible for some types of uncontrollable costs.[45] Although these reports are for individual cases and Whinston does not claim their generality, a survey conducted by Mautz indicates that about 24% of the participating diversified companies revealed negotiation as the basis for the setting of transfer prices between divisions.[46]

There are some fundamental objections to negotiation, in addition to those already discussed, as a basis for setting transfer prices. Dopuch and Drake, for instance, consider the negotiated price to be an unsatisfactory basis for the evaluation of divisional performance since this will, in fact, imply an evaluation of the power to

agement Controls: New Directions in Basic Research, C. Bonini, et al., eds. (McGraw-Hill, 1964), p. 221–2.

[42] D. Solomons, Divisional Performance, Measurement and Control (Financial Executive Research Foundation, Inc., 1965), p. 213.

[43] R. Cyert and J. March, A Behavioral Theory of the Firm (Prentice-Hall, 1963), p. 276.

[44] A. Whinston, "Price Guides in Decentralized Organizations," New Perspectives in Organizational Research, W. W. Cooper, et al., eds. (Wiley, 1964), pp. 411–7.

[45] Ibid., p. 416.

[46] R. K. Mautz, Financial Reporting by Diversified Companies, (The Financial Executives Research Foundation, 1968), p. 36.

negotiate rather than of performance itself.[47]

SUMMARY

After appraising the approaches to transfer pricing systems suggested by various researchers three disquieting observations may be gleaned: (1) Even though transfer prices may be determined by rather sophisticated techniques, they are often followed by negotiation and/or directives specified by headquarters. Under these circumstances, it would appear that a skill in collective bargaining may prove more useful than a skill in the quantitative methods of pricing. (2) Transfer pricing problems arose from the requirement of divisional autonomy in vertically intergrated organizations; and sophisticated approaches have been addressed to the profit center dilemma caused by a decentralized management orientation. In the context of decentralization, one observes sabotage and cheating. This counterproductive behavior is also observed in systems which transcend the firm, i.e., political systems. Numerous examples in the Soviet economy could be cited to show that the firm's management more often than not underestimates output, overestimates cost, and does not report any significant increase in output beyond the budget.[48] This problem has become known as the problem of success indicators which is not unique to the Soviet economy. Cyert and March have described a similar behavior as a result of "uncertainty avoidance." (3) Ridgway has successfully disclosed the weaknesses of a single criterion for performance measurement.[49] Since the inputs to the decision models are provided by divisions, and the accuracy of divisional performance depends on the accuracy of cost previously accumulated through transfer pricing, divisional profits may not prove to be the best single criterion for the measurement of divisional performance.

Although total profits of the firm may not be different, their distribution between divisions is necessarily influenced by the pricing of transfer goods. To the extent that transfer prices incorporate some avoidable inefficiencies, there will be a shift of profits from the last division in the process to the transferring divisions. In such a situation, divisional profit is not necessarily a good measure of performance. Nor is any positive motivation likely to be derived from any of the transfer pricing systems examined in this paper.

Accordingly, we offer the following propositions which in effect are applicable to all situations irrespective of the organizational design:

(a) The problem of imputing divisional profits is situational and varies with each specific case. Therefore, modeling without sufficient empirical evidence does limit the viability of these models.

(b) In many cases, transfer pricing unnecessarily complicates the organizational design and decision-performance controls.

(c) Performance evaluation does not have to be a function of profits. It can be a function of cost, of deviations from standards, and/or of physical units of output which may be incorporated into control systems.

(d) The analysis undertaken in this paper seems to indicate that transfer pricing may blur the evaluation perspective when the evaluation of performance is strictly profit-oriented.

(e) The authors suggest that the same degree of control and evaluation attempted through transfer pricing models may be effected through the setting of standards of divisional performance and the evaluation of deviations from these standards.

[47] Dopuch and Drake, p. 13.

[48] A: Nove, "The Problem of Success Indicators in Soviety Industry," *Economica*, N.S., Vol. XXV, No. 97 (February 1958), pp. 1–13.

[49] V. F. Ridgway, "Dysfunctional Consequences of Performance Measurements" *Administrative Science Quarterly*, I (September 1956), pp. 240–1.

Transfer Pricing:
A Behavioral Context

DAVID J.H. WATSON
University of Queensland

JOHN V. BAUMLER
Lewis and Clark College

THE accounting, management science, and economics literature contains numerous models addressing the resource allocation and transfer pricing problems. Some of the earliest statements on the transfer pricing problem are recorded by Hirshleifer (1956 & 1957), Dean (1955), and Cook (1955). These authors suggest solutions to the transfer pricing problem which reflect the analogy of the internal price problem to the determination of the (Competitive) market price of traditional economics. The advent of mathematical programming produced another stream of articles addressing the transfer price problem, especially after the relation between a decentralized firm and the Dantzig and Wolfe (1960) decomposition principle was stated by Whinston (1964) and Baumol and Fabian (1964).[1]

This paper represents an attempt to place the solutions proposed by the mathematical programming models as well as other traditional solutions in an appropriate context. Since the transfer pricing problem only arises within a recognizable social system (be it an organization or a socialist economy) the paper considers the solutions in a social system context.[2] The paradigm developed can then be used to evaluate the usefulness and limitations of the various proposed solutions.

DECENTRALIZATION AND DIFFERENTIATION

Decentralization is one approach to organizational design. Implicit in this approach is the segmentation of the organization into various specialities. Numerous reasons are provided in the transfer price literature for decentralization. For example, Dean (1955) suggests, " . . . the modern integrated multiple product firm functions best if it is made into a miniature of the competitive free enterprise system." Dopuch and Drake (1964) suggest that the division managers are in a better position to process information concerning resource allocation. Along a similar vein Ronen and McKinney (1970) argue that the division manager's nearness to the market place provides relevant information regarding changes in prices of inputs and outputs and that more effective coordination of production factors should be obtained at the divisional level. Reasons such as size and diversity of modern corporations and the promotion of morale (because of the decision-making autonomy of managers) are also offered in support of decentralization (Godfrey, 1971). While each of these reasons may be true, none of the authors has offered a coherent theory of decentralization. Consequently, the implications that the authors see of decentralization for

---

[1] As examples of this see the articles by Dopuch and Drake (1964); Godfrey (1971); Gordon (1970); Hass (1968); Ruefli (1971 a&b).

[2] In this paper we only consider an organizational context, but there seems to be a direct analogy to a planned (or socialist) economy.

---

transfer pricing are fairly restricted and pragmatic.

We consider the central problem facing complex organizations is one of coping with uncertainty. This is the view many current organizational theorists propose. Similarly, we identify the two major sources of uncertainty for a complex organization as its technology and its environment. An organization's design, then, represents a response to these sources of uncertainty.[3] Specifically, an organization may create parts to deal with the uncertainty and thereby leave other parts to operate under conditions of near certainty, i.e., the organization will departmentalize and decentralize.[4] Decentralization is a response to uncertainty.

Decentralization, however, does not quite explain the process involved. A consequence of the segmentation of the organization into parts (departments, divisions, etc.) is that the behavior of organizational members will be influenced by the segmentation. Because of the differences in the nature of the task and in the environmental uncertainty facing various segments, the organizational members will develop different mental processes and working styles, adopt different decision criteria, and may have varying perceptions of reality. A well-known example of this differentiation at the perceptual level is the research report of Dearborn and Simon (1958) which demonstrated that different executives can interpret differently the same organizational problem. The differences in interpretation reflect the departmental identification of the executives.

Therefore, we use the term *differentiation* to include not only the segmentation of the organization into specialized parts, but also to include the consequent differences in attitudes and behavior of organizational members. Requisite differentiation is a requirement for organizational success. That

is, each organizational unit must be designed so as to cope effectively with the demands of its technology and environment. Later we will discuss the role of management accounting and transfer pricing in achieving the requisite degree of differentiation between organizational units.

ORGANIZATIONAL INTEGRATION

The Concept

Differentiation is only one design problem facing the organization. The other side of the same coin, and another design problem, is integration: the process of insuring that efforts of the several organizational units, now appropriately differentiated, do collectively attain the goals of the total organization.

Lawrence and Lorsch (1967) in their research demonstrated that the most successful firms (in terms of the traditional measures of profitability) in the various industries studied were the firms that achieved the required differentiation and were then able to integrate the diverse units. Further, the research indicates that only firms that achieve these dual requirements can be successful. However, a basic organizational dilemma is that the more successful an organization is in achieving the requisite differentiation (especially those organizations requiring significant differentiation) the more difficulty the organization has in achieving the necessary integration. But, of course, the difficulties in achieving the required degree of differentiation and then integrating the total organizational effort is not uniformly distributed over all firms and industries.

[3] The exact roles technology and environment play in determining organizational design is still the subject of research: see Burns and Stalker (1961); Lawrence and Lorsch (1967); Mohr (1971); Thompson (1967); Woodward (1965).

[4] Even in the most dynamic industries manufacturing operations are often sufficiently buffered to allow the effective use of standard cost systems to control manufacturing processes.

Rather, the more diverse and dynamic (uncertain) the subenvironments faced by organizational units, the more differentiated they must be. The greater the degree of differentiation, the more difficult is integration.

We stated, originally, that the central problem facing organizational designers is one of coping with uncertainty. This problem has now been restated in terms of achieving requisite differentiation of organizational components while simultaneously coordinating (or integrating) their collective efforts. The magnitude of the differentiation problem is basically determined by uncertainty in technological and environmental factors. However, the magnitude of the integration problem is partly determined by uncertainty factors and partly by the state of interdependence between organizational components.[5] To summarize, the most challenging problems to those seeking integration arise when organizational components are strongly differentiated and highly interdependent. At the opposite extreme, mildly differentiated subunits which exhibit only minimal interdependencies do not pose significant integration problems.

Integrating Mechanisms

Integration is achieved by the use of integrating mechanisms of which there are obviously many. One list of such mechanisms is indicated below. This list is adapted from an article by Galbraith (1972).[6]

Rules, Routines, Standardization
Organization Hierarchy
Planning
Direct Contact
Liaison Roles
Temporary Committees (task forces or teams)
. Integrators (personnel specializing in the role of coordinating inter-subunit activities)

Integrating Departments (departments of integrators)
Matrix Organization (an organization that is completely committed to joint problem solving and *shared* responsibility)

The list is ordered from the least elaborate to the most sophisticated integrative mechanisms. All organizations employ the first several mechanisms on the list. These mechanisms are sufficient for integrating many organizational functions and are probably all that is needed by organizations facing minimal environmental and technological demands. However, when environmental and technological demands become more complex, organizations become more differentiated and this increases the problem of integration. Consequently, more sophisticated integrating mechanisms (the latter ones listed), in addition to the simpler mechanisms, are required.

[5] (i) We are considering interdependence basically from a technological (the actual technical processes employed) and resource allocation viewpoints, although interdependence may also arise through the environment (e.g., from operating in common input and output markets). Environmental interdependence is not excluded, although we believe the most important aspect of the environment is the uncertainty dimension.
(ii) We are using the term "interdependence" in the Thompson (1967) sense. He identifies pooled, sequential, and reciprocal interdependence. Pooled interdependence is a situation in which each part of the organization renders a discrete contribution to the whole and each is supported by the whole. The parts do not interact directly with one another. This is basically the situation where the only major common organizational link among subunits is some scarce organizational resource, e.g., capital. Sequential interdependence is a situation in which, in addition to the pooled aspect, direct interaction between the units can be pinpointed and the order of that interdependence specified. Reciprocal interdependence refers to the situation in which the outputs of two units become inputs for each other. The three types of interdependence are, in the order indicated, increasingly difficult to coordinate.
[6] (i) Galbraith actually expands this list somewhat especially with regard to organizational planning.
(ii) Thompson (1967) has provided a somewhat different list. He suggests three mechanisms for achieving integration, coordination by standardization, coordination by planning, and coordination by mutual adjustment. The first two mechanisms we present correspond to Thompson's No. 1, while mechanisms 4 to 9 (lateral mechanisms in Galbraith's terminology) correspond to Thompsons No. 3.

Differentiation, Integration, and Management Accounting

The amount of differentiation required is determined primarily by technological and environmental demands, and an organization's adaptation to these demands is reflected in the first instance by the organizational design. The accountant, in designing the management accounting system, needs to consider the requisite degree of differentiation as a constraint. That is, the accountant cannot create or demand differentiation when behavioral factors dictate otherwise.

This is not to say that the management accounting system has no part to play in organizational design. In fact, the accounting system can be designed to facilitate or enhance the differentiation achieved. For example, each of the concepts—expense center, profit center, and investment center—may be employed, depending upon the differentiation required by the technological and environmental demands. When the appropriate accounting techniques are used in conjunction with required organizational design we expect the claimed benefits of decentralization to be realized.[7]

We are now in the position to consider the role of the accounting system in integration. An accounting system is a well-defined, formal information system within an organization. Basically, it is a set of rules and standard procedures. The accounting system can thus be classified as an integrating mechanism primarily of the first type listed above.[8] In more complicated integrating situations, although the accounting system (or, more precisely, the costs and prices generating by the accounting system) may be helpful in obtaining integration, this will only be *one* input to the integrating process.

Differentiation, Integration, and Transfer Pricing

Essentially we have argued that the re-quisite differentiation has to be taken as given by the accountant when he designs an organization's formal control and reporting subsystems. In some cases there will be a one-to-one mapping between the differentiated units and the accountant's responsibility centers, i.e., the expense, profit, and investment centers. However, when there is not this convenient mapping we would argue that the behavioral factors dominate, and that the accountant should not try to impose differentiation through the creation of artificial responsibility centers. Organizational design is a complete task. Numerous variables must be simultaneously considered. The accountant must accept the organizational structure as given. Restructuring the organization merely to facilitate the management accounting system is not recommended.

What then is the role of transfer pricing? Obviously, once responsibility centers are established, goods and services transferred among these units need to be priced. This helps separate and pinpoint responsibility for different aspects of the firms functioning. In other words, to some extent, the transfer pricing mechanism *enhances* differentiation. But, we have also demonstrated above that differentiation is only one part of the problem. Integration is another facet of this problem. Can the transfer pricing mechanism be used to help achieve the required integration? Again the answer is obviously "yes." In many cases the pricing mechanism is a routine or standardized process, a formula like, for example, standard cost, cost plus, marginal cost, a fixed price, etc. This type of transfer pricing is at least applicable in simple integrating situations, although in more com-

---

[7] For one listing of these claimed benefits "automatically" arising from decentralization see Horngren (1972), p. 693.

[8] Budgeting and planning are also usually considered part of the management accounting system. Notice, however, that planning has also been classed as a fairly simple or routine integrating mechanism.

plicated integrating situations it may be only one input to the integrating process.

MATHEMATICAL PROGRAMMING SOLUTIONS TO THE TRANSFER PRICING PROBLEM

As stated in the introduction to this paper many of the papers proposing programming solutions to the transfer price problem rely on the interpretation of the decomposition principle as a model of decision making in a decentralized firm. While the analogy is undoubtedly useful for analyzing some situations, the methodology appears to have some limitations.

The first limitation of these approaches is that they maintain only the facade of decentralized decision making. The last phase of the process is usually dictated by central management. For example, in the Baumol and Fabian (1964) model, although the optimal divisional plan will be a weighted average of the plans submitted by the division, the weights are entirely determined by central management. Godfrey (1971, pp. 289–90) in evaluating the Baumol and Fabian article and the more recent refinements to their model says:

Despite the appeal of the decomposition technique, in our opinion, it is still a highly centralized decision making procedure. The divisions are at the mercy of central headquarters and would probably not agree that they enjoy the autonomy of decision making that is intended.[9]

There seems to be two explanations for this problem. The first is that many authors of the programming solutions are primarily interested in the mathematical properties (or elegance) of their solutions and only secondarily in the model's organizational implications. The second is that most authors in the transfer price literature are asking the question, "What transfer price will result in the decentralized firm maximizing joint (or corporate) profits?" Since the emphasis is on the maximization of joint profits whenever

conflict arises between this goal and the decentralization philosophy, the latter tends to be sacrificed. The solution is always centralized decision making whether this is through some stated price rule, a wishful appeal to competitive market prices and their surrogates, or to mathematical programming solutions. The result is predictable since none of these authors has offered a coherent theory for decentralization. On the other hand, we have offered a theory for explaining decentralization, and under this theory it is not clear that decentralization should be sacrificed or that sacrificing decentralization will optimize decision making.

A second limitation of this approach is that they concentrate on the behaviorally simple integration problems.[10] The environments are stable and the interdependencies are of the simplest kinds. This is true even of recent articles in the area. Ruefli (1971a), for example, develops a decomposition model which can be interpreted as a representation of decision making in a three-level hierarchial organization. Ruelfi greatly restricts the degree and incidence of interdependent relationships within his tri-level hierarchy.[11]

[9] Godfrey also uses the decomposition approach in his short-run planning model but freely admits it is a centralized decision making model.

[10] (i) We are using mathematical programming models as the example. However, the same argument could be made against the economic solutions and against the traditional accounting solutions.

(ii) We are not arguing against the future development of programming models. Even the development of more efficient algorithms for handling solved problems is undoubtedly important.

[11] (i) Ruefli's model, as he notes, is easily generalized to an n-level hierarchial model.

(ii) In a second article Ruefli (1971b) does mention, with regard to behavioral externalities, the question of bidirectional effects (reciprocal interdependence) for operational units within a management unit. However, he does not propose any solution. Ruefli even proposes an integrating mechanism (a behavioral center) which he says could be a liaison arrangement, a joint planning committee, etc. However, this behavioral center seems to act very similarly to the central management unit and consequently be subject to the same "centralization" criticism.

The Case Against Negotiated Prices

The use of negotiated prices has rarely been seriously entertained by those writing in the transfer price literature. Joel Dean (1955) pressed for negotiated prices, but in such a way that they simulated a competitive market. The foundation for his recommendations really lay in the availability of markets outside the decentralized firm. Cook (1955) also discussed the use of "free negotiation" but proceeds to point out two disadvantages: (1) the amount of executive time it is likely to take, and (2) negotiated prices may distort the profit center's financial reports.[12] However, Cook (1955, p. 93) does suggest, " . . . if managers are sophisticated and equipped with good accounting data on their operations, such a free negotiation system could satisfy the basic criteria outline above; that is, a transfer price that will not lead to transfers which will reduce the company's profit but will permit and encourage any transfer which increases the company's profit."[13] Dopuch and Drake (1964, p. 13) also seem to be concerned about Cook's second point above when they state:

In evaluating the resulting performance of the divisional managers, however, the central management may be evaluating their ability to negotiate rather than their ability to control economic variables. Accordingly, the information economies of decentralization may be more apparent than real.

Later, in their paper, when discussing the decomposition procedure solutions Dopuch and Drake (1964, p. 18) suggest:

The relevant point is that, if this method can be applied in practice, it will provide a basis for negotiation between the departmental and central management levels. In this respect it would not be necessary for the divisional managers to negotiate with each other. This in itself may be an advantage since situations of negotiation between divisional managers may degenerate into personal conflicts.

Although there is undoubtedly some truth to each of these observations, that is, at times negotiated transfer prices may have these dysfunctional effects, we believe a very strong case can be made for the use of negotiated transfer prices. In presenting this case we will also be suggesting a way for obtaining suitable transfer prices for the complicated integrating situations.

Transfer Prices and Conflict Resolution

Lawrence and Lorsch (1967) in their research were able to isolate three conflict resolution mechanisms in the firms they studied. One of their most interesting results was that the successful firms facing uncertain environments were able to resolve effectively interdepartmental conflict, and the most important means of resolving this conflict was confrontation, i.e., negotiation.[14] This effective resolution of interdepartmental conflict seemed to be an important reason why these successful firms could achieve a high degree of integration as well as the high degree of differentiation demanded by their uncertain environment.

A second point worth noting is that within a complex organization conflict is going to be multidimensional. In a highly differentiated organization this will at times involve the transfer and pricing of goods and services within the organization. But it may also include design and engineering changes, production and delivery schedules, and quality control. Seen in this light, the transfer pricing question be-

[12] One, often mentioned, example of this is when one division occupies a monopoly position.

[13] Unfortunately, (technically) sophisticated managers and good accounting data are probably not sufficient conditions for insuring proper integration. Dean (1955) also suggests the position of "price mediator" for a company when *initially* installing his system. These ideas are similar to the concepts of an integrator which we will discuss later.

[14] Forcing was also an important back-up means. Smoothing was the third method and generally was the least effective.

248

comes one facet of a multidimensional conflict resolution process.[15] If the appropriate conflict resolution process is negotiation, then it appears the transfer price should be one arrived at through negotiation.[16] Specifically, determination of transfer prices could be part of the integrative process. Note that this is not a wholesale endorsement of negotiated transfer prices in all cases. There are undoubtedly instances in which unalterable formulas could be employed (e.g., the least difficult integration situations). Such formulas may be necessary to guard against obvious diseconomies or, more importantly, to enhance requisite differentiation. But if the requisite degree of differentiation is achievable and the problem is to obtain adequate integration, one of the integrative tools available might well be negotiating intrafirm prices. If organizational subunits seek to resolve conflict by confrontation—possibly with the aid of an integrator—and negotiate their differences, negotiated transfer prices might well be the desired result.

IMPLICATIONS FOR RESEARCH ON TRANSFER PRICING

The obvious implication is that we need to know something about the conflict resolution processes. In particular, we would like to know how accounting data are, or can be, used in a conflict situation. It may be, for example, that accounting data are completely irrelevant or unimportant in the more difficult integrating situations. Alternatively we may find some accounting data useful and other accounting data less useful. It may even be that we need to develop new kinds of data for these tougher areas.

Let us for the moment consider a difficult integrating situation—one that requires a formal integrator to integrate successfully the differentiated units. What can we say about this situation? First,

although the protagonists may have somewhat different working styles, time horizons, decision criteria, and perceptions of reality (because they are part of a differentiated firm facing different subparts of the organizational environment), they are still members of the one organization and consequently have some attributes in common. There is some basis therefore for believing agreement can always be attained. Second, successful integration will depend largely on the skill of the integrator and how the personnel in the differentiated units perceive him.[17] Third, from a strict accounting viewpoint, instead of giving point estimates to all the parties on the "correct" transfer price (as, for example, the output of a mathematical program) we may wish to provide guides to simply bound the solution area.[18] These bounds could then reflect other accounting re-

[15] Hence, it makes little sense to be concerned about a possible monopoly position by one department. It is unlikely, if at all possible, in uncertain environments or reciprocally interdependent situations (or both) that one department will have a monopoly position on all dimensions of the conflict.

[16] This general argument for negotiated prices could probably be extended into the simpler integrating situations. Resolving conflict in part depends upon how close the protagonists' expectations of a suitable solution point are (see Schelling for a clearly stated exposition of this point). The similarity of expectations is also a function of the complexity of the situation. Thus, it could be argued that, when environmental demands or organizational interdependencies or their interaction are least complex, expectations of a mutually agreeable solution point are closest and so the conflict is easily resolved. This seems to be, for example, the conditions when a competitive market transfer price can be established. In other words, the market-based transfer price is a limiting (or simple) case of negotiated prices. See Schelling (1960).

[17] Again notice Dean (1955) argues along a similar line when discussing his successful price mediator. He suggests the prime role of the mediator is not to dictate a price but to keep the negotiations flowing until that is a settlement.

[18] (i) For example, the variable costs of the input units may represent a lower bound, and the selling price less the variable costs of the output units may represent an upper bound. We may also give the integrator various other combinations of cost data to facilitate his integrating role (e.g., full costs (plus a markup), the mathematical programming solutions, etc.)

(ii) These behavioral questions obviously require future empirical verification or falsification.

straints on the transfer price (e.g., the fact that the transfer price may be used in the evaluation of the economic performance of the units). However, within the guides set, the final transfer price is a result of the confrontation process.

If we move to a more complicated integrating situation requiring an integrating department, some members of this department may need to be experts in internal financial matters. The implications of this and the wider implications of a matrix organization, for management accounting practice, are still very open questions. We are saying that at times the management accounting process must perform more than a mere scorekeeping or attention-directing function. The integrator has one of the most crucial roles within the organization. Certain aspects of the managerial accounting system—specifically, resolving transfer price disputes—must perhaps be merged within the integrator's total activities.

Further, little empirical evidence has been gathered on how transfer prices are established in various organizations. In gathering such evidence in the future, it is suggested that assessments of the states of differentiation and integration between buyer and seller subunits, the degree of interdependence between them, and the mode of conflict resolution utilized be made. This will allow the transfer pricing techniques to be viewed in terms of the relevant organizational and behavioral

variances. Finally, it might be worth while to investigate the relative trade-offs between nonoptimal transfer prices and the dysfunctional consequences of removing this subject from the integrator's purview.

CONCLUSION

We have attempted to place the transfer pricing question in a relevant behavioral setting. Briefly, we have suggested the management accountant needs to consider organizational differentiation a constraint in designing the management accounting system. Working within this constraint we suggested the management accounting system can be designed to enhance the organizational differentiation achieved or to facilitate organizational integration. The transfer pricing mechanism, being part of the management accounting system, can be used to enhance organizational differentiation and to facilitate organizational integration. The transfer pricing mechanisms will probably play the role of enhancing differentiation in those instances in which integration is easily attained. This may well be achieved by the use of formula pricing mechanisms. In other cases, integration will be a major organizational problem. Consequently, the transfer pricing mechanism could be utilized to facilitate integration. An appropriate transfer price mechanism in this case seems to be negotiated pricing. Further areas of research suggested by this conclusion were discussed.

REFERENCES

Baumol, W. J. and Fabian, T., "Decomposition, Pricing for Decentralization and External Economics," *Management Science* (September 1964), pp. 1–32.

Burns, T. and Stalker, G. M., *The Management of Innovation* (London: Tavistock Institute, 1961).

Cook, P. W., "Decentralization and the Transfer Price Problem," *Journal of Business* (April 1955), pp. 87–94.

Dantzig, G. B. and Wolfe P., "Decomposition Principles for Linear Programs," *Operations Research* (February 1960), pp. 101–11.

Dean, J., "Decentralization and Intracompany Pricing," *Harvard Business Review* (July–August 1955), pp. 65–74.

Dopuch, N. and Drake, D. F., "Accounting Implications of a Mathematical Programming Approach to the Transfer Pricing Problem," *Journal of Accounting Research* (Spring 1964), pp. 10–24.

Galbraith, J. R., "Organization Design: An Information Processing View," in J. W. Lorsch and P. R. Lawrence, eds., *Organizational Planning: Cases and Concepts* (Georgetown, Ontario: Irwin-Dorsey Limited, 1972).

Godfrey, J. T., "Short-Run Planning in a Decentralized Firm," THE ACCOUNTING REVIEW (April 1971), pp. 282–97.

Gordon, M. J., "A Method of Pricing for a Socialist Economy," THE ACCOUNTING REVIEW (July 1970), pp. 427–43.

Hass, J. E. "Transfer Pricing in a Decentralized Firm," *Management Science* (February 1968), pp. B-310–B-331.

Hirshleifer, J., "On the Economics of Transfer Pricing," *Journal of Business* (July 1956), pp. 172–84.

———, "Economics of the Divisionalized Firm," *Journal of Business* (April 1957), pp. 96–108.

Lawrence, P. R. and Lorsch, J. W., *Organization and Environment* (Irwin, 1967).

Mohr, L. B., "Organizational Technology and Organizational Structure," *Administrative Science Quarterly* (December 1971), pp. 444–59.

Ronen, J. and McKinney, G., "Transfer Pricing for Divisional Autonomy," *Journal of Accounting Research* (Spring 1970), pp. 99–112.

Ruefli, T. W., "A Generalized Goal Decomposition Model," *Management Science* (April 1971), pp. B-505–B-518.

———, "Behavioral Externalities in Decentralized Organizations," *Management Science* (June 1971), pp. B-649–B-657

Schelling, T. C., *The Strategy of Conflict* (Oxford University Press, 1963).

Thompson, J. D., *Organizations in Action* (McGraw-Hill, 1967).

Whinston, "Pricing Guides in Decentralized Organization," in W. W. Cooper et al., eds., *New Perspectives in Organizational Research* (Wiley, 1964).

Woodward, J., *Industrial Organizations: Theory and Practice* (Oxford University Press, 1965).

The Significance and Investigation of Cost Variances: Survey and Extensions

ROBERT S. KAPLAN*

Carnegie-Mellon University

1. Introduction

Standard cost systems can produce as many variances each period as there are accounts for which standards are set, since actual costs for a period will rarely equal the standard or budgeted cost for any process worth controlling.[1] Nevertheless, no one seriously advocates taking action and investigating every cost variance that occurs each period. Managers recognize that many variances are insignificant and caused by random, noncontrollable factors. Since any investigation will involve a certain expenditure of effort and funds, managers will attempt to take action on only the most significant and correctible variances. An investigation should only be undertaken if the benefits expected from the investigation exceed the costs of searching for and correcting the source of the cost variance.

Many articles have appeared in statistical and accounting journals that directly deal with determining whether a process is in or out of control and, hence, whether it is worthwhile to intervene in the process. Despite the widespread use of quality control techniques in industry, however, the application of these ideas in actual standard cost accounting settings can generously be characterized as minimal. For example, in 1968, Koehler reported that "in some general inquiry from some prominent corporations, I was unable to find a single use of statistical procedures for variance control."[2] He attributes this paucity of applications not to the inherent

---

* Professor, Carnegie-Mellon University. Many helpful comments on an earlier draft were received from Professors Nicholas Dopuch, Thomas Dyckman, Robert Magee, and Roman Weil. The opinions and interpretations still remaining in this paper are solely the author's responsibility.

[1] I am excluding the budgeting of expirations of accrued costs such as depreciation or prepaid expenses which should equal planned levels in each period. These expenses represent allocations of prior expenditures and, hence, are not interesting to control on an item-by-item basis each period.

[2] Koehler (1968): 35.

---

inapplicability of such procedures but to "the fact that accountants have not recognized a conceptual distinction between a significant and an insignificant variance."[3] Koehler proceeds to advocate the use of a simple testing procedure which I will consider later in the paper.

In contrast to Koehler's view, that the fault lies with the lack of formal statistical training among practicing accountants, other observers conclude that statistical procedures are rarely used in practice because the procedures themselves are inappropriate for assessing the significance of accounting variances. For example, Anthony, in a review article on management accounting observed that "researchers continue to explore the possibility of finding a mathematical way of stating whether a variance between planned and actual cost is or is not significant."[4] He concludes, though, that

> The differences between the data on a production process that is repeated several times a day and data on the overall costs of a department that are measured once a month are so great that few if any managers believe that statistical techniques in the latter case are worth the effort to calculate them. They prefer either to establish control limits by judgment or to run down the report item by item and determine, without any numerical calculation, whether a difference between planned and actual costs is worth investigation.[5]

He also states that "attempts to be even more sophisticated and to apply Bayesian probability theory or dynamic programming to the control chart idea do not strike me as being very promising."[6]

The final judgment on the appropriateness of formal statistical and mathematical models for cost variance analysis must be based on empirical studies. To date little such evidence is available. There are reasons to believe, however, that some form of screening model would be beneficial to managers by eliminating the need for them to examine extensive variance reports item by item in order to detect a significant variance. A formal screening model could also scan detailed variance reports more efficiently than a manager, thereby permitting a more disaggregate collection of costs. Moreover, there is extensive evidence in the psychological literature[7] that persons consistently underestimate the importance of

---

[3] *Ibid.*, p. 35.

[4] Anthony (1973): 52.

[5] *Ibid.*, p. 52.

[6] *Ibid.*, p. 51.

[7] For surveys of this literature, see Edwards (1968) and Slovic and Lichtenstein (1971). The evidence seems very strong that persons do not process sample evidence very well in complex environments. For example, Slovic and Lichtenstein conclude (p. 714), "[Man as an] intuitive statistician appears to be quite confused by the conceptual demands of probabilistic inference tasks. He seems capable of little more than revising his response in the right direction upon receipt of a new item of information (and the inertia effect is evidence that he is not always successful in doing even this)." Also (p. 724), "We find that judges have a very difficult time weighting and combining information, be it probabilistic or deterministic in nature. To reduce cognitive strain, they resort to simplified decision strategies many of which lead them to ignore or misuse relevant information."

sample evidence in forming probability judgments about events. In other words, a manager with strong prior beliefs that everything is all right with a given process will interpret sizable variances as still being consistent with an in-control situation, whereas a statistical model would clearly signal a low probability that such large deviations could arise from an in-control situation. A statistical model may also indicate that an occasional large variance is consistent with fluctuation that has occurred in the past so that immediate action may not be warranted.

The purpose of this paper is to provide a comprehensive survey of techniques that are potentially useful for assessing the significance of cost variances. A simple taxonomy of various approaches will be described which should help to classify the basic assumptions and purpose of each type of proposed procedure. Important techniques commonly used in industrial quality control will be briefly surveyed and related to proposals made in the accounting literature. Several widely referenced articles in the accounting literature will be reviewed and a number of fundamental errors and hidden assumptions in some of these papers will be noted. Finally, I will suggest extensions and describe a model, new to the accounting literature, that may eventually prove useful for aiding the variance investigation decision.

Before embarking on this survey, it is useful to indicate some aspects of the variance investigation decision I will *not* be considering. First, since I will deal only with a single process and a single variance reported from this process, then models which are designed to identify or isolate the most important variances from a large set [see Lev (1969)] will not be treated. I will not be involved with the actual investigation process [Demski (1970)] and methods for aggregating variances to enhance the reporting and investigation process [Ronen (1974)]. As an aside, Demski (1970), classifies five separate sources of cost deviations and after assuming that we are able to estimate the time to investigate each source as well as the prior probability that the deviation came from each source, describes an algorithm which will minimize the expected time until the source is uncovered. In a more general setting, DeGroot (1970) describes an algorithm when there is a cost, c_i, of investigating each source as well as a probability, α_i, of not detecting the cause even when investigating the true source of the deviation (i.e., imperfect investigation).[8]

I will also deal only briefly with relating the significance of the accounting variance to possible changes in decision models.[9] I am assuming that the significant variances being considered here are, for the most part, correctible and hence should not require changes in the firm's decisions but this point will be mentioned again in Section 6B.

---

[8] DeGroot (1970): 423–29; and Kadane (1971).

[9] This topic is developed in Dopuch, Birnberg, and Demski (1967) and Demski (1967).

2. *A Taxonomy of Variance Investigation Models*

All the papers and models that will be reviewed in this paper can be classified along two dimensions. The first dichotomy is whether the investigation decision is made on the basis of a single observation or whether some past sequence of observations, including the most recent one, is considered in the decision. I refer to this distinction as single-period versus multi-period models. An example of a single-period model is a control chart approach in which a variance is investigated if it falls outside a pre-specified limit, e.g., 2σ or 3σ from the expected value. An example of a multi-period approach occurs if all the most recent observations are used to estimate the current mean of the process to determine whether the process is within its control limits. The second dichotomy is whether or not the model explicitly includes the expected costs and benefits of the investigation in determining when to investigate a variance. A simple control chart or hypothesis test with preset (and arbitrary) levels of a Type I error is an example of a model which does not explicitly include decision relevant costs in the analysis. Economically designed control charts, however, in which control limits are set as a function of the cost of an investigation as well as the cost of making Type I and Type II errors would be an example of a model that included relevant costs in the analysis. Models which use statistical decision theory approaches such as Duvall (1967), Kaplan (1969), and Dyckman (1969) are other examples of this type of model.

Thus, we may classify the papers on the variance investigation decision into a 2×2 table as shown below. An additional sub-classification is useful in the lower right-hand category of multi-period decision theory models.

A Taxonomy of Deviation Investigation Models

	Costs and Benefits of Investigation not Considered	Costs and Benefits of Investigation Considered
Single-Period	Zannetos (1964) Juers (1967), Koehler (1968) Luh (1968), Probst (1971) Buzby (1974)	Duncan (1956) Bierman, Fouraker, and Jaedicke (1961)
Multi-Period	Cumulative-Sum Chart as in Page (1954). Also Barnard (1959) Chernoff and Zacks (1964)	Duvall (1967) Kaplan (1969) Dyckman (1969) Bather (1963)

Some models, such as Kaplan (1969) and Dyckman (1969), assume that the process being controlled can only be in a discrete set of states. Typically, only two states are assumed (in control and out of control) but it is also possible to use a finer classification in which discrete amounts of "out-of-controlness" are allowed. In fact, models such as Duvall (1967) and Bather (1963) allow the mean of the process to vary continuously so that there is an infinite set of states for the process. This leads to slightly different procedures to estimate the current state of the process and, hence, it is useful to introduce this sub-classification of discrete versus continuous process states. In the remainder of the paper, we analyze each compartment in the table, including the sub-classification just described, to indicate the assumptions, strengths, and weaknesses of the proposed models.

3. *Decision Models Based on a Single Observation; No Costs of Investigation or Misclassification*

In the simplest control formulation, the objective is to determine whether a shift in the probability distribution of the process generating outputs has occurred. Usually, the shift is identified with a change in the location parameter (e.g., the mean) of the distribution though it is, of course, possible to test for any shift in the distribution [see Luh (1968)]. No costs of misclassification are considered and information from previous observations on the process is ignored. The classic example of such a procedure is the simple $\bar{x}$ chart suggested by Shewhart (1931) and widely used in industry. With this procedure, a target mean is established and a standard deviation, σ, is estimated for the process when it is in control. Control limits are typically set so that the probability of an in-control process with normally distributed outcomes producing a signal beyond these limits (a Type I error) is very small (e.g., .01 or .002). In practice, Shewhart charts are modified on an ad hoc basis to detect a run of observations in excess of 1σ or 2σ, but there is no generally accepted modification to the classic Shewhart control chart.

Many articles in the accounting literature are essentially variations of a simple Shewhart chart in which a distribution is assumed under the null hypothesis that the process is in control. An investigation is signaled when the probability that any single observation could have come from this in-control distribution falls below a given level, usually assumed to be .05. For example, the papers by Buzby (1974), Juers (1967), Koehler (1968), Luh (1968), Probst (1971), and Zannetos (1964) are all of this type. Some of these papers [Buzby (1974), Zannetos (1964)] also suggest the use of Chebyschev's inequality to compute the probability of an extreme observation if one does not believe that observations from the in-control distribution are normally distributed (or some other parametric form).

Luh's paper is at a much more disaggregate form of analysis from any of the other papers. Rather than dealing with the total or average cost of a period, he assumes that we will measure the components of actual cost (usage and rate; material and labor) of every item that is produced in a period. The distribution of outcomes from each cost component is then compared with the assumed in-control distribution via a goodness-of-fit test (Kolmogorov-Smirnov or Chi-squared) to see if a significant shift in the distribution has occurred. Thus, Luh is able to detect not only shifts in the mean of the distribution but also shifts in the shape or scale of the distribution. This test will, therefore, signal an investigation much more often than a system which only monitors potential shifts in the mean. In addition, Luh's system requires the collection of far more detailed information than is typically required for traditional control chart-like systems so that the cost of operating this procedure may become a significant factor, especially relative to the incremental benefits the procedure might offer.

To summarize, procedures described in the papers referenced in this section only control for the distribution of outcomes when the process is in control. They test for significant departures from this null distribution based on a single-period's observation. Previous observations are not aggregated together when the statistical test is performed, and no costs of investigation or of failing to correct an out-of-control process are explicitly considered.

4. Decision Models Based on Multiple Observations; No Costs of Investigation or Misclassification

The procedures described in the previous section treat successive observations from the same process as being independent samples. No attempt is made to combine the information from previous observations with the current observation to reach a statistical conclusion as to whether the process is currently in control. These procedures, therefore, ignore a lot of the potentially useful information available from a systematic examination of trends. The use of prior observations should enable a mean shift to be detected much earlier than by successively testing single observations at a low α (probability of Type I error) risk.

The cumulative sum (cusum) procedure, introduced by Page (1954), is the most common procedure that uses previous observations for detecting a shift in the mean of a process. With this procedure, the target mean, μ, is subtracted from the current observation, x_r, and a series of partial sums formed, S_r, where

$$S_r = \sum_{i=1}^{r} (x_i - \mu).$$

Under the null hypothesis, these partial sums should follow a random walk with zero mean. But if a shift in the mean has occurred (away from μ), the partial sums will start to develop a positive or negative drift. While an analytic test to detect a drift is not hard to develop, many writers advocate a graphical approach for the cusum technique. Successive partial sums, $S_r = S_{r-1} + x_r - \mu$, are plotted ($S_r$ on the vertical axis, r along the horizontal axis) and a V-mask applied from the most recent observation (see figure 1). If any previous cumulative sum (S_i, $i = 1, \cdots,$ $r - 1$) is covered by the V-mask, a significant shift in the mean is deemed to have occurred. Cusum charts can be made sensitive to small changes in the mean of a process since these will cause the trajectory of cumulative

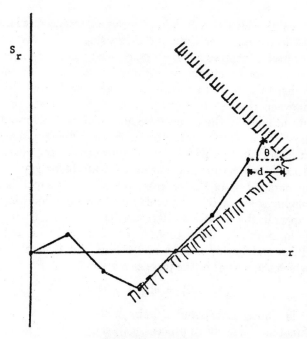

F_IG. 1.- Cumulative sum procedure.

sums to drift away from previous observations until one limb of the V-mask cuts across a prior point to signal an out-of-control condition.

The two design parameters of a cusum V-mask are the offset distance, d, and the angle of the mask, θ. These can be set based on (1) an assumed shift in the mean of the process of μ, (2) the average run length in control before a false investigate signal is generated, and (3) the average run length out of control (mean shift of μ) before an investigate signal is given [see Ewan and Kemp (1960) and Goldsmith and Whitfield (1961)]. In practice, these parameters are frequently set by experimenting with different values for d and θ on charts derived from past data from the process being controlled until the right incidence of false and true signals is achieved.

A more formal model of a multi-period nonstationary process is described by Barnard (1959) who formulates the control problem as one of estimation rather than hypothesis testing. In order to use all the past data to estimate the current mean of the process, a specific stochastic process of how mean shifts occur needs to be formulated. Barnard assumes that shifts or jumps in the mean occur according to a Poisson process. Conditional on a jump occurring, the amount of the jump is assumed to be a normally distributed random variable with a zero mean and known variance. From this process, Barnard derives an expression for a mean likelihood estimator (the maximum likelihood estimator would be very difficult to estimate) which is a weighted mean of recent observations with the weights decreasing over time and decreasing if there is a large jump between successive observations. Barnard also suggests an approximate graphical procedure to obtain an estimate of the current mean of the process. Perhaps the most important message from Barnard's paper is to realize that when we wish to aggregate prior observations to estimate or test the current mean of the process, we need to specify a formal stochastic model of how changes in the mean occur. For the nonstationary processes we are considering in this paper, simple unweighted aggregations of past data, such as sample means and variances, will not be good estimates of the current parameters of the process. We will return to this point later when discussing some of the proposals made in the accounting literature.

Other papers in the statistical literature have also dealt with estimating the change in mean of a noisy process. For example, Chernoff and Zacks (1964), Hinich and Farley (1966), and Farley and Hinich (1970) treat a model in which the output of the process is given by

$$x(t) = \theta(t) + n(t)$$

where $n(t)$ is Gaussian distributed noise with zero mean and known covariance function.[10] The mean process, $\theta(t)$, is assumed to undergo discrete shifts according to a Poisson distributed process. These papers assume that the total observation time is less than the mean time between jumps so that the possibility of two or more jumps in the observed interval can be ignored. Efficient estimators of the mean process, $\theta(t)$, are developed as a function of the sequence of observations. These papers and Barnard's can be used to develop an estimator of the current mean of a noisy nonstationary process. Within a standard cost accounting context, such an estimate would correspond to the current level of average cost for the process being controlled. Presumably, if this current level were sufficiently far away from the standard level, an investigation would be signaled. Note, however, that neither the cost of an investigation nor the value of waiting for additional sample information is explicitly included in this analysis.

To date, no article in the accounting literature has advocated the use of the cusum or the other sophisticated statistical techniques described in this section which make use of the entire history of observations to signal an out-of-control situation. Such procedures do represent an improvement over simple control charts and successive hypothesis tests on single observations since they specifically model the stochastic dependence of successive observations. Nevertheless, they are still an incomplete representation of the problem since they do not include the cost and benefit structure of the investigation decision.

---

[10] For the processes discussed in this paper, we have assumed that successive observations are statistically independent so that the covariance matrix would be diagonal.

5. *Decision Models Based on a Single Observation; Cost of Investigation and Misclassification Included*

A third category of papers generalizes the simple hypothesis testing ideas described first to include the cost of investigation and the potential benefit to be achieved from an investigation. In the quality control literature, Duncan (1956) devised a scheme for the economic design of $\bar{x}$ charts. Duncan's model assumed the following types of benefits and costs: (i) Income when the process is in control, (ii) Income when the process is out of control, (iii) Cost of looking for a cause when none exists, (iv) Cost of looking for a cause when one exists, and (v) Cost of charting. With these costs and assuming a specific alternative hypothesis (i.e., a mean shift of known magnitude) Duncan computed control limits that approximately maximized average income per period. Duncan's analysis was subsequently extended by Goel, Jain, and Wu (1968) and Gibra (1971). Note that even though their approaches minimized costs or maximized income over extended periods of time, the decision to investigate is still based on whether the most recent observation falls outside the control limits. Thus, information from previous observations is not used in the investigation decision.

In the accounting literature, Bierman, Fouraker, and Jaedicke (BFJ) (1961) were the first to introduce the costs and benefits of an investigation into the investigation decision. Their paper treated a single-period model and assumed, as did the papers listed in section 3, that management could specify the distribution of outcomes when the process is in control. Given a particular observation, the probability, p, that this observation came from the null (in-control) distribution was computed. With an investigation cost of C and a potential benefit from correcting an out-of-control situation of L, an investigation was signaled if $C < (1 - p)L$. One problem with this formulation is the difficulty of estimating or even interpreting L. BFJ do not devote much discussion to estimating L but in a footnote explain, "In situations where the inefficiency will be repeated, L should be defined as the present value of the costs that will be incurred in the future if an investigation is not made now."[11] Unfortunately, these future cost savings are not easy to estimate. In situations where the inefficiency will be repeated, one would have opportunities in the future to correct the process. Therefore, the discounted future costs assuming no future investigation is an overestimate of L. But L will not equal the one-period costs, assuming an investigation occurs next period, since a good realization may occur next period even when operating somewhat inefficiently so that no investigation would be signaled. Therefore, the benefit, L, depends upon future actions, and models which do not specifically include the consequences of future actions will have a hard time defining, much less estimating, what is the benefit from current actions. BFJ could reply that they are dealing with one-period nonrepetitive situations so

---

[11] Bierman, Fouraker, and Jaedicke (1961), footnote 1, pp. 414–15.

261

that future costs and actions are not relevant. Such situations do occur in practice. But some of the papers to be discussed in the next section purport to treat multi-period aspects and still fail to deal with this crucial aspect of estimating the incremental benefits from an investigation now rather than in future periods.

Dyckman[12] has criticized the BFJ model for basing the investigation decision on only the most recent observation, thereby ignoring prior information—either sample information from previous periods or subjectively determined priors. To the extent that the outputs from the process are believed to be dependent random variables from a stochastic process, then a reasonable decision should make use of prior observations as well as the most recent one. We turn now to a discussion of such procedures.

6. *Discrete State Decision Models with Multiple Observations; Cost of Investigation and Misclassification Included*

CONTROL CHARTS

We have already described cusum charts which can signal an investigation based on the relation of the current observation with all prior observations. In a manner analogous to that done by Duncan for $\bar{x}$ charts, Taylor (1968) and Goel and Wu (1973) develop procedures to design cusum charts that minimize long-run average cost. Both papers assume a cost structure similar to Duncan's and a process in which a single shift in the process mean of known magnitude occurs at a random time. Economically determined values of d, the V-mask offset distance, and θ, the angle of the V-mask, are determined based on the magnitude of the shift, the parameters of the distribution of time the process remains in control, the investigation costs, and the costs of operating in or out of control. The optimal design of control charts, however, is optimal in only a special sense. In effect, the form of the optimal policy is predetermined by the characteristics of the control chart, and only the parameters of the control chart are optimized. It is analogous to finding the optimal (s, S) policy in an inventory problem even though an (s, S) policy is not the globally optimal one.

Traditional control charts tend to be non-Bayesian in that no prior information about in- or out-of-control probabilities is combined with sample evidence. An exception is provided by Girshick and Rubin (1952) who considered a two-state model (in and out of control) with a Markov chain describing transitions between the two states in successive periods. Assuming a constant cost of investigation and a constant cost per period for operating out of control, an optimal investigation policy was determined that minimized long-run average cost.

---

[12] See "A Correction," pp. 114–15 in Ozan and Dyckman (1971).

Kaplan (1969) adapted the Girshick and Rubin procedure for the accounting variance investigation decision. Rather than having to derive a cost from operating out of control, Kaplan used the actual costs when operating in or out of control to derive optimal policies. Thus, a decision to delay investigating for one period incurred the risk of operating one more period out of control, that is, obtaining a cost realization from the higher cost, out-of-control distribution, rather than from lower cost, in-control distribution. Balanced against this risk was the certain cost of an investigation which might find that the system was still in control. Note that the loss function in the accounting variance setting arises directly from the nature of the problem. In the control chart approach, the cost of operating in or out of control must be imputed. In the accounting setting, the incremental costs of operating out of control arise directly from the higher costs that accrue when operating away from standard. Thus the cost variance decision may be more amenable to an economically based decision theory treatment. Dynamic programming was used to compute optimal policies that minimized discounted future costs. Discounted future cost was used as the criterion, rather than long-run average cost as used by Girshick and Rubin, because the time interval between successive accounting reports made the time value of money a relevant consideration. But since the computation of optimal policies in this situation is not very sensitive to the assumed discount rate, the long-run average cost criterion could be achieved simply by using a discount factor of unity (or arbitrarily close to unity) and adopting the policy to which the n-period optimal policy converges.

A key feature of the two-state Markov model used by Girshick and Rubin and by Kaplan is that all the relevant information from the prior observations, since the last investigation was made, could be summarized by a single state variable—the probability that the system is currently operating in control. This variable is updated after each observation via Bayes' theorem to incorporate information from the most recent observation. Assuming a specific form for the transition matrix—in this case geometric distribution for the time until the system goes out of control—provides a tremendous reduction in the amount of information that must be stored about previous realizations of the process. One could even relax the geometric distribution assumption of constant probability of going out of control without a great increase in the complexity of the procedure. Of course, this would require more information about the specific probabilities of going out of control as a function of time. In general, one could define g_k as the probability that, in period k, the system will remain in control given that it was in control at the start of the period. For the geometric distribution, $g_k = g$ for $k = 1, 2, \cdots$, with an arbitrary distribution for going out of control, the discrete state variable k would be appended to the state description and the optimization done with respect to this state variable as well as the one summarizing the current probability that the system is in control. The main difference would be that the operator $\tau_x q$[13] which updates the probability, q, of being in control after receiving an observation x would now become a function of k—the number of periods since the last investigation; i.e.,

$$\tau_{x;k}q = g_k[1 + \lambda(x)(1 - q)/q]^{-1}$$

where $\lambda(x) = f_2(x)/f_1(x)$ is the likelihood ratio of the out-of-control distribution to the in-control distribution. The functional equation for $C_n(q)$ then becomes one for $C_n(q; k)$, where $C_n(q; k)$ is the minimum expected discounted cost with present estimate of q of being in control and k periods since the last investigation. The steady state equation for $C_n(q; k)$ is given by

$$C(q; k) = \min \{K + \int [x + \alpha C(\tau_{x;0}g_0; 1)]f_{g_0}(x)\, dx;$$
$$\int [x + \alpha C(\tau_{x;k}q; k + 1)]f_q(x)\, dx\}$$

where K is the cost of the investigation, α is the discount rate and $f_q(x)$ = $qf_1(x) + (1 - q)f_2(x)$, a weighted sum of the in-control and out-of-control density functions.

The first set of terms (before the semi-colon) is the current and expected future costs when an investigation is made now. The second set represents the expected costs when no investigation is made now. The derivation of the functional equation is along the lines developed in Kaplan (1969). Roughly speaking, the density function $f_q(x)$ gives the probability of getting an observation x when q is the probability the observation comes from the in-control density function. After an investigation, the system is reset so that there is a probability g_0 (perhaps equal to 1) that the system will remain in control for one full period after an investigation has taken place. This is why the probability is g_0 that the observation immediately after an investigation comes from the in-control distribution. To solve the equation, some reasonable upper bound on k must be assumed. Perhaps the value such that the a priori probability is .95 or .99 that the system will be out of control after that number of periods is a reasonable upper bound for k.

The infinite period function equation serves as a convenient approximation to a long but unspecified planning horizon. In fact, the infinite period optimal policy is typically very similar to the optimal policy with only 10 or 15 periods remaining. In any case, the infinite period optimal policy is computed as the limit of the finite horizon optimal policies so that one has the information to use the policy optimal for whatever planning horizon one thinks is appropriate.

There are at least two other assumptions that may limit the applicability of this approach. One is the heroic simplification of the process to

---

[13] See pp. 34–35 in Kaplan (1969).

a two-state system, in control and out of control, with sudden transitions between the states. While we have seen that this model is frequently used in the quality control literature, the process by which a controllable cost process suddenly moves from in control to out of control is rather difficult to articulate. Intuitively it is more appealing to consider a process that gradually drifts away from standards through an evolutionary process of neglect and lack of proper supervision. In such a case, the forced dichotomy between in control and out of control may be an unrealistic aggregation of reality. One solution is to expand the number of states to allow for varying degrees of out of controlness. For example we might allow S states ($S =$ 5 or 10, say) with state 1 representing perfectly in control, state 2 representing slight deterioration, and state S being well out of control. Each state would be associated with a different distribution of cost outcomes, with the average cost increasing from state 1 to state S. For each state s in S, we would have a density function $f_s(x)$ of outcomes arising from a process while in state s. We could then define an $S \times S$ Markov matrix, P, describing how one-period transitions are made from state to state. If the process is expected to just deteriorate over time, P would be an upper block triangular matrix with no entries below the main diagonal. Unfortunately, the state space would require $S - 1$ states (q_1, q_2, $\cdots$, q_{S-1}) with q_i being the current probability that the system is in state i.[14] Given an observation, x, the posterior probabilities, $q_i{}^*(x)$, that the system was in state i when observation x was produced could be computed from

$$q_i{}^*(x) = \frac{f_i(x)q_i}{\sum_{j=1}^{s} f_j(x)q_j}.$$

These posterior probabilities $\mathbf{q}^* = (q_1{}^*(x), \cdots, q_S{}^*(x))$ would then be multiplied by the transition matrix P to yield the q_i's for the system in the next period. While this procedure is not difficult to describe, optimal policies may become difficult to compute for S larger than 4 or 5.

An extended version of such a model was treated by Ross (1971). He assumed that a process could be in a countable number of states i, ($i = 0$, 1, 2, $\cdots$), with quality a function of the state. He assumed that costs of production, inspecting, and revision were all functions of the current state, i. A Markov chain described the movement from state to state of the process for each transition. The state variables of the system consisted of the probability vector $\mathbf{q} = (q_0, q_1, \cdots)$ where q_i is the current probability that the system is in state i. Three actions are possible—produce without inspection, produce with inspection (to learn the current state), and revise the process, to state 0. For this very general formulation, Ross was able

---

[14] Since the q_i's must sum to one, we only need to explicitly consider $S - 1$ probabilities. The omitted probability is determined implicitly by subtracting the sum of the $S - 1$ probabilities from 1.

to obtain only the most general results. He determined that the steady state optimality function $V(\mathbf{q})$ is concave in $\mathbf{q}$ and that the inspection and revision regions are convex. Some more specific results are obtained for a two-state process (good and bad) in which he demonstrated an example for which the "produce without inspection" region could consist of two disjoint regions, a region being defined by those values of q, the probability that the system is in the good state at the start of the period, for which a given action is optimal ($0 \leq q \leq 1$).

In addition to the two-state limitation of Kaplan's model, the model is also limited by the assumption that the process can always be returned to the in-control distribution. The decision model is based on the assumption that if an out-of-control situation is discovered, the process can be corrected so that future costs will likely arise from the in-control cost density function, $f_1(x)$. But, occasionally, fundamental shifts in the process may occur that are not reversible even after discovery. Prices may have risen or operating procedures developed which may be impossible or at best difficult to reverse. Therefore, an investigation undertaken in anticipation of realizing the benefits from a restoration to the historical standard cost may never realize these benefits and, hence, the benefits expected from the investigation will have been overestimated. This feature represents one of the fundamental differences between the traditional quality control setting for which most of the described techniques have been developed and the cost variance setting considered in this paper. The physical processes being monitored in the quality control environment can almost always be reset from an out-of-control situation to the desired setting once such a situation is discovered. The benefits from investigating these processes can, therefore, be measured by the almost certain return to the in-control state.

The feature of the cost variance setting in which the previous standard may no longer be attainable seems difficult to capture in a simple practical model. One could always define a probability that an out-of-control situation is not correctible but then one would have to be concerned with controllable and noncontrollable deviations from the new, but still not completely known, standard and the problem rapidly escalates. About the only ameliorating factor here is that there is some benefit in learning about a fundamental shift in the cost or technology of a process. Such a shift may affect the firm's decision model[15] and thereby effect some savings, though not as much as had been anticipated at the time the investigation decision was made. In a similar vein, the model has difficulty capturing the benefits that may accrue from investigating a below-average cost. If a lower than expected cost performance can be made permanent by resetting the cost standard to adjust to the more efficient process, then a long-term benefit can be achieved. This benefit is ignored in the model which as-

---

[15] See Dopuch, Birnberg, and Demski (1967) and Demski (1967).

266

sumes that the process is always returned to its original cost standard. Also, the model in its present formulation does not adequately handle problems with below-average costs due to use of lower-quality materials or labor. It always assumes that lower cost is better than higher cost, i.e., it assumes the quality of output remains constant.

The above situations describe one set of reasons why the system may not always be returned to the in-control state after an investigation has occurred. It is also possible to consider the situation in which the investigation fails to detect an out-of-control situation when one exists. This possibility is not considered in Kaplan's model but an extension to allow for imperfect investigations will be discussed shortly. Other extensions to the basic model are discussed in Kaplan (1969). These extensions allow (1) for a delay between the time the investigation decision is made and the time the system is restored to the in-control state, (2) the system to be self-correcting, and (3) the cost of investigation to be a function of the state the system is actually in.

DYCKMAN'S MODEL

Dyckman (1969) dealt with a model very similar to Kaplan's except that the multi-period cost structure was suppressed. The stochastic process with a Markov chain describing transitions between an in-control state and out-of-control state was used with Bayesian updating of the probability of being in either state after each observation from the process. Thus the limitations of the two-state process, just described, apply to this model too.

As in the single-period BFJ model, though, Dyckman assumes a constant saving, L, from investigating an out-of-control situation. Dyckman does not offer much more guidance as to the interpretation or estimation of L. He calls it the "present value of the savings obtainable from an investigation when the activity is out of control," then notes that "where a corrective action is not forever binding, the calculation of L needs to be adjusted to reflect the possibility of future out-of-control periods" and then concludes that "the precise determination of the savings for each future period is not an easy matter."[16]

The difficulty, of course, arises because Dyckman suppresses the sequential decision-making nature of the problem and therefore cannot evaluate the benefits from delaying the investigation for another period when more sample evidence may be obtained. Difficulties with interpreting what L represents, similar to those expressed here, were raised by Li (1970) who observes that "dynamic programming is more appropriate to use under this situation."[17] Dyckman's reply concurs with the logic of this suggestion but claims that "the difficulties attendant on solving large and complex real dynamic programming problems can limit the successful

---

[16] Dyckman (1969): 218.

[17] Li (1970): 283.

267

application of this technique."[18] It is true that dynamic programs are difficult to solve when there are a large number of state variables. But the model treated by Dyckman can be summarized by a single-state variable [see Kaplan (1969)] and dynamic programs with a single-state variable are quite easy to solve. Therefore, computational costs should not be high relative to the benefits from including the effect of future decisions and actions into the analysis.

Dyckman eventually concludes that L should be measured by the savings over the planning horizon which is taken to be the minimum of the average time until the process goes out of control again and the time until standards need to be revised.[19] This does not settle the issue, however, since some problems inherently remain in his nonsequential decision model. For one thing, L must then be a function of n, the number of periods since the process started. If L is the discounted savings over the planning horizon, then as a number of periods pass, there are fewer periods remaining in the planning horizon so the potential savings last for fewer periods. Hence, L must decrease with increasing n. Dyckman extends in Some Extensions, Section A (pp. 228–30) the traditional two-action space (Investigate, Don't Investigate) model by allowing for an exploratory investigation which costs less than a full investigation but has probability h, with $h < 1$, of detecting an out-of-control situation when one exists. This is certainly a worthwhile extension and can easily be incorporated into the dynamic programming framework already developed. There are two outcomes from the exploratory investigation; either an out-of-control situation is discovered or it is not. If the probability that the system is in control is q, then the probability of finding it out of control with the exploratory investigation is $(1 - q)h$. When the process is found to be out of control, it is reset and a new cycle starts. Conversely, the probability that the system is not found to be out of control by the exploratory investigation is $1 - (1 - q)h$. But in this case, the investigation is not a complete failure since we get some new information about the probability that the system is in control. If q was the probability of the system being in control before the unsuccessful exploratory investigation, the posterior probability of being in control can be obtained via Bayes theorem as $q/[1 - h(1 - q)]$ which is greater than q. Therefore, the decision to undertake an exploratory investigation must include not only the potential benefit from cheaply discovering an out-of-control situation but also the expected future benefits to be achieved by an increase in our estimate of the probability of being in control. Formally, if K' is the cost of the limited investigation, the expected infinite horizon future cost from undertaking an exploratory investigation is given by:

$$K' + (1 - q)h \int [x + \alpha C(\tau_x g)]f_o(x)\, dx$$
$$+ [1 - (1 - q)h] \int [x + \alpha C(\tau_x q')]f_{q'}(x)\, dx$$

---

[18] Dyckman's reply, in Li (1970): 283.

[19] *Ibid.*; also in Ozan and Dyckman (1971): 98.

268

with $q' = q/[1 - h(1 - q)]$ and $g =$ one-period probability of going out of control. Dyckman recognizes that the probabilities of being in or out of control should be revised to reflect the exploratory investigation outcome but advises against this if it will raise one of the probabilities.[20] He incorrectly neglects the value of this anticipated revision (in effect the expected value of sample information) in his decision to conduct the exploratory investigation.

For a more general treatment still, we might let the amount of money spent on an investigation be a continuous variable, z, and define a function $h(z)$ as the probability of detecting an out-of-control situation when one exists. Presumably $h(0) = 0$, $\lim_{z \to \infty} h(z) = 1$ and $h(z)$ is a nondecreasing function of z. The decision then becomes one of not only deciding whether to investigate or not but how much to spend on the investigation. If q is the prior probability that the system is in control, an amount z is spent on an investigation and an out-of-control situation is not found, the posterior probability that the system is in control (after the investigation) is

$$q'(z) = q/[1 - h(z)(1 - q)].$$

Therefore, we may formulate the infinite horizon decision problem as:

$$C(q) = \min_{z \geq 0} \{z + (1 - q)h(z) \int [x + \alpha C(\tau_x g)]f_o(x) \, dx$$

$$+ [1 - (1 - q)h(z)] \int [x + \alpha C(\tau_x q')]f_{q'}(x) \, dx\}$$

where q' is a function of z as defined above and setting $z = 0$ with $h(0) = 0$ and $q'(0) = q$ yields the expected cost when no investigation is undertaken.

Returning to Dyckman (1969), in Some Extensions, Section C (pp. 231–33), n consecutive observations are used to develop posterior probabilities about the states of the process. The sample mean, $\bar{x}$, of these n observations is used as a sufficient statistic to summarize these sample results. But the sample mean of a normal process (with known variance) can only be the sufficient statistic of a *stationary* process. That is, the procedure of combining n sample results into a sufficient statistic, $\bar{x}$, is valid only if one assumes that the process is in a given state at the start of the string of observations and *remains* in that state for all n observations. But since we are dealing with a nonstationary process, the sample mean cannot summarize all the information contained in the first n observations.[21] When drawing statistical conclusions from the observations on a process whose mean can shift over time, the order in which the observations occur provides important information.

A subsequent paper by Ozan and Dyckman (1971) expands on Dyckman's model by defining different types of controllable and noncontrollable variances. Some guidance is offered as to how to estimate some of

---

[20] *Ibid.*, p 230.

[21] A similar error is made by Duvall (1967) and will be discussed in the next section.

the many different probabilities this model requires but the formulation is still in terms of using myopic decision rules which entails the difficulties already discussed. Ozan and Dyckman (1971) eventually derive a reward function similar to that used by Duvall (1967) in a paper discussed in the following section.

In conclusion, attempting to reduce an essentially multi-period problem to a simplified single-period one may produce more difficulties than any potential benefits gained from the simplification. While there are some limitations to the two-state dynamic programming approach, as previously discussed, these still remain under the model with single-period decision rules introduced by Dyckman. Since dynamic programming over a uni-dimensional state space, especially in a two- or three-action space setting, is straightforward and easy to implement, I am skeptical that adopting single-period decision rules will produce a net benefit in situations where the two-state model is a reasonable representation of reality.

7. Continuous State Decision Models with Multiple Observations, Cost of Investigation and Misclassification Included

DUVALL'S MODEL

Duvall (1967) develops an interesting model which allows the state of the system to be the level of controllable costs, a continuous variable. He assumes, as is traditional, that in-control costs are normally distributed with mean μ, equal to standard cost, and variance equal to σ_w^2. An observed deviation away from standard therefore consists of a noncontrollable component, w, (with $w \sim N(0, \sigma_w^2)$) and a controllable component y. The controllable component, y, is also assumed to be normally distributed and statistically independent of the noncontrollable component, w. Duvall develops procedures which allegedly allow the parameters of the distribution of y to be estimated from the observed deviations.

Duvall's reward function from an investigation is a direct function of the continuous variable, y, and I find this an appealing feature of the model. In particular, future savings are assumed to be proportional to the size of the deviation, y. This allows for savings to occur if the deviation is negative, representing the value of resetting standards at lower cost levels. It is intuitively appealing that the savings from an investigation be made a function of the degree of out-of-controlness of the system, and this procedure gets us away from having to impose a simplified discrete state world on an inherently continuous process. There is still a problem as to how to measure the savings from an investigation, since this model does not incorporate the possibility of investigations in the future; e.g., Duvall writes, "Conceptually, it is easy to say that if an investigation revealed that a certain amount could be saved each time period for the life of the project, then the present value of these future savings could be obtained."[22] But this assumes a constrained model in which the current time is the only possible opportunity for an investigation. Nevertheless, there may be circumstances in which this is not an unreasonable assumption.

There are more fundamental problems with Duvall's procedure, however, which raise questions about the validity of his entire procedure. Duvall uses a sequence of 25 observations to compute a sample mean and standard deviation. Just how we know that 25 is the right number of observations to be taken for estimating sample means and standard deviations is never discussed. Nor are we told what to do if some of the early observations indicate an out-of-control situation. Must we still wait until we get the full 25 observations before taking action? These difficulties arise because Duvall has not developed a sequential strategy that, after each observation, compares the value of obtaining additional information with the cost of operating another period at a too high, controllable cost level. But even granting the static nature of the analysis and the heuristic of estimating from an arbitrary number of observations, Duvall's procedure is not even internally consistent. Duvall uses the sample mean and standard deviation of departures from standard, $(\bar{x}, \sigma_x{}^*)$, computed from these 25 observations to estimate the mean and standard deviation of the distribution of controllable costs, y. Since the mean of noncontrollable costs, w, is assumed to be zero, the mean of y is estimated as the sample mean; i.e., $\mu_y{}^* = \bar{x}$. Also, with y and w assumed to be statistically independent, the variance of y is estimated from the sample variance as

$$\sigma_y{}^{*2} = \sigma_x{}^{*2} - \sigma_w{}^{*2}$$

where $\sigma_w{}^*$ has been previously estimated from an arbitrary period of time during which it was somehow determined that standard conditions prevailed ($y = 0$). This procedure, however, is only valid if the mean, μ_y, of the controllable cost distribution shifted before the first observation was taken. The above procedures treat each observation equally and symmetrically and this can only be done for a stationary process, one in which the parameters do not shift over the course of the observation period. I find this to be an unrealistic assumption. It seems far more likely that a shift in the distribution of y will occur arbitrarily in the interval and it even seems reasonable that multiple jumps could have occurred (recall Barnard's model in Section 4) during the observation period.

After describing the estimation procedure, an inference is done on only the most recent observation, and it is claimed that this inference will enable us to determine whether to investigate or not. While the previous assumption of stationarity might be classified as unrealistic, the procedure of basing an investigation decision on only the most recent observation is obviously inconsistent. For if the process is stationary, then the investi-

---

[22] Duvall (1967): 638.

271

gation decision should be based on all the observations, not just an isolated one. But if the most recent observation is deemed to be more informative than prior observations, there is a strong presumption of nonstationarity which implies that the procedure to estimate the parameters of the process is incorrect.

Duvall's problems arise because he failed to specify the stochastic process which leads to changes in the distribution of y. As previously noted, when we deal with noisy nonstationary processes it is vital that we identify the source of the nonstationarity before we estimate the parameters of the process. Otherwise we will be unable to separate out the effects of normal fluctuations (noise) from changes in the level of the process.

BATHER'S MODEL

In fact, a model which overcomes the previously described difficulties in Duvall's procedure had already appeared in the statistics literature. Bather (1963) describes a process which, like Duvall's, has a state described by a single continuous variable which represents the performance level of the process. Costs are similarly assumed to be a function of this continuous variable. Let y_t be the unknown performance level of the system at time t (assume that $y_t = 0$ is the state representing no deviation from standard) and let x_t be the observation at time t. As before, we assume that $x_t \sim N(y_t, \sigma^2)$.[23] Bather, however, postulates a process by which the performance level changes from period to period:

$$y_t = y_{t-1} + z_t,$$

where $z_t \sim N(0, \rho^2)$; i.e., the process mean undergoes a random walk without drift over time. Successive changes in the process mean are independent and identically distributed with zero mean and constant standard deviation, ρ. This process is the limit of the Barnard Poisson jump process as the Poisson parameter, λ, goes to infinity to yield a continuous string of infinitesimal changes.

Assume, initially, that the process is reset with some error to the standard level of performance so that $y_0 \sim N(0, v_0)$ where v_0 is the initial level of uncertainty in the current mean of the process. Then, since y_t is the sum of independent normally distributed random variables, $y_t \sim N(u_t, v_t)$, with u_t and v_t to be determined from $(x_1, \cdots, x_t)$, the observed values. The conditional distribution of y_{t+1} given just $(x_1, \cdots, x_t)$ is

$$y_{t+1} \mid (x_1, \cdots, x_t) \sim N(u_t, v_t + \rho^2)$$

and the distribution of x_{t+1} given y_{t+1} is

$$x_{t+1} \mid y_{t+1} \sim N(y_{t+1}', \sigma^2).$$

---

[23] This notation denotes that x_t is normally distributed with mean y_t and variance σ^2.

272

Therefore, by Bayes theorem,

$$y_{t+1} \mid (x_1, \cdots, x_{t+1}) \sim N(u_{t+1}, v_{t+1})$$

where

$$\frac{1}{v_{t+1}} = \frac{1}{v_t + \rho^2} + \frac{1}{\sigma^2}$$

and

$$\frac{u_{t+1}}{v_{t+1}} = \frac{u_t}{v_t + \rho^2} + \frac{x_{t+1}}{\sigma^2}.^{24}$$

Since the sequence $v_0, v_1, \cdots, v_t$ is deterministic (not affected by sample outcomes, x_t), u_t by itself is a sufficient statistic for this process. Note that u_t is *not* the sample mean. Even though the process outcomes are normally distributed, the nonstationarity of the process causes the sample mean to be an uninteresting characterization of the process. The posterior variance v_t converges (geometrically) to v, with

$$v = \frac{1}{2}\rho^2 \left[\sqrt{1 + \frac{4\sigma^2}{\rho^2}} - 1 \right]$$

which represents the long-run tracking variance of the process. In effect, it represents a minimal level of uncertainty of the current mean of the process which cannot be reduced even by taking longer sequences of observations. If we make the simplifying and not unreasonable assumption that the process is reset with an uncertainty equal to this tracking variance (i.e., that $v_0 = v$), then we have the convenient result:

$$v_t = v \qquad \text{for all } t$$

and

$$u_t = \frac{v}{v + \rho^2} u_{t-1} + \frac{v}{\sigma^2} x_t.$$

Defining $\gamma = v/(v + \rho^2)$, so that $1 - \gamma = v/\sigma^2$, we have

$$u_t = (1 - \gamma)(x_t + \gamma x_{t-1} + \cdots + \gamma^{t-1} x_1),$$

an exponential moving average of prior observations.

Define $k(y)$ to be the cost of investigation and subsequent repair when the true process mean is y. This is a more general treatment than previous cost investigation papers which assumed this function to be a constant [but see Ross (1971)]. Let $g(y)$ be the cost of continuing to operate, for one period only, when the present state is y. We will assume the following sequence of events for the Bather model: A cost report is received, followed

---

[24] This development is analogous to the Bayesian analysis on the mean of a stationary normal process; see DeGroot (1970): 167. A more detailed derivation appears in the Appendix.

by an immediate decision whether to investigate the process or allow it to operate for another period. If the process is investigated, it is assumed that the process can always be reset back to the desired initial state in which $y_0 \sim N(0, v)$. Thus the previously mentioned difficulties of modeling situations for which it is impossible to reset the standard back to the desired level and for which it is possible to reset the standard to a lower cost level for the future are still not captured by the Bather model.

If u is the best estimate of the current mean of the process, the expected investigation cost is

$$K(u) \equiv \int k(y) f_N(y \mid u, v) \, dy$$

where $f_N(\cdot \mid u, v)$ is the density function of a normally distributed random variable with mean u and variance v. The expected one-period cost of operating when the best estimate of the current mean of the process is u will be denoted $G(u)$ with

$$G(u) \equiv \int g(y) \, f_N(y \mid u, v) \, dy.$$

The only remaining term needed for the dynamic programming equation is the prediction of the next period's state variable given the current period's state variable. We know that

$$u_{t+1} = \gamma u_t + (1 - \gamma) x_{t+1}$$

and we can write x_{t+1} as

$$x_{t+1} = y_t + (y_{t+1} - y_t) + (x_{t+1} - y_{t+1}).$$

Each of the three terms on the right is, by assumption, normally and independently distributed with means and variances given, respectively, by: (u_t, v); $(0, \rho^2)$; and $(0, \sigma^2)$. Therefore $x_{t+1} \sim N(u_t, v + \rho^2 + \sigma^2)$ and

$$E(u_{t+1} \mid u_t) = u_t.$$

Also,

$$\begin{aligned}
\text{Var}(u_{t+1} \mid u_t) &= (1 - \gamma)^2 \, \text{Var}(x_{t+1}) \\
&= (1 - \gamma)^2 (v + \rho^2 + \sigma^2) \\
&= \rho^2
\end{aligned}$$

where the last equality follows from the definition of γ.[25] We therefore

---

[25] Since $1 - \gamma = \dfrac{v}{\sigma^2} = \dfrac{\rho^2}{v + \rho^2}$, we have that

$$\begin{aligned}
(1 - \gamma)^2 (v + \rho^2 + \sigma^2) &= \frac{v}{\sigma^2} \frac{\rho^2}{v + \rho^2} (v + \rho^2 + \sigma^2) \\
&= v\rho^2 \left[\frac{1}{\sigma^2} + \frac{1}{v + \rho^2} \right] \\
&= \rho^2 [(1 - \gamma) + \gamma] \\
&= \rho^2.
\end{aligned}$$

have that

$$u_{t+1} = u_t + z \quad \text{with} \quad z \sim N(0, \rho^2).$$

While Bather computes optimal policies to minimize expected (undiscounted) costs per unit time I will reformulate the problem to minimize total expected discounted costs in the future. For convenience in notation, I assume an infinite horizon problem with a discount factor, α, less than one. Some mild regularity conditions on the cost functions $k(\cdot)$ and $c(\cdot)$ will ensure the geometric convergence of the finite period optimality functions to a unique steady state minimum expected cost function, $C(u)$. We can write $C(u)$ as

$$C(u) = \min \{K(u) + C(0); G(u) + \alpha E[C(u + z)]\}.$$

The first term in the minimization is the expected investigation cost, $K(u)$, and the effect of immediately resetting the process to its desired mean, 0. The second term consists of the expected costs of operating for one period at the current level plus the discounted expected future costs, one period in the future. The expectation of this latter term is taken with respect to the random variable z defined above ($z \sim N(0, \rho^2)$). Of course, the actual state variable, u', for the next period will become known after the next period's cost report, x, is received:

$$u' = \gamma u + (1 - \gamma)x.$$

The solution to the above functional equation can be easily obtained by taking the limit of the optimal policies of the finite horizon optimality equation:

$$C_n(u) = \min \{K(u) + C_n(0); G(u) + \alpha E[C_{n-1}(u + z)]\}.$$

The preceding formulation could represent only the starting point for more elaborate models. Additional features such as adding a third action alternative of an exploratory investigation could be included as we have already discussed. Also, if one wanted to assume a gradual increase in controllable costs over time, the distribution of z could have a small positive mean. In a private communication, Dyckman has suggested the possibility that y_t be modeled as a mean reverting process, rather than a random walk, due to corrective actions undertaken by subordinates. A particularly interesting possibility to pursue would involve attempting to model the reduction in future cost due to investigating a process whose mean has drifted below the previously set standard. If such a procedure could be developed, we might similarly be able to model those situations for which a higher current level of costs would become the new standard because of our inability to reset the process back to its original standard. These extensions represent opportunities for further research. Carter

(1972) has already extended Bather's model to allow for assignable causes to occur at exponentially distributed inter-arrival times rather than continuously.

8. *Summary and Conclusions*

This paper has surveyed papers in the accounting, statistics and management science literature dealing with the significance and investigation of realizations from a process which deviate from preset standards. A simple 2 x 2 classification scheme was developed which distinguished (i) models using only the most recent observation for decisions from those that used all observations since the last action time, and (ii) models which were mainly concerned with estimation or hypothesis testing from those whose actions were imbedded in a decision model which attempted to assess the costs and benefits from alternative actions. A number of questions were raised with respect to some models that have been proposed for the accounting cost variance decision and, it is hoped that, at the very least, the key assumptions and limitations behind all these models have been identified.

To gain some closure on this issue, suppose a hypothetical situation in which I must design a system that would track cost variances. Given the large number of alternative models surveyed in this paper and their limitations and assumptions, which would I choose to implement in a real-life ongoing situation? My short-range solution would probably be to install a cusum chart to track the accounting variances. This procedure is already widely used in quality control and would likely be reasonably robust with respect to the causes of nonstationary behavior. Initially, I would set the parameters of the cusum chart using prior data from the processes to establish the right tradeoff between false alarms and failures to detect changes quickly. With more time, I would try to estimate the cost and benefits from an investigation and use these to design "economic optimal" cusum charts [Taylor (1968), Goel and Wu (1973)]. In the long run, I would attempt to develop a continuous state model (e.g., along the lines of Bather) by attempting to directly model the source of nonstationary behavior and build this into the decision model.

My bias therefore is to first implement a procedure that systematically and sensibly processes the current data with all prior observations (i.e., the cusum chart). With this as a benchmark, I would then attempt to develop models that are closer to being "right" from a cost-benefit analysis. As more experience and data develop from such a process, I would then feel more comfortable about directly modeling the underlying stochastic process and implementing procedures which are optimal for that particular stochastic process. For the present, our most pressing need is for empirical research to uncover a set of plausible stochastic processes to describe the accounting cost variance environment.

APPENDIX

Derivation of Sufficient Statistics (u_t, v_t) in Bather's Model

Assume that $y_t \mid x_t \sim N(u_t, v_t)$, with u_t, v_t to be determined from $x_t = (x_1, x_2, \cdots, x_t)$. Since $y_{t+1} = y_t + z_{t+1}$ with $z_t \sim N(0, \rho^2)$ and with y_t and z_{t+1} independently distributed, we have that

$$y_{t+1} \mid x_t \sim N(u_t, v_t + \rho^2).$$

Also, $x_{t+1} \mid y_{t+1} \sim N(y_{t+1}, \sigma^2)$ by definition. Therefore, the likelihood function for y_{t+1} given $(x_1, x_2, \cdots, x_{t+1}) \equiv x_{t+1}$ (denoted by $\Lambda(y_{t+1} \mid x_{t+1})$) can be written (using the rule of conditional probability and Bayes Theorem) as

$$\Lambda(y_{t+1} \mid x_{t+1}) = k_1 \Lambda(y_{t+1}, x_{t+1} \mid x_t)$$
$$= k_2 \Lambda(x_{t+1} \mid y_{t+1}) \Lambda(y_{t+1} \mid x_t)$$

(where k_1 and k_2 are known constants). We write the two likelihood functions on the right-hand side of the above equation as:

$$\exp -\frac{1}{2}\left[\frac{1}{\sigma^2}(x_{t+1} - y_{t+1})^2\right] \exp -\frac{1}{2}\left[\frac{1}{v_t + \rho^2}(y_{t+1} - u_t)^2\right]$$

$$= \exp -\frac{1}{2}\frac{1}{\sigma^2(v_t + \rho^2)}\left[(v_t + \rho^2)(x_{t+1} - y_{t+1})^2 + \sigma^2(y_{t+1} - u_t)^2\right]$$

$$= \exp -\frac{1}{2}\left[\frac{1}{\sigma^2} + \frac{1}{v_t + \rho^2}\right]\left[y_{t+1} - \frac{(v_t + \rho^2)x_{t+1} + \sigma^2 u_t}{v_t + \rho^2 + \sigma^2}\right]^2 + k_3$$

where the last expression is obtained by completing the square and rearranging terms, and k_3 is a complicated expression involving terms such as v_t, ρ, x_{t+1}, etc., but *not* y_{t+1}.

Therefore if we identify u_{t+1} as

$$u_{t+1} = \frac{(v_t + \rho^2)x_{t+1} + \sigma^2 u_t}{v_t + \rho^2 + \sigma^2} \quad \text{and} \quad \frac{1}{v_{t+1}} = \frac{1}{\sigma^2} + \frac{1}{v_t + \rho^2}$$

we may write

$$\Lambda(y_{t+1} \mid x_{t+1}) = k_4 \exp -\frac{1}{2}\left[\frac{1}{v_{t+1}}(y_{t+1} - u_{t+1})^2\right]$$

so that $y_{t+1} \mid x_{t+1} \sim N(u_{t+1}, v_{t+1})$ with u_{t+1} and v_{t+1} defined above. Thus, the posterior distribution of y_{t+1} conditional on the previous realizations $(x_1, x_2, \cdots, x_{t+1})$ is a normal distribution with mean u_{t+1} and variance v_{t+1}.

REFERENCES

ANTHONY, R. N. "Some Fruitful Directions for Research in Management Accounting." In N. Dopuch and L. Revsine (Eds.), *Accounting Research 1960–1970: A Critical Evaluation* (Center for International Education and Research in Accounting: University of Illinois), 1973.

BARNARD, G. A. "Control Charts and Stochastic Processes." *Journal of the Royal Statistical Society, Series B* XXI (1959): 239-57.

BATHER, G. A. "Control Charts and the Minimization of Costs." *Journal of the Royal Statistical Society, Series B* XXV (1963): 49-70.

BIERMAN, H. AND T. DYCKMAN. *Managerial Cost Accounting* (New York: Macmillan). 1971.

——, L. E. FOURAKER, AND R. K. JAEDICKE. "A Use of Probability and Statistics in Performance Evaluation." *The Accounting Review* XXXVI (July 1961): 409-17.

BUZBY, S. L. "Extending the Applicability of Probabilistic Management Planning and Control Systems." *The Accounting Review* XLIX (January 1974): 42-49.

CARTER, P. "A Bayesian Approach to Quality Control." *Management Science* XVIII (July 1972): 647-55.

CHERNOFF, H. AND S. ZACKS. "Estimating the Current Mean of a Normal Distribution Which Is Subjected to Changes in Time." *Annals of Math. Statistics* XXXV (December 1964): 999-1018.

DEGROOT, M. H. *Optimal Statistical Decisions* (New York: McGraw-Hill), 1970.

DEMSKI, J. "An Accounting System Structured on a Linear Programming Model." *The Accounting Review* XLII (October 1967): 701-12.

——. "Optimizing the Search for Cost Deviation Sources." *Management Science* (April 1970): 486-94.

DOPUCH, N., J. G. BIRNBERG, AND J. DEMSKI. "An Extension of Standard Cost Variance Analysis." *The Accounting Review* XLII (July 1967): 526-36.

DUNCAN, A. "The Economic Design of $\bar{x}$ Charts Used to Maintain Current Control of a Process." *Journal of the American Statistical Association* LI (June 1956): 228-42.

DUVALL, R. M. "Rules for Investigating Cost Variances." *Management Science* XIII (June 1967): 631-41.

DYCKMAN, T. R. "The Investigation of Cost Variances." *Journal of Accounting Research*, Vol. 7 (1969): 215-44.

EDWARDS, W. "Conservatism in Human Information Processing." *Formal Representation of Human Judgment*, B. Kleinmuntz, Ed. (New York: Wiley), 1968.

EWAN, W. D. AND K. W. KEMP. "Sampling Inspection of Continuous Processes with No Autocorrelation Between Successive Results." *Biometrika* XLVII (1960): 363-80.

FARLEY, J. AND M. HINICH. "Detecting 'Small' Mean Shifts in Time Series." *Management Science* XVII (November 1970): 189-99.

GIBRA, I. N. "Economically Optimal Determination of the Parameters of $\bar{X}$-Control Charts." *Management Science* XVII (May 1971): 635-46.

GIRSHICK, M. A. AND H. RUBIN. "A Bayes Approach to a Quality Control Model." *Annals of Math. Statistics* XXIII (1952): 114-25.

GOEL, A. L., S. C. JAIN AND S. M. WU. "An Algorithm for the Determination of the Economic Design of $\bar{X}$-Charts Based on Duncan's Model." *Journal of the American Statistical Association* LXIII (1968).

—— AND S. M. WU. "Economically Optimum Design of Cusum Charts." *Management Science* XIX (July 1973): 1271-82.

GOLDSMITH, P. L. AND H. WHITFIELD. "Average Run Lengths in Cumulative Chart Quality Control Schemes." *Technometrics* III (February 1961): 11-20.

HINICH, M. AND J. FARLEY. "Theory and Application of an Estimation Model for Time Series with Nonstationary Means." *Management Science* XII (May 1966): 648-58.

JUERS, D. A. "Statistical Significance of Accounting Variances." *Management Accounting* XLIX (October 1967): 20-25.

KADANE, J. "Optimal Whereabouts Search." *Operations Research* XIX (July-August 1971): 894-904.

Kaplan, R. S. "Optimal Investigation Strategies with Imperfect Information." *Journal of Accounting Research*, Vol. 7 (1969): 32–43.

Koehler, R. W. "The Relevance of Probability Statistics to Accounting Variance Control." *Management Accounting* L (October 1968): 35–41.

Lev, B. "An Information Theory Analysis of Budget Variances." *The Accounting Review* XLIV (October 1969): 704–10.

Li, Y. "A Note on 'The Investigation of Cost Variances'." *Journal of Accounting Research*, Vol. 8 (1970): 282–83.

Luh, F. "Controlled Cost: An Operational Concept and Statistical Approach to Standard Costing." *The Accounting Review* XLIII (January 1968): 123–32.

Ozan, T. and T. Dyckman. "A Normative Model for Investigation Decisions Involving Multi-Origin Cost Variances." *Journal of Accounting Research*, Vol. 9 (1971): 88–115.

Page, E. S. "Continuous Inspection Schemes." *Biometrika* XLI (1954): 100–15.

Probst, F. R. "Probabilistic Cost Controls: A Behavioral Dimension." *The Accounting Review* XLVI (January 1971): 113–18.

Ronen, J. "Nonaggregation Versus Disaggregation of Variances." *The Accounting Review* XLIX (January 1974): 50–60.

Ross, S. "Quality Control Under Markov Deterioration." *Management Science* XVII (May 1971): 587–96.

Shewhart, W. A. *The Economic Control of the Quality of Manufactured Profit* (New York: Macmillan), 1931.

Slovic, P. and S. Lichtenstein. "Comparison of Bayesian and Regression Approaches to the Study of Information Processing in Judgment." *Organizational Behavior and Human Performance* VI (November 1971): 649–744.

Taylor, H. M. "The Economic Design of Cumulative Sum Control Charts for Variables." *Technometrics* X (August 1968): 479–88.

Zannetos, Z. A. "Standard Cost as a First Step to Probabilistic Control: A Theoretical Justification, An Extension and Implications." *The Accounting Review* XXXIX (April 1964): 296–304.

A Behavioral Extension
to the Cost Variances
Investigation Decision

SHAHID L. ANSARI
New York University

MASAO TSUJI*
Waseda University, Tokyo

Introduction

There are two main approaches to the study and design of organizational control systems. The first approach, here referred to as the "structural" or "engineering" approach, is exemplified by the literature on cybernetics, mathematical control and communication theory.[1] This view of control tends to be mechanistic and places primary emphasis on structural variables such as information flows. The other approach, here referred to as "behavioral" originates in the management and organization behavior literature. Its intellectual origins are the so-called behavioral sciences such as organizational-sociology, social psychology, etc. This view of control regards human motivation and leadership as central to the problem of control.[2]

The focus of this paper is on the control models used for investigating variances in budget control systems. It argues that most existing variance investigation decision (VID) models are engineering oriented and are based on simplistic or untenable organizational-behavioral assumptions. Some of the assumptions used are inconsistent with the available empirical evidence about the behavior of people in budget control systems. One key assumption, the lack of feedback between the control policy and the subsequent behavior of the control system, is examined in this paper. The analysis here will contrast the results of the engineering approach, which does not recognize such feedback, with that of the behavioral approach which does recognize such feedback. It will show that: (a) existing closed form mathematical solutions to the VID problem are unlikely and that the optimal solution to the VID problem is likely to require the use of simulation techniques; (b) research to specify the nature of the feedback relationship between a control policy and control system behavior must precede the solution of the optimal VID model; and (c) a wider range of variables, such as, reward and penalty structure, strictness of enforcement, etc. will have to be incorporated in the system to solve for the optimal control policy.

The following discussion is divided into five parts. The first part introduces the background and research setting for the problem. This is followed by a section which presents a simple representational model of the variance investigations decision. The next two sections present the engineering and behavioral

*The authors are respectively, Associate Professor of Accounting at New York University, and Associate Professor of Accounting at Waseda University, Tokyo. They are grateful to Steve Lippman, Jan Bell and Jim Manegold for their helpful suggestions on earlier versions of this paper, and also to Kuldip Shastri who provided invaluable help in checking out the mathematical formulations. (Paper received July 1980, revised July 1981)

approaches respectively to the problem, and the final section is devoted to a comparison of the two approaches with implications for further research.

Background and Problem Setting

The purpose of this section is to show that most existing VID models reflect the engineering or structural view of control. No comprehensive survey of the numerous models is provided since an excellent compilation is available in Kaplan (1975). Instead of duplicating that discussion, the attempt here is to selectively cite the literature to highlight the generic approach common to all such models.

Ansari (1977) has developed and defined what he terms as the "structural" and "behavioral" approaches to control. He shows that the structural approach is rational and mechanistic. It views a control system as an interconnected information network, and defines the problem of control as essentially one of designing an optimal information structure. The extreme cybernetic view best exemplifies this philosophy. Using Ashby's (1956, Ch.11) terminology, consider the following five variables:

D = A set of environmental disturbances.

T = Those parts of a system in contact with the environment and buffering the system against it.

E = The essential or controlled variable.

R = The regulator.

η = The acceptable subset of the values of E.

Given these variables, the problem of control is to stop the disturbances D from throwing values of the essential variable E out of the acceptable range η (Ashby, 1956, Ch. 11). To keep the disturbances D from reaching E, R and T are coupled together to form a regulatory mechanism. Ashby analyzes this problem as one in which an information sender D and an information receiver E are to be blocked from communicating with each other — an important reason why this type of work was picked up by communications engineers such as Shannon. (See Shannon and Weaver, 1969.)

To illustrate, consider Figure 1, which is reproduced from Ashby (1956, p.223).

FIGURE 1

THE ERROR CONTROLLED REGULATOR

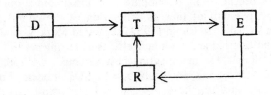

The above configuration represents an information network in which D has to go through T to get to E. The first buffer between D and E is thus T. When D does succeed in reaching E, such information is fed to a regulator, R, which, acting in concert with T, takes corrective measures when the values of E are outside the acceptable range η. Obviously, η in such cases represents tolerable errors which can be used as signals by R to take corrective measures. The classic example of this type of "error-controlled servo mechanism" is the thermostat. Such feedback type control systems are now common and widely used in many different types of control problems.

One important application of error controlled regulation is in the field of production quality control. Most statistical quality control (SQC) models utilize the ability to learn from small errors to take timely corrective action. The information feedback in a typical SQC model is provided by frequent sampling of product quality. Here product quality, appropriately defined, is E, the machine operation is R, and the controls within the machine, T. The specification of the acceptable values of E, i.e., η. ("tolerance limits" in quality control terminology) is the key problem of SQC.

To specify η, the point at which corrective actions will be taken by R, SQC models specify the underlying probability distribution of E when operating in-control. Upper and lower bounds are then established for values of E and the system is considered out of control when a value of E is outside these "control limits". A critical assumption in this system is that a regulator's choice of control limits does not affect the behavior of D and E.

The pioneering work in production quality control was done by Shewhart (1931). He suggested the use of the now familiar $\overline{X}$ or mean charts. Control limits in Shewhart's system are specified by assuming that successive sample means from a process in control will be normally distributed. Thus a decision maker can choose an appropriate confidence interval, such as ± two standard deviations, to set control limits. If a sample mean in some period falls outside these limits, the process is stopped and an investigation and correction is undertaken.

Shewhart's basic model has been considerably refined over the years. The non-economic approach to setting control limits was replaced by Duncan (1956) with a procedure which recognizes the costs and benefits of investigation. Page (1954) extended the single period model by suggesting a cumulative sum procedure that uses prior observations for detecting a nonrandom change. Taylor (1968) extended Page's procedure by developing an approximate formula for the long run average cost per unit of time as a function of the cumulative sum chart. Others, such as , Girshik & Rubin (1952) suggested Markov models as a way of incorporating multiperiod and economic effects of setting control limits.

Accounting models for investigating cost variances are applications of the quality control models and are analagous to SQC models. For instance: (i) instead of product quality, the controlled variable is cost; (ii) the standard or budgeted cost is the mean of the distribution when the system is in control; and (iii) the tolerance limits for product quality are replaced by control values of cost variances at which investigation and corrective action is undertaken. Not surprisingly, therefore, the development of the various VID models in accounting has followed a path very similar to the one described for the development of SQC models above. For instance, early VID models were essentially applications of the $\overline{X}$ (mean) and $\overline{R}$ (range) charts being used in production quality control. Gaynor (1954) is an example of this approach. Bierman, Fouraker and Jaedicke (1961) proposed a model which, like Duncan's (1956) SQC model, incorporated the costs and benefits of investigation. It also used a statistical decision theory approach which could be easily extended to incorporate Bayesian probability revisions. Finally, the Markovian multiperiod SQC models developed by Girshik & Rubin (1952) was incorporated in several accounting models starting with Kaplan (1969).

As indicated previously, no attempt has been made to survey all the various VID models in the literature since Kaplan (1975) has done this. In his survey, Kaplan used a two dimensional taxonomy to classify the existing models. The first dimension was whether a model had single period or multiperiod decision orientation. The other dimension was whether it included the costs and benefits of the decision. The previous discussion shows that accounting VID models have followed the SQC models in moving from single-period-noneconomic orientation to mutli-period-economic orientation. Thus, VID models in accounting have inherited the engineering or structural orientation of cybernetics incorporated in production quality control models.

While the mechanistic view point of the engineering approach is suitable for a production situation it is *a priori* unsuitable to budget control systems. This is because the central assumption of statistical quality control – the independence between the control policy and the subsequent behavior of the control system – is unlikely to hold for budget control. Unlike machines, people do react to control policies such that the prior and posterior behavior cannot *a priori* be assumed to be from the same causal system.

This proposition is supported by research on the motivational effects of budgets which indicates that control limits used for investigating variances may influence participant behavior for two reasons. First, control limits define the range of performance considered acceptable by an employee's superior. It thus determines how easy or difficult it is for a subordinate to meet budget goals. Literature on the effects of goal difficulty shows that a person's actual performance may be affected by his perception of goal difficulty. The higher the perceived goal difficulty, the greater the chances that actual performance may be lowered by a fear of failure. The other factor relates to the ability of control limits to engender feelings of success or failure for subordinates by providing feedback information on performance. Negative feedback lowers aspiration levels which in turn lowers effort and performance levels and vice-versa. Empirical results supporting this finding in a budget context were reported by Stedry (1961). Thus, these findings on goal difficulty and negative feedback suggest that control limits in budget systems are likely to influence subsequent employee performance. The impact that such behavioral feedback has on the determination of the optimal control policy is considered next.

A Representational Model for Investigating Variances

To contrast optimal policies and philosophies embodied in the engineering and behavioral approaches, it is necessary to use a simple model to represent the decision process. Such a model is needed to state the essential elements of the decision and to provide a setting against which differing assumptions can be compared or contrasted.

The choice of one model to represent the VID is problematic since, as stated earlier, there are numerous such models currently available. To avoid unnecessary computational complexities, the paper uses a single-period, rather than a multi-period formulation. This is not a serious problem since the main conclusions of the paper are valid for any multi-period extension. Within the single period category it was decided to use a composite model which would combine SQC characteristics, as in Duncan (1956), with the decision theory-economic approach of Bierman et al. (1961). Features from other models such as Duvall (1966) are added to provide a general comprehensive single-period representation of the VID including cost-benefit analysis. The model is thus more comprehensive and richer than the various models it borrows from.

Specifically, consider a decision maker (DM) whose objective is to minimize cost-variances in a budget control system. Every period the DM receives a variance report summarizing the positive and negative deviations from budgeted costs. Given an observed variance, x, the DM's problem is to decide whether to investigate and correct the system or let it operate for one more period. If the system is considered in control there is no investigation and next period's cost is the same as this period, i.e., x. If an investigation is undertaken, it will *always* uncover the cause for the deviation.

Using the SQC convention, cost variances x are assumed to have a continuous probability density function. The DM seeks a one-tail SQC type control limit, k, to trigger the investigations. That is, the decision rule is,

Investigate, if x > k, where 0 < k

Do not investigate if x < k

and the DM seeks that optimal control limit, k*, which will minimize the long run expected cost of the decision.[3]

The following costs are associated with the decision to investigate.

First, the cost of investigation I(x). For generality this cost is assumed to have a fixed and a variable component. The latter is assumed to depend on the size of the variance; this represents a situation in which size is used as a basis for deciding the amount of resources to be spent uncovering the underlying cause for a variance.

Second, there is a probability, p, that an investigation will reveal a *controllable* cause for all or part of the variance. If so, a cost of correction J(x) will have to be incurred. Again, for generality, the correction cost is assumed to have both fixed and variable components. The size of the variance, x is used as a surrogate for estimating the cost of correction. Corrective actions will ensure that future variances are less than the current period's variances.

Finally, there is a probability, (1-p), that an investigation will uncover an *uncontrollable* cause. Since no corrective action is possible, the standard cost for the next period will be adjusted by a fixed amount, E.

An example may help to clarify the above assumptions. Assume that the budgeted labour cost per unit is $20 for a process. The actual cost during a period is $25; thus the reported variance, x is $5. Assume that an investigation reveals that $3 resulted from a controllable cause, such as poor scheduling, and $2 was uncontrollable because of equipment shortage. Since nothing can be done about the $2, the budget for the next period is adjusted to $22. Thus, next period's cost will be $2 (E) higher than the current period's cost. Better work scheduling can be undertaken for the controllable part so that next period's variance is less than $3. Finally, if no investigation is undertaken, the variance next period will be the same as in the current period or $5.

It is important to emphasize that the assumptions outlined above are distilled from the existing single-period economic models of the VID. While it is possible to question individual assumptions related to the costs, and probabilities in the model, such parameter specification problems are secondary to this paper. The purpose here is to show that even if the problems of parameter specifications were to be overcome, the usefulness of such VID models would be limited by the realism of their fundamental premises. These fundamental premises as formulated in the engineering and behavioral approaches are examined in the next two sections. Before turning to that discussion, however, it may be useful to summarize the costs a DM faces if he uses a control limit k as the policy. If the above assumptions hold, the costs are as shown in Table 1.

TABLE 1

PAYOFFS ASSOCIATED WITH THE SELECTED CONTROL POLICY

Size of Variance (Observations)	Cost Associated with Control Policy
$-\infty < x \leq k$	x (Favorable or Unfavorable variances)
$k \leq x \leq \infty$	$I(x) + \left(\begin{array}{l} J(x), \text{ if x is controllable} \\ E, \text{ if x is uncontrollable} \end{array} \right.$

Optimal Control Policy — The Engineering Formulation

As discussed in the section headed Background and Problem Setting, above, most existing models follow the engineering approach and assume no feedback between the control policy, k, and subsequent cost variances, x. Given this independence, the optimal k* now can be solved for by combining the costs shown in Table 1 with the probability density function of x and the probabilities p and 1-p of x resulting from controllable causes. Since k does not affect the probability distribution of x, and future values of x do not depend on *when* investigations are undertaken, the total costs U(k) for the decision are:

$$U(k) = \int_{-\infty}^{k} x f(x)\, dx + \int_{k}^{\infty} I(x) f(x) dx + p \int_{k}^{\infty} J(x) f(x) dx$$

$$+ (1\text{-}p) \int_{k}^{\infty} E f(x) dx \qquad \cdots \cdots \cdots \cdots \quad (1)$$

Since each term in (1) is expressed by a definite integral, variable x will drop out in the process of calculation and the expected total costs can be described as a function of k. The optimal k is obtained by minimizing U(k).[4] The optimal k* will be the critical level k° which satisfies the equation:

$$U'(k°) = \frac{dU(k°)}{dk°} = 0 \qquad \cdots \cdots \cdots \cdots \cdots \quad (2)$$

provided that U(k) is convex at k°, i.e.,

$$U''(k°) = \frac{d^2 U(k°)}{dk°^2} > 0 \qquad \cdots \cdots \cdots \cdots \cdots \quad (3)$$

287

and that $k°$ is unique and positive:

$$k° > 0 \quad \ldots \ldots \ldots \ldots \ldots \ldots \ldots \ldots \ldots \quad (4)$$

Differentiating each integral with respect to its lower or upper limit in (1), one has, for $k = k°$,[5]: $\dfrac{d}{dk} \int_a^k f(x)\, dx = f(k)$

$$U'(k°) = f(k°) \{ k° - I(k°) - pJ(k°) - (1 - p)E) \} \quad \ldots \ldots \quad (5)$$

The second derivative of (1) for $k = k°$ is calculated as follows:

$$U''(k°) = f'(k°) \{ k° - I(k°) - pJ(k°) - (1 - p)E \}$$

$$+ f(k°) \{ 1 - I'(k°) - pJ'(k°) \} \quad \ldots \ldots \ldots \ldots \ldots \quad (6)$$

To illustrate with a specific case, suppose that the costs of investigation and correction are given as a linear function of x:

$$I(x) = C + cx \qquad (C \geq 0,\ c > 0)$$
$$J(x) = D + dx \qquad (D \geq 0,\ d \geq 0) \quad \ldots \ldots \ldots \ldots \quad (7)$$

Substituting (7) into (5) and setting (5) equal to zero, one obtains:

$$k° = \frac{C + pD + (1-p)E}{1-c-pd} > 0 \quad \text{if } 1 - c - pd > 0 \quad \ldots \ldots \ldots \quad (8)$$

Without loss of generality, it can be assumed $(1 - c - pd)$ to be positive since, *a priori*, an investigation will be undertaken only if the benefits from it exceed its costs. Since the quantity $(c + pd)$ represents the cost of investigation and correction, there is no economic incentive to undertake an investigation if it is greater than one. Calculting the second derivative for $k = k°$, one gets:

$$U''(k°) = f(k°) (1 - c - pd) > 0 \quad \ldots \ldots \ldots \ldots \ldots \quad (9)$$

Since $k°$ given in (8) satisfies the conditions set forth in (3) and (4), it represents the optimal control limit, $k*$, in cost variance investigation, i.e.:

$$k* = \frac{C + pD + (1 - p)E}{1 - c - pd} \quad \ldots \ldots \ldots \ldots \ldots \ldots \quad (10)$$

It is interesting to note that the numerator in (10) represents the expected fixed costs of investigation and correction while the denomination represents the expected marginal benefit (cost saving) yielded by investigation and correction. The optimal value k* is the ratio of these quantities. It represents a break-even point since the critical cost variance level equates the expected benefits (cost savings) to expected costs of investigation and correction. Therefore, the range of values within which no investigation is undertaken $(-\infty, k*)$ will increase when the fixed (C,D,E) and marginal cost terms (c,d) increase.

This analysis is consistent with the results of studies which use a similar formulation and employ minimization of expected costs as a decision criterion. For instance, Bierman et al.'s decision rule for the critical probability, P*, is a ratio of the fixed investigation cost and the marginal cost savings from investigation and correction. The results in (10) are more general since they do not assume fixed costs of investigation and correction nor the certainty of finding a controllable cause for deviations. They use observed cost variances rather than probabilities to trigger investigations. Also, since x has an unrestricted probability distribution, k* in (10) can be applied to any kind of continuous distribution with a positive density function.

Optimal Control Policy — The Behavioral Approach

An alternative formulation for the model described in the section headed A Representational Model for Investigating Variances, is to assume that the cost variances x are affected by the control policy k. This effect may be *real* in as much as it actually alters the behavior of the participants in the control system or it may be a *reported* change in the behavior.

To illustrate, assume a "Hawthorne" type situation in which a group of workers is given a task, such as assembling telephone parts.[6] The group's output has some prior probability distribution. A standard is set and a tight control limit is used to investigate all deviations. With the control policy in place, the prior distribution is likely to change because workers at the lower tail of the distribution may be frustrated by being constantly under budget and may stop trying — the aspirational level effect. Conversely, effective policing with the tight limits may actually reduce any existing budget slack and thus reduce the dispersion in the distribution lowering its mean and variance.

While both of the above changes result from participants changing their actual output, observed changes in the probability distribution may be caused by invalid reporting of data. If, for example, workers decide as a group (as they did in the original Hawthorne experiments) to limit productivity at a level specified by a group norm, then one method will be for efficient workers not to report their full actual output. Here the shift in the mean and variance in response to the control limits is a reporting rather than actual behavioral phenomena. For control purposes, however, both have the effect of increasing labor costs per unit of time.

Since people tend to anticipate the consequences of a control policy, their behavior (actual or reported) responds to such policies. Sometimes, these responses are difficult to predict and may be dysfunctional for the system. In any event, it is inappropriate to assume the same prior and posterior distributions when control policies are introduced or changed. For the VID, it means that the solution of the optimal limit, k*, requires an assessment of *how k affects the probability density function of x*. The decision maker is thus confronted with a conditional distribution of x, given a control limit, k. This type of behavioral situation can be generally stated as:

x=f(k;ε), where ε, is a random error term.

For the Hawthorne type situation described above, assume that the introduction of tight control limits causes a reduction of any slack in the budget previously available to workers. This means that the mean and variance of the probability distribution will be different. Increased efficiency will lower the observed mean of the deviations and decrease their variance. Such a shift may be generally specificed as:

$$x = m(k) + s(k) u \quad . \quad . \quad . \quad . \quad . \quad . \quad . \quad . \quad . \quad . \quad . \quad . \quad (11)$$

where m and s are the mean and standard deviation respectively and u is a multiplicative error term. Therefore:

$$m(k) = \int_{-\infty}^{\infty} x f(x;k) \, dx$$

$$s(k) = \left[\frac{\int_{-\infty}^{\infty} \{ x - m(k) \}^2 \, f(x;k) \, dx}{\sigma_u^2} \right]^{1/2}$$

u = random variable with mean zero and a constant finite variance, σ_u^2

Using the cost function defined in (7), equation (1) can be rewritten as:

$$U(k) = \int_{-\infty}^{k} x f(x;k) dx + \int_{k}^{\infty} \{ C + pD + (1 - p)E + (c + pd)x \} \, f(x;k) dx.$$

Substituting the value of x defined in (11), this may be rewritten as:

$$U(k) = \int_{-\infty}^{\frac{k-m(k)}{s(k)}} \{ m(k) + s(k)u \} \, g(u) du$$

$$+ \{ C + pD + (1 - p)E \} \int_{\frac{k-m(k)}{s(k)}}^{\infty} g(u) du$$

290

$$+ (c+pd) \int_{\frac{k-m(k)}{s(k)}}^{\infty} \{m(k) + s(k)u\} \ g(u) \, du$$

$$= m(k) \ F(k) + s \ (k)W(k) + \{C + pD + (1-p)E\} \{1 - F(k)\}$$

$$= m(k) \ (c + pd) \ \{1 - F(k)\} - s(k) \ (c + pd)W(k) \quad . \quad . \quad . \quad . \quad (12)$$

where:

$$F(k) = \int_{-\infty}^{\frac{k-m(k)}{s(k)}} g(u) du$$

$$W(k) = \int_{-\infty}^{\frac{k-m(k)}{s(k)}} u g(u) du$$

Differentiating (12) with respect to k and setting it equal to zero, the following equation is obtained:

$$U'(k) = m'(k) F(k) + m(k) \ Y(k) \ Z(k)$$

$$+ s'(k) \ W(k) + s(k) \ (\frac{k-m(k)}{s(k)}) \ Y(k)Z(k)$$

$$- \{C+pD+(1-p)E\} \ Y(k)Z(k)$$

$$+ (c+pd) \ m'k \ \{1-F(k)\} - (c+pd) \ m(k) \ Y(k)Z(k)$$

$$- s'(k) \ (c+pd)W(k) - s(k) \ (c+pd) \frac{k-m(k)}{s(k)} \ Y(k)Z(k)$$

where

$$Y(k) = g \left(\frac{k-m(k)}{s(k)} \right) \quad . \quad . \quad . \quad . \quad . \quad . \quad . \quad . \quad . \quad . \quad . \quad . \quad (13)$$

$$Z(k) = \left[\frac{s(k)-m'(k)s(k)-ks'(k)+m(k)s'(k)}{\{ s(k)^2 \}} \right]$$

If $U''(k)$ is positive in the region where $U'(k) = 0$, then the positive k which satisfies (13) is at least a local minimum. To find an optimal k*, it is necessary to compare the local minima and identify the one which yields the smallest value of $U(k)$. If this value is less than $U(k)$ as k approaches zero and infinity, then this point is the optimal control limit. Also, to solve for k*, the distribution of the error tern u must be specified.

In the situation described the control limit, k, causes a change in future variances, x. Assume further, that the error term u has a standard normal distribution and m(k) is specified as m.k, where $(-1 < \bar{m} < 1)$; then (13) can be rewritten as:

$$U'(k) = \bar{m} \ (c+pd) + \bar{m} \ (1-c-pd)F(k)$$

$$+ \frac{(1-\bar{m})}{\sigma} \left[k(1-c-pd) - \{ C+pD+(1-p)E \} \right] g \left(\frac{k-\bar{m}k}{\sigma} \right) \quad . \quad . \quad . (14)$$

where:

$$g(u) = \frac{1}{\sqrt{2\pi}} e^{-\frac{1}{2}u^2}$$

$$F(k) = \int_{-\infty}^{\frac{k-\bar{m}k}{\sigma}} \frac{1}{\sqrt{2\pi}} e^{-\frac{1}{2}u^2} du$$

The result in (14) cannot be used to solve explicity for k because there are two unknown parameters (m and σ) in that single equation. Therefore, the local minima which satisfy (14) can be found only by trial and error. What is apparent from (14) is that for the Hawthorne type situation in which the control policy shifts the mean and variance of the distribution, there is no explicit solution for the optimal limit k*.

To appreciate the difficulty of obtaining closed form solutions, the analysis can be simplified further. Consider the situation in which productivity is determined by a group norm. Since control limits define a band around the mean, the group can define its mean in a way to allow most of its workers to be within the control limit. In this situation the response is to change the reporting rather than the actual behavior. The mean of the distribution of cost variances, therefore, is a simple linear function of k. That is:

$$x(k) = x + \bar{m}.k$$

The probability distribution of cost variances now can be represented by a triangular distribution. For simplicity, let us say that the lower limit of this distribution is $-a+\bar{m}k$ and the upper limit is $b+\bar{m}k$. The resulting density function will be:

$$\frac{h}{a}(x - \bar{m}k) + h \qquad \text{if} \quad -a+\bar{m}k \leq x \leq \bar{m}k$$

$$f(x;k) = \quad - \frac{h}{b}(x - \overline{m}k) + h \quad \text{if} \quad \overline{m}k \leq x \leq b + \overline{m}k \quad \ldots \ldots \quad (15)$$

This distribution, whose unknown parameter is h, is depicted in Figure 2.

FIGURE 2

TRIANGULAR DISTRIBUTION OF COST VARIANCES (x)

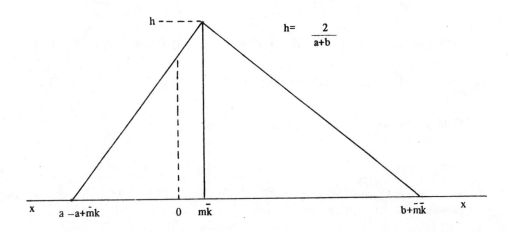

Using the triangular distribution, the expected total costs in (1) may be reformulated as follows:

$$U(k) = \int_{-a+\overline{m}k}^{\overline{m}k} x \left\{ \frac{h}{a} (x-\overline{m}k) + h \right\} dx + \int_{\overline{m}k}^{k} x \left\{ -\frac{h}{b} (x-\overline{m}k) + h \right\} dx$$

$$+ \int_{k}^{b+\overline{m}k} \{ C + pd+(1-p) E + (c+pd) x \} \left\{ -\frac{h}{b} (x-\overline{m}k)+h \right\} dx$$

$$= \frac{h}{6b} \left[(1-c-pd) (3\overline{m} - \overline{m}^3 - 2) \right] k^3$$

$$+ \frac{h}{2} \left[2\overline{m} (1-\overline{m})+(1-\overline{m}^2) (1-c-pd)+\frac{(1-m)^2}{b} \{ C+pD+(1-p)E \} \right] k^2$$

$$+ h \left[\frac{\overline{m}}{2} (a+c+pd) (b) - (1-\overline{m}) \{ C+pD+(1-p)E \} \right] k$$

$$+ \frac{h}{6} \left[(c+pd)b^2 - a^2 + 3b \{ C+pD+(1-p)E \} \right] \quad \ldots \ldots (16)$$

Differentiating (16) with respect to k and setting it equal to zero yields:

$$\frac{dU(k)}{dk} = Kk^2 + Lk + M = 0$$

Where:
$$K = \frac{h}{2b} \left[(3\bar{m} - \bar{m}^3 - 2(1-c-pd) \right]$$

$$L = h \left[2\bar{m}(1-\bar{m}) + (1-\bar{m}^2(1-c-pd) + \frac{(1-\bar{m})^2 \{ C+pD+(1-p)E \}}{b} \right]$$

$$M = h \left[\frac{\bar{m}}{2} (a+c+pd)(b) - (1-\bar{m}) \{ C+pD+(1-p)E \} \right] \quad \ldots (17)$$

There will be two real roots for the above equation:

$$k+ = \frac{-L + \sqrt{L^2 - 4KM}}{2K} \qquad k- = \frac{-L\sqrt{L^2 - 4KM}}{2K} \quad (k \# 0) \quad . (18)$$

provided that $L^2 - 4KM > 0$.

The optimal control limit k* in this case will depend on the sign of the three quantities K, L, and M. Table 2 summarizes the various possibilities with respect to K, L, and M and the resulting sign of the two real roots in (18). It shows that for most cases, the optimal control limit, k*, is always conditional. The control limits associated with each of the several possible values of K, L, and M are shown in the last column of Table 2.

Concluding Remarks

This paper has contrasted the engineering and behavioral approaches to the design of control systems in the context of the budget variance investigation decision. It has shown that most existing VID models are largely applications or adaptations of statistical quality control models from industrial engineering. The SQC models in turn are based on a structural view of control which ignores behavioral considerations. A fundamental premise of the engineering models of the VID is that cost variances are independent of the control policy, k. This assumption is inappropriate in budget control situations because variance information affects participant aspiration levels, feelings of success or failure and determines other intrinsic and extrinsic rewards. These psychological and pecuniary variables may influence effort and performance levels. Thus actual or

TABLE 2
OPTIMAL CONTROL LIMIT FOR A TRIANGULAR DISTRIBUTION OF x

Sign of K L & M	Sign of k^+ & k^-	Condition	Optimal Control Limit
$K>0, L>0, M>0$	$k^+<0, k^-<0$		$k^*=0$
$K<0, L<0, M<0$	$k^+<0, k^-<0$		$k^*=n^*$
$K>0, L>0, M<0$ $K>0, L<0, M<0$	$k^+>0, k^-<0$	if $k^+>n$	$k^*=n$
$K>0, L<0, M>0$	$k^+>0, k^-<0$	if $k^+<n$	$k^*=k^+$
$K<0, L>0, M>0$ $K<0, L<0, M>0$	$k^+<0, k^->0$	if $U(0)>U(n)$	$k^*=n$
		if $U(0)<U(n)$	$k^*=0$
$K<0, L>0, M<0$	$k^+>0, k^->0$	if $U(k^+)<U(n)$	$k^*=n$
		if $U(k^+)<U(n)$	$k^*=k^+$
$K=0, L>0, M<0$		if $-\dfrac{M}{2L}>n$	$k^*=n$
		if $-\dfrac{M}{2L}<n$	$k^*=-\dfrac{M}{2L}$
$K=0, L<0, M>0$		if $U(0)>U(n)$	$k^*=n$
		if $U(0)<U(n)$	$k^*=0$
$K=0 L>0, M>0$			$k^*=0$
$K=0, L<0, M<0$			$k^*=0$
$K=0, L=0, M<0$			$k^*=n$
$K=0, L=0, M>0$			$k^*=0$.

* Here n = upper limit or $b + \bar{m}k$.

reported changes in participant behavior will occur as a response to changes in control policies. In such situations there exists a feedback between a control policy, k, and future cost variances, x.

A preliminary model incorporating behavioral feedback effects was introduced in the paper. The analysis was based on recognizing that the appropriate variable for determining a control limit, k, was not the *independent* cost variances, x, but rather, the cost variances *dependent* on k, that is, x(k). To specify x(k), two simple behavioral situations of the type reported in the Hawthorne experiments were postulated. The first situation was assumed to shift the mean and the statistical variance of cost deviations. A normal distribution to specify this shift produced an equation which could not be solved explicitly. The other, a simpler mean shift model using a triangular distribution produced an explicit solution but only under restricted conditions. Both these situations produced far more mathematically intractable solutions than the corresponding engineering approach using x as the optimization variable.

There are three major implications of the analysis presented here. First, when behavioral considerations are present, the specification of the feedback relationship between control policies and control system behavior must *precede* the solution of an optimal policy. The behavioral situations examined in this paper are extremely simple and were chosen for illustrative purposes rather than for their realism. Since there is little empirical research on the nature of the feedback between a policy k and future deviations, x, any specification of this relationship at this stage would be empirically arbitrary. Thus, there is need for empirical research to determine the change in the probability density function of x caused by the introduction of k. This will indicate how many and which parameters of the distribution are affected by the control policy. Also, for multiperiod extensions, empirical research must be undertaken to specify whether x, if uncorrected, undergoes a random walk or progressively decays. Without an answer to such questions, all formulations of the variance investigation decision are likely to be speculative.

Second, even for the simple behavioral situation presented here, it is clear that the nature of the feedback will depend upon several attendant variables. For instance, how workers respond to a control policy will be determined by what rewards and penalties are attached to the policy, the strictness of enforcement, task familiarity, etc. The optimal control policy thus becomes a *package of actions only one of which is k**. That is, the optimal policy will now take the form of specifying a set of actions such as k*, reward structure, strictness of enforcement, etc. Thus, k* is likely to be one part of an over all control policy. It is even likely that a quality control type k* may be totally unsuited for budget control because of other factors present in the situation. For example, in the control of expense centers, such as a Legal Department, the feedback information from variances plays a limited role in control. Rather, it is the process of participating in budget preparation and accountability for inputs which accomplishes control. Future research must therefore specify the other variables which, together with k, form the optimal control policy.

Finally, the analysis shows that when behavioral considerations are recognized and the simple single period model is abandoned in favor of more realistic multi-period analysis, the optimal policy k* is unlikely to yield simple closed form mathematical solutions. The solution will most likely require the use of simulation techniques, particularly because several scenarios incorporating other control variables may have to be included in the determination of an optimal policy.

The variance investigation decision provides an excellent example of how a particular orientation to control may lead to an incorrect formulation of a control problem. The engineering orientation to the variance investigation problem has produced a bias in favor of adopting quality-control type formulations. The fact that many of the assumptions are inconsistent with evidence on the behavior of participants in a cost system may explain why these models have not been applied in practice.

A broader orientation which integrates both structural and behavioral variables formulates the problem in a different manner. It suggests that the optimal solution is more complex and requires the development of a general theory of control which is capable of dealing with both structural and behavioral variables.[7] Without such a theory there will be a tendency to look for and solve control problems "where the light is better".

NOTES

[1] For a representative sample of this approach to control see Ashby (1956), Aoki (1969), Bellman (1962), Emery (1969), Shannon & Weaver (1969).

[2] There are several important works which reflect this particular view on control. Some examples which provide comprehensive surveys are Blau (1974), Bonini et al. (1964), Lawler & Rhode (1976).

[3] A similar hypothesis is stated by Dittman & Prakash (1979, p.359). In talking about the feedback effects of a control policy on those being controlled they state: "Information inductance (their term for feedback) will make the parameters of cost generating process a function of the control policy".

[4] The general procedure used in this paper was suggested by the late Professor Jacob Marschak. For the analysis of management-by-exception information structures, see Marshak and Radner (1972 pp.206-217).

[5] The derivative of a definite integral with respect to the upper limit of integration is equal to the value of the integrand at this upper limit: $\frac{d}{dk} \int_a^k f(x)dx = f(k)$

[6] For a discussion of the Hawthorne experiments see George Homans, *The Human Group* (New York, Harper & Row, 1950).

[7] For a more detailed discussion of the need to adopt an integrated view of control systems, see Ansari (1977).

297

REFERENCES

Ansari, S. L. (1977), "An Integrated Approach to Control System Design", *Accounting, Organizations & Society*, 2, 2, (1977) pp.101-112.

Aoki, M. (1967), *Optimization of Stochastic Systems*, (New York: Academic Press, 1967).

Ashby, W.R. (1956), *An Introduction to Cybernetics*, (London: Chapman & Hall, 1956).

Beer, S. (1964), *Cybernetics and Management*, (New York: John Wiley & Sons, 1964).

Bellman, R.E. (1962), *Adaptive Control Processes: A Guided Tour*, (Princeton, N.J.: Princeton University Press, 1962).

Bierman, H., L.E. Fouraker and R. K. Jaedicke (1961), "A Use of Probability and Statistics in Performance Evaluation", *The Accounting Review* (July 1961), pp.409-17.

Blau, P.M. (1974), *On the Nature of Organization*, (New York: John Wiley, 1974).

Bonini, C.P., Robert R.K. Jaedicke and H. M. Wagner (1964), eds. *Management Controls: New Direction in Basic Research*, (New York: McGraw Hill, 1964).

Dittman, D.A. and P. Prakash (1979), "Cost Variance Investigation: Markovian Control Versus Optimal Control", *Accounting Review*, (April, 1979), pp.358-373.

Duncan, A.J. (1956), "The Economic Design of x Chart Used to Maintain Current Control of a Process", *Journal of the American Statistical Association* (June 1956).

Duvall, R.M. (1967), "Rules for Investigation Cost of Variances", *Management Science* (June 1967), pp.631–41.

Emery, J. C. *Organizational Planning and Control Systems*, (New York: McMillan Co., 1969).

Gaynor, E.W. (1954), "Use of Control Charts in Cost Control", *N.A.C.A. Bulletin* (June 1954). In W.E. Thomas ed. *Readings in Cost Accounting Budgeting and Control*, (Cincinnati: South-Western Publishing Co., 1968). pp.835-45.

Girshick, M.A. and H. Rubin (1952), "A Bayes Approach to a Quality Control Model", *Annals of Mathematical Statistics* (1952), pp.114-25.

Kaplan, R.S. (1969), "Optimal Investigation Strategies with Imperfect Information", *Journal of Accounting Research* (Spring 1969), pp.32-43.

————— (1975), "The Significance and Investigation of Cost Variances: Survey and Extensions", *Journal of Accounting Research* (Autumn, 1975), pp.311-337.

Lawler, E.E. III and Rhode, J.R. (1976), *Information and Control In Organizations*, (Pacific Palisades, Ca.: Goodyear Publishing Co., 1976).

Marschak, J. and Radner (1972), *Economic Theory of Teams*, Stamford, Conn.: Yale University Press, 1972).

Page, E.S. "Continuous Inspection Schemes", *Biometrika* (1954), pp.100-115.

Schiff, M. and Lewin, A.Y. (1968), "Where Traditional Budgeting Fails", *Financial Executive* (May, 1968), pp.57–62.

Shannon, C. and Weaver, W. (1969), *A Mathematical Theory of Communication* (Urban, I11), University of Illinois Press, 1969).

Shewhart, W.A. (1931), *Economic Control of Quality of Manufactured Product* (Princeton: Van Nostrand, 1931).

Taylor, H. M. (1968), "The Economic Design of Cumulative Sum Control Charts for Variables", *Technometrics* (August 1968), pp.479-88.

PART IV
PERFORMANCE MEASUREMENT

The final section of the reader is devoted to the issue of performance measurement. Cost allocation, a controversial accounting practice affecting performance evaluation, has been addressed in different frameworks. Thomas rejects allocations in general purpose financial statements because they violate a qualitative objective of accounting: neutrality. Ferrara uses the "flexible" approach and suggests specific technical allocation methods when results are to be used for performance evaluation. Bodnar and Lusk suggest technical approaches to allocation that can motivate subunit managers to achieve nonfinancial organizational goals. They are explicitly trying to influence managers' behavior by selecting an allocation base that formally structures motivational considerations into the design of the planning and control systems.

Articles are also included on return on investment (ROI), a performance evaluation tool made popular by decentralization. It has suffered criticisms in recent years and has been called outdated. Bierman's paper reviews the use of ROI as a performance measure and suggests that it is a useful technique, which would improve with better measures of income and investment. Ridgeway criticizes the use of a single quantitative performance measurement such as ROI, and advocates the use of multiple or composite measures coupled with a better understanding of organizational behavior when using such measures. This book ends with an article by Hopwood which discusses *if* and *how* people use accounting data in performance evaluation.

The articles in this section provide useful insights into subparts of the performance evaluation issue. All together they are a foundation for an emerging integrated perspective for performance evaluation.

Useful Arbitary Allocations (With a Comment on the Neutrality of Financial Accounting Reports)

ARTHUR L. THOMAS
University of Kansas

I N A recent monograph I concluded that most of financial accounting's allocations are arbitrary, and that this renders them useless for the general purposes which financial accounting attempts to serve.[1] Several friends have been kind enough to point out that an allocation may be unsuitable for general purposes yet highly useful for some specific purpose.[2] Although this does not alter the financial accounting conclusions of SAR #3, it should be evident by the end of this paper that the existence of useful arbitrary allocations has implications for managerial accounting which deserve further study. These implications are not pursued here; instead, what follows is merely an initial examination of *when* arbitrary allocations will be useful.[3]

RANGE OF AMBIGUITY

The concept of the "range of ambiguity" of an allocation was applied briefly in SAR #3 to situations in which various allocation methods are available and no conclusive reasons for choosing any individual possibility can be demonstrated. An accounting allocation divides a monetary magnitude among recipients (inputs to the firm, accounting periods, and so forth). If different allocation methods are possible, the amounts which could be attributed to individual recipients will vary. The *range of ambiguity* of an allocation with respect to an individual input is the extent to which the amounts attributed to that recipient may vary by virtue of choice of allocation methods.

To get down to specifics, SAR #3 discusses allocations (such as depreciation) in which the costs of nonmonetary inputs are written off. It points out that financial accounting theory requires that two kinds of allocations be performed in the amortization of nonmonetary inputs. First, a series of *contribution allocations* must be made in which the total net revenues of the

---

[1] *The Allocation Problem in Financial Accounting Theory*, Studies in Accounting Research #3 (American Accounting Association, 1969), hereafter designated "SAR #3." A reply to certain criticisms of this monograph and a study of its implications for revenue-recognition controversies are now (March 1971) in process.

[2] Of these friends, Alfred Rappaport and Yuji Ijiri were the most persistent. In addition, this paper benefited greatly from criticism by my colleague, L. G. Eckel, and from technical assistance by Kathleen S. Martin. Background research was in part supported by a 1970 McMaster University Summer Research Stipend.

[3] As a preliminary analysis, I have tried to keep this presentation brief. For example, only a single line of argument is used to support the conclusions reached in the next section and the Appendix, despite the broad implications of these conclusions.

---

firm during successive periods are allocated to the various inputs which are deemed to generate them; this yields a pattern of periodic net revenue contributions which have been attributed to the individual non-monetary input. This pattern is used to determine the *amortization allocation* of that input's cost to different accounting periods.

Ambiguities of the Two Allocations

With respect to the contribution allocations, SAR #3 distinguishes between the separate effects of the individual inputs and their interaction effects. A major part of the allocation problem in financial accounting is that at present there is no conclusively defensible way to allocate these interaction effects to the individual inputs. (An illustration of this difficulty is given later in this paper.) There is a similar problem of interaction among the total inputs of different accounting periods which afflicts the amortization allocation (independently of the difficulties experienced with the contribution allocations).

SAR #3 demonstrated (page 72) that the range of ambiguity in the *amortization* allocation is at least as large as the difference between the cost of the input and the total of the net-revenue contributions which are attributed to that input during all accounting periods. This difference may be perceived as the combined interaction effect of the contributions made by the input during the several periods. Similarly, the range of ambiguity in the *contribution* allocation of any period with respect to any individual input will be at least as large as the difference between the total net revenues generated by the particular input alone or in combination with other inputs and the total separate effects of these inputs; this may be designated the "combined interaction effect during the period of the individual input and all other inputs with which it interacts to generate net revenue," or, for brevity, the *combined interaction effect*.

As is also illustrated below, there is no way to determine decisively whether any one allocation of this combined interaction effect is preferable to any other. Therefore, allocation of the entire combined interaction effect to any one input is just as defensible as allocation of none of the combined interaction effect to that input. From this it follows that the range of ambiguity in the contribution allocation of any one period must be at least as large as the combined interaction effect.

Ambiguity in the Individual Amortization Charge

For financial accounting purposes, the most important range of ambiguity is that of the amortization charges for individual inputs during individual accounting periods (such as the depreciation charge for a particular asset during a particular year). For brevity, this will be designated as *the range of ambiguity in the individual amortization charge*. This range of ambiguity is a function of the ranges of ambiguity in the input's amortization and contribution allocations. SAR #3 argued that this range of ambiguity was apt to be enormous—large enough to swamp the amortization charge calculation. The Appendix to this paper attempts to show that, paradoxical as this may seem, this range of ambiguity in the individual amortization charge usually will be at least as large as the total historical cost of the input.

It is easily proved that any amortization in an individual period which *exceeded* the input's historical cost would require negative amortization (appreciation) of the input in at least one other period. Such recognition of appreciation raises issues which are best reserved for a study of the impact of the allocation problem on revenue recognition; therefore, the simplifying assumption that negative amortization is inappropriate will be made instead. All of this leads to the following minimum conclusion (which, though probably much more conservative than the truth, will suffice for the purposes of this paper):

The range of ambiguity in an individual financial accounting amortization charge usually will equal the total historical cost of the related input.

This situation (in which any amortization of a nonmonetary input from zero to complete write off is as defensible as any other) will for brevity be designated as one of *total ambiguity* in the related allocation.

Significance of this Conclusion

But how significant is this? Are there circumstances in which totally ambiguous allocations are useful to recipients of accounting data? The rest of this paper suggests that totally ambiguous allocations can be useful in some situations and for some purposes. Unfortunately, though, it will turn out that this demonstration does not alter the severe conclusions of SAR #3.

Allocations which are totally ambiguous yet perhaps useful may be classified into two broad categories:[4]

1. Some totally ambiguous allocations are embodied in laws, regulations, and custom. When an entity is required by an external authority to allocate, the resulting allocation automatically is useful to the entity (regardless of how large the allocation's range of ambiguity may be) merely because it satisfies that requirement. For example, if tax regulations prescribe that depreciation allocations be made, such allocations are thereby rendered useful; similarly, if authoritative custom requires that manufactured inventories be reported at "cost," the necessary allocations will be useful even if they are totally ambiguous. Cases of this kind are discussed in the report of the American

Accounting Association's Committee on Foundations of Accounting Measurement,[5] and are not examined in detail here (though they will be referred to in the final section of this paper); for brevity, they may be termed allocations which are *useful for institutional purposes.*

2. A totally ambiguous allocation may be useful to an entity if this allocation serves the purposes of that entity; it also may be useful if it serves a common purpose of two or more entities. Whatever the size of the range of ambiguity, if those individuals and groups who are affected by an allocation have similar enough purposes in common to override any conflicts of their separate interests, they may find it possible to develop mutually useful allocations. These kinds of allocations, characterized by a community of interest and designated *mutually satisfactory allocations*, are discussed below.

An Example

A simple example may be used to illustrate two things simultaneously: first, that the range of ambiguity in the contribution allocation is at least as large as the combined interaction effect and, second, that entities with a sufficient community of interest can develop mutually satisfactory allocations even when the related ranges of ambiguity are large. The particular allocation situation illustrated is one in which the range of ambiguity, though substantial, is not total. Such a situation gives a clear insight into the nature of the ambiguity in contribution allocations. For simplicity, the example chosen utilizes only two interacting inputs and does not involve an amortization allocation. However, all of the following

---

[4] This is for convenience in exposition, not for rigor; it is likely that these categories overlap.

[5] Committee on Foundations of Accounting Measurement, American Accounting Association, "Report of the Committee on Foundations of Accounting Measurement," The Accounting Review, Supplement to Vol. XLVI, 1971, pp. 1–48.

illustrated points may be extended without modification to the more severe and complicated allocation situations which are encountered in financial accounting.[6]

Let us suppose that two graduate students Fast and Slow, have been hired to grade an examination at a rate of 50¢ per paper. (For reasons that will become apparent later, it is also assumed that Fast is married.) Working alone, Fast can grade five papers an hour; working alone, Slow can grade three papers an hour. For efficiency, each has "specialized" in grading part of the examination; this allows them, working together, to grade twelve papers per hour. The separate effects of Fast and Slow on physical output may be perceived as five and three papers an hour, respectively; net revenues and total revenues are identical, and the two students' separate effects on net revenues will be $2.50 (50¢×5) and $1.50 (50¢×3) per hour. Total revenues are $6.00 (50¢×12) per hour, resulting in a combined interaction effect of $2.00 ($6.00−$2.50−$1.50) per hour.

How shall Fast and Slow divide the total $6.00 per hour between them? SAR #3 contends that in situations like this (where two or more inputs interact to produce an output) there will be no single, conclusively defensible, answer. The table indicates a few possibilities.

WAYS IN WHICH THE $6.00 PER HOUR MIGHT BE ALLOCATED BETWEEN FAST AND SLOW

	Fast	Slow
1. Split the whole amount 50/50...	$3.00	$3.00
2. Attribute 7 papers per hour to Slow, on the basis that if he quit, total output would drop from 12 to 5 papers per hour............	2.50	3.50
3. Attribute 9 papers per hour to Fast, on the basis that if he quit, total output would drop from 12 to 3 papers per hour...........	4.50	1.50
4. Attribute each grader's separate effects to him, then split the interaction effect 50/50.............	3.50	2.50
5. Split the whole amount in proportion to each grader's separate effects........................	3.75	2.25

Comparison of methods (2) and (3) demonstrates that the range of ambiguity in this allocation is at least as large as the entire combined interaction effect of $2.00 per hour; this will always be true of contribution allocations.[7]

Method (2) is to Slow's short-term financial advantage. It attributes the entire combined interaction effect to him by a calculation which parallels that of the marginal analysis (something which should make method (2) even more attractive to Slow, since such reasoning is widely respected in contemporary accounting theory). Slow could defend method (2) quite as forcefully as Fast could defend any alternative allocation approach. Of course, Fast could defend method (3) equally well against any alternative that was proposed by Slow.

DEVELOPMENT OF A MUTUALLY SATISFACTORY ALLOCATION

For the purposes of this paper, however, the most important thing to recognize is that in practice the two graders usually would manage to agree upon a mutually satisfactory method of allocation. This process is much too complicated for its details to be discussed here; besides, only a summary of it is needed to support the conclusions that are reached in the next section. In this example, ignorance of the other grader's capacities ordinarily would be a factor in reaching a mutually satisfactory allocation, but four other factors seem

[6] I am grateful to Wadsworth Publishing Company, Inc., for its permission to paraphrase some of what follows from the author's forthcoming accounting principles textbook to be published in 1972.

[7] Technically, once the two graduate students have agreed to grade the exam, the minimum amount which must be paid to either grader is whatever it will take to keep him grading. This might be less than $1.50 per hour for Slow or $2.50 per hour for Fast; therefore in theory the range of ambiguity could exceed an amount equal to the combined interaction effect. But in actual business situations forces of competition should prevent the range of ambiguity from exceeding the combined interaction effect in this way (except, possibly, in the very short run).

involved, too. First, people who work together day after day (as graduate students often do) develop various mutual goals which are best furthered by co-operation; excessive emphasis on purely financial interests can jeopardize other, nonfinancial, interests. Second, even on strictly financial grounds it may not pay either grader to become so greedy that the other will refuse to team with him on future projects. (This will be true even from Fast's standpoint if Slow is more efficient on other jobs.) Third, there seem to be pervasive institutional pressures which encourage individuals who are in the same station of life to share things fairly equally. Finally, in the graders' situation, bargaining may take place between what resemble two duopolists. (There is an extensive amount of theoretical literature about this kind of bargaining.)

The reader is asked to notice, though, that if Fast and Slow reach a mutually satisfactory allocation here, it is either because they have common goals which override their short-run financial interests, or because in some sense Society constrains the bargaining process.

Perhaps Fast and Slow agree that a 50/50 split would be fair. The resulting allocation then will be useful to them despite the fairly large ($2.00) range of ambiguity.[8] However, from the standpoint of someone else who does not share their common goals, or who is not subject to the same social constraints, this 50/50 allocation may be quite unsatisfactory. For example, let us suppose that Mrs. Fast is trying to raise three children on a graduate student's earnings and doesn't give two hoots for Slow; from her point of view the 50/50 allocation may be unsatisfactory, even though it is satisfactory to her husband.[9]

In general, allocations with large ranges of ambiguity may be useful to an entity whose total advantage is maximized by that allocation, or who is constrained to accept it. Other entities will find the allocation unsatisfactory (unless, of course, in their judgment the gap between the results of the allocation method actually employed and those of whatever allocation method would be to their maximum over-all advantage is not material).

APPLICATION TO FINANCIAL ACCOUNTING

Certain qualities or characteristics make financial information useful. Providing information that has each of these qualities is an objective of financial accounting. These qualitative objectives are relevance, understandability, verifiability, neutrality, timeliness, comparability, and completeness.

* * *

Neutrality. Neutral financial accounting information is directed toward the common needs of users and is independent of presumptions about particular needs and desires of specific users of the information. Measurements not based on presumptions about the particular needs of specific users enhance the relevance of the information to common needs of users. Preparers of financial accounting information should not try to increase the helpfulness of the information to a few users to the detriment of others who may have opposing interests.[10]

We may conclude by contrasting these graders with individuals who are affected by financial accounting's allocations.

---

[8] Several individuals who have responded to SAR #3 in private correspondence have gone further and would contend that the allocation would not be *arbitrary* from the standpoint of Fast and Slow, either. I have no real objections to saying this as long as it is recognized that "arbitrary" is being used here in a limited sense which differs from the more general sense employed in SAR #3.

[9] An important parallel situation arises here with transfer prices. For instance, a transfer price may be mutually satisfactory to a parent company and its foreign subsidiary, yet be unsuitable from the standpoints of other affected parties in the host country—see "Transfer Prices of the Multinational Firm: When Will They be Arbitrary?" forthcoming in *Abacus.*

[10] *Basic Concepts and Accounting Principles Underlying Financial Statements of Business Enterprises,* Statement of the Accounting Principles Board No. 4 (American Institute of Certified Public Accountants, October, 1970), pages 10 and 37.

There are substantial differences between the two cases. First, most financial accounting allocations are totally ambiguous. Second, individuals and groups whose interests are affected by financial accounting's allocation practices (hereafter designated *the affected entities*) are not in the position that Fast and Slow were to develop mutually satisfactory allocations by bargaining. Nevertheless, we have seen that even total ambiguity need not always be a barrier. There appears to be a slow process in lieu of bargaining whereby the interests of affected entities often are eventually reflected in generally accepted accounting principles. One may still ask, accordingly, whether the totality of affected entities might manage to develop mutually satisfactory allocations, or whether the financial accountant might develop these for the affected entities.

The prospects are not encouraging. Society's guidance to the affected entities seems to discourage co-operation, sharing things evenly, and so forth; instead, maximization of immediate financial advantage is encouraged. Moreover, there are relatively few common goals to be advanced by entities partially sacrificing their financial interests. Part of the problem here is that too many individuals and groups are affected by financial accounting reports. Consequently, a sense of community is difficult to develop. Finally, there are abundant current and potential sources of conflict between affected entities in which different allocation decisions will favor the interests of one set of contending parties over those of others.

Thus, the chances of financial accounting developing mutually satisfactory allocations are at a minimum. This is serious, since financial accounting's traditional role has been as a kind of general-purpose reporting which supposedly is neutral with respect to conflicts among its users. If the analysis in this paper is correct, financial accounting *cannot* be neutral in this sense because it usually cannot provide mutually satisfactory allocations (except for institutional purposes, as defined earlier).[11] But if this is so it follows that much of financial accounting's traditional social justification and much of its traditional role in legitimizing social institutions are at least partly founded on illusion.[12]

APPENDIX

THE RANGE OF AMBIGUITY IN THE AMORTIZATION OF AN INDIVIDUAL INPUT DURING AN INDIVIDUAL ACCOUNTING PERIOD

What follows is an attempt to demonstrate that usually the range of ambiguity in an individual amortization charge will

[11] One reviewer of an earlier version of this paper commented that this will depend upon how these allocations are used and upon how resourceful the users are in compensating for the limitations of the allocations. It is worth emphasizing again that if financial accounting is to be independent of the desires of special interests it must report data which are *mutually* satisfactory to contending affected entities, and that the limitations encountered usually are ones of total ambiguity. At present, many of financial accounting's readers cope with (or at least tolerate) such ambiguity. But the probable explanations of this are not especially comforting: reliance upon nonaccounting data instead of accounting's allocations, acquiesence to present rules because of institutional compulsion or because they provide the "only game in town," ignorance of the ambiguity or of its extent, or indifference to the allocation because the reader's interests are unaffected by it (or because he is unaware of any effect). Similarly, if someone is tolerating a possible error of six hours in his watch one concludes either that he is using some other timepiece, has despaired of learning the time, is unaware of the ambiguity, or simply doesn't care what time it is. Finally, of course, some readers cope with financial accounting's allocation rules because they are lucky, clever, or powerful enough to benefit from these rules or to influence development of rules which favor their own financial interests.

[12] In contrast, the allocations that are employed in managerial accounting often need to be satisfactory only to a single user or to a small number of users who share common purposes. I tentatively conclude, therefore, that accounting's allocation problems do not always have as serious consequences in managerial accounting as they do in financial accounting. Further research seems warranted.

be total—will be at least as great as the historical cost of the related nonmonetary input. The reader is warned that what follows is tentative and subject to refutation. Let:

$R(X)$ = the range of ambiguity in any allocation, X

j = any input to the firm, $j = 1, 2, \cdots, q$

i = any accounting period, $i = 1, 2, \cdots, p$

N_{ij} = the total net revenue of the firm in period i that was generated by input j alone, or in combination with other inputs

n_{ij} = the net revenue contribution of input j in period i, as determined by the contribution allocation

s_{ij} = the separate effects of input j in generating N_{ij}

I_{ij} = N_{ij} minus the separate effects of all inputs which generate N_{ij}—the combined interaction effect in period i of input j and all other inputs with which it interacts to produce net revenues

H_j = the historical cost of input j

$R(C_{ij})$ = the range of ambiguity in the contribution allocation in period i, with respect to the amount allocated to input j

$R(A_j)$ = given n_{ij} for each period, the range of ambiguity in the amortization allocation for input j

$R(AC_{ij})$ = the range of ambiguity in the amortization charge for input j in period i.

This notation is used only to clarify the matters to be discussed; what follows should not be regarded as a mathematical proof. SAR #3 evidenced that the range of ambiguity in the amortization allocation

equals the difference between the input's total net-revenue contributions and its cost:

$$R(A_j) = \sum_{i=1}^{p} n_{ij} - H_j.$$

Were there no ambiguity in the contribution allocations, the range of ambiguity in the amortization charge for input j in period i would equal the range of ambiguity in the amortization allocation. To the extent that there is ambiguity in the contribution allocations with respect to input j, $R(AC_{ij})$ will be greater than or equal to $R(A_j)$, since one cannot reduce total ambiguity by additional ambiguity.

This paper argues that the range of ambiguity in the contribution allocation of period i with respect to input j equals the combined interaction effect in period i of input j and all other inputs with which it interacts:

$$R(C_{ij}) = I_{ij}.$$

Therefore, n_{ij} may vary anywhere from s_{ij} to $(s_{ij} + I_{ij})$. Since each $R(C_{ij})$ is independent of each other, $\sum_{i=1}^{p} n_{ij}$ may vary anywhere from $\sum_{i=1}^{p} s_{ij}$ to $\sum_{i=1}^{p} (s_{ij} + I_{ij})$. Looking to the most extreme case, if for each i, $n_{ij} = s_{ij} + I_{ij}$, then:

$$R(A_j) = \sum_{i=1}^{p} (s_{ij} + I_{ij}) - H_j.$$

Now the total range of ambiguity in the amortization charge for input j in period i must encompass this case, along with all other cases resulting from varying allocations of the N_{ij}'s to the n_{ij}'s. Accordingly, $R(AC_{ij})$ itself cannot be less than $\sum_{i=1}^{p} (s_{ij} + I_{ij}) - H_j$:

$$R(AC_{ij}) \geq \sum_{i=1}^{p} (s_{ij}) + \sum_{i=1}^{p} (I_{ij}) - H_j.$$

But SAR #3 argues that the combined interaction effects of most inputs in any period usually are substantial: most of the total net revenues of the firm are such interaction effects and most inputs interact with most other inputs. Because of this it seems very likely that for most inputs $\sum_{i=1}^{p} (I_{ij})$ will be at least twice as large as H_j, and that:

$$R(AC_{ij}) \geq H_j.$$

That is, the range of ambiguity in the amortization of any given input for any given accounting period usually will be at least as large as the historical cost of that input. This in turn implies that anything from zero amortization to complete write-off will be appropriate for the input in any given period.

Overhead Costs and Income Measurement

WILLIAM L. FERRARA
Pennsylvania State University

A T THE present time there are two basic assumptions involved in the accounting for manufacturing overhead costs as it relates to income measurement. These assumptions are:

1) A fixed-variable cost segregation is best for income measurement purposes.
2) Unit costs should not be allowed to vary with volume.[1]

The fixed-variable cost separation is admitted to be a difficult process, but as usual, all that is asked of practitioners is to do the best that can be done in a difficult situation. Once the cost elements are separated into fixed and variable components, each group (fixed and variable) can be allocated to production on appropriate bases, e.g., variable costs on the basis of actual service and fixed costs on a readiness to serve basis. The readiness to serve allocation for fixed costs is based on a number of different measures of plant capacity or readiness to serve.

Under each measure of capacity, variable overhead costs would be allocated to products on the basis of actual output. Presumably each unit of output is charged with those elements of variable overhead to which it gave rise. *All* variable overhead would thus be allocated to output, for without output there would be no variable overhead costs. Under each capacity measure, fixed overhead allocated to production is represented by the portion of capacity utilized multiplied by the fixed costs. The method of capacity measurement affects the measure of utilized capacity costs.

Allocation of fixed costs under three of the most commonly mentioned capacity measures (practical capacity, normal capacity, and cycle capacity) can be illustrated by the following diagram.

Fixed overhead costs associated with unutilized plant capacity are called idle capacity costs which are treated as a loss since they are considered a form of waste. Fixed overhead costs associated with utilized plant capacity are considered costs of production and thus as an element in the computation of inventory values and cost of goods sold.

The meaning of "measure of capacity" for each of the three capacity concepts would be as follows:

Capacity Concept	Measure of Capacity
Practical	Physical Output Potential (maximum theoretical capacity less expected idle time and other expected operating interruptions.)
Normal	Average Sales Expectations
Cycle	Average Sales Expectations

[1] A few examples of accounting literature in which these assumptions are explicitly or implicitly stated are:

R. Lee Brummet, *Overhead Costing*, Michigan Business Studies, Vol. XIII, No. 2 (Ann Arbor, Michigan: University of Michigan, 1957), pp. 59–72.

William J. Vatter, "Accounting Measurements of Incremental Costs," *The Journal of Business*, XVIII (July, 1945), p. 156.

Charles F. Schlatter and William J. Schlatter, *Cost Accounting*, 2nd ed. (New York: John Wiley and Sons, Inc., 1957) pp. 401–4.

Adolph Matz, Othel J. Curry, and George W. Frank, *Cost Accounting*, 2nd ed. (Cincinnati: South-Western Publishing Company, 1957), pp. 263–273.

Practical capacity thus represents the physical ability of the plant to produce during the regular working hours with special allowances made for expected operating interruptions. These expected operating interruptions do not include those caused by inability to sell. Practical capacity is based solely on ability to produce. On the other hand normal and cycle capacity represent ability to sell. Ability to sell in this case does not represent the ability to sell in a particular year; it represents an average of annual sales expectations.

Capacity utilized would be actual output under all capacity concepts, and unutilized capacity under each of the three capacity concepts would represent the following:

Capacity Concept	Meaning of Unutilized Capacity
Practical	Idle capacity in a strict physical sense, considered a loss.
Normal	Idle capacity due to less than average use of fixed assets, considered a loss.
Cycle	Unused costs due to less than average use of fixed assets, considered deferred fixed costs to be utilized in the future when greater than average use of fixed costs occurs.

Unutilized capacity under the practical capacity concept is simply a matter of measuring the unused productive ability of a plant. Unutilized capacity under the normal and cycle overhead concepts is measured in the same way, that is as the difference between capacity utilized and average sales expectations. However the meaning of unutilized capacity is considerably different in each case. Unutilized capacity is considered a loss under the normal overhead concept while it is considered a deferred charge under the cycle overhead concept.

Under normal and cycle capacity, actual output can be greater than average sales expectations. Thus the previous illustration would have to be changed as follows:

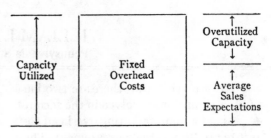

Overutilized capacity would represent a special gain due to greater-than-average use of fixed costs under normal capacity, and a deferred credit due to greater-than-average use of fixed costs under cycle capacity. The deferred charges and deferred credits associated with the cycle capacity concept are treated as offsetting items. Overutilized capacity cannot ordinarily exist under the practical capacity concept, since practical capacity is defined as physical output potential which cannot be exceeded.[2]

Two other capacity measures are sometimes spoken of in accounting literature. They are maximum theoretical capacity and expected output for the year. Maximum theoretical capacity is generally repudiated since it does not recognize human frailties, i.e., the occurrence of operating interruptions. Expected output for the year is generally repudiated as a basis for allocating fixed overhead costs to product since it yields a unit cost which will vary with the volume of production activity.

Each of the capacity measures introduced is ordinarily identified by the names and descriptions given above.[3] However,

[2] Actual output could exceed practical capacity where the estimate of operating interruptions is in error or when plant and equipment are used for more hours than expected or when the productivity of plant, equipment, and facilities is above expectations.

[3] Adolph Matz, Othel J. Curry, and George W. Frank, *op. cit.*, pp. 532–4.
Charles F. Schlatter and William J. Schlatter, *op. cit.*, p. 435.
John J. Blocker and W. Keith Weltmer, *Cost Accounting*, 3rd. ed. (New York: McGraw-Hill Book Company, 1954), p. 313.

"normal capacity" is often considered as including some of or all the capacity concepts mentioned here.[4] In one significant study, normal and cycle capacity as defined in this paper are considered as two aspects of "average activity."[5]

The above illustrations of capacity concepts (practical capacity, normal capacity, and cycle capacity) and the treatment of overhead costs show how overhead costs are divided and allocated for income measurement purposes. Fixed overhead costs are assumed to be one lump sum which is cut into slices of equal cost for allocation to individual units of output. Each unit of output then has an equal fixed cost allocation.[6] Thus, unit costs are not allowed to fluctuate with volume, that is, the fixed costs of a period are not allowed to be allocated to the actual output of the same period[7] which would yield a varying fixed cost per unit based solely on changes in production volume. The possibility of unit costs fluctuating with volume is eliminated by means of the special treatment of unutilized and over-utilized fixed overhead costs.

Thus far, the assumptions concerning the fixed-variable cost breakdown and constancy of fixed overhead costs per unit have been illustrated. Both assumptions are inherent in the three generally recognized measures of capacity. However, objection is necessary to both of these assumptions. A fixed-variable cost breakdown is not best for income measurement and unit costs should be allowed to vary with volume, under the conditions to be spelled out in succeeding pages.

Overhead Cost Segregation for Income Measurement

For income measurement purposes, overhead costs should not be segregated into the familiar fixed-variable dichotomy. A threefold categorization of manufacturing overhead would be best to illustrate the recommended approach to income measurement. The segregation is as follows:

1) Acquisiton costs of long-lived assets (fixed assets).
2) Semi-variable cost inputs related to salaries of supervisory personnel, practically all the costs of service departments, and practically all the expenses incurred by the plant superintendent's office and the manufacturing vice-president's office.
3) All other overhead costs; these are primarily the costs of operating equipment and facilities.

At first there may not seem to be a great distinction between the twofold and the threefold categorizations of overhead costs. Categories (1) and (2) of the new threefold grouping can almost be described as a breakdown of the old fixed cost category, while category (3) can almost be described as the old variable cost category. However, category (2), semi-variable inputs, consists of cost elements which are separated into fixed and variable components for purposes of refining the usual fixed-variable cost breakdown. In addition to the threefold cost categorization recommended, there is another very important difference (perhaps the most important) in the approach to income measurment to be recommended. Each of the three cost groups is to be allocated to production in a different manner. The acquisition costs of long-lived assets are to be allocated to production on a unit-of-production basis. In other words, depreciation *is not* to be calculated on a straight-line basis; depreciation *is* to be calculated on a unit-of-production basis. Under straight-line depreciation the useful life of fixed assets is

[4] N.A.C.A. Research Study, "Practice in Applying Overhead and Calculating Normal Capacity," *N.A.C.A. Bulletin*, XIX, Brummet, *op. cit.*, p. 72.
[5] Brummet, *op. cit.*, p. 62.
[6] Each unit of output also has an equal variable cost allocation.
[7] One exception to this is under expected annual output as a measure of capacity wherein all fixed costs are allocated to actual output.

calculated in terms of years. Under the unit of production method the useful life of fixed assets is calculated on the basis of expected output during the time the fixed asset is expected to be used.[8] Fixed assets are purchased in order to produce units of product. Thus it seems quite reasonable to allocate fixed asset costs on the basis of units of product expected to be produced during the lifetime of the fixed asset.

Semi-variable cost inputs are to be allocated to actual output produced. Semi-variable cost inputs are costs that come in chunks. It is absolutely necessary to incur these "chunks" in order to obtain any output within the range of output serviced by the semi-variable cost inputs. These "chunks" are added when production reaches a certain level, and they are absolutely necessary to all output possibilities starting where the "chunk" is first added and ending at the point where it is necessary to add another "chunk." The salaries of all classes of supervisory personnel are good examples of semi-variable cost inputs or "chunk costs." Since these semi-variable cost inputs are absolutely necessary for production, they must all be considered costs of production no matter what output is within the range for which they are absolutely necessary.

On the basis of these semi-variable cost inputs, unit costs can and must vary with volume. For example, if the addition of one more supervisor yields the possibility of adequately supervising a range of outputs from the present output limit (in terms of adequate supervision) of 200,000 units to an output limit of 240,000 units, all the costs associated with the supervisor are costs of whatever output is produced within the 200,000–240,000 output range for which the supervisor is absolutely necessary. The supervisor must be acquired in his entirety for he is an indivisible cost input. The supervisor is as necessary for the first unit as he is for the 40,000th unit. If the added supervisor's salary is $8,000, the added supervisory costs per unit of output would have a range from $8,000 per unit for the first unit above 200,000 to $.20 per unit for the 40,000th unit above 200,000. The fluctuation in the added supervisory costs per unit within the 200,000–240,000 output range would certainly yield a total unit cost that would vary with volume.

If costs are absolutely necessary for production, they cannot be considered other than true costs of production and thus allocable to units produced. A system of accounting which will not allow unit costs figures to fluctuate on the basis of production volume and indivisible cost inputs is inaccurate. Such an accounting system takes the indefensible position of describing an absolutely necessary cost element as "waste" (an idle capacity loss).

Describing an absolutely necessary cost element as "waste" is a natural concomitant of those cost systems which will not allow unit costs to fluctuate with production volume. If the unit cost is stabilized at the top of the "chunk cost" output range (practical capacity), the cost per unit would be stabilized at its lowest possible level. If production is at any point in the output range below the top point, the justifiable increase in unit costs would not be allowed. The unit cost increase would be removed from production costs and classified as "waste" due to unutilized facilities in a strict physical sense (practical capacity).

If the unit cost is stabilized at an average of expected output within the "chunk cost" range (normal and cycle capacity), the cost per unit would be stabilized at an average unit cost level. If production is at any point above the average, the justifiable

---

[8] The calculability of unit-of-production depreciation will be considered in succeeding pages under "Some Objections Considered."

decrease in unit costs would not be allowed. The cost decrease would be removed from production costs and considered as a special gain under normal capacity and a deferred credit under cycle capacity. If production is at any point below the average, a justifiable unit cost increase would not be allowed. The cost increase would be removed from production costs and considered as a loss under normal capacity and a deferred charge under cycle capacity.

Thus, under any of the three capacity concepts an absolutely necessary cost of production could be considered as a loss due to unutilized capacity or as a deferred charge. Under normal and cycle capacity, when output is above average, unit costs would be stabilized at an inflated level. The inflated unit costs would be offset by the bookkeeping manipulation of a special gain or a deferred credit due to greater than average use of "chunk costs." It seems hardly necessary to restate that unit costs should be allowed to fluctuate on the basis of whatever output is achieved within the range for which "chunk costs" are absolutely necessary. None of the capacity concepts considers this possibility, and therefore all three concepts are in error. What are absolutely necessary costs of production cannot sensibly be considered otherwise.

The third category of overhead costs is essentially variable in nature. These costs are incurred only if there is production, and thus they should be allocated to units produced.

In the case of all three cost categories, costs are allocated to actual production, for it is actual production which gives rise to these costs. Note that the actual production basis is usable for depreciation because depreciation is recognized on a unit-of-production basis. Actual production is usable for semi-variable cost inputs

because the semi-variable cost inputs are absolutely necessary to produce actual output. Actual production is usable for the third cost category because of the variable nature of these costs.

The fact that it seems quite reasonable to allocate fixed asset costs on a unit-of-output basis plus the fact that both "chunk costs" and variable costs are absolutely necessary cost inputs gives rise to two conclusions, viz.

1) The threefold categorization of manufacturing overhead provides an excellent approach to the measure of income as it relates to overhead costs, and
2) Unit costs should be allowed to vary with volume within the confines of the chunk cost range of output.

These conclusions automatically repudiate the two basic assumptions inherent in the present-day treatment of manufacturing overhead as it relates to income measurement which are that a fixed-variable cost segregation is best for income measurement purposes and that unit costs should not be allowed to vary with volume.

Some Objections Considered

It would seem that there are three possible objections to the method of accounting for overhead costs recommended in the preceding pages. Objection one relates to the practicality of calculating depreciation on a unit-of-output basis. Objection two relates to the possibility of subjecting certain "chunk costs" (particularly supervisory salaries) to a unit-of-production cost amortization plan. Objection three relates to the direct costing ideology.

For those who claim that they use a normal capacity concept for allocating fixed overhead, there should be no problem in calculating unit-of-production depreciation. The normal capacity concept yields an excellent approximation to unit-of-production depreciation if under-and-overabsorbed straight-line depreciation are treated as adjustments of the allowance for depreciation or as deferred balance sheet items.

The normal overhead concept has been applied in actual practice.[9] In fact, one study (1948) by the National Association of Cost Accountants shows without doubt that the normal overhead concept was predominant in seventy-two industrial concerns. This predominance was revealed in the following quotation from the published report.

"The standard overhead rate is usually based upon a volume of production which is intended to provide for recovery of overhead costs over a period of years Used for costing production it avoids the disturbing effect of fluctuations in production volume which tend to increase unit costs in periods of low activity and to decrease unit costs in periods of high activity.[10]

There is no suggestion here that one should revert to a normal capacity concept. All that is suggested is that the average sales expectations of normal capacity can yield an approximation to unit-of-output depreciation if under-and-overabsorbed depreciation are treated as adjustments of the depreciation allowances or perhaps as deferred balance sheet items (in effect the cycle capacity concept).

The only costs that would be subject to the revised normal or cycle concept would be depreciation costs and possibly the taxes and insurance on depreciable property. The taxes and insurance on depreciable property are a part of the cost of utilizing equipment. In addition taxes and insurance are automatically incurred because of a fixed asset expenditure decision and thus it seems quite logical they should be amortized over the useful life of the fixed asset acquisitions.

The following illustration should show the similarity of the revised normal capacity concept (in effect the cycle capacity concept) and the unit of production

method of amortization. A single asset and depreciation costs will be used as the basis of the illustration.

Unit-of-Production Depreciation on a Single Asset

Cost (less salvage).................. $3,000
Expected output during five-year expected life..................... 150,000 Units
Depreciation cost per unit.......... $.02

Years	Output	Depreciation Charged to Product
1	20,000	$ 400
2	25,000	500
3	30,000	600
4	35,000	700
5	40,000	800
	150,000	$3,000

Cycle Capacity Applied to Depreciation Costs on a Single Asset

Cost (less salvage).................. $3,000
Useful life........................ 5 years
Depreciation per year.............. $ 600
Expected output during useful life..... 150,000 units
Average expected output per year (150,000 ÷ 5)..................... 30,000 units

Years	Actual Output	Ratio of Actual Output to Average Output	Depreciation per Year	Depreciation Charged to Product	Depreciation (under) or Overabsorbed
1	20,000	20/30	$ 600	$ 400	($200)
2	25,000	25/30	600	500	(100)
3	30,000	30/30	600	600	—0—
4	35,000	35/30	600	700	100
5	40,000	40/30	600	800	200
	150,000		$3,000	$3,000	—0—

As shown in the above illustrations, the amount of depreciation charged to production is the same in each year under the unit-of-production and the cycle capacity methods. An extension of the argument presented here from one fixed asset and

[9] N.A.C.A. Research Study, "Practice in Applying Overhead and Calculating Normal Capacity" *op. cit.*, p. 930.
N.A.C.A. Research Study, "Accounting for Excess Labor Costs and Overhead Under Conditions of Increased Production," *N.A.C.A. Bulletin*, XXII, Sec. 3 (August 15, 1941), pp. 1565-70.
[10] *How Standard Costs Are Being Used Currently*, (New York: National Association of Cost Accountants, 1950), p. 60.

depreciation costs to all fixed assets and insurance and taxes as well as depreciation is not difficult. All that is necessary is recognition of the fact that for purposes of expediency the cycle concept could not be applied to individual assets. The useful lives and expected actual outputs of individual fixed assets would have to be averaged for groups of fixed assets or for all fixed assets as a whole. This is not much different than what is done for all group or composite methods of depreciation used in financial accounting. In addition to the averaging, estimates of real property taxes and insurance on real property would have to be made.

Today in many business enterprises manufacturing facilities are leased rather than purchased. Thus a question arises concerning the allocation of lease rentals to output. Since the lease is only another way of acquiring the service utility of property, there should be no new problem here. A lease involves the acquisition of property with someone else's money rather than with the purchaser's money. The periodic payments on a lease can be regarded as regular installments paid for the total useful service potential of the property during the life of the lease. Thus the total lease payments can be added and divided by useful life in terms of units of output in order to yield a unit-of-production method of cost allocation for the lease costs. The unit-of-production method is defensible in the case of a lease, since a lease still represents the acquisition of the expected output use of an asset during the life of the lease. Of course, as an approximation to the unit-of-production amortization plan, the individual lease payments can be subjected to the cycle capacity concept in the same manner as straight-line depreciation.

An extension of the unit-of-output amortization plan (equivalent to the cycle capacity concept) for lease rentals can possibly be made to supervisory salaries.

Under an argument which states that supervisory salaries should be made subject to a unit-of-output amortization plan there is one implicit assumption, viz., salary payments are not given for services in the year or month paid, they are only periodic payments given as an installment on the total useful service potential of the supervisor. Such an assumption was accepted above for leasehold rentals, but it is difficult to use the same assumption for supervisory salaries or for any of the items identified as semi-variable cost inputs ("chunk costs"). Supervisors and other semi-variable cost inputs are paid for whatever usefulness they can render within the volume range for which they are necessary. Thus it is necessary to classify supervisory costs as semi-variable cost inputs and to accept the overhead cost categories presented in this paper.

If one were to accept the direct costing idea that only variable costs are to be considered costs of production, the ideas presented in this paper would certainly not be acceptable.[11] However, the advocates of direct costing who use economic marginalism and break-even analysis as the foundation of their arguments should remember that neither marginalism nor break-even analysis is a form of income measurement. Marginalism is a technique designed to concentrate on the strategic factors involved in the short-run price and output decisions of a firm. Break-even analysis is essentially a process which focuses attention on the strategic factors involved in short-run decision-making. Both marginalism and break-even analysis are short-run decision-making processes related to in-

---

[11] In one sense the ideas presented in this paper would be acceptable to direct costing enthusiasts. The conversion of fixed costs related to fixed assets into variable costs via a unit-of-output amortization plan would yield a sympathetic relationship between net income and sales, a goal of direct costing. However, there still remain varying unit costs due to indivisible cost inputs which would have a tendency to offset this greater sympathy between sales and net income.

come maximization, a far cry from income measurement which is a long-run concept. The lack of consideration given to fixed costs by marginalism and break-even analysis does not mean that fixed costs are *not costs* of production, it only means that fixed costs are *not relevant* to short-run decision-making.

The three possible objections to the accounting for overhead costs recommended in this paper are not valid. A unit-of-production method of depreciation is not easy to quantify. All that is recommended is that practitioners either make the attempt to quantify the unit-of-production method or use an approximation thereto. The approximation would be the revised normal or cycle overhead concept applied to depreciation and to insurance and taxes on depreciable property also. The normal overhead concept has been used in practice and thus an approximation to the unit-of-production method for depreciation is calculable on a practical basis. Supervisory costs as well as other "chunk costs" cannot logically be considered a form of lease rental so they must be considered as costs of producing whatever output is produced within the relevant volume range. Direct costing cannot be accepted for income

measurement purposes since it is directly opposed to the long-run implications of income measurement.

Summary

Income can be measured properly only when every attempt is made to segregate and allocate overhead costs to units of output so that costs of products may be matched or associated with the revenues derived from the sale of merchandise. To accomplish this task the generally accepted fixed-variable cost breakdown should be discarded for income measurement purposes. The straight-line amortization of costs associated with fixed assets should also be discarded. In place of straight-line amortization, a unit-of-output amortization plan or an approximation thereto should be used. The approximation would be the cycle overhead concept. The fixed cost portion of semi-variable cost inputs should be reassociated with their variable counterparts and then allocated to the output for which they were absolutely necessary elements of production. Finally, unit costs should be allowed to fluctuate with volume within the range for which semi-variable cost inputs are absolutely necessary costs of production.

Dysfunctional Consequences of Performance Measurements

V.F. RIDGWAY
California State University, Sacramento

Although quantitative measures of performance are undoubtedly useful, their behavioral side effects should be carefully considered to gauge their net benefits. The consequences of using single, multiple, and composite criteria for performance measurement are examined. Each of these three types of criteria can lead to undesirable consequences for overall organizational performance. Further research is required if we are to understand the motivational potentials of various performance measurement systems.

There is today a strong tendency to state numerically as many as possible of the variables with which management must deal. The mounting interest in and application of tools, such as operations research, linear programming, and statistical decision making, all of which require quantifiable variables, foster the idea that if progress toward goals can be measured, efforts and resources can be more rationally managed. This has led to the development of quantitative performance measurements for all levels within organizations, up to and including measurements of the performance of a division manager with profit responsibility in a decentralized company. Measurements at lower levels in the organization may be in terms of amount of work, quality of work, time required, and so on.

Quantitative measures of performance are tools, and are undoubtedly useful. But research indicates that indiscriminate use and undue confidence and reliance in them result from insufficient knowledge of the full effects and consequences. Judicious use of a tool requires awareness of possible side effects and reactions. Otherwise, indiscriminate use may result in side effects and reactions outweighing the benefits, as was the case when penicillin was first hailed as a wonder drug. The cure is sometimes worse than the disease.

It seems worthwhile to review the current scattered knowledge of the dysfunctional consequences resulting from the imposition of a system of performance measurements. For the purpose of analyzing the impact of performance measurements upon job performance, we can consider separately single, multiple, and composite criteria. Single criteria occur when only one quantity is measured and observed, such as total output or profit. Multiple criteria occur when several quantities are measured simultaneously, such as output, quality, cost, safety, waste, and so forth. Composite criteria occur when the separate quantities are weighted in some fashion and then added or averaged.

SINGLE CRITERIA

A single criterion of performance was in use in a public employment agency studied by Peter M. Blau.[1] The agency's responsibility was "to serve workers seeking employment and employers seeking workers." Employment interviewers were appraised by the number of interviews they conducted. Thus the interviewer was motivated to complete as many interviews as he could, but not to spend adequate time in locating jobs for the clients. The organization's goal of placing clients in jobs was not given primary consideration because the measurement device applied to only one aspect of the activity.

Blau reports another case in a federal law enforcement agency which investigated business establishments. Here he found that work schedules were distorted by the imposition of a quota of eight cases per month for each investigator. Toward the end of the month an investigator who found himself short of the eight cases would pick easy, fast cases to finish that month and save the lengthier cases till the following month. Priority of the cases of investigation was based on length of the case rather than urgency, as standards of impartiality would require. This is one of many instances in which the existence of an "accounting period" adversely affects the overall goal accomplishment of the organization.

Chris Argyris also reports this tendency to use easy jobs as fillers toward the end of a period in order to meet a quota.[2] In this case, a factory supervisor reported that they "feed the machines all the easy orders" toward the end of the month, rather than finish them in the sequence in which they were received. Such a practice may lead to undue delay of the delivery of some customers' orders, perhaps the most profitable orders.

David Granick's study of Soviet management reveals how the attention and glory that accrue to a plant manager when he can set a new monthly production record in one month lead to the neglect of repairs and maintenance, so that in ensuing months there will be a distinct drop in production.[3] Similarly, the output of an entire plant may be allowed to fall off in order to create conditions under which one worker can make a production record, when the importance of such a record is considered greater than overall plant production.

Joseph S. Berliner's report on Soviet business administration points out sharply how the accounting period has an adverse effect upon management decisions.[4] The use of monthly production quotas causes "storming" at the end of the month to reach the quota. Repairs and maintenance are postponed until the following month, so that production lags in the early part of the month, and storming must again be resorted to in the following month. This has impact upon the rate of production for suppliers and customers who are forced into a fluctuating rate of operations with its attendant losses and wastes.

Standard costs as a criterion of performance is a frequent source of dissatisfaction in manufacturing plants.[5] The "lumpiness" of indirect charges that are allocated to the plants or divisions (indirect charges being unequal from month to month), varia-

---

[1] Peter M. Blau, *The Dynamics of Bureaucracy* (Chicago: University of Chicago Press, 1955).

[2] Chris Argyris, *The Impact of Budgets on People* (New York: Controllership Foundation, 1952).

[3] David Granick, *Management of the Industrial Firm in the U.S.S.R.* (New York: Columbia University Press, 1954).

[4] Joseph S. Berliner, "A Problem in Soviet Business Management," *Administrative Sicence Quarterly*, 1 (1956), 86–101.

[5] H. A. Simon, H. Guetzkow, G. Kosmetsky, G. Tyndall, *Centralization vs. Decentralization in Organizing the Controller's Department* (New York: Controllership Foundation, 1954).

tions in quality and cost of raw materials, or other factors beyond the control of the operating manager, coupled with inaccuracies and errors in the apportionment of indirect charges, cause distrust of the standards. A typical reaction of operating executives in such cases seems to be to seek explanations and justifications. Consequently, considerable time and energy is expended in discussion and debate about the correctness of charges. Only "wooden money" savings accrue when charges are shifted to other accounts, and there is no increase in company profits. It should be pointed out, however, that having charges applied to the proper departments may have the advantage of more correctly directing attention to problem areas.

Granick discusses two measures of the success of the Soviet firm which have been considered and rejected as overall measures by Soviet industrial leaders and economists.[6] The first, cost reduction per unit of product, is considered inadequate because it does not provide a basis for evaluating new products. Further, variations in amount of production affect the cost reduction index because of the finer division of overhead costs, quality changes, and assortment. The second overall measure of a firm's performance, profitability, has been rejected as the basic criterion on the grounds that it is affected in the short run by factors outside the control of management, such as shortages of supplies. Profitability as a measure of success led to a reduction in experimental work and deemphasized the importance of production quantity, quality, and assortment. Neither cost reduction nor profitability was acceptable alone; each was only a partial index. The Soviets had concluded by 1940 that no single measure of success of a firm is adequate in itself and that there is no substitute for genuine analysis of all the elements entering into a firm's work.

Difficulties with single criteria have been observed in operations research, where one of the principal sources of difficulty is considered to be the choice of proper criteria for performance measurement.[7] The difficulty of translating the several alternatives in their full effect upon the organization's goal forces the operations researcher to settle for a criterion more manageable than profit maximization, but less appropriate. The efficiency of a subgroup of the organization may be improved in terms of some plausible test, yet the organization's efficiency in terms of its major goal may be decreased.

In all the studies mentioned above, the inadequacy of a single measure of performance is evident. Whether this is a measure of an employee at the work level or a measure of management, attention is directed away from the overall goal. The existence of a measure of performance motivates individuals to effort, but the effort may be wasted, as in seeking "wooden money" savings or may be detrimental to the organization's goal, as in rushing through interviews, delaying repairs, and rejecting profitable opportunities.

MULTIPLE MEASUREMENTS

Recognition of the inadequacies of a single measure of success or performance leads organizations to develop several criteria. It is felt then that all aspects of the job will receive adequate attention and emphasis, so that efforts of individuals will not be distorted.

A realization in the employment office studied by Blau that job referrals and placements were also important led eventually to their inclusion in measuring the per-

[6] Granick, *op. cit.*

[7] Charles Hitch and Roland McKean, "Suboptimization in Operations Problems," in *Operations Research for Management*, ed. J. F. McCloskey and Flora F. Trefethen (Baltimore: Johns Hopkins Press, 1954).

formance of the interviewers.[8]   Merely counting the number of referrals and placements had led to wholesale indiscriminate referrals, which did not accomplish the employment agency's screening function.   Therefore, to stress the qualitative aspects of the interviewer's job, several ratios (of referrals to interviews, placements to interviews, and placements to referrals) were devised.   Altogether there were eight quantities that were counted or calculated for each interviewer.   This increase in quantity and complexity of performance measurements was felt necessary to give emphasis to all aspects of the interviewer's job.

Granick relates that no single criterion was universally adopted in appraising Soviet management.[9]   Some managers were acclaimed for satisfying production quotas while violating labor laws.   Others were removed from office for violating quality and assortment plans while fulfilling production quotas.   Apparently there is a ranking of importance of these multiple criteria.   In a typical interfirm competition, the judges were provided with a long list of indexes.   These included production of finished goods in the planned assortment, an even flow of production as between different ten-day periods and as between months, planned mastery of new types of products, improvement in product quality and reduction in waste, economy of materials through improved design, and changing of technological processes, fulfillment of labor productivity tasks, and lowering of unit cost, keeping within the established wage fund, and increase in the number of worker suggestions for improvements in work methods and conditions and their adoption into operation.   But no indication of how these indexes should be weighted was given.   The pre-eminence of such indexes as quantity, quality, assortment of production, and remaining within the firm's allotment of materials and fuels, brought some order into the otherwise chaotic picture. The presence of "campaigns" and "priorities" stressing one or more factors also has aided Soviet management in deciding which elements of its work are at the moment most important.

Without a single overall composite measure of success, however, there is no way of determining whether the temporarily increased effort on the "campaign" criteria of the month represents new effort or merely effort shifted from other criteria. And the intangibility of some of these indexes makes it impossible to judge whether there has been decreased effort on other aspects. Hence even in a campaign period the relative emphases may become so unbalanced as to mitigate or defeat the purpose of the campaign.

The Soviet manager is working then under several measurements, and the relative influence or emphasis attached to any one measurement varies from firm to firm and from month to month. Profits and production are used, among other measurements, and these two may lead to contradictory managerial decisions. Granick hypothesizes that some managers have refused complicated orders that were difficult to produce because it would mean failure to produce the planned quantities. Acceptance of these orders would have been very profitable, but of the two criteria, production quantity took precedence.

Numerous American writers in the field of management have stressed the importance of mulitple criteria in evaluating performance of management. Peter Drucker, for example, lists market standing, innovation, productivity, physical and financial resources, profitability, manager performance and development, worker performance and attitude, and public responsibility.[10] This list includes many of the same items as the list used by Soviet management.

[8] Blau, *op. cit.*

[9] Granick, *op. cit.*

[10] Peter M. Drucker, *The Practice of Management* (New York: Harper & Row, 1954).

The consensus at a round-table discussion of business and professional men[11] was that although return on investment is important, additional criteria are essential for an adequate appraisal of operating departments. These other criteria are fairly well summed up in Drucker's list above.

Thus we see that the need for multiple criteria is recognized and that they are employed at different levels of the organization—lower levels as in the employment agency, higher levels as considered by Granick and Drucker. At all levels these multiple measurements or criteria are intended to focus attention on the many facets of a particular job.

The use of multiple criteria assumes that the individual will commit his or the organization's efforts, attention, and resources in greater measure to those activities which promise to contribute the greatest improvement to overall performance. There must then exist a theoretical condition under which an additional unit of effort or resources would yield equally desirable results in overall performance, whether applied to production, quality, research, safety, public relations, or any of the other suggested areas. This would be the condition of "balanced stress on objectives" to which Drucker refers.

Without a single overall composite measure of performance, the individual is forced to rely upon his judgment as to whether increased effort on one criterion improves overall performance, or whether there may be a reduction in performance on some other criterion which will outweigh the increase in the first. This is quite possible, for in any immediate situation many of these objectives may be contradictory to each other.

COMPOSITES

To adequately balance the stress on the contradictory objectives or criteria by which performance of a particular individual or organization is appraised, there must be an implied or explicit weighting of these criteria. When such a weighting system is available, it is an easy task to combine the measures of the various subgoals into a composite score for overall performance.

Such a composite is used by the American Institute of Management in evaluating and ranking the managements of corporations, hospitals, and other organizations.[12] These ratings are accomplished by attaching a numerical grade to each of several criteria, such as economic function, corporate structure, production efficiency, and the like. Each criterion has an optimum rating, and the score on each for any particular organization is added to obtain a total score. Although there may be disagreement on the validity of the weighting system employed, the rating given on any particular category, the categories themselves, or the methods of estimating scores in the A.I.M. management audit, this system is an example of the type of overall performance measurement which might be developed. Were such a system of ratings employed by an organization and found acceptable by management, it presumably would serve as a guide to obtaining a balanced stress on objectives.

A composite measure of performance was employed in Air Force wings as reported by K. C. Wagner.[13] A complex rating scheme covering a wide range of activities

[11]William H. Newman and James P. Logan, *Management of Expanding Enterprises* (New York: Columbia University Press, 1955).

[12]*Manual of Excellent Managements* (New York, 1955).

[13]Kenneth C. Wagner, "Latent Functions of an Executive Control: A Sociological Analysis of a Social System under Stress," *Research Previews*, Vol. 2 (Chapel Hill, N.C.: Institute for Research in Social Science, March 1954), mimeo.

was used. When the organizations were put under pressure to raise their composite score without proportionate increases in the organization's means of achieving them, there were observable unanticipated consequences in the squadrons. Under a system of multiple criteria, pressure to increase performance on one criterion might be relieved by a slackening of effort toward other criteria. But with a composite criterion this does not seem as likely to occur. In Wagner's report individuals were subjected to tension, role and value conflicts, and reduced morale; air crews suffered from inter-crew antagonism, apathy, and reduced morale; organization and power structures underwent changes; communications distortions and blockages occurred; integration decreased; culture patterns changed, and norms were violated. Some of these consequences may be desirable, some undesirable. The net result, however, might easily be less effective overall performance.

These consequences were observable in a situation where goals were increased without a corresponding increase in means, which seems to be a common situation. Berliner refers to the "ratchet principle" wherein an increase in performance becomes the new standard, and the standard is thus continually raised. Recognition of the operation of the "ratchet principle" by workers was documented by F. J. Roethlisberger and William J. Dickson.[14] There was a tacit agreement among the workers not to exceed the quota, for fear that the job would then be rerated. Deliberate restriction of output is not an uncommon occurrence.

Although the experiences reported with the use of composite measures of performance are rather skimpy, there is still a clear indication that their use may have adverse consequences for the overall performance of the organization.

CONCLUSION

Quantitative performance measurements—whether single, multiple, or composite—are seen to have undesirable consequences for overall organizational performance. The complexity of large organizations requires better knowledge of organizational behavior for managers to make best use of the personnel available to them. Even where performance measures are instituted purely for purposes of information, they are probably interpreted as definitions of the important aspects of that job or activity and, hence, have important implications for the motivation of behavior. The motivational and behavioral consequences of performance measurements are inadequately understood. Further research in this area is necessary for a better understanding of how behavior may be oriented toward optimum accomplishment of the organization's goals.

[14]F. J. Roethlisberger and William J. Dickson, *Management and the Worker* (Cambridge, Mass.: Harvard University Press, 1939).

Motivational Considerations in Cost Allocation Systems: A Conditioning Theory Approach

GEORGE BODNAR
Dusquesne University

EDWARD J. LUSK
University of Pennsylvania

ABSTRACT: A basic question is how cost allocations may be used to motivate. This research addresses this question in terms of a specific behavioral theory. The basic components of cost allocation are provided for in a programming format which structures the parameters necessary for conditioning. The model is used to generate allocations in a manner sensitive to organizational behavioral considerations. The proposed model functions as a control technique in the sense that it may be used to reinforce selected behavior.

THE evaluative focus of most organizational control systems is on the management of the institution's financial resources. However, controlling on only one aspect of institutional performance often results in dysfunctional decisions [Caplan, 1971; Dalton and Lawrence, 1917]. Therefore, important managerial accounting problems found in both the private and public sectors are (1) how to select nonmonetary performance measures and (2) how to integrate them into the organizational control system.

Conceptually, the problems are straightforward. The accountant must select one of the established financial accounting systems and modify it so that subunit performance as it affects non-financial performance evaluation also is reflected in the financial accounting system. A financial accounting system available for such modification is the cost allocation system, in particular the allocation of joint costs. The accountant may view cost allocation from the standpoint of providing management control data and/or expense measurement [Vatter, 1945]. These perspectives may conflict. As a consequence, selection of cost allocation criteria and, hence, selection of the bases by which costs may be allocated should be approached with concern for the motivational dimension present in any allocation which affects financial performance.

The authors' interest in this subject arose attendant to the implementation of a responsibility accounting system at a university. The treatment of joint costs was an important issue in the design of the university's responsibility accounting system. Two problems which confronted the university were: (1) choosing a set of criteria for cost allocation and (2) treating nonfinancial considerations within a financial-based control system.

327

The university required an accounting procedure that would satisfy the requirements for allocation, but would do so considering the behavioral sensitivities involved. This paper suggests a process by which cost allocation systems may be made responsive to the behavioral dimension of organizational control.

A Critique of Allocation Models

Attempts to refine the traditional approach to cost allocation are numerous and varied. Some deal with the computational aspects of allocation [for example, Churchill, 1964; Williams and Griffin, 1964; Livingstone, 1965; and Manes, 1965]. The works of these authors consider cost allocation problems ex post; given a matrix of allocation coefficients (a summarized presentation of the previously selected allocation bases), the various models seek a computationally efficient way of determining particular allocations. The technique commonly used in these approaches is matrix algebra.

An alternative approach to cost allocation problems deals with the development of allocation models ex ante so as to predictably affect the behavior of the subunit's management. This class of models focuses on financial planning. These models are formulated in terms of profit maximization and differ mainly in the nature of solution algorithms.

Models based on linear programming have been suggested by Ijiri, Levy and Lyon [1963], Samuels [1965] and Kaplan and Thompson [1971]. The Ijiri, Levy, Lyon model considers all joint costs as period costs; accordingly, there is no attempt to allocate joint costs within their model. Criticism of this approach centers on the effect of joint costs on the optimal solution. The Kaplan-Thompson model develops a procedure to reconcile the differences between direct and full costing by presenting an allocation method that allocates joint costs (to satisfy full costing) but does so in such a manner that the relative profitability of products is not distorted (to satisfy direct costing). The basic scheme is to charge overhead to products on the basis of their utilization of scarce resources. The information necessary to accomplish this allocation is extracted from the dual solution to the primal programming problem.

Samuels develops an allocation procedure based on opportunity cost that is similar to the procedures suggested by Kaplan and Thompson. Samuels' approach differs in that he does not reformulate the initial program to incorporate information from the dual solution; rather, he proceeds directly from the dual solution to an allocation of the joint costs. The fundamental difference between Samuels' and Kaplan and Thompson's approach is that the Samuels model incorporates charges for lost opportunities (measured by the shadow prices of the optimal solution), while the Kaplan and Thompson model is concerned with allocating actual overhead to the products on the basis of the shadow prices of the optimal solution.

Except for Colantoni, Manes and Whinston [1969], all the models mentioned assume conditions of perfect competition. In practice, this assumption is rarely reasonable; thus, prices are usually determined by the firm. Programming models of the type developed by Colantoni et al. consider the role of joint costs in several contexts. However, as the conditions of the problem become more realistic, the models must become so complex as to limit their implementation. In addition, these approaches have failed to consider explicitly behavioral factors in the cost allocation process.

Several authors [Anthony, 1970, Horn-

328

gren, 1972] discuss behavioral issues in terms of specific examples, such as the allocation of maintenance costs but always conclude, "It depends"; the behavioral issue usually is ignored in the literature. For example, in stressing the theoretical decision-making aspects of the problem, Shubik [1960] assumes away the psychological aspects. Such approaches fail to recognize that control involves individual decision makers, and their behavioral sensitivities cannot be assumed away realistically.

CONDITIONING THEORY APPLIED TO COST ALLOCATIONS[1]

Behavior in organizations is determined largely by the relationship between actions and outcomes [Nord, 1969]. Important aspects of behavior can be attributed to the immediate environment within which individuals function; the potential exists to structure and restructure formal organizations in a manner to promote desired behavior [Bariff and Lusk, 1977]. In the terminology of operant conditioning, a control technique will be effective if it reinforces desired outcomes. Thus, control involves the manipulation of reinforcement contingencies available to the organization. According to Nord [1969, p. 398]:

> If you want a certain response and it does not occur, you had better change the reinforcement contingencies to increase its probable occurrence. The first step in the direction of designing organizations on this basis involves defining explicitly the desired behaviors and the available reinforcers. The next step is to then make these rewards dependent on the emission of the desired responses.

The task is then to recognize that cost allocations may be useful as a reinforcer within a responsibility accounting system. We suggest that the allocation base selection decision be made contingent on subunit activity judged as it affects the nonfinancial organizational goals. While pragmatic measurement considerations usually make the selection of allocation bases arbitrary, if allocations of joint costs are to be made, bases must nontheless be selected. From a costing perspective, this decision is the choice of a particular allocation mode within a range of acceptable cost assignments. It is important to note that the set of allocation bases itself results from management's behavioral disposition.

For instance, in considering the allocation of a central library's costs to schools within the university, the administration may suggest the following bases: number of students, number of faculty, a distribution of books purchased by school, usage records kept by the library, flat percentages and proration on direct costs, among others. Each of these allocation bases is defensible in that it has some logical relationship to the costs of operating a library. In practice, the length to which one may go to establish such logical relationships is, itself, somewhat arbitrary. There are alternatives which one probably would not consider in this case, such as square footage per school on courses taught per school, although one would likely consider these for other cost allocations. The selection of an allocation basis usually is rationalized by appealing to some selection criterion such as "fairness" or "ability to bear." The subjective nature of such criteria are well known.

We suggest that selection of an allocation base affords a unique opportunity to formally structure motivational considerations into the organization's control system. What is required is to integrate the effect of subunit activity on

[1] The authors refer the interested reader to the following operant conditioning literature: Glaser and Klaus [1966], Marx [1970] and Glaser [1971].

329

various nonfinancial measures of performance into the financial reporting system. Specifically, subunit activity would be evaluated as it affects particular nonfinancial measures of performance; this evaluation then generates the cost allocation scheme.

We suggest that management would a priori specify a set of performance measures, a set of bases for cost allocation and an allocation criteria functional, such as fairness or ability to bear. During the period, data concerning performance and activity relative to the set of allocation bases would be accumulated. Alternative cost allocations then would be generated based on activity statistics. The specific allocation scheme would be selected ex post based on a review of subunit performance relative to the allocation criteria functional.

In terms of the operant conditioning paradigm:

1. The operant is defined as a set of nonfinancial performance measures.
2. Management specifies a set of possible cost allocation bases and an allocation criterion functional.
3. The response rate (periodic performance measurement) is determined by an ex post analysis of activity relative to the operant measures.
4. Management evaluates the subunits' responses relative to the criterion functional thereby effecting a particular allocation.
5. The resulting allocations are feedback to the subunits' management, which then assesses the relation between their behavior and their financial environment, that is, conditioned learning.

FIGURE 1
COST ALLOCATION BASED UPON THE OPERANT CONDITIONING PARADIGM

I. *Ex Ante*
  1. Managerial specification of possible allocation bases: Note these bases as:

$$\{B_1, B_2, \cdots, B_h\}$$

  2. Managerial specification of the m criteria used to evaluate subunit performance: Note the ith criterion as C_i.

$$\text{The Operant} \equiv \{C_1, C_2, \cdots, C_m\}$$

  3. Management specifies a cost allocation criteria functional: Note this functional as Z.

- -

  Performance: Note subunit performance (response) as Φ_i for the ith subunit.
     : *Financial* performance is taken to mean revenue less all costs except for allocated joint costs.

- -

II. *Ex Post*
  1. Evaluation of subunit performance on the m a priori criteria which generates the following matrix:

$$P = \begin{bmatrix} P_1^1 & P_2^1 & P_3^1, \cdots, P_m^1 \\ P_1^2 & P_2^2 & P_3^2, \cdots, P_m^2 \\ \vdots & & & \vdots \\ P_1^k & P_2^k & P_3^k, \cdots, P_m^k \end{bmatrix}$$

where: P_j^k represents the evaluation of the performance of the kth subunit on the jth (C_j) evaluation criteria: $P_j^k = \Phi_k(C_j)$

  2. If appropriate, P may be used to determine the specific weighting of the allocation criterion functional Z.
  3. Given the allocation bases $\{B_1, B_2, \cdots, B_h\}$ and Z, management determines a particular allocation scheme and allocates joint costs which then finally determines the subunits *financial* performance.
  4. Subunit managerial analysis and systems learning then occur (The Operant Conditioning Paradigm).

330

This process then is intended to signal a relationship between the financial control system and nonfinancial aspects of performance. (See Figure 1).

Jablonsky and DeVries [1972] have argued that behavioral change in an organization is more probable if multiple sources of contingencies all reinforce similar responses. The allocation procedure suggested here is desirable as it established contingencies which, given the operant conditioning paradigm, are consistent with the overall control process. Subunit activity is evaluated relative to nonfinancial goals; therefore, reinforced directly through the cost allocation process (that is, the financial dimension). In addition, reinforcement occurs by evaluating subunit activity as it affects the nonfinancial evaluation criteria. By entering nonfinancial performance criteria into the financial control process, one subjects such activities to multiple sources of reinforcement. The additional set of reinforcement contingencies derived through cost allocations strengthen the class of responses elicited and bring these responses under the control of a stimulus. The stimulus (the allocation procedure) does not elicit responses as a reflex; it merely sets the environment within which the response is more likely to occur in the *next* evaluation period. This, of course, assumes that subunit financial performance is evaluated and either rewarded or sanctioned as is appropriate.

AN EXAMPLE: A UNIVERSITY

The following example indicates how the basic components of the operant conditioning paradigm are structured to affect subunit cost allocations. The model used is goal programming [Lusk and Bodnar, 1973]. We shall assume the organization is structured on a responsibility accounting system, that there are one or more classes of joint costs and that there is an *a priori* set of alternative allocation bases for each class of joint costs.

Assume that the educational institution is composed of a central administration and three colleges. The administration has decided to allocate joint costs and is considering three different allocation bases. Table 1 shows the allocation bases under consideration and the base statistics associated with each college:

TABLE 1

BASE STATISTICS FOR THREE ALLOCATION BASES

College	Number of Faculty (Base 1)	Number of Major Students (Base 2)	Course Units Taught (Base 3)
1	14	50	125
2	10	30	100
3	6	20	75
Total	30	100	300

Table 2 summarizes the development of the cost allocations, using $600 as the period's joint cost to be allocated.

TABLE 2

POSSIBLE COST ALLOCATIONS

College	Number of Faculty (Base 1)	Number of Major Students (Base 2)	Course Units Taught (Base 3)
1	$280	$300	$250
2	200	180	200
3	120	120	150
Total	$600	$600	$600

We further assume that the institution uses the most common form of responsibility center report, an income statement.

After the activity for the period *but* prior to the allocation of joint cost, each school has a net revenue of $200. The above data may be structured as the constraint set to a goal programming model as follows:

$$200 - .E_i + Y_i^+ - Y_i^- = 0 \quad (1)$$

$$280X_{11} + 300X_{12} + 250X_{13} = E_1$$
$$200X_{21} + 180X_{22} + 200X_{23} = E_2 \quad (2)$$
$$120X_{31} + 120X_{32} + 150X_{33} = E_3$$

$$\sum_{j=1}^{3} X_{ij} = 1 \quad (3)$$

$$\sum_{i=1}^{3} E_i = 600 \quad (4)$$

$$Y_i, E_i, X_{ij} \geq 0, \forall_{i,j}$$

where:

E_i represents the joint cost assigned to the ith subunit;

Y_i^+ the underachievement (loss) of the ith college;

Y_i^- the overachievement (income) of the ith college;

X_{ij} the cost allocated to the ith college from the jth base.

These base statistics form a solution space of feasible cost assignments. Equation (1) is an algebraic representation of income statements for the subunits. Equations (2) identify potential cost assignment to the ith subunit (E_i). Equations (3) and (4) constrain the solution to entirely allocate the joint costs.

The university administrator (or accountant) now faces the problem of selecting a particular base (or combination of bases) to be used in the subunit performance report (net income statement). In a programming format, this is equivalent to the construction of a functional. Bodnar [1975] uses this example to show how several allocation criteria may be operationally defined as func-

tionals and how they may be used to effect allocation schemes.

For example, consider the fairness criterion. Fairness may be defined operationally as the minimization of total absolute deviations from breakeven. Under this criterion, one would attain an "equitable" allocation in the sense that all deviations are valued equally. The formulation of this "fairness" functional is:

$$\text{Min } Z = Y_1^+ + Y_1^- + Y_2^+ + Y_2^-$$
$$+ Y_3^+ + Y_3^-.$$

Using this functional, the programming solution of the problem (that is, Min Z given Equations 1, 2, 3 and 4) is:

$$X_{13} = X_{23} = X_{33} = 1$$
$$Y_1^+ = 50, Y_3^- = 50$$
$$E_1 = 250, E_2 = 200, E_3 = 150$$

All the other program variables are equal to zero.

The program indicates that Base 3, course units taught, would best conform to the breakeven goal, for example, better than Base 1 or Base 2, under the fairness criterion.[2] Given course units taught as the allocation system for joint cost, the following subunit income statements are generated:

	College		
	1	*2*	*3*
Net Revenue	$200	$200	$200
Indirect Cost Allocated (E_i)	250	200	150
Subunit Income	$(50)	$-0-	$ 50

[2] This simple illustration results in a single allocation base. In more complex examples, multiple bases may result. Given the programming formulation of the problem, multiple bases are integrated easily into the analysis, and equation set (4) ensures that overhead allocations are allocated precisely that is, that they are not over- or underabsorbed.

332

Sensitizing the Cost Allocation to Behavioral Considerations

Since the goal-programming functional may be altered (weighted and re-weighted), one may modify the selected functional so as to establish the operant environment in recognition of the appropriate behavioral sensitivities. We shall adopt the term "behavioral weighting" to mean the assignment of pre-emptive priority factors. This is a concept which was introduced and used in goal-programming models by Ijiri [1965, pp. 110–113] to weight elements in the functional.

Consider further the case of a university preparing responsibility reports for its colleges. Table 3 presents some nonfinancial performance indicators for colleges within a university.

TABLE 3

PERFORMANCE INDICATORS IN A UNIVERSITY SETTING

Goal Measures	Surrogate Representative of Organizational Goal
Degrees granted	Knowledge dissemination
Current publications	Contribution to professional literature
Number of research grants	External recognition of the faculty's ability to do research
Credit hours taught	School workload—courses offered
National school ratings	Quality of school
Public seminars, etc. presented	Public service
Credit hours per terminated student	Student time invested without receiving a degree

If the university desires to increase and promote knowledge, a college's publication record may be deemed a reasonable surrogate to measure congruency with this goal. Although one cannot strictly commeasure publications in different fields of knowledge, one may rank schools on the basis of publication records, per-haps best by converting the quantity measure to a unit (an "efficiency") measure. Assuming that this is done, one then may assign behavioral weights to reflect this ranking, modify the functional of the model and, hence, influence the cost allocations with nonfinancial considerations.

Assume that the administration assigns behavioral weights on the basis of each college's publication record for the period under consideration. The operational data and, hence, the constraint set of the original model are unchanged. Table 4 presents hypothetical publication data from which the behavioral weights are to be assigned:

TABLE 4

HYPOTHETICAL PUBLICATION DATA

College	Items Accepted for Publication during the Period	Number of Faculty	Publications per Faculty Member
1	3	14	.21
2	4	10	.40
3	3	6	.50

Behavioral weights P_i are assigned by management on the basis of publications per faculty member—the higher the ranking, the lower the weight.[3] With this data, College 3 would be assigned the lowest weighting factor. The behaviorally weighted functional may appear as:

$$\text{Min } Z = -(P_3 Y_1^- - P_3 Y_1^+ + P_2 Y_2^- \\ - P_2 Y_2^+ + P_1 Y_3^- - P_1 Y_3^+)$$

where:

$$P_1 > P_2 > P_3.$$

[3] There is nothing fundamental about making the behavioral weights inverse relative to a subunit's performance on the selected evaluation criteria. Clearly, it is a Darwinian approach; more humanistic weighting schemes may be selected. This, again, is a matter of choice which must enter into the selection process.

333

With this functional, the solution is to select Base 2, number of major students, as the allocation scheme. The assignment of behavioral weights alters the solution generated; Base 2 is selected as opposed to Base 3. The resulting allocation yields the following income statements:

	College		
	1	*2*	*3*
Net Revenue	$200	$200	$200
Indirect Cost Allocated (E_i)	300	180	120
Subunit Income	$(100)	$ 20	$ 80

BEHAVIORAL RATIONALE: PERFORMANCE CONDITIONING

The responses of interest to management are those subunit activities which result in goal attainment, that is, periodic performance; the "organism" is the decentralized subunit. In the university example, items such as publications, degrees granted and public seminars are subunit activities that are presumed to relate to university goals. These activities are ongoing and exist naturally in a university environment, that is, they are not contrived for purposes of assignment only. From the university's standpoint, the relative priority of these activities may vary over time. By assigning behavioral weights on the basis of these activities, management establishes a priority scheme which, when reflected in cost assignments to the subunits, will tend to reinforce the strength of these various performance responses from the colleges.

Although publications and degrees among schools are topologically different, this need not be a concern in defining the operant, which is defined as a class of responses upon which reinforcement is contingent. For a university, the operant would be identified as a group of activities which affect various quantitative measures that relate to university goals, such as "number of publications" or "number of degrees granted."

Empirically, reinforcement refers to any conditions introduced into a particular environment to increase the probability that a given response will reoccur. The allocation procedure, in particular the process of behavioral weighting, should be reinforcing in that it systematically affects the financial environment of subunits. Therefore, nonfinancial performance which was previously neutral with respect to both the allocation process and the financial control system becomes associated with the subunit's financial environment. Goal measures as included in the operant acquire a capacity to signal the occasion of financial reinforcement.

In the operant conditioning framework, the reinforcement schedule is important as it affects systematic behavior. We consider the suggested allocation process as a fixed interval variable ratio reinforcer. The interval depends upon the number of subunit reporting periods. While the timing is fixed (the length of the reporting period), the reinforcement magnitude is variable since reinforcement is dependent on the subunits' performance as weighted relative to overall subunit performance. Allocations are derived from a combination of both operational and behavioral considerations. Operational considerations determine the constraint set, the set of operationally feasible, that is, noncapricious, cost assignments. Behavioral weightings provide a figure of merit for generating an allocation scheme that is sensitive to overall organizational considerations. The interactions between these two dimensions ensure that the perceived reinforcement schedule will be variable ratio in nature.

The appropriateness of behavioral weighting depends on one's assumptions concerning behavior in an organization. In the operant conditioning framework, behavioral weighting structures an additional source of reinforcement contingencies. Traditional cost allocation under a responsibility accounting system structures a set of reinforcement contingencies which are generally insensitive to and, hence, do not serve to reinforce subunit performance relative to nonfinancial goal measures. In excluding nonfinancial considerations, traditional allocation is potentially dysfunctional *as a control procedure.*

Behavioral weighting structures and, theoretically, promotes a learning situation in which subunit performance is conditioned in the responsibility accounting cycle through the allocation procedure. Over time the subunit "learns" that performance measures which define the operant influence the financial environment. Activities which are not included in the definition of the operant do not directly affect the subunit's financial environment. Conditioning theory suggests that the reinforced activities will be strengthened over time. Given the dominant and objective features of financial control, behavioral modification is likely.

NEGOTIATION VERSUS CENTRALIZATION OF THE BEHAVIORAL WEIGHTING PROCESS

The derivation of the behavioral weights is a most complex task. Even though our purpose is not to suggest a process for derivation of the specific behavioral weights, we wish to note that the set of allocation bases to be specified should result from management interchange and negotiation. Although negotiation a priori would seem to increase the probability of ultimate acceptance of a particular allocation scheme, establishing the behavioral weights (See Lusk [1977]), by negotiation is another matter.

The complexities in formalizing a behavioral weighting arise from the recognition that a negotiated weighting would be taken as the explicit recognition of the organizational priority scheme. Given the usual complex organizational implications of decentrally formalizing a preemptive priority weighting, it is suggested that the priority rankings be done centrally.

It is presumed that central management best understands the behavioral disposition of the decentralized decision makers and the desired expansion path of the organization. Further, since communication of the weighting scheme may alter the reinforcement contingencies to a point where it would be possible for a subunit to perceive the reinforcement schedule, that schedule may lose its desirable variable ratio property and become a fixed ratio schedule. For these reasons, we suggest that the subunits should not be privy to the centrally derived behavioral weights.

POSSIBLE GAMING LIMITATIONS

Gaming possibilities exist (as they always do), but the game is complex because there are two sets of data used in the model. The first set is basic operating data, that is, costs and activity statistics. If subunits misstate net revenue figures, the cost allocations may be affected. If the organization has a centralized accounting system or an ex post review of subunit systems, such possibilities are minimized. The joint cost elements are, centralized, by definition, thus subunit manipulation of these figures is not possible. As the allocation bases are identified ex ante, it is possible for subunits to manipulate activity statistics; however, such possibilities exist in all approaches to cost allocation. Manipulation is more complex under the procedures herein: Although bases are ex ante identified, the actual base(s) used are determined ex post. Thus, the possibilities of successful manipulation seems minimal.

Other gaming possibilities relate to the role of behavioral weighting. The suggestion that behavioral weighting be done centrally stems primarily from the recognition of the complexities involved in formalizing a weighting which would be recognized as an explicit identification of the organizational priority scheme. A centralized approach removes gaming possibilities that would arise from negotiation of the weighting scheme. It also minimizes the possibilities of gaming performance measures to the extent that subunits could concentrate solely on measures with the highest priority if the scheme were identified. Such behavior would benefit the subunit (as the preemptive weights influence allocations) but may be dysfunctional to the organization as a whole. The tendency to pursue a single goal to the exclusion of others is well documented when weights are identified a priori. The uncertainties that exist when weights are not specified a priori are essential to structuring variable ratio reinforcement contingencies in the cost allocation process.

RECOMMENDATIONS AND CONCLUSIONS

The control process suggested in this research has as its objective the structuring of an organizational environment in which multiple sources of reinforcement contingencies motivate desired subunit behavior. The appropriateness of subunit behavior usually is related to a set of goal measures. This paper suggests that the cost allocation process provides an additional source of reinforcement contingencies for motivating particular behavior relative to this goal set.

In order to operationalize the suggested cost allocation system we suggest the following:

1. The operational statistics (allocation bases) to be used in the modeling process should be reviewed periodically to ensure *ex ante* appropriateness.
2. The operant model requires careful specification of (1) the set of goal measures, (2) their measurement surrogates, (3) the definition of periodic responses and (4) the process by which responses are evaluated relative to the allocation criterion functional. It is recommended that each subunit have some form of participation in specification of these four elements. Participation itself generally is considered to be a source of control and reinforcement, hence, a positive factor in the implementation of a control technique [Tannenbaum, 1968]. Agreement on the evaluative dimension of the control system should enhance its effectiveness since organizational control inevitably involves manipulation of human behavior [Kelman, 1965].
3. It is recommended that simple, objective (that is, easily quantifiable) measures be used and that these measures be unitized or normalized to account for subunit size differences. Subjective measures should be considered to be inappropriate for this application owing to the disagreement which often accompanies measurement of subjective evaluative indices [Peters, 1972].
4. It is recommended that the assignment of behavioral weights be done centrally, based upon management's

perception of the overall state of the organization, behavioral disposition of the decentralized units, and the desired expansion path of the organization.

Recommendations 1 through 3 are concerned with promoting acceptance of the proposed control technique through subunit participation in the basic design of the process. These recommendations do not encompass the establishment of an explicit ranking or weighting scheme to be used in the behavioral weighting process.

In some situations, it may be desirable to generate tentative cost allocations ex ante. The use of the suggested conditioning model in such cases would require estimates of subunit operant behavior. If these could be obtained, cost allocations could be generated. This issue, however, deserves a good deal of research as it involves an evaluation of forecasted performances, that is, how to evaluate performance relative to its forecast. Excellent papers in this area are provided by Peters [1972] and Ijiri Kinard and Putney [1968].

Some behavioralists object to the view that reinforcement which is contingent upon a class of responses is sufficient to maintain and generate a sub-stantial activity [Skinner, 1969]. As a consequence, there is substantial research into the identification of appropriate and inappropriate rewards. A related paper in the area is provided by Cherrington and Cherrington [1973]. The determination of what constitutes "appropriate" reinforcement is necessarily a subjective judgment and, therefore, situational. The above paper explores this topic in relation to budget setting.

It should be noted that conditioning may be viewed as but one way in which managers learn and assess the numerous variables which affect their behavior, as in the Livingstone and Ronen [1975] presentment of the expectancy model of budgetary behavior. However, throughout all the various theories of "why" reinforcement works (that is, drive reduction, sensory feedback, information processing, incentive effects), the *operational* definition of reinforcement has remained stable. Behavior is acquired and modified through contingent relations between responses and consequent events [Glaser, 1971]. Motivation implies the ability to "change something." In this sense, this research has addressed the question of motivation in cost allocation systems.

REFERENCES

Anthony, R. N., *Management Accounting Principles*, rev. ed. (Irwin, 1970).

Bariff, M. and E. Lusk, "A Study of the Utilization of Cognitive and Personality Tests for the Design of Management Information Systems," *Management Science*, Vol. 23, No. 8, (April 1977), pp. 820–829.

Bodnar, G., "A Behavioral Analysis of Cost Allocation in Responsibility Accounting Systems" (Ph.D. diss., University of Pennsylvania, 1975).

Caplan, E. H., *Management Accounting and Behavioral Science* (Addison-Wesley Publishing Co., 1971).

Cherrington, D. J. and J. O. Cherrington, "Appropriate Reinforcement Contingencies in the Budgeting Process," paper presented at the Accounting Empirical Research Conference (University of Chicago, May 1973).

Churchill, N., "Linear Algebra and Cost Allocations: Some Examples," THE ACCOUNTING REVIEW, (October 1964), pp. 894–904.

Colantoni, C. S., R. P. Manes and A. Whinston, "Programming, Profit Rates and Pricing Decisions," THE ACCOUNTING REVIEW, (July 1969), pp. 467–481.

Dalton, G. and P. Lawrence, *Motivation and Control in Organizations* (Irwin, 1971).

Glaser, R., ed., *The Nature of Reinforcement* (Academic Press, 1971).

Glaser, R. and D. Klaus, "A Reinforcement Analysis of Group Performance," *Psychological Monographs: General and Applied*, Vol. 80, No. 13, Whole No. 621, 1966.

Horngren, C., *Cost Accounting: A Managerial Emphasis*, 3rd ed. (Prentice-Hall, 1972).

Ijiri, Y., *Management Goals and Accounting for Control* (North-Holland Publishing Co., 1965).

————, F. Levy and R. Lyon, "A Linear Programming Model for Budgeting and Financial Planning," *Journal of Accounting Research*, (Autumn 1963), pp. 198–212.

————, J. Kinard and F. Putney, "An Integrated Evaluation System for Budget Forecasting and Operating Performance," *Journal of Accounting Research* (Spring 1968).

Jablonsky, F. and D. DeVries, "Operant Conditioning Principles Extrapolated to the Theory of Management," *Organizational Behavior and Human Performance* (Octoner 1972), pp. 340–358.

Kaplan, R. and G. Thompson, "Overhead Allocation via Mathematical Programming Models," THE ACCOUNTING REVIEW (April 1971), pp. 352–364.

Kelman, H. C., "Manipulation of Human Behavior: An Ethical Dilemma for the Social Scientist," *Journal of Social Issues*, Vol. 21, No. 2 (1965), pp. 31–46.

Livingstone, J. L., "Matrix Algebra and Cost Allocation," THE ACCOUNTING REVIEW (July 1965), pp. 640–643.

———— and A. Ronen, "An Expectancy Theory Approach to the Motivational Impact of Budget," THE ACCOUNTING REVEW (October 1975), pp. 671–685.

Lusk, E. and G. Bodnar, "Operationalizing Cost Allocation Criteria: A Goal Programming Approach," Proceedings of the National Meeting of the American Institute of Decision Sciences (November 1973).

————, "Behaviorally Weighting the Operant Conditioning Functional: An Eigenvalue Priortization Approach" (Wharton School Working Paper, 1977).

Manes, R. P., "Comment on Matrix Theory and Cost Allocation," THE ACCOUNTING REVIEW, (July 1965), pp. 640–643.

Marx, M., *Learning: Theories* (Macmillan Co., 1970).

Nord, W. "Beyond the Teaching Machine: The Neglected Area of Operant Conditioning in the Theory and Practice of Management," *Organizational Behavior and Human Performance*, Vol. 4, No. 11 (November 1969), pp. 375–401.

Peters, D., "Reward Functions to Reinforce a Goal-Based Management Process," *Management Science* (August 1972), B663-B675.

Samuels, J. M., "Opportunity Costing: An Application of Mathematical Programming," *Journal of Accounting Research* (Autumn 1965), pp. 182–192.

Shubik, M., "Incentives, Decentralized Control, the Assignment of Joint Costs and Internal Pricing," *Management Science* (February 1960), pp. 325–343.

Skinner, B. F., *Contingencies of Reinforcement: A Theoretical Analysis* (Meredith Corp., 1969).

Tannenbaum, A. S., *Control in Organizations* (McGraw-Hill, 1968).

Vatter, W., "Limitations of Overhead Allocation," THE ACCOUNTING REVIEW (April 1945).

Williams, T. H. and C. H. Griffin, "Matrix Theory and Cost Allocation," THE ACCOUNTING REVIEW (July 1964), pp. 671–678.

ROI as a Measure of Managerial Performance

HAROLD BIERMAN, JR.
Cornell University

The measure of ROI can and should be improved. If it is, it can be used to provide a much-needed indication of managerial performance.

Several authors have investigated the use of return on investment (ROI) or alternatives to ROI for measuring the performance of profit centers. John Dearden has suggested that ROI is obsolete. David Solomons and Dearden recommend the use of residual income as a substitute for ROI, and Keith Shwayder suggests the use of interest adjusted income as a substitute for residual income. (See bibliography.) This article will attempt to answer some of the objections to ROI raised by Dearden and to extend the residual income method so that it may be reconciled to ROI. The objective is to evaluate the use of ROI as a performance measure device, not as a means of evaluating investments (there are better ways of evaluating investments).

IN DEFENSE OF ROI

Says John Dearden, "In the management control field, I think we should recognize that ROI financial control was a very useful innovation when it was first developed, but that it is now obsolete." (Dearden, "The Case Against ROI Control," p. 135.) Why would ROI be useful in the '50s and '60s but obsolete in the '70s? There were good reasons for the introduction of ROI as a performance measurement device and these reasons still exist. And they will not go away in the future.

Unfortunately it is easy to confuse the ROI issue with difficulties that are only tangentially related to ROI. For example, consider a multi-divisional firm with inter-connecting transactions among the divisions that give rise to the necessity for transfer pricing and the joint use of assets by several divisions. It is not clear that profit centers should be used in such a situation. While factors involved in the profit center concept differ to a larger extent from those in ROI, in one respect they are similar. To compute either the ROI or the profitability of an operating unit, it is necessary to arrive at an income measure, which implies that the unit's product is sold and that the revenue can be measured in a useful manner.

Advocating the use of ROI implies that it provides a better measure of performance than is obtained from using just the cost of the product. But ROI is not equally appropriate in all situations. One can argue in favor of the use of ROI in a specific situation without taking the position that all subsidiary operating units should be judged using ROI. For many operating units marketing efforts are not autonomous, and it will be more appropriate to use cost minimization than profit maximization (or its near equivalent, maximization of ROI, subject to constraints). Thus, the discussion contained in this article will be limited to entire firms, self-contained operating components of a firm, or components that are not self-contained but for which there is a reasonable transfer pricing procedure.

Dearden indicates that the most important limitation of ROI is that "ROI oversimplifies a very complex decision-making process." While we would agree that some managers tend to place too much faith in an ROI measure and that measurement of performance is much more difficult than is sometimes assumed, we cannot conclude that ROI is therefore not a valuable aid. ROI is not the best or only measure of performance, but it can be very useful. Consider what an ROI measure can accomplish: before concluding whether a particular income level is satisfactory, we relate that income to the amount of assets used to earn it. The necessity of making this comparison is obvious ($1 million of earnings may be considered to be very good, but if the operating unit used $100 million of capital to earn it, your opinion might well change).

The use of ROI to evaluate performance can affect investment decisions, since the manager knows that the results of operations of each investment he accepts will affect the measurement of his performance. Thus the divisional (or other sub-component) manager tends to reject investments that yield a lower return on investment than is earned on assets currently owned. Top management should be concerned not only with the return on investment of the assets being used, but also with the growth in assets and income. Growth as well as return on investment is important! A static division earning 30 per cent ROI may well be evaluated as badly managed, while it may be concluded that a division earning 15 per cent but is growing is well managed.

The investment decision problem resulting from a desire to maintain a high ROI highlights the necessity of relying on more than one measurement technique, and of bringing in sufficient measures to restrain the impulses of persons trying to circumvent the control-evaluation system.

COMPUTATION OF ROI

It is widely known that straight-line or accelerated depreciation, except in very well defined and specific situations, will distort ROI and that the ROI for each year will differ from the return computed at the time of acquisition even when the expected results are realized.

The solution of this difficulty is simple to state but difficult to implement. If the return at time of acquisition is correctly computed (that is, if a discounted cash flow procedure is used) and if the ROI each year after acquisition is correctly computed, the two measures will be identical for each year of operation (assuming the events forecasted at the time of making the decision actually occur). To accomplish this objective, depreciation must be defined in a theoretically correct manner and the computation of depreciation must be consistent with this definition.

Let us define depreciation as "the decrease in value of the investment during the time period." (The definition becomes more complex if additional investments are made during the period.) This definition must be used to compute the income that is used in the ROI calculations. The following example shows that return on investment, when properly calculated, gives at least as much information as the "residual income method"; in fact the two calculations can be reconciled.

Assume the net cash flows (and net revenues) associated with an investment costing $3,000 at time zero are as follows:

Time	Cash Flow
1	$1,300
2	1,200
3	1,100

The firm uses straight-line depreciation and has a time value of money of 10 per cent. This investment has a yield (rate of return) of 10 per cent.

Table 1 shows the incomes and investments for each of the three years of use.

The fact that each year has identical returns on investment equal to the yield of the investment seems to be a coincidence.

TABLE 1

Year	Cash Flows or Net Revenues	Depreciation	Income	Investment at the beginning of the year	ROI (Income divided by investment)
1	1,300	1,000	300	3,000	.10
2	1,200	1,000	200	2,000	.10
3	1,100	1,000	100	1,000	.10

TABLE 2

Time	Cash Flows	Period 1 Present Value Factors	V_0 Present Values	Period 2 Present Value Factors	V_1 Present Values	Period 3 Present Value Factors	V_2 Present Values
1	1,300	.9091	1,182				
2	1,200	.8264	992	.9091	1,091		
3	1,100	.7513	826	.8264	909	.9091	1,000
			$V_0 = 3,000$		$V_1 = 2,000$		$V_2 = 1,000$

TABLE 3

Net revenues		$1,300
Capital consumption $1,300 × .9091		1,182
Income before interest		$ 118
Interest cost on investment of $1,182:		
$1,182 × .10	− 118	
Interest revenue on entire		
investment of $3,000:	+ 300	182
Residual income		$ 300

TABLE 4

		Period 2	Period 3
Net revenues		$1,200	$1,100
Capital consumption $1,200 × .8264		992	
$1,100 × .7513			826
		$ 208	$ 274
Interest			
$ 992 × .10 + 1,091 × .10 = $ −208			
2,000 × .10 = $ 200		−8	
$ 826 × .10 + 909 × .10 + 100 = −274			
1,000 × .10 + 100			−174
Residual income		$ 200	$ 100

However, if we inspect Table 2 showing the present value of the investment at four moments in time (V_i is the value at time i), we see that in each period the decrease in value is $1,000 (the value of V_3 is zero), and that in this very special situation the use of straight-line depreciation is correct (if the cash flows are different the depreciation schedule would be different).

The procedure illustrated works with any set of cash flows. ROI does not have to be distorted by the method of depreciation. In this simplified example, the yield of the investment is equal to the firm's time value of money and the cash flows of each period equal the net revenues. Different assumptions would add to the complexity of the calculations but they can be solved.

RESIDUAL INCOME METHOD

Using the residual income procedure, interest is deducted from income to obtain a resid-

ual income. This procedure is acceptable if we properly define income and investment, if the correct interest rate is used, and if interest is appropriately assigned to time periods.

Unfortunately these requirements will not be fulfilled in a manner that will give theoretically sound (and useful) results if one uses conventional accounting. Using the same example, we will illustrate a correct application of the residual income method.

Define income as net revenue less a capital consumption adjustment and the interest cost on the investment and add the implicit interest revenue earned on the investment during the period. The capital consumption is assumed to be equal to the amount paid at acquisition for the expected cash flows of the period and that this is equal to the present value of the cash flows. For period 1 we would have residual income determined as in Table 3.

The residual income of $300

for period 1 is the same amount of income as was obtained in the ROI calculation. But the ROI calculation relates the income to the investment and provides a percentage that has meaning to a manager.

The results for periods 2 and 3 are shown in Table 4.

Again the amounts of residual income are the same as those obtained with the ROI calculation. The two methods will not consistently produce identical results unless depreciation is defined as the decrease in value of the investment in computing the return on investment and the capital consumption, the interest cost, and the interest revenue are defined in a manner consistent with the above example and calculations.

INTEREST ADJUSTED INCOME

Keith Shwayder suggests the use of "interest adjusted income," a modification of residual income. My interpretation of Shwayder's article leads me to conclude that he would be in agreement with an allocation of interest cost typified by the example I have used. In addition he would define interest cost as the default-free rate rather than as the more vague time value of money used in my example or the cost of capital used by other authors. I am sympathetic to his desire to remove the risk adjustment from the interest rate used to evaluate performance.

TIME ADJUSTED REVENUES

Instead of assuming that the cash flows and the revenue measures are the same for each period, let us assume that the timing of cash flows and revenue recognition differ (an example would be the receipt of cash advances in payment for a service not yet performed).

Continuing the example, assume the facts in Table 5 apply.

The revenue used is a sophisticated "time-adjusted revenue" measure rather than a naive measure coinciding with the amount of cash received. For example, if $1,000 were to be received one year from now but the revenue is to be recognized now, the time-adjusted revenue would be $1,000 $(1+r)^{-1}$. Expenses would have to be time adjusted in like manner.

Applying the present value factors to the revenue measures, we obtain the values at different points in time and the resulting depreciation as shown in Table 6.

The computations of incomes and returns on investment for each period would be as in Table 7.

It should be noted that time-adjusted revenues and cash flows are very much tied together and that they rigorously define the depreciation (the decrease in value) of a period.

POSITIVE NET PRESENT VALUE

The example used to this point sets the net present value of the investment at zero; that is, the yield of the investment is equal to the time-value factor for the firm. Obviously this will only rarely be the situation. We would expect most investments to have anticipated returns in excess of the return required by the firm. For example, let us assume that the investment costs $2,760 instead of $3,600. The net present value of each period would be as in Table 7.

the investment at time of acqu sition is $240 and its yield .15. There are now several po sible ways to look at the cas The most straightforward woul be to use .15 as the rate of di count to compute the deprecia tion expenses and returns o investment.

Using .15 as the rate of di count, we obtain the resul shown in Table 8.

The primary difficulty wit this view is that the time valu of money was previously e tablished at .10, not .15. Thu the values of the investment each time period are greate than those shown in Table 8. second approach is to adju the value of the investment $3,000, the present value of th benefits, despite the fact tha the investment only cost $2,76 This procedure would not be a ceptable for financial accoun ing purposes because of the in plicit threat of manipulation, bu it would be perfectly acceptabl for internal managerial pu poses. It is a very appealin procedure because it is re atively simple and yet is corre from the standpoint that the ac counts reflect values.

The third solution is a con bination of the first two. Th value of the investment at tim zero is defined as $3,000, bu the $240 of value increment treated as being initially u realized. The $240 is realize through time as the asset operated. Returning to the e ample where the cash flows an revenues are the same, w would have for each period th results shown in Table 9.

For period 1, excluding th $116 would result in a 10 pe cent return on investment. I cluding the $116 in income an using the investment base $2,760 would result in an RC of 15 per cent.

TABLE 5

Period	1	2	3	4
Cash flows	1,300	1,200	1,100	
Revenues		1,430	1,320	1,210

TABLE 6

Time	Value	Depreciation for period
0	3,000	
1	3,300	– 300
2	2,200	1,100
3	1,100	1,100
4	0	1,100

TABLE 7

Period	Revenues	Depreciation	Income	Investment	Return on Investment
1	0	– 300	300	3,000	.10
2	1,430	1,100	330	3,300	.10
3	1,320	1,100	220	2,200	.10
4	1,210	1,100	110	1,100	.10

TABLE 8

Period	Revenue	Depreciation	Income	Investment	ROI
1	1,300	844	416	2,760	.15
2	1,200	919	281	1,876	.15
3	1,100	957	143	957	.15

TABLE 9

Time	Value using .10	Value using .15	Value differences (remaining unrealized value)	Original un-realized income which should be recognized during the period
0	3,000	2,760	240	
1	2,000	1,876	124	116
2	1,000	957	43	81
3	0	0	0	43

INCENTIVE CONSIDERATION

The use of book value based on cost (the denominator in the ROI calculation) to measure the investment or even estimates of value by the accountant is subject to severe criticism. There is no reason why a system based on managerial values cannot be used for internal purposes. But, as Dearden indicates (p. 128), "most managers [are reluctant] to be evaluated on the basis of values that seem to be artificially created by the economist or accountant."

But suppose that, rather than asking the accountant or the economist to supply the number by which the manager is to be judged, let us ask the manager himself to supply it. The procedure would be simple. Take a set of eligible managers and ask them to "bid" periodically for the assets they want to manage and for which a change in management is appropriate. The bid that is accepted takes the asset and becomes the accounting base for performance evaluation. If a manager's bid is too high, he will find it very hard to meet the return on investment requirements. If he bids too low, he may lose the asset to a competing manager or the "board" may reject the bid and ask him to resubmit a bid.

This procedure would have many advantages. It would establish an investment base whose measure is acceptable to both the operating manager and to the top level of management (the former sets the value and the latter must accept it). The accountant and economist serve the very important and proper function of supplying the information used by the managers in making their judgments and bids. The ROI measure is improved since the investment base is appropriate to the specific investment and manager being evaluated rather than the result of a series of historical accidents (such as the year of purchase and the method of depreciation). Most importantly, it requires managers to set, describe, and quantify their plans for the utilization of the assets. It ties together planning, decision making, and control.

The one major difficulty with this procedure is that managers can rig the time shape of projected earnings so that early targets can be easily attainable. This tendency would have to be controlled if this procedure were to be adopted.

CONCLUSIONS

The measure of ROI can and should be improved. If it is, it can be used to provide a picture of managerial performance. This is necessary if top management is to measure the utilization of assets controlled by persons at different levels of the firm. While the return on investment provides a very useful means of accomplishing this objective, it is successful only if efforts are made to measure income and investment in theoretically correct ways.

BIBLIOGRAPHY

1. Anthony, R. N., Dearden, John, and Vancil, R. F., "Accounting for Capital Costs," Management Control Systems: Cases and Readings (Homewood, Ill., R. D. Irwin, 1965) pp. 343–348.

2. Bierman, H., Jr., "Depreciable Assets—Timing of Expense Recognition," The Accounting Review, October 1961.

3. Bierman, H., Jr., "A Further Study of Depreciation," The Accounting Review, April 1966, pp. 271–274.

4. Dearden, John, "The Case Against ROI Control," Harvard Business Review, May–June 1969.

5. Dixon, R. L., "Decreasing Charges Depreciation—A Search for Logic," The Accounting Review, October 1960, pp. 590–597.

6. Hirshleifer, Jack, "On the Economics of Transfer Pricing," Journal of Business, July 1956, pp. 172–184.

7. Hirshleifer, Jack, "Economics of the Divisionalized Firm," Journal of Business, April 1957, pp. 96–108.

8. Schwayder, Keith, "A Proposed Modification to Residual Income—Interest Adjusted Income," The Accounting Review, April 1970, pp. 299–307.

9. Solomons, David, Division Performance: Measurement and Control, (Financial Executives Research Foundation, 1965.)

Harold Bierman, Jr. is the Nicholas H. Noyes professor of business administration in the Graduate School of Business and Public Administration at Cornell University. He also serves as faculty coordinator of the financial management section of Cornell's Executive Development Program. He has been a consultant for several major business firms as well as the Ford Foundation. Professor Bierman, who holds a PhD from the University of Michigan, is the author or co-author of several books, including The Capital Budgeting Decision and Financial Policy Decisions, and many articles.

Leadership Climate and the Use of Accounting Data in Performance Evaluation

ANTHONY G. HOPWOOD
London Graduate School of Business Studies

THE final effectiveness of any management accounting system is dependent not only upon its design and technical characteristics, but also upon the precise manner in which the resulting data are used. In the extreme, of course, a system contributes little or nothing to the efficiency of an organization's operations if the data are ignored. More generally, however, despite any amount of thought and consideration which may have gone into its design, no management accounting system ever achieves a perfect representation of the underlying structure of economic events. A careful use of the data is always essential to compensate for their many unavoidable inadequacies.

But it remains so much easier naively to acknowledge that the data should be used carefully than to specify what this entails in terms of managerial actions. Yet such an understanding is an essential prerequisite for the intelligent management of change and improvement. The present study was accordingly designed to investigate empirically some of the managerial factors which influence an accounting system's organizational and personal impacts. Particular consideration is given to the relationship between wider managerial behaviors and the use which is made of accounting data in performance evaluation.

DIFFERENT WAYS OF USING ACCOUNTING DATA IN PERFORMANCE EVALUATION

The investigation is based upon an analysis of the managerial determinants of the following three distinct styles of using budgeted and actual cost information in performance evaluation.

1. *A Budget Constrained Style.* Despite the many unavoidable problems in using accounting data as comprehensive measures of managerial performance, the manager's performance is primarily evaluated on the basis of his ability continually to meet the short-term budget.

2. *A Profit Conscious Style.* The manager's performance is evaluated on the basis of his ability to increase the long-term effectiveness of his unit in relation to the goals of the organization. The accounting data, although indicating whether the budget has been met, do not necessarily indicate whether long-term effectiveness is being attained. Therefore, while important, they are used with some care in a flexible and creative manner, and where

The author wishes to acknowledge the helpful comments and advice of Professor L. Richard Hoffman of the University of Chicago.

necessary, supplemented by alternative sources of information.

3. *A Nonaccounting Style.* Accounting data play a relatively unimportant part in the evaluation of the manager's performance.

Previous empirical research has demonstrated that these three ways of using accounting data have significantly different organizational and personal effects.[1] Although both the Budget Constrained and Profit Conscious styles resulted in a higher degree of involvement with costs than the Nonaccounting style, only the Profit Conscious style succeeded in attaining this without resulting in either emotional costs for managers or defensive behavior which was dysfunctional for the organization. The Budget Constrained style resulted in a belief that the evaluation was unjust, in widespread tension and worry on the job, and in feelings of distrust and dissatisfaction with the supervisor. Not only were the managers who were evaluated in this way found to manipulate the accounting data and make decisions which resulted in higher long-term processing costs for the company as a whole, but the consequent conflict and rivalry between colleagues impeded the cooperation which was so essential for controlling their interdependent activities. In contrast, the Profit Conscious style, while seen as very demanding, was accepted. It resulted in levels of tension and in satisfaction with the supervisor and colleague supportiveness similar to those which prevailed under a Nonaccounting evaluation.

FACTORS INFLUENCING THE USE MADE OF ACCOUNTING DATA

As Argyris noted in this study of the personal impact of budgets in four industrial organizations, the way in which a manager uses budgetary data is only one aspect of his more general approach to the job.

. . . It became obvious that the way people expressed their interest in budgets, and the way in which they described and used them, were directly related to the pattern of leadership in their daily industrial life.[2]

Many recent studies have made a distinction between the instrumental or task aspects and the socio-emotional aspects of managerial behavior. In this study, these two aspects of behavior are characterized in terms of the two dimensions of the Ohio State University Leadership Behavior Description Questionnaire (LBDQ), namely, Initiation of Structure and Consideration.[3] The Initiation of Structure dimension reflects the extent to which a manager defines both his own work role and those of his subordinates. A high score is indicative of clearly delineated roles and attempts to establish clear channels of communication, patterns of organization, and detailed job instructions. The Consideration dimension reflects the extent to which a manager is friendly, trusting, and respectful of his subordinates. A high score is indicative of a manager who is willing to explain his actions and who tries to maintain warm and personal relationships with his subordinates.

A manager who is seen as using a Budget Constrained style of evaluation is expected to have a leadership style characterized by a high score on the Initiation of Structure dimension of the LBDQ and a low score on the Consideration dimension. Because accounting data have an aura of objectivity and clarity, their use in a rather direct manner should appeal to a manager who is concerned with establish-

[1] A. G. Hopwood, "An Empirical Study of the Role of Accounting Data in Performance Evaluation," *Empirical Research in Accounting: Selected Studies, 1972,* Supplement to Vol. X, *Journal of Accounting Research.*
[2] C. Argyris, *The Impact of Budgets on People* (School of Business and Public Administration, Cornell University, 1952), p. 24.
[3] E. A. Fleishman, "A Leader Behavior Description for Industry," in *Leader Behavior: Its Description and Measurement,* edited by R. M. Stogdill and A. E. Coons (Bureau of Business Research, Ohio State University, 1957), pp. 120–33.

ing well-defined work procedures and means for evaluation.[4] To use the data in such a manner, however, the manager must also be relatively insensitive in his interpersonal relations, being more concerned with the task and goal attainment than with the maintenance of cordial and trusting relations with people. A more considerate supervisor is more likely to have that degree of empathy, and perhaps the open communications with his subordinates, which allow him to see the threat and the subsequent defenses which a rigid concern with the accounting data is capable of creating.[5]

It is, however, impossible to provide any adequate understanding of managerial evaluative behaviors without also considering the complex nature of the interrelationships between different levels of an organizational hierarchy. Since a manager himself is subject to an evaluation which may take on a similar form to those already described, it is necessary to look at the ways in which the demands and pressures are passed down from one level in the hierarchy to the next. In his simulation study of a firm's information and decision systems, Bonini[6] called such a process a "contagion effect," a term which is used in the present context to refer to any tendency for managers to evaluate their subordinates as they themselves are evaluated.

The contagion effect is particularly pertinent for a Budget Constrained style of evaluation because of the additive nature of accounting data. If a manager's superior pays attention to the extent to which the budget is met, the manager can satisfy this objective only by similarly paying attention to the budget variances of his own subordinates.

The above arguments can be summarized in terms of the following hypotheses which are discussed in this paper:

A manager is more likely to be seen as using a Budget Constrained style of evaluation if (a) he has a leadership style which is characterized by low Consideration and high Initiation of Structure; (b) he is himself evaluated on the basis of a Budget Constrained style.

RESEARCH SITE

The manufacturing division of a Chicago-based company which served as the site for the study had a labor force in excess of 20,000 persons and an annual revenue of several hundred million dollars. The division's management accounting system had been in operation for over a decade and it was based on flexible budgets, standard costing techniques, and the allocation of certain overhead costs. All levels of management received monthly reports comparing their actual and budgeted costs; these were supplemented by daily and and weekly reports on such matters as production, labor, and supplies.

The division was organized on the basis of a series of areas, departments, and cost centers. Each area included several departments; and each department, a series of cost centers. A simplified organization chart is shown in Figure 1. The cost centers were usually under the responsibility of a general foreman, although some foremen and assistant departmental supervisors also had responsibilities at this level. One person could also be in charge of several cost centers. At the time the study was conducted, there were over 350 cost

[4] P. Weissenberg and L. Grunefeld, "Relationships Among Leadership Dimensions and Cognitive Style," *Journal of Applied Psychology* (October 1966), pp. 392–5.

[5] See E. A. Fleishman and J. A. Slater, "Humanizing Relationships in a Small Business: the Relationship Between the Leader's Behavior and His Empathy Toward Subordinates," *Advanced Management* (March 1961), pp. 18–20.

[6] C. P. Bonini, *Simulation of Information and Decision Systems in the Firm* (Prentice-Hall, 1963). Mann and Baumgartel provided some evidence that a manager's general attitude towards costs influenced his subordinates' concern with them: F. Mann and H. Baumgartel, *The Supervisor's Concern with Costs in an Electric Power Company* (Survey Research Center, Institute for Social Research, University of Michigan, 1953).

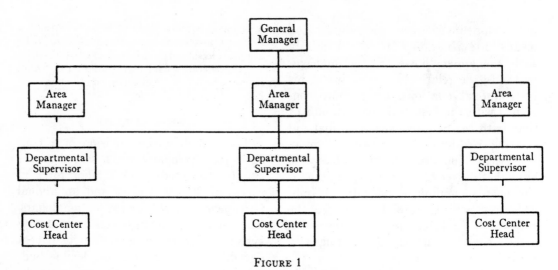

FIGURE 1

ORGANIZATION CHART FOR SUBJECT COMPANY

centers under the responsibility of 193 cost center heads.

Questionnaires were sent to 27 departmental supervisors and the 193 cost center heads. When a respondent failed to return the questionnaire two follow-up letters were sent to him. The final response rate was very high: 96% (26 out of 27) for the supervisors and 87% (167 out of 193) for the cost center heads.

MEASUREMENT OF THE VARIABLES

It was preferable to test for the presence of a contagion effect on the basis of independent reports from at least two levels in the organizational hierarchy so as to avoid any tendency for persons at just one level to report in a consistent manner. Therefore, the departmental supervisors were asked to report on the evaluative styles of the area managers and the cost center heads on the supervisors' styles.

The Area Manager's Style of Evaluation

The major methodological problem confronting the investigation concerned the means for empirically distinguishing among the different styles of using accounting data in performance evaluation. Although a broad set of behaviors had been isolated for each style, their operational definition necessitated an understanding of the meanings which the managers attached to these behaviors and the language which they used to describe them.

During a series of exploratory interviews, it was found that all levels of management referred to patterns of evaluative behaviors which were in agreement with the distinctions described above. In particular, a Budget Constrained orientation was referred to in terms of "meeting the budget" and a Profit Conscious orientation in terms of "concern with costs." These two phrases had distinct meanings which were known to all the managers interviewed, and therefore they were used as the basis for operationally defining the three styles of evaluation.

Each departmental supervisor was presented with a list of eight performance criteria which included both meeting the budget and concern with costs, as well as cooperation with colleagues, getting along with the boss, effort put into the job, concern with quality, attitude towards the work and company, and ability to handle the men. He was asked to rank-order the

348

three factors which he saw as being most important in his own evaluation, and the following operational definitions of the evaluative styles were then defined on the basis of the rankings.[7] The number of respondents in each group is shown in parentheses.

1. *Budget Constrained Style* (BC): meeting the budget ranked among the top three criteria (6).[8]

2. *Profit Conscious Style* (PC): concern with costs, but not meeting the budget, ranked among the top three criteria (10).

3. *Nonaccounting Style* (NA): neither meeting the budget nor concern with costs ranked among the top three criteria (10).[9]

The Departmental Supervisors' Style of Evaluation

Although the 167 cost center heads completed an identical series of questions on their supervisors' styles of evaluation, the same operational definitions could obviously not be used because several subordinate cost center heads reported on the style of each of the 27 supervisors. Furthermore, in some departments, as is discussed subsequently, the cost center heads' perceptions were not in agreement. Some means of characterizing the *dominant* style reported by the cost center heads in each department was therefore required.

The following operational definitions of the supervisors' styles of evaluation are used in the study. The number of supervisors assigned to each style is shown in parentheses.

1. *Budget Constrained Style:* at least 40% of the cost center heads in a department reported that meeting the budget was one of the three most important criteria in their evaluation (12).

2. *Profit Conscious Style:* at least 40% of the cost center heads reported that concern with costs was one of the three most important criteria used in their evaluation, but less than 40% reported that meeting the budget was similarly important (7).

3. *Nonaccounting Style:* less than 40% of the cost center heads in a department reported that meeting the budget and concern with costs were amonst the three most important criteria in their evaluation (8).

Forty percent was selected since it was the median percentage for the relative importance of concern with costs, and although slightly above the median for the relative importance of meeting the budget, it took advantage of a break in the series.

The Departmental Supervisors' Leadership Style

The 48 items of the Ohio State Leadership Behavior Description Questionnaire were included in the questionnaire sent to the cost center heads. The responses were coded to provide scores for the Consideration and Initiation of Structure dimensions of leadership behavior. The totals for all responding cost center heads under a departmental supervisor were then averaged to arrive at values of the dimensions for each supervisor. The range of the values of the Consideration dimension was found to be 50 to 92 (the possible range

---

[7] A discussion of the evidence on the validity of the operational procedures is given in Hopwood, "An Empirical Study of the Role of Accounting Data in Performance Evaluation."

[8] In an analysis of the cost center heads' perceptions of the departmental supervisors' styles of evaluation which was reported in the previous paper, a distinction was made between a Budget Constrained (BC) and a Budget-Profit (BP) style. The BC style referred to cases where meeting the budget, but not concern with costs, was ranked among the three most important criteria, and the BP style to cases where both the accounting-related criteria were in the top three. Subsequent analysis showed that the BC orientation dominated in the BP situation. There were no significant differences between the effects of the two styles, although the BP style did result in significantly different consequences than the pure PC style. In view of this evidence and the small size of the sample, the pure BC and BP styles are combined into a single Budget Constrained style in this analysis.

[9] The operational definition of the Nonaccounting style should be interpreted as implying a low *relative* importance to the accounting related criteria. It neither precludes some importance being attached to them nor their use for nonevaluative purposes.

TABLE 1

RELATIONSHIP BETWEEN THE REPORTED STYLE OF EVALUATION AND THE EXTENT TO WHICH
THE COST CENTER HEADS MET THE BUDGET FOR DEPARTMENTS WITH DISAGREEMENT

Relationship Between Actual Costs and the Budget for 6-Month Period Prior to Receipt of Questionnaire	Cost Center Head Reports a Budget Constrained Style of Evaluation	Cost Center Head Does Not Report a Budget Constrained Style of Evaluation	N
On average at least met the budget	9	17	26
On average did not meet the budget	16	12	28
N	25	29	54

$\chi^2 = 2.69$; 1 d.f.; $P < 0.11$.

was 0–112); the mean value, 75.6; and the standard deviation, 10.6. The range for the Initiation of Structure scores was 30 to 58 (with a possible range of 0–80); the mean value, 46.9; and the standard deviation, 7.0. The two dimensions were found to be independent (Kendall's Tau $= -0.04$).[10]

SELECTIVE USE OF A BUDGET CONSTRAINED STYLE

The cost center heads in some departments were not in agreement over whether or not their supervisors used a Budget Constrained style of evaluation. While at least two-thirds of the responding cost center heads in 19 of the 27 departments agreed that their supervisors either did or did not use this style, only 40% to 57% of the cost center heads in the remaining 8 departments reported that he did. Before proceeding with the main analysis, it was important first to investigate whether these differences in opinions were due to inaccurate perceptions or the insensitivity of the measurement procedures or a real selective use of this style by some supervisors. An analysis was therefore made of the factors influencing the style of evaluation reported by the 54 cost center heads employed in the 8 departments where there was substantial disagreement.

The analysis indicated that the cost center heads reporting a Budget Constrained style in these 8 departments tended to have been less successful in meet-

ing their budget. In Table 1 the 54 cost center heads are divided on the basis of (1) whether or not they reported a Budget Constrained evaluation and (2) whether or not they had, on average, met their budget over the 6-month period prior to the receipt of the questionnaire. There is a difference between the two criterion groups, but the difference is only significant at the 11% level.[11]

Prevention might, however, have been seen as being preferable to cure. An analysis was therefore made to see whether the supervisors of these 8 departments focused their Budget Constrained approach on the large cost centers which had the greatest potential to influence the overall departmental results. The cost center heads were divided on the basis of whether or not they were responsible for a cost center or a series of cost centers which dealt with total annual costs above, equal to, or less than the departmental median. From Table 2 it can be seen that these supervisors were more likely to be seen as using a Budget Constrained style by per-

[10] A review of the relationships between the two dimensions of the LBDQ is given by P. Weissenberg and M. J. Kavanagh in "The Independence of Initiating Structure and Consideration: A Review of the Evidence," *Personnel Psychology* (Spring 1972), pp. 119–30.

[11] There was no significant difference between these two criterion groups when the analysis was based on the average performance in the 9-month period prior to the receipt of the questionnaire. For the remaining 19 departments where there was substantial agreement over whether or not the supervisor used a Budget Constrained style, there was no relationship between the reported style and performance in either the 6- or 9-month period.

TABLE 2
RELATIONSHIP BETWEEN THE REPORTED STYLE OF EVALUATION AND THE RELATIVE SIZE OF THE COST CENTERS FOR DEPARTMENTS WITH DISAGREEMENT

The Total Annual Costs of the Cost Center(s) in Relation to the Median Cost for Its Department	Cost Center Head Reports a Budget Constrained Style of Evaluation	Cost Center Head Does Not Report a Budget Constrained Style of Evaluation	N
Above the departmental median	16	10	26
Equal to or less than the departmental median	9	19	28
N	25	29	54

$\chi^2 = 5.23$; 1 d.f.; $P < 0.05$.

TABLE 3
RELATIONSHIP BETWEEN LEADERSHIP STYLE AND THE SUPERVISORS' STYLE OF EVALUATION

Leadership Style	The Cost Center Heads' Perception of the Supervisors' Dominant Style of Evaluation			Significance of Paired Comparison[a]
	BC	PC	NA	
Mean Initiation of Structure	48.0	51.3	41.9	BCvNA: $p<0.01$ PCvNA: $p<0.05$
Mean Consideration	70.6	80.9	79.4	BCvPC: $p<0.05$ BCvNA: $p<0.05$
N	12	7	8	

[a] Significance of paired comparisons is based on the Mann-Whitney U Test. Unless otherwise stated, a paired comparison is not significant at the 5% level.

sons in charge of the *relatively* large cost centers in a department.[12]

The findings suggest that the supervisors of the 8 departments where there was substantial disagreement over their style of evaluation used the Budget Constrained style with discretion, emphasizing it where it was seen as likely to have the greatest impact on the departmental results. As such, the evidence is in agreement with other studies which have shown that managers do not necessarily use one personal style of management irrespective of their circumstances and subordinates.[13]

LEADERSHIP STYLE AND THE USE OF ACCOUNTING DATA

As can be seen from an examination of Table 3, both the Budget Constrained and Profit Conscious supervisors were seen as creating a structured job environment geared to the attainment of their perceptions of the organization's goals. The Budget Constrained supervisors, however, were seen as showing significantly less consideration for the feelings and opinions of their cost center heads than either their Profit Conscious or Nonaccounting colleagues. Yet without the maintenance of such a considerate managerial climate, the structured concern with the financial aspects of performance was seen in terms of

[12] There was no relationship between the reported style and the *absolute* size of the cost centers. Also no significant relationship was found between the reported style and either relative or absolute size in the nineteen departments with substantial agreement.

[13] See E. Kay and R. Hastman, *An Evaluation of Work Planning and Goal Setting Discussions* (General Electric Behavioral Research Service, 1966), and A. Lowin and J. R. Craig, "The Influence of Level of Performance on Managerial Style: An Experimental Object Lesson in the Ambiguity of Correlation Data," *Organizational Behavior and Human Performance* (November 1968), pp. 440–58.

a threatening emphasis on the accounting data in isolation of their organizational context. The findings are therefore supportive of hypothesis (a).

THE CONTAGION EFFECT

The contagion effect was very strong for the Budget Constrained style of evaluation. With supervisors divided on the basis of whether or not their perceptions of the area managers' styles of evaluation were in agreement with their cost center heads' perceptions of their own dominant style, it can be seen in Table 4 that only one of the 6 supervisors who reported a Budget Constrained evaluation did not pass down the same style to his cost center heads.[14] In contrast, there was no evidence of a contagion effect for either the Profit Conscious or Nonaccounting styles. For the Profit Conscious style, however, many of the supervisors maintained a concern with the accounting data, although the concern was just as likely to be rigidly tied to the short-term budget variances as it was to longer-term cost effectiveness. Four of the 10 supervisors who were evaluated on this basis evaluated their cost center heads in a Budget Constrained manner compared with the 3 who maintained the Profit Conscious style.

TABLE 4

RELATIONSHIP BETWEEN THE AREA MANAGERS'
AND THE DEPARTMENTAL SUPERVISORS'
STYLES OF EVALUATION

Relationship between the Cost Center Heads' Perception of the Supervisor's Dominant Style of Evaluation and the Supervisor's Perception of the Area Manager's Style	Supervisor's Perception of the Area Manager's Style of Evaluation			
	BC	PC	NA	N
Agreement	5	3	4	12
Disagreement	1	7	6	14
N	6	10	10	26

Supervisors were seen as passing on a Budget Constrained style even though they *intended* to do otherwise. All the departmental supervisors were asked to report how they thought that they evaluated their cost center heads, the responses being referred to as the supervisor's intended style of evaluation. It can be seen in Table 5 that only 2 of the 6 supervisors who reported being evaluated on the basis of a Budget Constrained style intended to evaluate their cost center heads in the same way. The other 4 supervisors intended to use a Profit Conscious style. In comparison, a majority of the supervisors who were evaluated on the basis of either a Profit Conscious or a Nonaccounting style intended to evaluate their cost center heads in the same manner, although they did not necessarily possess the requisite managerial abilities to put this into effect.[15]

The supervisors whose performance was evaluated upon the basis of their departments' short-term budget variances were in a conflict situation. It was easy for them to feel that it was necessary to evaluate similarly their cost center heads in order to obtain the desired results. Yet from their own experience they knew that this was an unfair evaluation which was likely

[14] While the Budget Constrained style might have been easier to resist if the departmental variances had been consistently favorable, the single supervisor who was the exception to the rule resisted the contagion effect despite having had unfavorable departmental variances for most of the fifteen months prior to the receipt of the questionnaire. His cost center heads saw him as having an average concern with a structured job environment (his Initiation of Structure score of 47 equals the median for the sample of supervisors), but an exceptionally high consideration for their feelings and opinions. His Consideration score of 89 was the second highest in the sample, and compared with the median of 79.

[15] Recent evidence relating self-reported leadership behavior to subordinate descriptions of behavior has also found that the two are not necessarily equivalent. See M. G. Evans, "Leadership Behavior: Demographic Factors and Agreement Between Subordinate and Self-Descriptions," *Personnel Psychology* (Winter 1972), pp. 649–53, and W. K. Graham and T. Olena, "Perceptions of Leader Behavior and Evaluation of Leaders Across Organizational Levels," *Experimental Publications System* (February 1970), p. 144A.

TABLE 5

RELATIONSHIP BETWEEN THE AREA MANAGERS' STYLE OF EVALUATION AND THE DEPARTMENTAL SUPERVISORS' INTENDED STYLE OF EVALUATION

Relationship Between the Supervisor's Perception of the Area Manager's Style and the Supervisor's Intended Style	Supervisor's Perception of the Area Manager's Style of Evaluation			
	BC	PC	NA	N
Agreement	2	7	7	16
Disagreement	4	3	3	10
N	6	10	10	26

to result in excessive tension and worry. One of them described his own experiences in the following way:

"When I'm in the red [the Area Manager] will always blame you. I'll get a black eye. Even if I'm not to blame, I'll still get a black eye. I like a good budget to shoot at but when you have obvious discrepancies in the budget, then it's difficult to show what you are doing. A good budget is a good thing, but a bad budget is a bad thing."

Yet he felt that he had to pass on the Budget Constrained style since his own superiors "will generally criticize me if I'm unfavorable, regardless of reason." So for some of his cost center heads, "if they're in the red, I'll probably know why, but I'll ask *them* why and I'll tarpoon [sic] a few things with them." He was, however, aware of the anxiety and undesirable behaviors which this could cause.

"The accounting numbers are a big thing for most of [the cost center heads]. It gets down to personalities; it's bound to. Generally [a cost center head] has to get a reasonable product to get a reasonable result. Well, he may want good relations with those who supply him with [his material], but then he wants to make himself look good, and to do that he makes others look poor."

With such problems in mind, he tried not to evaluate two of his cost center heads on the basis of their short-term budget variances because he thought that their highly skilled subordinates would react to the subsequent pressure by leaving the company. Since the two cost centers were also "low in real dollars," he was prepared to use a different style of evaluation.

All 5 of the supervisors who were seen as passing down their own Budget Constrained evaluation used a similar means of resolving the conflict with which they were confronted. They were, in fact, responsible for 5 of the 8 departments where there was disagreement over this aspect of the supervisor's style of evaluation and in which, as we have already seen, the more rigid style was used for the larger cost centers and possibly those with a poor budget record.[16]

DISCUSSION

In supporting the hypotheses, the evidence allows the initial distinctions which were made among the three styles of using accounting data in performance evaluation to be placed in a wider managerial perspective. For the final impact of an accounting system on managerial behavior has been shown to depend on its interaction with the forms of social- and self-controls which are reflected within the various leadership climates and the personal motives and defenses which they activate.

In being responsive to the feelings and opinions of their cost center heads, the Profit Conscious supervisors recognized and responded to the threat which the financial concerns and structured job environment were capable of creating. But, in addition, the supportive organizational climate encouraged the cost center heads to discuss openly their budgetary problems with the supervisor.[17] This might, of

[16] The percentage of cost center heads in the 5 departments reporting a Budget Constrained style were: 40%, 50%, 50%, 50% and 57%.

[17] In a field study conducted in three major industrial organizations Read found that trust in the supervisor resulted in accurate upward communications. See W. H. Read, "Upward Communication in Industrial Hierarchies," *Human Relations* (February 1962), pp. 3–15.

course, be viewed as a means of avoiding responsibility, although this would be an inappropriate description of the situation in these departments. The Profit Conscious supervisors, while listening to explanations, certainly did not readily accept them. In the words of one cost center head:

"[A Budget Constrained supervisor] takes the budget to heart, while what [a Profit Conscious supervisor] does is to accept it upon himself and if he doesn't agree with it, then he'll reject the budget. He's a real tough guy and it's difficult to argue with him. You have got to have some good arguments, but if he agrees with you, then out goes the budget. [The Budget Constrained supervisor] can be stubborn. He aims to stay right on his budget and that's it."

The budgetary pressures associated with the Profit Conscious style of evaluation were seen, in the words of another cost center head, as being applied "where they [were] appropriate." The cost center heads were aware of both the supervisors' willingness to listen and, in turn, explain the reasons for accepting and rejecting explanations. As a result, the supervisors were provided with the alternative sources of information which enabled them to test continually the validity of the accounting data and keep the job environment devoid of the rigidities of the Budget Constrained approach. In contrast, the cost center heads subject to a Budget Constrained evaluation hardly felt free to offer realistic explanations. One such cost center head described his supervisor's attitude in terms of "just don't do it, rather than asking for explanations."

Unfortunately the study did not directly investigate the relationship among the three styles of using accounting data and the overall effectiveness of operations.[18] The observed leadership style configurations are, however, of interest in this respect since studies using the LBDQ dimensions have found that, although the Initiation of Structure and Consideration scores were designed to be independent, supervisors who are rated high on both dimensions are considered to be more effective by their superiors, as well as favorably influencing their subordinates' morale and improving indices of productivity and labor turnover. Fleishman and Harris,[19] for instance, found that for production supervisors scoring high on both dimensions, the structured job environment was seen as less threatening and had little or no effect on grievances and turnover. That a number of other studies have come to similar conclusions[20] provides some indirect evidence on the potential benefits of the Profit Conscious style, although it should be stressed that such findings are no more than suggestive in the present context.

However, while recognizing the need for further research on the overall effects of the various styles, the findings do point to a number of implications for both accounting practice and the study of the behavioral impact of accounting data. At the very least, they serve to emphasize the importance of the accountant's educational function. With the increasing complexity of management accounting pro-

[18] A review of the evidence on the differential effects of the various styles did provide some basis for concluding that the Profit Conscious style was likely to be more effective than the Budget Constrained style in situations which required a careful consideration of a wide variety of information, a high degree of interunit coordination, a long time horizon, and an ability to respond in a flexible manner to unexpected circumstances: see the discussion in Hopwood, *op. cit.*

[19] E. A. Fleishman and E. F. Harris, "Patterns of Leadership Behavior Related to Employee Grievances and Turnover," *Personnel Psychology* (Spring 1962), pp. 43–56.

[20] E. A. Fleishman and J. Simmons, "Relationship Between Leadership Patterns and Effectiveness Ratings Among Israeli Foremen," *Personnel Psychology* (Summer 1970), pp. 169–72; A. W. Halpin, "The Leader Behavior and Effectiveness of Aircraft Commanders," in Stodgill and Coons; H. Oaklander and E. A. Fleishman, "Patterns of Leadership Related to Organizational Stress in Hospital Settings," *Administrative Science Quarterly* (March 1964), pp. 520–32. A survey of the relationship between the two dimensions of the LBQD and various criteria of organizational effectiveness is given in A. K. Korman, " 'Consideration,' 'Initiating Structure' and Organizational Criteria—A Review," *Personnel Psychology* (Winter 1966), pp. 349–61.

cedures, it is unrealistic to expect managers to use the data in an appropriate manner without adequate preparation and training. But they need to be informed not only of the objectives and advantages of the accounting system, real though they may be, but also of the inadequacies of the data and the consequences of attaching too much importance to the short-term reports—a far more difficult task.

The different ways of using the data were not, however, simply based on ignorance. They were associated with much more widespread differences in managerial attitudes and behaviors, and for the Budget Constrained style, with the evaluative style of the superiors. Even the most carefully designed educational program is unlikely to provide an easy solution to the problem, and it would certainly require the active cooperation of specialists in organizational development. Hence, consideration needs to be given to how the use which is made of the data can be explicitly recognized as a factor in the design of accounting systems. This does not mean that accountants should immediately strive to stifle the undesirable responses by filling the obvious loopholes in their systems. Rather, there is a need for system designs to take account of the constraints and opportunities of their managerial environment in the manner that Wildavsky has contrived to design federal budgeting procedures which are congruent with the political process.[21]

Such a task requires both practical experimentation and systematic research. But, so far, many of the studies of the effects of accounting data on decision behavior have ignored their managerial context. They have all too often merely presented reports based on different accounting methods to samples of financial analysts, managers, and students, and observed whether their decision behaviors were dependent upon the type of data received. The present findings suggest, however, that the relationship between accounting data and decision behavior is moderated by the leadership style and social context of the decision maker. Much greater explicit consideration needs to be given to these factors in further research, although, in so doing, there may be a need to rely less on the abstractions of laboratory experimentation and more on the complexities of field research.[22]

---

[21] A. Wildavsky, *The Politics of the Budgetary Process* (Little, Brown, 1964) and *Toward a Radical Incrementalism: A Proposal to Aid Congress in Reform of the Budgetary Process* (American Institute for Public Policy Research, 1965).

[22] This is not to deny that some aspects of the problem can be studied in controlled experiments. Lowin and Craig showed the potential for simulating different leadership styles in the laboratory, and among others, Mock *et al.* have recently reported experiments on the effects of cognitive style on decision behavior: See T. J. Mock, T. L. Estrin, and M. A. Vasarhelyi, "Learning Patterns, Decision Approach, and Value of Information," *Journal of Accounting Research* (Spring 1972), pp. 129–53. Nevertheless, there are formidable difficulties in trying to simulate hierarchical patterns and organizational contexts within the analytical and time constraints of the experimental method.

Social Accounting for Corporations: Private Enterprise versus Public Interest

Tony Tinker, Editor

An introduction to the contemporary debate concerning the accounting profession and corporate disclosure: for students of Business Policy, Corporate Responsibility, and Advanced Management Accounting.

- Introduction by Tony Tinker, New York University

- Accountability of Private Enterprise. Private No Enterprise Yes. by Charles E. Lindblom, Yale University

- Double Entry, Double Think, Double Speak by Abraham L. Briloff, Baruch College, CUNY

- Accounting and Realism by Stanley Sporkin, previously Enforcement Director, Securities and Exchange Commission

- Accounting for Unequal Exchange: Wealth Accumulation versus Wealth Appropriation by Tony Tinker, Chairman, Public Interest Section, AAA & NYU

ISBN 0-910129-17-7   190pp. $18.95

send order to: MARKUS WIENER PUBLISHING, INC.
540 Barnum Avenue, Bridgeport, Conn. 06608

DIVISIONAL PERFORMANCE: MEASUREMENT AND CONTROL

by David Solomons

Wharton School of Finance and Commerce
University of Pennsylvania

When this book was originally published in a hardbound edition by The Financial Executives Institute, it was honored with the American Institute of Certified Public Accountants Award for Notable Contributions to Accounting Literature.

This study deals with the possibilities of avoiding conflict between divisional and corporate interests.

Some of the problems discussed are:
- How should responsibilities be divided between corporate staffs and divisions?
- How far should the devolution of authority to divisions go?
- Is the impact of the computer likely to reverse the trend to decentralization?
- Are "generally accepted accounting principles" directly relevant to divisional accounting?
- What is the best measure of success for divisional management?
- How should accounting methods chosen for tax advantages be modified so as to meet management's needs for information?
- How should transfers of products between divisions be priced so as best to serve both the interests of the division and of the parent corporation?

Decision-making errors, motivation, the efficiency of ROI (Return on Investment), and budgets are among the diverse subjects analyzed to provide insights into ways of measuring and controlling divisional performance.

MARKUS WIENER PUBLISHING, INC.
540 Barnum Avenue, Bridgeport, Conn. 06608

ISBN 0-910129-00-2